The State of Welfare

The Economics of Social Spending

SECOND EDITION

MARIA EVANDROU

MARTIN EVANS

JANE FALKINGHAM

HOWARD GLENNERSTER (EDITOR)

JOHN HILLS (EDITOR)

JULIAN LE GRAND

POLLY VIZARD

OXFORD UNIVERSITY PRESS

1998

Oxford University Press, Great Clarendon Street, Oxford OX2 6DP

Oxford New York
Athens Auckland Bangkok Bogota Bombay
Buenos Aires Calcutta Cape Town Dar es Salaam
Delhi Florence Hong Kong Istanbul Karachi
Kuala Lumpur Madras Madrid Melbourne
Mexico City Nairobi Paris Singapore
Taipei Tokyo Toronto Warsaw

and associated companies in
Berlin Ibadan

Oxford is a trade mark of Oxford University Press

Published in the United States
by Oxford University Press Inc., New York

British Library Cataloguing in Publication Data
Data available

Library of Congress Cataloging in Publication Data
The state of welfare II: the economics of social spending / Martin
Evans . . . [et al.]; Howard Glennerster, John Hills [editors].
p. cm.
Includes bibliographical references.
1. Public Welfare—Great Britain. 2. Great Britain—Social policy.
3. Welfare state. I. Evans, Martin (Martin J.)
II. Glennerster, Howard. III. Hills, John.
HV245.S73 1998 361.6'5'0941—dc21 97–31997

ISBN 0–19–877591–1
ISBN 0–19–877590–3 (Pbk)

10 9 8 7 6 5 4 3 2 1

Typeset by Hope Services (Abingdon) Ltd.
Printed in Great Britain
on acid-free paper by
Bookcraft Ltd.,
Midsomer Norton, Somerset

QAS T
D 771
(Cge)
2060

0198775911

Acknowledgements

The origins of this book lie in a paper by A. B. Atkinson, John Hills, and Julian Le Grand (1987) on trends in public spending and their outcomes in the period between 1970 and 1985. This was an early product of the Welfare State Programme at the London School of Economics. The first edition was a much-expanded version of that paper. It was designed as a comprehensive sourcebook and review of social service spending over the period 1974 to 1988 and a review of the results of that spending. It turned out to have a much wider audience than we originally expected and found its way onto many university reading lists as a basic text. It provided the only consistent time series of public and private spending on the basic services in the United Kingdom—education, health, personal social services, housing, and social security. Government statistics keep changing their basis and fail to take account of changes in the prices of the raw materials these services use—mainly people! However, both policy and spending patterns have changed much since 1988. The end of the long period of Conservative administration forms a natural break-point. Did their major reforms in the years after 1988 make any difference? Did they dismember the welfare state?

In this book we keep the same format as in the first edition, but take the story forward from 1974 up to 1997 in policy terms and as far forward as we can in expenditure (1995/6) and outcomes, taking into account new research on these areas, including the outputs of the LSE Welfare State Programme over its whole existence from 1985 to 1997.

We owe a considerable debt to all those who contributed to this book on top of all their normal duties, to Phil Agulnik for many of the spending figures, to Sophie Sarre, who did all the bibliographical checking, to Jane Dickson, who coped with the manuscript, to Nic Warner and John Wild for their computing support, and to all the colleagues in the Suntory and Toyota Centres (STICERD) at the LSE for all their expertise and help unstintingly given.

Earlier drafts of particular chapters benefited from helpful suggestions made by Nicholas Barr, Bleddyn Davies, Martin Knapp, David Piachaud, Anne Power, Hilary Steadman, Anne West, Steve Wilcox, Jennifer Dixon, Rudolf Klein, and colleagues in STICERD. We are also grateful to those involved in the first edition of this book, especially Nicholas Barr, Fiona Coulter, Will Low, Beverley Mullings, David Winter, and Francis Woolley, on whose earlier work we were able to draw.

We are very grateful to the Michio and Yoko Morishima Fund for support and to STICERD for a grant that enabled us to pay for the able research assistance we had and for some of the authors' time. We have been helped by many government departments who have responded to our requests for unpublished material and for explanations of published data. Material from the General Household Survey made available through the Office for National Statistics and the ESRC Data Archive has been used by permission of the Controller of the Stationery Office. We are also grateful to the ESRC for their support for the work that contributed to the first edition of the book and is repeated here.

London School of Economics
July 1997

Contents

List of Figures

List of Figures

List of Tables

List of Tables

List of Tables

Abbreviations

AA	Attendance Allowance
ABI	Association of British Insurers
APU	Assessment of Performance Unit
CAF	Charities Aid Foundation
CBO	Congressional Budget Office
CHR	Centre for Housing Research
CIPFA	Chartered Institute of Public Finance and Accountancy
CSA	Child Support Agency
CSO	Central Statistical Office
DEE	Department for Education and Employment
DES	Department of Education and Science
DfE	Department for Education
DHSS	Department of Health and Social Security
DLA	Disability Living Allowance
DoE	Department of the Environment
DoH	Department of Health
DSS	Department of Social Security
ERS	Earnings-Related Supplement
FC	Family Credit
GDP	Gross Domestic Product
GHS	General Household Survey
GNP	Gross National Product
HAT	Housing Action Trust
HBAI	households below average income
HCHS	Hospital and Community Health Services
HIP	Housing Investment Programme
HRA	Housing Revenue Account
IAEP	International Assessment of Educational Progress
ICA	Invalid Care Allowance

Abbreviations

ILEA	Inner London Education Authority
IMF	International Monetary Fund
IS	Income Support
IVB	Invalidity Benefit
LEA	local education authority
LLSI	limiting long-standing illness
LSI	long-standing illness
MA	Mobility Allowance
MHLG	Ministry of Housing and Local Government
MISG	Mental Illness Specific Grant
MoH	Ministry of Health
n/a	not available
NCVO	National Council for Voluntary Organizations
NHS	National Health Service
NHSE	National Health Service Executive
NSPCC	National Society for the Prevention of Cruelty to Children
OFSTED	Office for Standards in Education
ONS	Office for National Statistics
OPCS	Office of Population Censuses and Surveys
PFI	Private Finance Initiative
PMI	Private Medical Insurance
PSS	personal social services
QALY	Quality-Adjusted Life-Year
SB	Supplementary Benefit
SBC	Supplementary Benefits Commission
SDA	Severe Disablement Allowance
SMP	Statutory Maternity Pay
SMR	Standardized Mortality Ratio
SSA	Standing Spending Assessment
SSD	Social Services Department
SSP	Statutory Sick Pay
STG	Special Transitional Grant
STICERD	Suntory and Toyota International Centres for Economics and Related Disciplines
UB	Unemployment Benefit
WHO	World Health Organization

1 Introduction

Howard Glennerster and John Hills

THIS BOOK is about what has happened to the welfare state in the United Kingdom during nearly a quarter of a century of profound economic, social, and political change. Our period begins with the oil price shock that shook the world economy and was shortly followed by the spending cuts associated with the Labour Government's agreement with the International Monetary Fund at the end of 1976. Hard on the heels of those painful decisions came the official abandonment of the post-war Keynesian strategy of demand management to sustain full employment. Then came the election of a Conservative Government with a strong ideological opposition to the public sector as a whole and deep suspicion of public 'welfare' in particular. That Government was to remain in office for eighteen years. Surely, then, the picture we shall be painting will show the continuous 'rolling back' of cherished institutions which were once 'the envy of the rest of Europe'.

The detailed study which we report in these pages may come as a surprise. It is true that, by most measures, the welfare state has not grown since the mid-1970s in the way that it had before. It is also true that particular services within the welfare state have been reduced in extent, some quite dramatically, like council housing. Others have grown, equally dramatically, notably social security. More generally, there have been important changes in the structure and organization of services and in the balance of spending within them. Yet, by 1996, the last full year of the Conservative Government, the share of the Gross Domestic Product (GDP) spent on state-funded welfare services was somewhat greater than in 1974. It accounted for a quarter of all spending in the economy. We chart that growth and the changed spending patterns in subsequent chapters. We also measure what that spending has achieved and the growing demands on it. As we said in the last edition of this book (Hills 1990), reports of the death of the welfare state have, like Mark Twain's, been greatly exaggerated.

The society that social policy has had to respond to has altered more in the past twenty years than it did in the previous thirty. We shall analyse the altering demands on the system, caused by age structure, unemployment, sickness and disability, and the growing inequality of original incomes. We then look at the outcomes of spending and structural change, given the changing pattern of demand. Standards of educational achievement, health gains, housing standards, standards of care of the elderly, income distribution, and poverty are all indicators we shall use. Here again, there may be a group of readers who expect to read a gloomy story of failure. This group will include those who have in their minds what Titmuss (1968: 26) described as the 'burden' model of welfare, in which public spending on welfare services is simply money thrown down an expensive drain. The very title of an influential early book in our period, Bacon and Eltis's *Britain's Economic Problem: Too Few Producers* (1976), reflects that view, as did the stark first paragraph of the 1979 Conservative Government's initial public spending White Paper—'Public expenditure is at the heart of Britain's present economic difficulties' (HM Treasury 1979b: l). The model was elaborated in a more sophisticated way reflecting modern public choice theory in later writing, well represented by a paper in the *Economic Journal* by Denis Snower (1993). State welfare institutions perform badly and thus drag down the nation's economic performance, he and others argue. Yet many of the reforms undertaken in the period of Conservative office were directed at changing that perceived situation. Did they succeed?

Critics on the left and centre of politics have also been critical of the achievements of social welfare institutions. They blame lack of resources, failings in the education system, and the very same 'market reforms' the Conservatives imposed on the services in their period of office. These critics, too, may find our results a surprise. The picture is neither so black nor so white as many of the protagonists claim. If we are to have a serious debate on 'the future of the welfare state' it would be as well to begin with fact rather than fiction. We report improved educational outcomes, improved housing standards, better performance by the National Health Service, more redistribution towards the poor. Why, then, is there so much concern and dissatisfaction with the state of welfare?

The answer is that the non-welfare world has not stood still in the last quarter of a century. There has been a marked growth in the inequality of incomes derived from the labour market (Hills 1996), a growth in unemployment, and, for those who have prospered, a growth in expectations of quality and service standards. The growing demands made on the taxpayers' pockets have come from the unemployed and the no longer employed. They have squeezed the money available to the basic services like health and education. Yet consumers' expectations of high standards have continued to grow. Average household expenditure in real terms grew by well over half in our period. People's purchases of household goods nearly doubled in real terms from 1971 to 1995, their spending on travel and communication more than doubled, their spending on recreation, entertainment, and education nearly trebled (ONS 1997b). So, of course, people have demanded more of their social services, despite the fact that much the same share of their income was taken to pay for them and that costs per item delivered have steadily risen. Rising expectations, rising demands, and a lid on the budget: that has been the story of the past twenty-five years. 'Has done reasonably well in all the circumstances but must do better', might be the report card.

The Scope of the Book

The core of this book is concerned with five areas—education, the National Health Service, housing, personal social services, and social security. Together we take public policy in these areas to constitute 'the welfare state'. A primary focus is on public spending and the results of that spending. In 1996/7 (that is, the financial year ending on 31 March 1997) total UK public spending on these areas came to £190 billion (HM Treasury 1997). If nothing else, its scale suggests that it is important to examine the way in which such a sum is spent.

At this point, we should make clear that 'the welfare state' is not a term that we are entirely happy to use. Like others before us (e.g. Titmuss 1958) we would rather consider the term within quotation marks. But the term does have a popular meaning and resonance, so we shall continue to use it, developing and expanding it as we go. However, there are other 'states of welfare' than that provided by direct public spending alone. These include what Titmuss identified as 'fiscal welfare' operating through what has come to be called 'tax expenditure' (income tax relief for mortgage interest payments being perhaps the best known) and 'occupational welfare' operating through employers (for instance, in providing occupational pensions). To this we shall add 'legal' or 'regulated welfare'. The actions of both courts and government may require individuals and firms to spend money in certain ways that supplement or replace state welfare (Burchardt and Hills 1997; Glennerster 1997; Le Grand 1997). Examples are statutory requirements for individuals to take out private pensions or for employers to pay for sick leave or maternity or paternity leave or that require men to pay for the child for which they are responsible. We shall assess the trends in these complementary states of welfare.

It would also be a mistake to look at public spending in isolation. While the public sector is dominant in many of the areas which we examine—education, health, and non-pension-related social security—it plays a smaller role than the private sector in others—housing and many areas covered by the personal social services (where unpaid informal carers carry out most of the work).

Even where the public sector is dominant, it is important to maintain a distinction between public *finance* (or resources provided in kind) and public *provision*. The National Health Service provides a model where provision is largely by public employees paid for through tax-financed public spending. This is, however, by no means a universal feature of the welfare state. Where charges are made for publicly provided services—for instance, rents for local authority housing—it is private sector resources which are paying for public provision. Meanwhile, public sector finance of privately provided services is becoming more important: one example is 'contracting out' of previously publicly provided services; another was the use of social security payments to meet the costs of privately run residential homes. Even in areas where provision of a service is both private (profit-making or voluntary/informal) and is paid for privately, public sector regulation may still have very important effects. We have therefore looked at public sector services where appropriate in the context of this 'mixed economy of welfare' (although we would not want to claim that our coverage of private/occupational welfare is complete). We elaborate some of these ideas about complementary and competing systems of welfare in the last chapter.

We have examined the period since 1974, in particular, for three reasons. The most important is that it bridges the gap between a period of continuous growth and development in social policy and that following the economic crisis and public expenditure cuts of the mid-1970s, which marked a break in the history of ideas about social policy. We discuss this discontinuity and some of the continuities in Chapter 2. Second, the period covers the terms of office of the Labour Government from 1974 to 1979 and of the long period of Conservative rule from 1979 to 1997. For technical reasons the detailed examination of outcomes and real spending has to end in 1995/6.

Finally, we have been able to look at the use and distribution of many welfare services using data from the Government's annual General Household Survey (GHS), which covers more than 10,000 households (containing more than 25,000 individuals) each year. This became available at the beginning of our period and provides a consistent series on service outcomes through the period. Unfortunately, as we write, it seems it may be abandoned. We have used raw data from the survey for individuals and households for a number of years, using in particular the surveys carried out in 1974, 1979 (or 1980), 1985, 1990, and 1994 to compare the performance of the welfare state over the two and a half decades, supplemented by material from a wide range of other sources.

Public discussion of the welfare state is often confused by the messy state of the data describing it. Politicians can pick the figures to suit their case. We have attempted to provide consistent time series which we hope will provide a useful source of coherent data. In the analysis we therefore concentrate on quantitative measures and indicators. This should not be taken to imply that we regard qualitative analysis and information as unimportant, but rather reflects the constraints of length and our aim of providing directly comparable material on the different service areas and on trends over time. For similar reasons we provide little in the way of international comparisons; again, that is not to imply that they are unimportant, simply that they require a different book.

Structure of the book

In Chapter 2, Howard Glennerster elaborates on the importance of the mid-1970s as a breakpoint in the history of social policy since the Second World War. This provides the background to the five core chapters of the book, in which we look in turn at education, health, housing, personal social services, and social security. Finally, in Chapter 8 we bring together some of the key findings of the earlier chapters to provide an overview of the 'state of welfare' and the emerging other 'states of welfare' and to speculate about their future.

The separation of the five service areas into different chapters will be convenient for those readers who have a particular interest in, say, education or social security. We have also tried, where this is possible without putting a strait-jacket on what are sometimes heterogeneous areas, to answer common questions about each area within a common format. The logic behind that format is sketched out in Fig. 1.1. Thus, for instance, someone who wanted to examine the way in which policy towards the whole of the welfare state had developed could read Chapter 2 and then the policy sections of the five succeeding chapters. Similarly, each of the core chapters contains sections on public expenditure, on the 'outputs' from that spending, and on 'outcomes' in terms of indicators of individual welfare. The book is thus designed to be read 'vertically' as well as horizontally. Someone who did not want to read very much could content themselves with the 'In brief' sections at the end of each chapter and with Chapter 8.

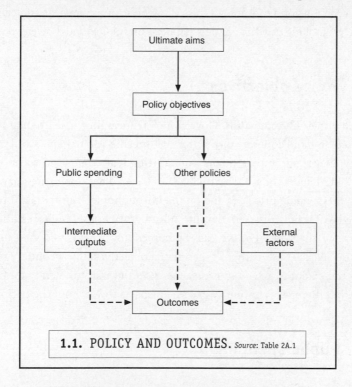

1.1. POLICY AND OUTCOMES. *Source*: Table 2A.1

Ultimate aims

At the start of each of the core chapters we discuss the ultimate aims of welfare policy in that area. What is the result of all this activity supposed to be, and why is the state involved in this area, rather than leaving it to the unaided market? This may seem unnecessary, but it often seems to be forgotten that the *objective* of health policy, for instance, is to do with *health*, not—ultimately—with the amount of *health care* provided. This specification of objectives helps to provide a framework against which outcomes can be measured at the end of each chapter. A recurring problem is, however, the vagueness or blandness of the specification of such objectives—'a healthy population' or 'a decent home for all at a price within their means', to give two examples. We have tried to tie such statements down in ways in which we can at least measure progress in the direction of their attainment, even where we cannot specify precisely what full achievement would entail. A further problem is that some of the objectives conflict, and in some areas (such as education) there has been considerable disagreement about the objectives of policy and changes in declared policy aims over time.

While there is some dispute, it will be evident from the discussion throughout the book that neither we nor those who have shaped the welfare state see its sole aim (or even in many cases its main aim) as being the provision of services for the poor. There are contested aims and the balance between them shifts over time, especially as the Government in power changes. Education is a good example of this. Many policies are unclear and can only be discerned, if at all, by looking at what actually happens on the ground—revealed policy.

Policy objectives

However clouded their ultimate aims, Governments more often specify their objectives for particular services in more concrete terms, through specific White Papers and through statements on individual programmes in the annual round of what used to be called Public Expenditure White Papers (now Departmental Reports). These objectives have a tendency to focus on public spending priorities and on the 'throughputs' (numbers of operations carried out or lengths of waiting lists) or 'outputs' (numbers of houses built) resulting from public spending, rather than on what we call 'outcomes'. As well as allowing us to examine progress in terms of each Government's own stated objectives, the account of policy in each chapter shows the extent to which, for instance, 1979 did mark the end of a previous consensus, or whether there was continuity in some respects throughout the period.

Public spending

Each of the core chapters contains a careful examination of public spending since the financial year 1973/4 (which provides the base for the examination of trends over the 'Labour' period up to its final full year of 1978/9). We take the series forward until 1995/6 for detailed spending analysis—the latest we have. Later figures for aggregate spending are included to bring the picture up to the end of the Conservative period of office where we can. This expenditure analysis over time is not an entirely straightforward exercise. First, there are problems of data. In a few cases detailed and consistent data for spending in the whole of the United Kingdom are available from the Central Statistical Office's (CSO's) *Annual Abstract of Statistics* for relevant years or from Public Expenditure White Papers. In most cases they are not.

Particular items move from programme to programme, or disappear entirely as a once explicit spending item is transformed into a tax expenditure. Some detailed information is available only for Great Britain excluding Northern Ireland, or for England and Wales but not for Scotland, or even only for England. We have used a variety of sources in order to present series which are as consistent as possible and we have tried to present most information on at least a Great Britain basis, but the latter has not always been possible.

A second problem relates to the *measurement* of public spending. Presentation of figures for spending in *cash* terms may be useful for accounting purposes, or even as political propaganda, but has few merits as a way of showing trends over a period when prices have changed as much as they have over the last twenty-five years. Much of the information we provide is therefore shown in *real* terms (sometimes called 'cost' terms), that is, with the cash figures adjusted by an index of general inflation (specifically by the 'GDP deflator' calculated by the ONS, which measures inflation throughout the economy). This gives the best guide to trends in the resources going to a particular area in terms of their opportunity cost to the rest of the economy, and is most useful as a way of measuring how resources going into a particular service are changing relative to other services and the rest of the economy.

Real spending does not necessarily tell us, however, what can be afforded by a particular spending programme. This is because the prices of what is being purchased by that programme (which could be goods such as school textbooks, or services such as paying teachers) may not have changed by the same proportion as prices as a whole—the *relative* price of what is being purchased may have changed. Thus, to take a hypothetical example, spending on doctors' salaries may have increased by 2 per cent per year over some period faster than prices in general, but this may have meant no change in the number of doctors being employed if all that happened was that their real salaries also increased by 2 per cent per year. In order to measure what *volume* of services is being provided by a particular programme, the cash spending figures have to be adjusted using an index for the prices of whatever it is spent on—an 'own price deflator'. Where this is possible and appropriate we also provide information on this basis.

Until 1982, public spending was planned in volume terms, with the figures presented in what were called 'Survey Prices' (once less kindly referred to as 'funny money'). The problem with planning in this way was that while it gave a good guide to, say, the number of doctors being provided, it did not necessarily give a good guide to how much tax revenue would be needed to pay for them. What became known as the 'Relative Price Effect'—a change in real spending which was invisible in the volume figures—undermined their credibility. The problem was not that the volume information was wrong or uninteresting, but rather that it shed light on only some of the important questions about public spending. To get a clear picture, one really needs *both* real *and* volume information, which is what we have tried to provide. We also show changes in spending in relation to the whole of general government expenditure (that is, by central government and local authorities, but not including public corporations) and as a share of Gross Domestic Product.

Real and volume information together still do not give the whole picture. A first problem is that it is very hard to measure the quality of what is being provided. To return to the example above, there may have been no change in the number of doctors employed, but it may be that their higher salaries reflect a higher level of training and quality of service. In this case, the volume figures could be misleading as a guide to the output of health care. One reason why some branches of the social services show much slower growth in volume terms than in real terms is that they are highly labour-intensive, and salaries tend to rise in real terms over time. The reasons for this lie partly in the need of the public sector to compete with increasing salaries elsewhere even if there is no productivity improvement possible in that particular service, but also in productivity improvement within the public sector itself. There is little we can do to measure this, however, other than to jump all the way to the kind of outcome measures which should reflect both quantity and quality of the service provided (but also reflect many other factors).

The second problem is somewhat more tractable. This is that one is not only interested in the volume of service being provided, but also in the relationship between this supply and the demand or *need* for it. Thus, for instance, much of the debate about spending on the National Health Service has concerned the extent to which spending has kept up with the increasing needs of an ageing population. If such needs are increasing, a constant total volume of spending will imply a declining level of service for equivalent conditions (as there are, for instance, more or more difficult cases to cope with). Again, where possible, we present figures on a per capita or demographically adjusted basis to give some idea of the relationship between the volume of service provided and such needs.

A third point to bear in mind is related to the difference between public funding and public provision which was noted above. Figures for public spending can be on a *gross* basis, or they can be *net* of charges. Where there is a change over time in the extent to which finance comes from charges, the gross and net figures will change in different directions, the gross figure giving a guide to public provision but the net figure to public funding. Chapter 5, for instance, examines the differences in trend between the net figure for current public spending on housing, including subsidies to public housing, and the gross amounts actually being spent on its day-to-day management and maintenance. Once again, figures on both bases are more illuminating than figures on either by itself.

Finally, the discussion of public spending in each area includes an examination of the tax expenditures which parallel (and often exceed) the explicit public spending programmes.

Intermediate policy objectives

Following the discussion of public spending we look at the *outputs* which result from that spending—numbers of houses built, numbers of meals on wheels delivered, and so on. These are closely related to the volume of spending (indeed, if there was only one variety of output and its price was calculated correctly, the two would show identical trends). Such measures are often used to formulate policy objectives—targets for nursery places in relation to the number of children under 5, to give an example from education policy. As well as looking at trends in the totals of such outputs, it is often possible to look at their *distribution* (and that of the 'outcomes' discussed below)—for instance, by income group or by region. This is of interest not only because policy objectives may have been stated for distributional goals (for instance, through the Resource Allocation Working Party system in the NHS), but also because concepts of *equity* in access to public services may form part of the ultimate objectives of policy in the area.

In four of the five areas (for data reasons, it was not possible in the case of social security) we have been able to draw on the General Household Survey as part of this exercise. This allows us to examine the distribution of the use of welfare services, or status in relation to the targets of those services, in a variety of ways, such as distribution by tenure, by region, by age, by socio-economic group, by parent's or head of household's birthplace (as a proxy for ethnic origin), and by income.

Distributional results by income are shown in relation to quintile groups, that is successive fifths of the population arranged by income. There are many ways in which this could be done. We have used gross family income, that is including social security benefits but before deducting taxes. We have also adjusted for family size, recognizing that a family of four with a particular income will not be as well off as a single person with the same income. This adjustment produces equivalent income to that of a single person (the scaling we use divides by 1 where the 'family unit' is a single person, and by 1.61 for a couple, adding 0.44 for each child; these relativities are a simplified version of those embodied in what used to be the 'ordinary' Supplementary Benefit scale rates). In the analysis, this level of gross equivalent family income was allocated to each individual (including children) within the family and each individual was then allocated to one of the five quintile groups, each containing 20 per cent of the individuals within each year of the GHS used.

This procedure gives a consistent way of allocating individuals by income over the period of study except in one respect. The inconsistency results from the change in the Housing Benefit system in 1982/3. Before then, those receiving Supplementary Benefit would have had included in their benefit payments—and hence their gross incomes on our basis—an amount reflecting their rates and rent (if tenants). After the 1982/3 change, these rebates were in most cases netted off rent and rates demands rather than being included in Supplementary Benefit payments. The rent and rates element thus disappears from our definition of gross income used in, for instance, allocating individuals to income quintile groups for 1985. This has advantages in bringing the treatment of those receiving Supplementary Benefit (now Income Support) into line with that of those receiving partial rent and rate rebates (which have always been netted off rent and rates demands and would not be included in gross income for earlier years either). It does mean, however, that the allocation of individuals between the first and second income quintile groups is not entirely comparable between 1975 and 1979 (or 1980) on the one hand and 1985 and later on the other. Comparisons on this basis between the two periods therefore have to be interpreted with some caution. Unfortunately the data did not permit a consistent definition of gross income, either including or excluding all Housing Benefit throughout.

Final outcomes

In Fig. 1.1 the final part of the picture is the box of what we call *outcomes*. The difference between these and the outputs discussed above is best explained with some examples. In education, the number of teachers per pupil would be given as an output from public spending, but the educational qualifications of the population would be an 'outcome'. In health, the number of operations carried out would be an output (sometimes called a throughput), but levels of morbidity and mortality would be outcomes. Of necessity, the accounts of outcomes in the different areas are fairly heterogeneous. However, we have tried to provide figures which match the objectives identified at the start of each chapter, and which give a guide to distribution as well as average or total levels of achievement.

In the figure the line linking the outputs from welfare spending to such outcomes is broken to stress that the link between the two may be tenuous. Mortality may be more related to public health in a wider sense than to health care by itself, for instance, and educational achievement may be influenced as much by home environment and the labour market as by teacher–pupil ratios. A full analysis of causality would have to specify counterfactuals as to what would have happened in the absence of the particular part of the welfare state, an exercise we have not been able to carry out. It should not be forgotten either that some of the other links in the figure are tenuous too—governments may set policy objectives, but the bureaucratic machine may be able to pursue others, so that public spending may not change automatically in the way in which the policy pronouncements would suggest.

In his analysis of social policy making Levin (1997) is critical of the whole approach taken in this book, arguing that many policies have no particular objective but are merely responses to particular interest groups or interdepartmental battles in Whitehall. Many stated objectives are just excuses for action that have other unstated objectives. We do not disagree. However, if politicians do set objectives and justify a policy with public statements of intention, a necessary part of the democratic process should be to see how far the stated intentions have been fulfilled. Other studies may wish to look for hidden goals and motives behind the scenes. That is not our purpose here.

In brief

In this book we attempt to provide a consistent picture of what has happened to the 'welfare state' as represented by public spending on and policy towards education, health, housing, personal social services, and social security (examining, where possible, comparable trends in private sector activity). We examine the data available on such services both in terms of their extent and in terms of the ultimate outcomes which they are intended to influence in so far as we can infer these from public statements of intent by governments. The picture we present will be a disappointment to those looking for simple overarching trends. The welfare state is not homogeneous; nor is what has happened to its component parts.

Further Reading

HILLS, J. (1997), *The Future of Welfare: A Guide to the Debate*, York: Joseph Rowntree Foundation.

GLENNERSTER, H. (1997) *Paying for Welfare: Towards 2000*, Hemel Hempstead: Prentice Hall/Harvester Wheatsheaf.

SNOWER, D. (1993) 'The Future of the Welfare State', *Economic Journal* 103, 700–17.

2 New Beginnings and Old Continuities

Howard Glennerster

I. A New Era

OUR STUDY begins in 1974. All dates are arbitrary starting-points in history but the defeat of the Conservative Government at the hands of the miners and the election of the Labour Government in that year makes it an important date for several reasons. Behind those political events lie deeper forces. One was the oil price rise of the previous year and the economic shocks that it brought with it. The oil shock was not, in itself, enough to change the course of history. The world's economies would have adjusted to it and, after a pause, resumed their previous pattern of growth in private and public prosperity. But the oil crisis brought to a head a longer-term accumulating crisis in Keynesian demand management and in the politics of public expenditure. It also produced a significant change in the economic philosophies of both the Conservative and Labour Parties and hence an eventual change in their social policies, too.

The politics of retrenchment are quite different from the politics of incremental growth, as both Reagan and Thatcher were to find (Pierson 1994). In the end, though, seeking to hold budgets down was not enough. Fundamental structural changes were called for. They did not happen immediately but the origins of structural change lie in this period.

Finally, the 1970s saw the beginning of a trend to growing inequalities in the earnings of those in the labour market. From some time in the mid-1970s the spread of original incomes earned in the workplace began to widen after a period of growing equalization. Instead of sailing with the tide the welfare state was now battling against it (Hills 1996).

Unemployment and inflation: a new trade-off

The promise to sustain a high and stable level of employment had been at the heart of post-war social policy. In 1944 the Coalition Government had accepted that post-war Governments should seek to achieve the goal of 'a high and stable level of employment' (HM Treasury 1944). However, the attempt to run the economy at a level of demand that generated full employment put both employers and unions in a strong position to pass on inflationary wage and price increases to consumers in the absence of some collective restraint as, indeed, the 1944 White Paper itself warned (HM Treasury 1944: para. 49). In each successive economic cycle since the Second World War in the United Kingdom the underlying level of inflation rose. The long-term consequences of this pattern were becoming unsustainable just at the point when the inflation induced by the oil shock hit home. The combined effect was to force a shift in economic priorities. Containing inflation became the prime goal of economic policy, not full employment. In 1975 the Labour Government reduced public spending despite the fact that there was a growing recession. The conversion from Keynesian orthodoxy to the new set of priorities was given formal expression in the famous passage from the new Prime Minister's speech to the Labour Party's Annual Conference in 1976. James Callaghan said:

We used to think that you could spend your way out of recession and increase employment by cutting taxes and boosting government spending. I tell you in all candour that option no longer exists, and in so far as it ever did exist, it only worked on each occasion since the war by injecting a bigger dose of inflation into the economy, followed by a higher level of unemployment as the next step. (Labour Party 1976)

The Conservative Government in 1979 took this fundamental change of emphasis further (Burk and Cairncross 1992). In the early 1980s the new government under Mrs Thatcher imposed a tight monetary regime and a tight fiscal one too, raising taxes and reducing the nation's borrowing during a time of recession. This would have been unthinkable a decade before. It was this which was to push unemployment above the three million mark. Yet, as the most articulate exponent of the new policy, Chancellor Nigel Lawson, was to argue, the Government was not abandoning its interest in the level of employment (Lawson 1984, 1992). It was asserting that the only contribution government could make to employment in the long run was first, to create conditions for relatively stable prices and second, to promote an internationally competitive and efficient economy through micro-economic policy— 'supply-side measures' as they came to be called. He put trade union reform high on his list of priorities to create a flexible labour market but improvements to education and training came to be agreed as key policies by both parties, as we shall see in the next chapter. The tolerance of high levels of unemployment and the primary emphasis on micro-efficiency measures had very important side-effects for social policy. Rapid increases in unemployment transformed the social security budget and reduced the amount available for other things.

The new emphasis on economic goals and supply-side measures changed education policy and much else.

Public expenditure: a new strategy

The second change of a fundamental kind that happened in the mid-1970s also coincided with the same economic shock but was more fundamental in character. For most of the twentieth century expenditure by the state on public assistance, health, education, and housing has risen much faster than the economy as a whole (see Fig. 2.1). Clearly this could not continue for ever. In the period from 1951 to 1976 nearly two-thirds of all the UK's economic growth had been devoted to finance public expenditure. The individual's own take-home pay was growing much more slowly than the economy was growing. There was a political limit to the extent that this could continue to be tolerated. The crisis of 1974–6 brought this problem to a head. Though consumer spending had been growing only slowly since the Second World War compared to many other countries, it had at least been growing. That ceased in 1974. Real consumer spending fell in 1974 and in 1975. It remained stable in 1976 but fell again in 1977. This had never happened since 1944. Consumers and taxpayers began to change their preferences. Public support for social spending waned (Whiteley 1981). Driven by the IMF, to whom it had appealed for help, the Labour Government reformed the way public expenditure was controlled, introducing cash limits on departments' budgets and checking the growth in public spending. The Conservative Government took these reforms further in 1983 (Thain and Wright 1995). During the 1980s, despite the large extra demands on the budget caused by unemployment, the share of the Gross Domestic Product (GDP) devoted to social welfare stopped rising.

New Conservatives

The experience of government and of defeat in 1974 as well as the economic crisis of 1976 had a profound effect on Mrs Thatcher, Keith Joseph, and others in the new leadership of the Conservative Party (Thatcher 1993; Timmins 1995). It caused them to rethink their beliefs and their policies (Thatcher 1993). Initially the rethinking concentrated on economic policy and the trade unions but later it included social policy too. In short, 1976 saw some important breaks in post-war continuities even if the immediate effects on social policy were varied. Tracing these and their impacts will be the subject of the subsequent chapters.

However, conflict and controversy were not new to social policy in the post-war world, as I have tried to show in more detail elsewhere (Glennerster 1995). Moreover, many of the debates about social policy in the period after 1974 can only be understood in the context of similar debates over the previous thirty years.

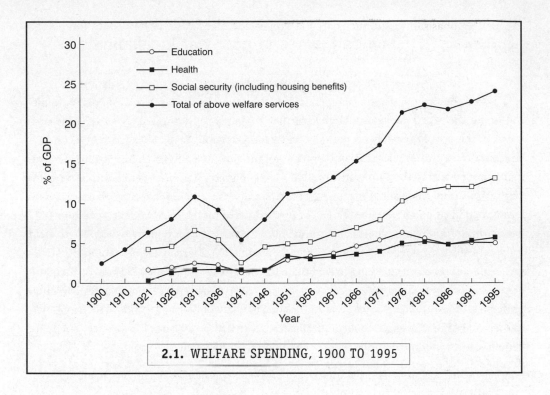

2.1. WELFARE SPENDING, 1900 TO 1995

New inequalities

Research undertaken for the Rowntree Inquiry into Income and Wealth (Joseph Rowntree Foundation 1995) and presented in full in Hills (1996) charts a remarkable and internationally experienced change in the pattern of incomes generated in the market place. Not only had post-war Governments been able largely to eliminate large-scale unemployment; the market place itself had generated more middle-income jobs in the 1960s and early 1970s. From 1977 to the early 1990s there was a very sharp widening in the gap between the wages of those at the top and the bottom of the earnings distribution. The lowest-paid male workers saw no real increase in their wages. Those at the median experienced a 35 per cent rise and those in the top decile a 50 per cent increase. The growth in inequality between households would have been even greater if women's earnings had not grown. From the time statistics on wages were first collected in the 1880s differentials had remained little changed. Now they were widening as the labour market demanded higher skills at one end and low labour costs at the other. Other forces were at work. Family structures were under threat as divorce laws and social attitudes changed. Marriage and family breakdown produced more single-parent families at young ages and labour markets pushed older men out of jobs much earlier than hitherto. The welfare state was being asked to work much harder merely to stand still and provide a safety net for the increasingly risky lives people were forced to live. The 1970s were, therefore, a watershed but there were continuities too.

II. Common themes in post-war legislation

The years from 1944 to 1948 were remarkable for the range of social legislation that was passed and the profound and lasting effect it had on the structure of social service adminis- tration for the next forty years (Glennerster 1995). Merely to list these Acts is to remind our- selves of the significance of this period. The 1944 Education Act established free secondary education as a universal right. It remained, until the Education Reform Act of 1988, the pri- mary statute setting the administrative structure and guiding principles of education policy. The 1946 Family Allowances Act created the first universal cash benefit (for second and sub- sequent children) paid to the mother. Though extended by the child benefit system in 1975 it was this Act which established the principle of paying a *cash* benefit to *mothers* to help defray the costs of a child. The 1946 National Insurance Act largely implemented the struc- tural changes recommended in the Beveridge Report (1942) though not the goal of adequate benefits as of right (Lowe 1993, 1994; Viet-Wilson 1994). The report set out six fundamental principles—flat-rate subsistence benefits (enough to live at a tolerable standard of living), flat- rate contributions, a single unified administrative structure for social insurance, adequate benefits, and a scheme that was adjusted to different kinds of employment.

It should not leave either to national assistance or to voluntary insurance any risk so general or so uni- form that social insurance can be justified. (para. 308)

The insurance scheme is one for all citizens irrespective of their means. (para. 309)

While no Government was to implement adequate benefits for all, the structure of national insurance remained in place until the 1980s (Hills *et al.* 1994).

The National Health Service Act 1946 was also, until the 1989 White Paper (DoH 1989*a*) and subsequent legislation, *the* essential foundation stone for the administration of health care in the United Kingdom. In setting out his objectives for the new service to his Cabinet colleagues in 1945, Aneurin Bevan said:

We have got to achieve as nearly as possible a uniform standard of service for all and to ensure that an equally good service is available everywhere. (Cabinet minutes for 5 October 1945, quoted by Buxton and Klein 1978)

The National Assistance Act 1948 created a single national means-tested allowance avail- able to all those not in employment whose financial resources fell below a standard set by Parliament. The Children's Act of 1948, the Housing Act of 1949, and the Town and Country Planning Act of 1947 complete the list of fundamental and long-lasting statutes.

Since they were all passed in such a short space of time, mainly by one Government, they incorporated common values and assumptions. First, they embodied the principle of a citi- zen's universal right of access to services of an equal standard regardless of geography or income. This principle differed sharply from practices in the 1930s, against which politicians of the centre as well as the left were reacting. There were sharp geographical inequalities. There were the indignities of public assistance. There was unequal access to health care, which depended on gender (women and children had very little access to the national insurance panel doctor), on generation, and on occupation (which affected the financial viability of workers' insurance schemes). These were all injustices that were strongly felt. Social services were primarily concentrated on some sections of the working class and on men, who were the insurance beneficiaries (Glynn and Oxborrow 1976). But in the new legislation, family allowances went to *all* mothers with two or more children. Every worker had to be a member of the National Insurance Scheme. The National Health Service (NHS) was available for all, not just those below average incomes. The Children's Act created a service for all children in need of care and protection. The Education Act of 1944 embodied the principle of free secondary education for all. Fees had been charged until then. The aim was to widen educational opportunity for everyone and at the same time to raise standards (see Kogan 1978).

The powers given to central departments enabled them to ration resources between local authorities. Local education authorities had to submit development plans to ensure there would be comparable standards of provision in different areas. Capital building was regulated and priorities set by central departments (Griffith 1965). Quotas were set to limit the employment of doctors and teachers in favoured areas. How effective these powers were we shall discuss later.

A second common principle was the setting of minimum standards. The National Insurance scheme sought to ensure that during periods of income loss for predictable reasons, such as when earnings were interrupted because of sickness or unemployment or more permanently after retirement, the citizen's standard of living did not fall below an acceptable minimum. Housing and public health legislation and regulations set minimum standards of fitness and overcrowding. Maximum class sizes were set by national regulations. This centrally set goal of minimum national standards and equal access for those in equal need was to remain an expectation of electorates. Governments that failed to deliver it would be held to account.

Much of the post-war legislation was not primarily concerned with redistribution from the rich to the poor. Beveridge was particularly clear on this. Everyone should contribute the *same* amount regardless of income, so that every citizen should feel themselves equally entitled to the benefits. (This was, of course, a considerable fiction in one sense because the taxpayer was to contribute a substantial portion of the eventual costs under the scheme's actuarial assumptions.) It *was* designed to achieve redistribution through a family's or individual's lifetime, to even out periods of misfortune or non-earning capacity. Indeed the *inclusion* of the middle classes for the first time as major beneficiaries of free health care and secondary education inevitably made the post-war welfare state even less redistributive in overall terms than its 1930s predecessor, which had embodied the principle of 'targeting'. The point was made powerfully in Abel-Smith's (1958) essay in *Conviction*. Goodin and Le

Grand (1987) suggest that middle-class capture is a common feature of welfare states. Those just excluded from the means-tested benefits press to be included and the service gradually becomes more universal. The providing professions, such as the doctors in poor areas, despite their leaders' protestations, were happy to have their livelihoods put on a more secure footing by being part of a national service. It was only in the 1950s and 1960s that the Labour Party and academic social reformers came to see redistribution as a goal of the welfare state, distinct, that is, from security and free access, which had been at the centre of campaigns of the 1930s and 1940s.

The structure of the welfare state and its financing mechanisms, especially in the case of social security, were ill-fitted to deliver equality. As those on the left analysed the extent to which welfare institutions were delivering egalitarian goals they were to be increasingly disillusioned (Townsend and Bosanquet 1972; Le Grand 1982).

The third common characteristic of the statutes of this period was stronger central power and administrative rationalization. Beveridge's national scheme replaced a multiplicity of tiny schemes and a mass of administrative complexity. Complex though the modern welfare state may look, it is simplicity itself compared with the schemes that preceded it. Eckstein (1959) maintained this was the main thrust of the reforms. Small district councils lost powers to county and county borough councils. The central departments assumed stronger powers of oversight and direction. Local authorities lost both public assistance powers and their hospitals. But as politics became increasingly concerned with social policy and political parties campaigned on delivering social policy promises, central control and initiative grew. This, too, was a trend that extended into the period of this study (Glennerster *et al.* 1991).

So far, we have been concerned with that spate of post-war legislation which was never matched until 1988. But politics did not stand still in the interim. Indeed, as Empire declined and the United Kingdom's international role diminished, 'social politics', as Crosland (1956) the socialist philosopher and politician called it, prospered. Social policy became the stuff of politics. The notion that somehow both parties agreed on the broad structure of the welfare state is far from the case. It may have been true for a time in the early 1960s but it was never true for the period as a whole. Debates about the appropriate scale of state activity, between universal or targeted benefits, and on the economic impact of social policy recurred throughout.

III. The swing of the social policy pendulum

Consolidation and reaction, 1948–1951

If the previous three years had been ones of legislative activity the period 1948–51 saw a growing economic crisis and relative inactivity in legislative terms. It might be called a period of consolidation. Most of the new services—the National Health Service, National Insurance, National Assistance—came into being on 4 July 1948. They involved a period of enormous administrative upheaval as the new authorities took over responsibility and much wider powers. Meanwhile, however, a reaction was developing to these big changes. In opposition the Conservative Party became increasingly critical of the whole trend to welfare statism. This was reflected publicly in their criticism and questioning of ministers in the House of Commons and in public speeches. In the debate on the 1949 devaluation of the pound the main target of attack was not the Chancellor but Aneurin Bevan, whose profligacy as Minister of Health was seen to be the main reason for the country's economic plight. This became a recurrent theme in Conservatives' speeches in the country. Moreover, the Conservative Party was developing a consistent alternative approach to social policy (Jones 1992; Glennerster 1995).

What emerged was not a meek acceptance of the Beveridge Report or the Labour Government's vision of a welfare state. Social services there should be, but they should have a Conservative face. The first opportunity to make a distinctive stand came with housing policy. Despite the large housing programme there was a popular desire to go faster, understandable in terms of the absolute housing shortage of the time and the enormous waiting lists for local authority housing. Small builders urged that they could do better if restrictions on their capacity to build were lifted. The party wanted to come out firmly in favour of owner occupation though it was reluctant to do so too clearly at this point. It favoured private renting and the removal of rent control. What it did do openly was to advocate a much higher building target of 300,000 houses compared to the existing 200,000 of the Labour Government. It was followed by vigorous support of owner occupation and private renting. These basic housing policy principles forged at this time were to stand the Conservative Party in good stead for the rest of the century.

The second major area of difference with the post-war Labour legislation was on social security. From the start the Conservative Party had been unhappy with the Beveridge scheme and the promise of adequate flat-rate benefits to all. Two young men who were working in the back rooms of the party in various capacities in this period were Enoch Powell and Ian Macleod, both of whom were to become Ministers of Health. The results of their work could be seen in a pamphlet produced by the Conservative Political Centre called *The Social Services: Needs and Means* (Macleod and Powell 1952). They argued that the multiplication of statutory social services had produced a decline in individual initiative and a reduction of personal and family responsibility. This had led to unnecessarily high levels of taxation and disincentives to work. The trend of post-war legislation had been fundamentally mistaken. Two major weaknesses were identified that were to recur in Conservative attitudes to the welfare state.

First, policy had moved away from the principle of insurance, for example in the Health Service, towards increasing levels of Exchequer contributions out of tax. What was needed, they argued, was a return to the insurance principle to finance the NHS. Secondly, they argued that post-war legislation had systematically moved away from charging. Hospital care was free, secondary education was free, and the effect was to involve an element of redistribution from the rich to the poor. This, they argued, should have no place in social policy philosophy. They concluded:

The question which therefore poses itself is not should a means-test be applied to a social service, but why should any service be provided without a test of need? (Macleod and Powell 1952: 5)

We see developing in the late 1940s an alternative philosophical position. Several studies by economists showed, or purported to show, that there had been a rapid redistribution of income since the 1930s away from the upper-income groups. Neither rich nor poor any longer existed in Britain, and indeed, if the process of redistribution continued, the economic health of the country would be endangered. The Labour Party responded to these kinds of attack by defending rather uncritically the institutions it had created. The new social services, it was often implied, were well-nigh perfect. They had eliminated poverty. They would provide a better life if only the Conservatives would leave them alone.

Retrenchment attempted, 1951–1958

The return of the Conservative Government in 1951 was part of the reassertion of individualistic values and the shift away from the universalist model of social policy. Tight limits were placed on spending. Internally the Treasury set up a special Social Services Committee to review spending on social services in the long term. Lowe (1989) shows how the spending departments essentially defeated its aim of major structural change. More publicly the Government set up a Committee of Enquiry on the cost of the National Health Service, the Guillebaud Committee (MoH 1956). The aim was to see what limitations could be placed on the growth of health expenditure, of which the Conservatives had been critical in opposition. They set up a parallel but internal Committee of Enquiry to consider financial provisions for old age and an internal review of housing policy drawing on the work of the party in opposition. It was the first to produce results. A White Paper on housing in 1953, *Houses: The Next Step* (MHLG 1953), set out a long-term strategy for Conservative housing policy. The aim was to reduce drastically the role of local authorities in housing provision and to rely instead on the private market to meet the needs of working people who required rented accommodation. Councils should be confined, it argued, to the role of replacing unfit property and the free market should be re-established in private rented accommodation. The Phillips Committee (Ministry of Social Security 1954) recommended the Government abandon any long-term aim of raising retirement pensions to a subsistence or adequacy level. It argued that in view of the rising numbers of retirement pensioners this would present an unduly heavy burden on the Exchequer. It was accepted by Government twelve years after the Beveridge Report had been published. His essential principle was abandoned. Flat-rate benefits were no longer to be gradually raised to subsistence level. Instead, pensioners who had to rely on state aid alone would have their pensions brought to subsistence level by the National Assistance Board.

The Government's housing White Paper was followed by two concrete measures. The first was the withdrawal of council house subsidies by the Exchequer, except in instances where local authorities were to replace slums or provide accommodation for old people. This process was begun in 1956. In the following year the 1957 Rent Act decontrolled higher-rented properties and provided for the gradual decontrol of any unfurnished property when a tenant moved. The aim was to restore, over a period, free market forces in housing once again. The Government did succeed, for a time, in checking the rising cost of Exchequer aid to local authorities for housing.

While the Guillebaud Committee was sitting the Government put a strict limit on NHS spending, and in the early 1950s the proportion of the Gross National Product (GNP) devoted to health fell. For a while, 1951–6, the total share of GNP going to welfare stabilized, but not for long. The White Paper on local government finance (MHLG 1957) argued that percentage grants should be replaced because they encouraged too much local authority spending. Under this system local authorities were given grants that met a percentage of their spending on a particular service. Under the new arrangement a flat sum of money would be given for a range of services in the hope that those authorities who spent more would be discouraged from doing so since the grant would not rise to meet additional spending. The National Insurance Act of 1959 introduced graduated contributions, which were an attempt to raise more money to meet the cost of pensions without putting an additional burden on general taxation. But none of these measures prevented a rise in social spending after 1956.

Restriction on social service spending in the early 1950s was beginning to show its effects in increasing frustration and criticisms of the welfare system. In 1956 the Guillebaud Committee reported, and although its original intention had been to suggest areas for economy, what it did, in fact, was to suggest that the Health Service was being *starved* of funds and that more should be spent on it. Unlike the Phillips Committee, which had drawn on advice from within government, the Guillebaud Committee had gone outside to appoint as its advisers the new Professor of Social Administration at the London School of Economics, Professor Richard Titmuss, and a young research worker called Brian Abel-Smith. The evidence which they presented to the Committee, and which can be read summarized at the beginning of the report, drew attention to the fact that the NHS was taking a declining share of the GNP, lower even than in the 1930s. This neglect was nowhere more obvious than in hospital building. No new hospital had been built since the war and capital expenditure was running at about a third of the level achieved by the numerous voluntary hospitals and small local authorities throughout the country in the 1930s. The Guillebaud Committee (MoH 1956) therefore recommended a major new hospital-building programme and the retention of the NHS on broadly the same pattern as then existed. In 1962, Enoch Powell, the backroom boy who had doubted the wisdom of the NHS, announced the largest hospital-building programme since the Victorian era. Finally, the Treasury disbanded its Social Services Committee and admitted defeat (Lowe 1989).

Expansion and convergence, 1959–1970

Guillebaud's was the first example of many Committees of Enquiry that were to focus attention on deficiencies in service provision and propose improvements in the late 1950s and early 1960s. The organized providing professions—the BMA, the Royal Colleges, the teachers' unions, the local authority associations—mobilized opinion and built links with the spending departments (Kogan 1978; Beer 1982; Klein 1995). The spending departments appointed a series of expert committees who produced volumes of research and began to win support in Cabinet (Heclo and Wildavsky 1974). After the Suez fiasco, social politics moved to the centre of the stage. The new generation of social scientists began to explore educational opportunity and the outcome of the 1944 Education Act (Floud *et al.* 1956), the reality of family life and the incomes of old people (Townsend 1957), the declining nutritional standards of families (Lambert 1964), and the extent of family poverty (Abel-Smith and Townsend 1965). Above all it was a period of major demographic change. After fears of population decline in the 1940s, births rose steadily. The number of schoolchildren began to rise. More children stayed on longer at school. More acquired qualifications that would gain entry to universities if only the places were available. The Russians' successful launch of the first space satellite provoked fears of Soviet domination and set off a rise in scientific and education spending throughout the Western world.

The elderly who had acquired rights under the post-war legislation were reaching retiring age. The country would be asked to deliver the fruits of those reforms and they would be costly. Thus, despite a decade in which a Conservative Government had sought to contain and reduce social spending, the dam began to break in the late 1950s and finally gave way in the early 1960s (see Fig. 2.1). It was the period of expansion for higher education, and of massive council house building. The reorganization of the social work services and the National Health Service were largely bipartisan.

Reaction begins, 1970–1974

In opposition in the late 1960s, the Conservatives started to develop the themes they had begun in the late 1940s. The public sector was making excessive demands on the economy. Levels of personal taxation were too high. Taxable capacity was insufficient to finance major improvements in *all* the social services. It was therefore better to concentrate public funds on the major services for which there was at present no private alternative—health and education. But in the fields of income maintenance and housing, measures were taken to build up alternatives to public provision. The two major Acts which gave legislative form to this new strategy were the Housing Finance Act of 1972 and the Pensions Act of 1973. The Housing Finance Act was designed to end the complex system of general Exchequer aid to housing authorities based on the number of houses they had built at various times in the past and replace it by a government subsidy which would give aid only to poorer tenants. A national system of reasonable rents would be fixed and rent rebates and allowances given to poorer tenants. This was accompanied by a policy of selling council houses to tenants to reduce the stock of public housing in general. In parallel with this was the 1973 Social Security Act. Its purpose was to rely on private occupational pension schemes. These would be regulated by Government but provision would be private. In the long run this would mean a declining role for National Insurance and leave employers with the primary responsibility for providing pensions for their workers. Thus, the twin strategies of a more managerial structure in the NHS and local government and the stabilization and long-term reduction of spending on housing and pensions did constitute a coherent selective strategy. It laid the foundations for the policies of the Thatcher era. In the end the pensions legislation was never implemented. It was to have come into force in 1975, but by that time a Labour Government had taken office and repealed it. The housing legislation was also repealed by the incoming Labour Government and there followed a brief last fling for that part of the 1960s agenda that remained uncompleted. Child benefit replaced tax relief for children; a major new pensions scheme was introduced. House-building increased. The economic crisis of 1976 put an end to all that.

IV. Outcomes

Measured against the kinds of objectives the politicians of the mid-1940s had set themselves the achievements of these thirty years were considerable (George and Wilding 1984; Wilding 1986). As Bradshaw and Deacon (1986) point out, egalitarian goals were discussed very little in the debates on National Insurance. James Griffiths, in his second reading speech, saw the purpose as the creation of a 'National Minimum Standard' with echoes of the Webbs (see Glennerster 1995). The means-tested National Assistance and Supplementary Benefit schemes *were* to play a much larger role than Griffiths or Beveridge envisaged. But to a large extent, up to the mid-1970s cash benefits did manage to provide a floor under those whose income in the market place would have been minimal. Supplementary Benefit and retirement pensions sustained their purchasing power relative to male manual earnings, that is, they had roughly doubled in real terms since 1948. In 1973 the average private or original income of the poorest tenth of all households in Great Britain was about £19 *a year*—most, remember, were pensioners. The income of the next decile was £283 a year (CSO 1974). If we look at the situation *after* the welfare state did its job and we include benefits in cash and kind we find the poorest tenth of households had a standard of living of not £19 a year but of £777 and the next decile an income of £896 a year, not a princely sum even in 1973 but a lot better than without the welfare state. This is a vivid illustration of Griffiths' National Minimum. What had been achieved was not equality, but a floor nevertheless. As Townsend *et al.*'s (1984) study of European systems showed, the British social security system was more successful than most others in putting an effective National Minimum in place, albeit a low one.

The same kind of story can be told of housing. If we take a combination of measures of inadequate housing—more than one household sharing a dwelling, overcrowding at twelve persons to a room, or lacking a basic amenity—we find from the 1951 Census that 70 per cent of all households suffered from at least one deficiency. By 1976 that was true of only 15 per cent of households. Indicators of maternal mortality, infant mortality, and perinatal mortality, all of which reflect on the standards of health provision as well as on nutrition and social conditions, had fallen dramatically in the thirty years. From eighty deaths of mothers per 100,000 live and still births in 1951 the figure fell to fourteen in 1979, for example. In 1950 only one primary class in three had thirty pupils or less. By the mid-1970s the figure was more than two in three.

By the mid-1970s, however, people had come to demand more. It was not that the social services were failing to meet the objectives of the 1940s. The question was, how far were they meeting the new consumer ambitions of the 1970s and 1980s?

V. In brief

In the period since the end of the Second World War there had been continuous debate about the scope and scale of public provision in the social services. It never was a period of consensus, but the economic crisis in the mid-1970s was to sharpen and deepen that debate. Much had also been achieved in those post-war years. We now go on to consider the changing goals of social policy after 1974, the changed spending climate, and the outcomes service by service. We begin with education.

Further Reading

GLENNERSTER, H. (1995), *British Social Policy since 1945*, Oxford: Blackwell.

HILLS, J., DITCH, J., and GLENNERSTER, H. (1994), *Beveridge and Social Security: An International Retrospective*, Oxford: Clarendon Press.

LOWE, R. (1993), *The Welfare State in Britain since 1945*, London: Macmillan.

TIMMINS, N. (1995), *The Five Giants: A Biography of the Welfare State*, London: HarperCollins.

ANNEXE

Table 2A.1. WELFARE SPENDING 1900 TO 1995 AS A PERCENTAGE OF GDP[a]

	1900	1910	1921	1926	1931	1936	1941	1946	1951	1956	1961	1966	1971	1976	1981	1986	1991	1995
Education			1.69	2.02	2.39	2.17	1.42	1.75	2.91	3.26	3.73	4.59	5.39	6.20	5.54	4.92	5.09	5.09
Health			0.41	1.41	1.69	1.69	1.68	1.72	3.46	3.11	3.28	3.69	4.02	4.91	5.19	4.91	5.47	5.74
Social security (including housing benefits)			4.26	4.65	6.71	5.30	2.47	4.53	4.82	5.16	6.16	6.94	7.86	10.18	11.45	12.02	12.04	13.13
Total of above welfare services	2.60	4.16	6.36	8.08	10.79	9.16	5.57	8.00	11.19	11.52	13.17	15.22	17.27	21.28	22.18	21.85	22.61	23.96

[a] GDP figures are taken from Feinstein (1972) for 1900, Hills (1992: table A3) for 1910–61, and HM Treasury (1997) for 1966 onwards. An adjusted series for money GDP is used for the years between 1946 and 1990. This has been constructed to remove the distortion caused by the abolition of domestic rates.

[b] The cost of Council Tax Benefit and its predecessor (rate allowance) is excluded throughout.

[c] Includes spending on Housing Benefit financed out of local authority housing revenues.

[d] Includes the cost of Child Benefit in the final four years and an estimate of the cost of child tax allowances in 1976. Estimates of the cost of child tax allowance in earlier years are not included.

Sources: Peacock and Wiseman (1967), Feinstein (1972), Hills (1992), HM Treasury (1997), and later chapters of this book.

Howard Glennerster

ANNEXE

Table 2A.2. REAL EXPENDITURE ON WELFARE, 1900 TO 1995 (£ BILLION AT 1995/6 PRICES)

	1900	1910	1921	1926	1931	1936	1941	1946	1951	1956	1961	1966	1971	1976	1981	1986	1991	1995
Education			2.3	2.7	3.4	4.0	3.2	3.6	7.3	9.5	12.4	17.5	23.4	29.9	28.0	29.4	33.1	36.1
Health			0.6	1.9	2.4	3.1	3.8	3.5	8.6	9.0	10.9	14.1	17.5	23.7	26.2	29.3	35.6	40.7
Social security (including housing benefits)[a][b][c]			5.9	6.3	9.5	9.8	5.6	9.2	12.1	15.0	20.4	26.5	34.2	49.1	57.8	71.8	78.3	93.0
Total of above welfare services	3.6	5.6	8.8	10.9	15.3	17.0	12.7	16.2	28.0	33.5	43.7	58.1	75.1	102.7	112.0	130.5	147.0	169.8

Note: The percentage of GDP devoted to welfare services in this table is lower than that in Table 8.2 because it excludes housing and PSS, for which a long-time series was not available.

[a] The cost of Council Tax Benefit and its predecessor (rate allowance) is excluded throughout.
[b] Includes spending on Housing Benefit financed out of local authority housing revenues.
[c] Includes the cost of Child Benefit in the final four years and an estimate of the cost of child tax allowances in 1976. Estimates of the cost of child tax allowance in earlier years are not included.

Sources: as for Table 2A.1, with the addition of Sefton and Weale (1995) and ONS (1997) to construct GDP deflators.

3 Education: Reaping the Harvest?

Howard Glennerster

I. Goals and policies

MORE THAN any other aspect of the welfare state we discuss in this volume education provokes disagreement not only about the means used to achieve its ends but about the very ends themselves. No universally agreed statement of goals can be set out against which to measure the system's achievements. This is illustrated in Fig. 3.1.

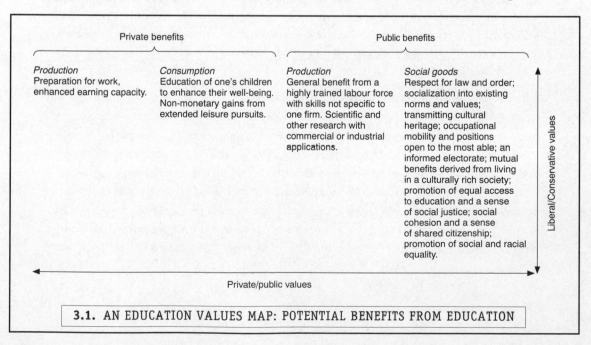

Private benefits | Public benefits

Production
Preparation for work, enhanced earning capacity.

Consumption
Education of one's children to enhance their well-being. Non-monetary gains from extended leisure pursuits.

Production
General benefit from a highly trained labour force with skills not specific to one firm. Scientific and other research with commercial or industrial applications.

Social goods
Respect for law and order; socialization into existing norms and values; transmitting cultural heritage; occupational mobility and positions open to the most able; an informed electorate; mutual benefits derived from living in a culturally rich society; promotion of equal access to education and a sense of social justice; social cohesion and a sense of shared citizenship; promotion of social and racial equality.

Liberal/Conservative values

Private/public values

3.1. AN EDUCATION VALUES MAP: POTENTIAL BENEFITS FROM EDUCATION

Howard Glennerster

There are clear private benefits individuals gain from being prepared for skilled work. These are most easily measured in the improved earnings such people receive in later life. In the words of the Robbins Report, education 'imparts skills suitable to play a part in the general division of labour' (DES 1963: para. 25). But as leisure time grows and working life shortens, the importance of learning as a private consumption good grows. The tuition costs at private colleges in the US are rising even faster than the costs of health care, as we shall see later (Clotfelter 1996). This might be seen as a form of conspicuous consumption by the very rich. Yet, many economic benefits are not just reaped by the individuals who receive the education but spill over to the rest of the economy. Firms are attracted to areas with concentrations of generally well-trained people. We all gain from living in a well-educated and law-abiding country that can support a varied cultural life. We gain from being able to converse with others, debate politics, watch serious TV, live in a democracy, enjoy music with others, go to the cinema and theatre, and travel abroad. Left to themselves parents might not fully appreciate the capacity of their child or wish to invest optimally in his or her education, never having enjoyed the fruits of a good education themselves. It seems plausible to argue that societies need a critical mass of educated people to provide the kind of seed-bed in which new ideas and technical innovations prosper. That is the essence of modern economic growth theory. But the gains may be more than economic growth. To quote the Robbins Report again, society has an interest in ensuring 'the transmission of a common culture and common strands of citizenship' (DES 1963: para. 28). For Tawney,

The fundamental aim of education is not difficult to state. It is simple because the needs of those it is designed to meet have themselves a terrible simplicity. Every year a race of 400,000 souls slips quietly into the United Kingdom—the purpose of the educationalist is to aid their growth. It should be easy to regard them, not as employers or workmen or masters and servants or rich and poor, but merely as human beings. Here, if anywhere, the spirit of equality might be expected to establish its Kingdom. (Tawney 1931: 141)

For some education may be a mere vehicle for ostentatious consumption, for others a way to an egalitarian Utopia, for yet others a means of instilling respect for tradition. No single measure of success is possible given this varied set of objectives and values. Yet politics is about responding to and leading shifts in values. During the period under study the objectives of government policy, the stated goals of both main parties, did change significantly. Under the shock of economic crisis and perceived school failure politicians in both parties began to shift their emphasis. They became more concerned with economic goals for education, with more emphasis on educational standards, traditionally measured as reading, writing, and numeracy, and less with the education system as a means of delivering social cohesion.

Convergent political concerns: basic standards and vocational 'relevance'

The economic crisis of 1976 helped tip the balance. In an influential book, the American historian Martin Weiner (1981) caught this mood. He argued that Britain's economic decline from the late nineteenth century on could be traced to an elite culture that was hostile to industrialization. Such attitudes had permeated the education system, spreading out from the old public schools and infecting the whole education establishment. They were common to aristocrats, conservatives, liberals, and romantic socialists alike. What Britain needed was a reawakening of pride in the vocational, in entrepreneurship, industry, and commerce. In a stream of studies through the 1980s Professor Prais of the National Institute for Economic and Social Research compared the standards achieved by British children at school and in their industrial training with their European counterparts. He found them lacking and in ways that undermined the capacity of their employers to be internationally competitive. (For an overview of this work see Prais 1995.) In America the new growth theorists saw education as a possible major source of innovation on which growth depended (Romer 1993). The shock of the 1976 débâcle and the UK's long-term relative decline produced a changed policy emphasis that is evident in the stated intentions of both the Labour Government before 1979 and in those of the Conservative administrations that followed it. Both produced White Papers that said very similar things in almost the same language. First, the Labour Government:

Young people need to reach maturity with a basic understanding of the economy and its activities, especially manufacturing industry, which are necessary for the creation of Britain's economic wealth. (DES 1977a)

Then, the Conservative Government:

By the time they leave school, pupils need to have acquired, far more than at present, the qualities and skills required for work in a technological age. (DES 1985a)

The Government believes that it is vital for our higher education to contribute more effectively to the improvement of the performance of the economy. (DES 1985b)

A similar bipartisan shift is clear in the growing concern with the poor basic standards achieved by pupils in school. (There was a similar concern in the USA; see Cohen 1996.) In the UK it was the so-called 'Black Papers' of the late 1960s and early 1970s that struck a chord with the media and, eventually, the electorate (Cox and Dyson 1969). Firmer evidence began to appear. Ever since the Second World War the old Ministry of Education and its successor had monitored the reading standards of school children. The results reported from 1948 to the mid-1960s had showed a steady improvement (DES 1966). The average reading age of 11-year-olds had improved by seventeen months and 15-year-olds by twenty to thirty months since the Second World War. The 1971 results (Start and Wells 1972) appeared to show that reading standards had ceased to rise and at junior level had fallen slightly. The caveats in the research report were significant but largely ignored. Mrs Thatcher, as Secretary of State for Education, appointed the Bullock Committee to investigate. Its report (DES 1975*a*) threw doubt on the more alarmist inferences. Amongst several problems with the survey was the fact that many children now found the tests originally set in 1948 *too easy*. Many scores were bunched at the 100 per cent mark, creating a 'ceiling effect'. The best children could not improve their scores and hence checked the average improvement registered.

There was other worrying evidence, however. A study in Aberdeen (Nisbet *et al.* 1972) analysed trends in reading standards by the social class of children's parents and found that, while children from professional and managerial homes had improved their standards, those from the lowest social groups had declined in recent years. Work in the poorest 'priority areas' suggested this effect might be more widespread. In 1974 the new Labour Government set up both the Assessment of Performance Unit (APU), with a remit to produce up-to-date national measures of school performance, and a unit to study ways of improving standards achieved by children from deprived backgrounds (DES 1974). Thus, right from the start of our period standards achieved in school were firmly on the political agenda.

In a well-publicized speech on 8 October 1976 at Ruskin College, Oxford, James Callaghan, the new Labour Prime Minister, both accepted that there was a genuine worry about educational standards and linked that with employers' concerns about the quality of their labour force. (At the end of 1996 Tony Blair, the Labour leader, returned to Ruskin to deliver much the same message.)

The time was ripe for the Department of Education (DES) to pursue what had been a long-term goal of influencing the *content* of school education nationally. This interest dated back at least to Sir David Eccles' failed attempt to create a Curriculum Study Group in the old Ministry of Education in 1962. The DES began to work gently and patiently to build a consensus around the notion of a national common curriculum to be followed by all state school children (DES 1978, 1979, 1985*d*, 1987). A White Paper published by Mrs Thatcher's Conservative Government was at pains to stress the bipartisan nature of this new, and what had been in the 1960s, a radical policy.

Since Sir James Callaghan's speech as Prime Minister at Ruskin College in 1976, successive Secretaries of State have aimed to achieve agreement with their partners in the education service on policies for the School Curriculum which will develop the potential of all pupils and equip them for the responsibilities of citizenship and for the challenges of employment in tomorrow's world. (DES 1987: para. 4)

The National Curriculum, legislated in the Education Reform Act of 1988, therefore originates in the actions of the Labour Government in 1976. The way the Curriculum was implemented, however, was to become controversial. It extended to a wider range of subject matter than had been originally envisaged, the contents became subject to political interference, the tests of children's attainment at successive ages and stages were published as school league tables. All this provoked the teachers' unions to anger and lost the consensus. Yet, even here the dispute was, to some extent, resolved. The central principle of tracking all children's attainment over time against an external standard came to be generally accepted. British and Continental European schooling systems have always had the advantage of externally set and assessed exams to set standards for schools but they had only applied at the end of the child's school life and only for the academically able groups of children taking the O and A level exams. Now external tests were to be applied to all children at regular intervals during their school life.

Politicians were not the only ones to voice concern over education standards. In August 1990 Sir Claus Moser made the state of education the centre of his Presidential Address to the British Association for the Advancement of Science. He called for a Royal Commission. The Government ignored his call and he raised the money to finance an enquiry from the Paul Hamlyn Foundation. The result was the National Commission on Education, whose report was published in 1993 (National Commission on Education 1993). It had many recommendations but summarized its proposals in seven goals:

1. High-quality nursery education for all 3- and 4-year olds.
2. Courses to bring out the best in schoolchildren—a wider choice within the National Curriculum and a voluntary extra Key Stage Five for 14 to 18-year-olds.
3. Better teaching quality achieved by better in-service support for teachers, tougher action on poor teaching, better selection and training of heads, and a maximum class size in primary schools of thirty within five years and twenty in deprived areas.
4. A lifelong entitlement to learning—five days' leave a year for education by the year 2000, funding for adults to reach a basic level of education.
5. The merging of ministerial responsibility for education and training at national level. (This happened in 1995 with the merging of the Departments of Education and Employment.)
6. More investment in education by government and a proposal to make students partly repay the cost of their education through a 'contribution' that could be paid as a higher social security contribution later in life (see Barr *et al.* 1994).
7. A national target that 90 per cent of young people under 18 should be working towards nationally recognized qualifications.

Most of these goals were not controversial—with the exception of the proposals to fund higher education, though even that was endorsed by the Committee of Vice-Chancellors and Principals in 1996. The Prime Minister accepted the goal of providing nursery education for all—at some time. Promising the money to do these things was quite another matter.

Some organizational changes legislated in the 1988 Act were also largely supported. The move to devolve budgetary control to schools as the 'local management of schools' had begun long before. Local authorities, like Hertfordshire, had given their head teachers and governors delegated budgets of a restricted kind since the 1950s. The Inner London Education Authority had begun to do so in the early 1970s and Cambridgeshire went the whole way, devolving virtually all its funding to schools in the 1980s. The 1964 Labour Government had proposed giving more powers to governors and including parents, teachers, and members of the local community as governors. This, too, was legislated in 1988, if anything giving parents less representation than many local authorities already had. So far, then, we can see a continuity of political purpose running through the whole period from 1974 to 1997 shared by the parties and expert opinion alike. There were conflicts, too.

Divergent goals

Labour If we look back to the beginning of the 1974 Labour Government, the Queen's Speech (12 March 1974) is reminiscent of a bygone age. It set the goal of a nationwide system of free state nursery education for all who wanted it. This echoed the commitment in Mrs Thatcher's own White Paper of a few years earlier when she was Secretary of State (DES 1972). The system of mandatory student grants was extended to students following the Higher National Diploma and teacher training. The Houghton Committee (DES 1975a) recommended a large increase in teachers' salaries. The stock of teachers was to be increased to 510,000 to ensure there would be no classes over thirty in primary schools. Circular 7/74 stated that the Government expected all local authorities to avoid the selection of pupils at 11-plus. Most had already been moving steadily to do so since the mid-1960s. When not all local authorities obliged, the Education Act of 1976 required them to submit plans to the DES to create a local system of comprehensive schools. Grants to the private but state-aided direct grant schools were to be phased out from 1976 onwards. Most of these schools became independent but a significant minority of Catholic schools, over a quarter, joined their local authority and became comprehensive. The Government announced, but had to scrap, a plan to give grants to children from poor homes to encourage them to stay on at school. There was considerable concern over the poor achievement of West Indian children, not least expressed by organizations representing their parents. The House of Commons Select Committee on Race Relations called for a high-level inquiry. One was appointed, the Swann Committee. It produced an interim report in 1981 (DES 1981). Its final report came out four years later (DES 1985c). Another committee on the education of handicapped children and those in need of special education was appointed, chaired by Mary Warnock.

Yet, for all its early ambitions, that Labour Government soon checked the growth in education spending after 1976 as part of its public spending strategy. Reform and growth urged on by committees of the great and the good, the pattern from 1954 to 1979, was to end.

Conservative The 1979 Conservative Government did set a new direction in education policy, but only a relatively modest one to begin with. One of its first acts was to repeal the 1976 legislation compelling local authorities to go comprehensive but very few local authorities wished to return to a system of grammar and secondary modern schools—and, with them, the old 11-plus. A few retained their grammar schools and some reintroduced them but on a very small scale. By 1995/6 only 5 per cent of all pupils in secondary schools in the UK were attending grammar schools (ONS 1997*b*).

Gradually, however, a distinctively new emphasis became evident in Conservative policy. It attempted to give parents a wider range of schools to choose from and to bring competitive pressures to bear on state schools. In this respect it shared a common theoretical origin with several developments we shall be meeting in other chapters—the creation of market-like competition, or 'quasi-markets', in the provision of welfare services (Glennerster 1991; Le Grand 1991*c*; Maynard 1991; Le Grand and Bartlett 1993). Much attracted by the idea of school vouchers, the new Conservative Secretary of State, Sir Keith Joseph, seriously pursued the idea of giving parents vouchers with which they could purchase education at state or private schools. He was finally convinced of the administrative difficulties and the cost (Blaug 1984; Seldon 1986). However, he did set in train a series of changes that went a long way toward introducing the principle of vouchers without the paper substance. The Conservative period ended with the introduction of a full voucher scheme for nursery provision abolished by the new Labour Government in 1997. (For a review of these reforms see Glennerster 1996 and West and Pennell forthcoming.)

This sequence of policy changes to increase choice and diversity began with the 1980 Education Act. This reversed the Labour Government's phased reduction of support for the old private direct grant schools. In its place a whole new group of private schools would receive state support that would enable them to give free or reduced fees to pupils with low-income parents. It was called the 'assisted places scheme'. A selected but small number of independent private schools could offer places to children and charge reduced fees depending on the parents' income. The difference between those fees and the full fee could be recovered by the schools from the Government. The scheme began in a small way in September 1981. 5,300 places were made available initially. The eventual target was raised to 35,000 and there it remained until 1995 when the Government announced plans to extend the scheme to primary schools and double the number of places. In 1989 86.5 per cent of the available first-year places were taken up. By 1992 this had risen to 100 per cent and the scheme remained fully booked (DES 1995). Even so it was a tiny scheme compared to the nearly four million children in secondary schools and amounted to about 5 per cent of all private school places.

In 1986 the Government introduced the City Technology Colleges Initiative—an attempt to encourage industry to fund a new kind of school that would give special emphasis to the teaching of technological subjects. This aroused rather little interest and support from industry.

More radical ideas were to wait for Mrs Thatcher's third term. The cornerstone was the 1988 Education Reform Act—the most important change in the administration of schools since 1944. The Act contained six main elements:

1. A National Curriculum was to be introduced with a series of levels or attainment targets to be achieved by given ages and common assessments set for children nationwide at ages 7, 11, 14, and the statutory school-leaving age.
2. Provision was made for schools to opt out of local authority control and to be funded directly from central government.
3. Local authority secondary, larger primary, and later virtually all schools had to have devolved budgets. The local authority was not able to retain more than 15 per cent of the money set aside for schools in its own hands for centrally provided services. The rest had to be devolved to schools and managed by the governors, who would include parents and local community representatives as well as some teachers.
4. Universities were to be funded by a Funding Council that would take much more central control of their affairs. Tenure for newly appointed academic staff was abolished.
5. Polytechnics moved from local authority control to become independent institutions under a separate Polytechnic Funding Council.
6. The Inner London Education Authority was abolished and education powers in London given to the local boroughs.

Later the 1992 Education (Schools) Act required schools to publish the exam results achieved by their pupils and the results of the National Curriculum tests. The White Paper of the same year—*Choice and Diversity*—was followed by the creation of the Funding Agency for Schools, which had the power to create new grant-maintained, centrally funded schools free of local authority control and to permit private schools to opt into the state sector as grant-maintained schools. Student funding also underwent a fundamental change. The Government announced that it would gradually reduce the real value of student grants and set up a student loans scheme to 'top up' the value of the grants. The loans would be repayable when the ex-student's income rose above 85 per cent of national average earnings. The Government returned with more proposals to restructure higher education only three years after the 1988 Act. It published a White Paper proposing to abolish the distinction between polytechnics and universities, funding all universities, new and old, on the same basis. Teaching and research would be separately funded by Higher Education Funding Councils—one for each of the separate countries of the UK. The universities would be free to charge what they liked for overseas students and to attract research grants as before. The 1992 Further and Higher Education Act transferred further education colleges from local authority control to independent corporate bodies competing for students funded on a modified per capita basis—'bums-on-seats funding' as the colleges put it.

The new funding arrangements for higher education enabled the Government to embark on a period of rapid expansion. Since teaching was to be separately financed it was possible to pay each college a smaller sum than before merely to pay for teaching, concentrating research money in a few institutions. Universities were also permitted to attract all the students they could and, for these extra students, merely receive the very low fees paid them by the local authorities who supported the students with mandatory grants. The Government announced its intention in the White Paper to raise the percentage of the 18-year-old group going to higher education from the one in five it was in 1991 to one in three by the end of the century. So eager were universities to expand their incomes that the numbers entering university rose to a third of the age group within a few years. Government then reimposed its limits on student places.

The early years of the 1990s were taken up with implementing this batch of legislation consolidated in the Education Act of 1996. Then, in the run-up to the next general election, more changes were legislated. The 1996 Nursery Education and Grant Maintained Act

1. gave the Secretary of State the power to make grants to both local authorities and private bodies to provide nursery education. Though the Act did not spell this out it gave the Government power to experiment with a pilot scheme that would give vouchers to parents of all 4-year-olds which they could then take to private and voluntary schools and playgroups as well as state schools. This was to be implemented generally in 1997. The value of the voucher would not meet the full costs of a nursery place, however;
2. gave grant-maintained, or opted-out, schools the power to borrow money to build facilities secured on their property or lands.

Public concern

In the midst of all this structural change public concern with educational standards grew and its desire to see greater priority given to education grew too. Professor Halsey's (1991) commentary on the British Social Attitudes Survey concluded:

there are increasingly widespread worries about a number of aspects of education. Large class sizes in state primary and secondary schools, shortages of books and equipment, early specialization, lack of discipline in the classroom, perceived disrespect for teachers and their declining real pay are all focal points of concern. Public perceptions of the performance of secondary schools in particular are decidedly gloomy. (Halsey 1991: 57)

What is very clear from these surveys is that the public wanted more money spent on education. Education held second place to the National Health Service in this regard but support for spending on education grew through the 1980s and 1990s. Support for the proposition that the Government should 'increase taxes and spend more on health, education and social benefits' rose from 32 per cent of respondents in 1983 to 58 per cent in 1994 (Taylor-Gooby 1995). Three-quarters of the population gave first or second priority to spending on the NHS in 1983–and almost the same in 1994. Half put education in that spot in 1983 but 60 per cent did so in 1994.

II. Expenditure trends

As in the rest of this book we distinguish two spending series. The first is based on 'real spending', that is cash spending deflated by the overall GDP deflator or an average price index for the whole economy. This shows us how much in resources education was taking from the rest of the economy—the opportunity cost of education. It is the series favoured by the Treasury. We begin with that (Table 3.1).

The column headed 'Total public expenditure on education' covers all levels and kinds of tax-financed spending not only on schools run by local education authorities but on government grants to students and to colleges. The preceding columns distinguish the broad components—current spending on primary, secondary, and post-school education, plus other related activities, followed by all capital spending lumped together. (More detailed breakdowns are given in the Annexe Table 3A.1.) The final component of public spending is that on student grants. All of this spending is net of any fees paid by individuals for a local college class, for example. Those fees, along with the total of private school fees and fees paid for things like private secretarial courses, come within the column headed 'Private expenditure on education'. (The Family Expenditure Survey provides the basis for the National Income Accounts to provide a consistent series.)

Until 1974/5 state education spending was rising, as it had done for the previous three decades. Through most of that period education spending had been rising by about 4 per cent per annum in real terms. Then comes the historic break in that pattern. There was a pause in spending in 1975/6 at just over £30 billion and then a fall of about £2.5 billion to £27.8 billion in 1977/8. That new lower level of spending was held to for almost a decade. The £30 billion figure, in 1995/6 prices, was only reached again in 1987/8. The largest proportionate change has been in capital spending. It was more than halved between 1973/4 and 1978/9. By the mid-1980s capital spending was running at little more than a quarter of its 1973 levels. Though recovering a little in the 1990s it was, by the end of our period, running at less than half the level of building activity taking place in 1974/5. The reduced school population (see below) explains some of this but surveys of school building standards in the 1970s (DES 1977b) suggested major deficiencies that required a large modernization programme.

The result of the public spending strategies of successive Governments was to reduce the share of the GDP allocated to publicly funded education from 6.5 per cent in 1975/6 to 4.7 per cent in 1988/9. The significance of this change should not be underestimated. No such previous reduction in education's share of the nation's resources had occurred this century, even following the Geddes 'cuts' of the 1920s or the retrenchment of the 1930s. It is not to be found in the experience of any other leading nation. There was some recovery in public spending in the 1990s but only to reach just above 5 per cent of GDP.

These basic figures, however, need some qualification. First, we take account of private spending and then of demographics.

Table 3.1. REAL EXPENDITURE ON EDUCATION, UNITED KINGDOM (£ BILLION AT 1995/6 PRICES, ADJUSTED BY GDP DEFLATOR)

	Current spending (net)						Total capital	Total student grants	Total expenditure on education	Private expenditure on education[c]	Public expenditure on education as % of GDP	Total expenditure on education as % of GDP
	Primary	Secondary	Higher, further, and adult education	Other[a]	Related[b]	Total current						
1973/4	5.5	6.5	5.9	1.6	2.5	22.0	4.3	1.2	27.5	1.6	5.8	6.1
1974/5	6.6	7.8	6.4	1.7	2.6	25.1	3.7	1.3	30.0	1.5	6.4	6.7
1975/6	6.7	8.0	6.4	1.8	2.7	25.6	3.4	1.4	30.3	1.6	6.5	6.8
1976/7	6.2	8.0	6.3	1.8	2.8	25.6	2.9	1.3	29.9	2.0	6.2	6.6
1977/8	6.2	7.7	6.0	1.8	2.5	24.4	2.2	1.2	27.8	2.2	5.6	6.1
1978/9	6.2	7.8	6.0	1.9	2.6	24.6	1.8	1.3	27.7	2.3	5.4	5.9
1979/80	6.1	7.6	6.1	2.0	2.7	24.4	1.7	1.4	27.5	2.3	5.2	5.7
1980/1	6.3	8.0	6.4	2.1	2.5	25.3	1.8	1.4	28.5	2.4	5.6	6.1
1981/2	6.2	8.2	6.3	2.1	2.4	25.2	1.4	1.4	28.0	2.6	5.5	6.1
1982/3	6.1	8.2	6.4	2.1	2.5	25.3	1.4	1.4	28.1	2.7	5.4	5.9
1983/4	6.1	8.3	6.6	2.2	2.5	25.7	1.4	1.5	28.5	2.5	5.3	5.8
1984/5	6.0	8.1	6.6	2.2	2.5	25.5	1.2	1.5	28.1	2.6	5.1	5.6
1985/6	6.0	8.1	6.6	2.2	2.5	25.4	1.2	1.4	27.9	2.6	4.9	5.4
1986/7	6.5	8.6	7.0	2.5	2.2	26.9	1.2	1.3	29.4	2.8	4.9	5.4
1987/8	6.9	8.8	7.2	2.5	2.2	27.6	1.2	1.2	30.1	2.9	4.8	5.3
1988/9	7.2	8.8	7.2	2.6	2.1	28.0	1.2	1.3	30.4	3.0	4.7	5.1
1989/90	7.6	8.8	7.5	2.8	2.2	28.8	1.6	1.2	31.7	3.4	4.8	5.3
1990/91	7.7	8.5	7.6	2.9	2.2	28.9	1.6	1.3	31.8	3.8	4.8	5.4
1991/2	8.1	8.7	7.7	2.9	2.4	29.9	1.7	1.6	33.1	4.5	5.1	5.8
1992/3	8.9	9.0	8.1	2.5	2.0	30.5	1.6	1.9	34.0	5.1	5.2	6.0
1993/4[d]	9.1	9.0	8.3	2.5	2.0	30.9	1.6	2.1	34.6	5.4	5.2	6.0
1994/5[d]	9.3	9.1	8.9	2.5	2.1	32.0	1.8	2.2	36.0	5.8	5.2	6.0
1995/6[e]	9.4	9.1	9.0	2.5	2.1	32.1	1.8	2.2	36.1	6.4	5.1	6.0

[a] Special schooling and other spending on administration.
[b] School health and welfare service, school meals, youth service, transport, VAT.
[c] Private consumer spending on education from ONS (1997d: table 4.7 and previous editions).
[d] Provisional data.
[e] Provisional data for England only, grossed up by author to provide UK figure.

For further detailed notes and sources see Annexe Table 3A.1.

So far we have been talking only of Governments' funding from taxation—'net' government spending after taking off any charges or private fee income. One strategy local government used to mitigate the consequences was to increase the fees it charged to attend courses in further education colleges. Universities were forced to charge higher fees to home and especially overseas students. Fees charged by private schools continued to rise and more people looked to private education to make up for what the state was not providing. We look at this in more detail below but in aggregate we can see from Table 3.1 that there was a steady rise in the funding of education from households' own pockets. Total private spending on education was only 0.3 per cent of the GDP in 1973/4 but rose to 0.9 per cent of the GDP by 1995/6 or £6 billion. People, or some people, were expressing their continued preference for education spending in a very clear way. Such an increase in private spending on education should not be equated with the growth in numbers going to private schools. The category covers far more spending than that, as we saw. But the percentage of the relevant age groups in the population going to private schools did rise a little in the twenty years—rising to a peak in the very prosperous years of the late 1980s and then falling back somewhat (see Table 3.2).

Table 3.2. PERCENTAGE OF PUPILS IN PRIVATE SCHOOLS

	2–4 years	5–11 years	12–15 years	16–18 years[a]	All school pupils
1974/5[b]	2.0	3.2	7.0	11.4	5.5
1979/80	4.8	4.5	6.9	18.3	5.8
1984/5	4.8	5.0	7.4	17.5	6.2
1989/90	5.7	5.1	7.7	16.9	6.7
1994/5	5.6	4.7	7.3	18.4	6.3

[a] State pupils in sixth form and Further Education colleges are not included in these calculations.
[b] On an England and Wales basis; on a UK basis in other years.

Source: DfE (1995b: table 12b; Table 13 in earlier editions).

Pearson *et al.* (1988) have shown that a rise in income amongst households in professional and managerial groups increases private school attendance. The 1980s were a period of very high additional incomes for the top decile and that would be expected to reflect itself in a rising demand for private education. Low spending per child in local education authority schools also tended to be associated with increased demand for private education. All in all it is, perhaps, the small rise in the proportion of schoolchildren going to private schools that is the surprise but it did reverse nearly a century-long decline in private schools' share of the school population (Glennerster and Wilson 1970).

The second caveat we must make about the crude spending figures above is that they take no account of demography. The numbers of children of primary school age fell from the beginning of our period, recovering only slightly after 1985. Secondary school numbers fell

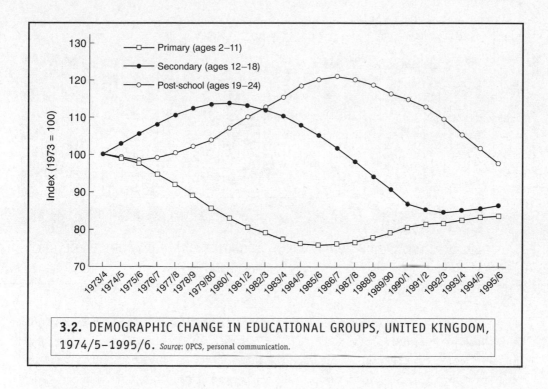

3.2. DEMOGRAPHIC CHANGE IN EDUCATIONAL GROUPS, UNITED KINGDOM, 1974/5–1995/6. *Source*: OPCS, personal communication.

through the 1980s. Yet the age group who could benefit from higher and further education rose sharply (see Fig. 3.2).

To get a better picture of changing resource levels we must take account of these demographics. But we must also take account of the price basis with which we have been working so far.

To this point we have confined our analysis to 'real' education spending—cash spending deflated by the broad GDP deflator or price index of all goods and services in the economy. For those working in education what matters is how much additional resources they have to work with—teachers or computers or buildings. To measure trends in the 'volume' of education provided we need to deflate cash spending by a series of indices that reflect how much the prices of the things schools and colleges use, above all teachers' salaries, have risen. The result is a measure of what volume of resources the education budget will buy. This picture is shown in Figs. 3.3 and 3.4. They smooth out the apparent jumps in educational spending in Table 3.1 that resulted from teachers' pay increases, for example.

What emerges is a quite extraordinary plateau in the volume of resources available to education for two decades, with a dip in the 1980s. Only at the end of the period did education spending financed from public sources regain the levels of the early 1970s, except for the election year of 1979/80! The decline in capital stands out again and so, too, do the consequences of expanding student numbers on the ' transfers', or student support, item in the 1990s. Fig. 3.4 shows the composition of current expenditure. What stands out is the relatively constant

Howard Glennerster

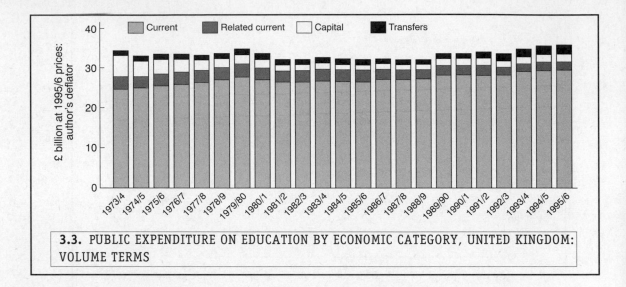

3.3. PUBLIC EXPENDITURE ON EDUCATION BY ECONOMIC CATEGORY, UNITED KINGDOM: VOLUME TERMS

share of the total taken by the different sectors. Given the very different demographic picture with which we started, a more varied pattern might have been expected. The 'equal pain' and 'inertia' theories of public budgeting seem to be alive and well (Glennerster 1980). In the face of falling rolls it is not so easy to sack primary teachers and close schools. Governments and

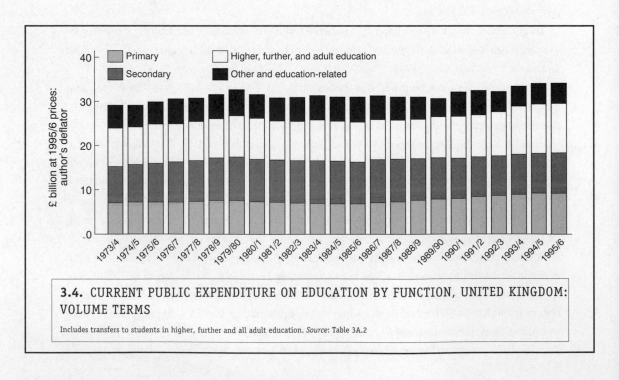

3.4. CURRENT PUBLIC EXPENDITURE ON EDUCATION BY FUNCTION, UNITED KINGDOM: VOLUME TERMS

Includes transfers to students in higher, further and all adult education. *Source*: Table 3A.2

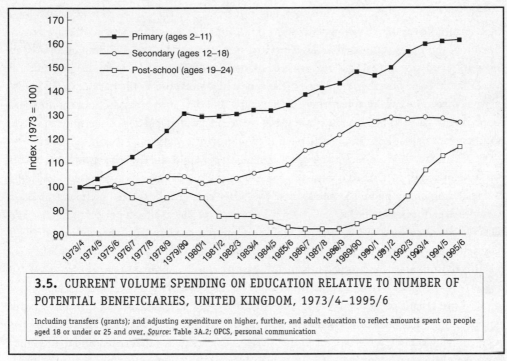

3.5. CURRENT VOLUME SPENDING ON EDUCATION RELATIVE TO NUMBER OF POTENTIAL BENEFICIARIES, UNITED KINGDOM, 1973/4–1995/6

Including transfers (grants); and adjusting expenditure on higher, further, and adult education to reflect amounts spent on people aged 18 or under or 25 and over. *Source:* Table 3A.2; OPCS, personal communication

local authorities appear to have put firm ceilings on all sectors' budgets and let demography do its worst or best.

If we now divide through these spending levels in volume terms by the numbers in the relevant age groups we can see what has happened to the resources available to the average young person in each age group (see Fig. 3.5).

Because the pre-primary and primary school population fell by nearly a quarter, the relatively stable spending overall in the 1970s and 1980s still permitted a significant rise in spending per head of that age group. Part of this was devoted to extending pre-school facilities to a larger percentage of the population and part to increasing the spending per primary school child (see Annexe Table 3A.3). The rising secondary population was forced to share a highly constrained pot of resources. Resources per pupil remained fairly constant until the mid-1980s. Then, as numbers in the age group began to fall, resources per pupil rose. Per-pupil spending in volume terms was a quarter higher by the end of our period compared to the beginning.

The story for the post-school age group is very different. University places were cut while the numbers in the age group who could have benefited rose. There was a 20 per cent cut in resources available for each young person who could have benefited from a place in higher or further education. The policy on access to higher education was reversed in 1988. This shows up clearly in Fig. 3.5. Resources per head of the population aged 19–24 did rise from 1988/9 on but the number of places in colleges of higher education rose even faster. That meant less per student. Per-pupil spending on post-school provision halved between 1973/4 and 1995/6. We show the reductions in spending per student in Annexe Table 3A.3.

The consequential reordering of spending priorities over the whole period does have a logic. From the time of the Plowden Report (DES 1967), at least, it had been officially recognized that the UK was unusual in devoting so little to primary school children compared to those in secondary school and university. If higher education was to expand significantly it was difficult to see how this could be done at such a high unit cost. In the period we are studying the Government were able to increase per-pupil spending on primary school children and reduce it for those in higher education using the financial stringencies of the time to tackle both issues. That, at least, is a charitable interpretation of events!

The relative stability in secondary school spending per child and the reduction in resources per student stands in marked contrast to trends in the United States. Between 1970 and 1990 real spending per pupil in US schools rose by 75 per cent (Burtless 1996). The comparison with private universities in the US is even more striking. There, after a period of relative stability in the 1960s and 1970s, average real spending per student rose sharply in the 1980s (Clotfelter 1996). Even taking account of growing concessions and scholarships, the real resource cost of attendance at US private universities rose by about 75 per cent from 1978/9 to 1991/2—a higher rate of increase than US medical costs! State universities' spending per pupil, more reliant on public funding, rose much less but still increased at just under 3 per cent per annum. In the world's richest society the demand for better-resourced education has been growing rapidly. It has to be said that there is little evidence that educational outcomes have been improving commensurately, at least in schools. If anything, standards of achievement have been falling for much of the period in US public schools (Hanushek 1996). Money, it seems, is far from being the solution to the problem of raising standards.

Before leaving the subject of educational spending we should remind ourselves that formal educational resources are only part, and probably not the most important part, of any child's education. Parenting time and the quality of parenting have significant explanatory power in analyses of childrens' school performance both in the US and the UK (Osborn *et al.* 1984; Osborn and Milbank 1987; Desai *et al.* 1989, 1990; Belsky and Eggebeen 1991; Robertson and Symons 1995). The current generation of schoolchildren has better-educated parents than its predecessors but it probably also has less of their time. In 1951 only a quarter of married women worked. Now the great majority do, including those with children. In 1994 46 per cent of mothers with children under 4 and 55 per cent of mothers with children of 5–10 were in paid work (CSO 1995). About a fifth of mothers with under-tens were working full-time. The proportions rise sharply for educated mothers. The majority of professional and managerial-class mothers are at work. There is little evidence that men have taken over serious parental duties to replace the time their wives are now devoting to paid work. (For a review of this evidence see Hobcraft and Kiernan 1995.) So, alongside a stable or declining formal educational input we may have also experienced a substantial decline in parental child care. On the other hand some parents may have been devoting more time to their children's education—poring over league tables or choosing schools as well as reading or helping with homework. The plain fact is that we do not know what has been happening to this crucial component in educational input.

III. Intermediate policy outputs

Politicians do not generally deal in readily quantifiable ultimate goals and objectives. They do sometimes set more practical intermediate targets. A clear example was the last 'educational growth' document of the era—the White Paper in 1972 for which Mrs Thatcher was responsible as Secretary of State for Education, *Education: A Framework for Expansion* (DES 1972). The Conservative Government set out targets which the subsequent Labour Government largely endorsed before the IMF crisis led it to abandon growth in education spending. It is a convenient starting point in reviewing the subsequent twenty-years.

Nursery education

The 1972 White Paper stated, '[The Government's] aim is that within the next ten years nursery education should become available without charge . . . to those children of three and four whose parents wish them to benefit from it' (DES 1972: para. 17). The estimate was that provision for 90 per cent of 4-year-olds and 50 per cent of 3-year-olds would meet the demand. The 1974 Labour Government reiterated that pledge. There was progress, helped by the decline in primary school numbers. Four-year-olds could be accepted in primary schools before they reached the statutory school entry age of 5. The number of under-fives in maintained state schools rose from 17 per cent of 3- and 4-year olds in 1970 to 44 per cent in 1987. By 1995/6 the figure for the UK had risen to about 55 per cent with a further 4 per cent of the age group in private nursery schools, making nearly 60 per cent all told (NSO 1997). This was still a long way from the targets set two and a half decades earlier. It was also well below the levels in many other European countries (see Table 3.3).

School buildings

The next priority was meant to be a major renewal programme for secondary schools to complement the one under way for primary schools and a new programme to improve special school facilities. The DES undertook a national survey of school building standards in the mid-1970s (DES 1977). It concluded that, at the levels of capital spending then under way, it would be possible to achieve only just over half of the relatively modest standards described in that document. In the next decade net capital spending on secondary schools was to fall dramatically from £2 billion to £290 million. It recovered but only to £540 million by the end of the period (see Table 3A.2). The fall in new money was offset, in part, by the sale of old school sites to fund new building. Conservative Government encouraged local authorities with falling school populations to close undersubscribed and old schools and sell the sites, often for housing, using the proceeds to finance school building. This means that in the 1990s the level of total gross spending has been a good deal higher than net spending. In 1994/5,

Table 3.3. PARTICIPATION OF 3- TO 5-YEAR-OLDS IN PRE-SCHOOL EDUCATION, 1991

	Age		
	3	4	5
Belgium	97	99	98
France	98	100	99
Germany	35	71	84
Netherlands	—	98	99
Spain	28	94	100
United Kingdom	32	72	100
USA	33	57	90
Canada	—	48	70
Japan	21	58	65

Source: CSO (1995).

for example, the gross total, with spending funded from sales, was running 75 per cent above the net figure. Even so, the building standards targets set in the 1970s must be a long way short of having been met.

A different equity issue arose in the 1990s. The new grant-maintained schools, created by the 1988 Act, were given separate allocations of capital from the local authorities. In 1994 these schools had 3.5 per cent of the school population (CSO 1996). In 1994/5 they were allocated 19 per cent of the Government's total provision for school building (DfE 1995: table 10).

Class size

Mrs Thatcher's 1972 White Paper set a 10 per cent improvement in staffing standards as its goal by 1981. The Labour Government promised to end classes over 30. This did not happen. By 1980/1 30 per cent of classes in English primary schools were still 31 or more (see Table 3.4). The average size of primary class as taught in England *did* fall from 27 to 25 between 1977 and 1980/81 as pupil numbers in primary schools fell but by 1995/6 the average class size had risen to 27 again. The number of primary school classes taught with over 30 pupils did fall as the number of primary age children fell but had risen again by 1995/6 as primary pupil numbers rose. In contrast the number of secondary classes of over 30 declined steadily from 20 per cent to 8 per cent in the two decades. The average class size changed little.

While state schools reduced their class sizes a little, private schools more than kept pace. In 1970/1 their average pupil–teacher ratio was 14 : 1 in the UK as a whole. By 1994/4 it was 9.9 : 1 (CSO 1996: table 3.13).

Table 3.4. CLASS SIZES AS TAUGHT, ENGLAND[a], 1977–1995/6

	Primary schools					Secondary schools				
	1977	1980/81	1985/6	1990/1	1995/6	1977	1980/81	1985/6	1990/1	1995/6
% of classes taught with										
1–20 pupils	9	11	10	7	5	28	29	31	32	24
21–30 pupils	48	59	64	67	63	52	58	59	62	68
31 or more pupils	43	30	26	26	32	20	13	10	6	8
Average size of class (no. of pupils)	27	25	26	26	27	21	21	20	20	22

[a] Public sector schools only. Excludes classes taught by two or more teachers and sixth form colleges.

Staying at school

Young people have left school in the UK earlier than in most other comparable countries since at least the 1950s though they have also begun formal schooling earlier. It is true that the numbers staying on rose from the mid-1950s through to the beginning of our period but not on the same scale as abroad. By 1973 about 18 per cent of boys and girls aged 17 in England and Wales were staying on at school. The figure was higher in Scotland, especially for boys at over 20 per cent, with girls just below 20 per cent.

Just as our period begins, this trend ceased. The numbers of both boys and girls staying on to 17 in Scotland fell to about 16 per cent by 1979. Numbers in England and Wales fell and then rose again a little, stabilizing at the 1973 level by 1979 (CSO 1979). This was the first serious check in twenty years. In the same way the number of young people gaining two or more A levels peaked in 1977 at about 13 per cent for girls and 15 per cent for boys. We discuss some of the possible reasons below. After a small rise after 1979 the numbers staying on at school and in further education colleges remained static until 1987/8. This was a decade lost, especially so in contrast to the rapid rises in staying-on rates happening in other European countries.

Then, a significant change begins to occur. The percentage of 17-year-olds staying at school and college begins to rise strongly after 1986. Increasingly young people were attending colleges rather than schools at this age and sixth-form colleges were breaking away from lower schools. We therefore need to look at the numbers of 17-year-olds attending schools and colleges full-time. In England this figure rose from below 24 per cent in 1979 to nearly 40 per cent in 1989/90 and then to over 60 per cent in 1994/5. This still left the UK below the levels reached in other countries (Green and Steedman 1993). Germany, the Netherlands, Belgium, and France had about 80 per cent of their 18-year-olds in education and training, with other European countries mostly reaching 60 per cent by 1992. Moreover, there were signs of a slowing down or halting in the rising trend by the mid-1990s. Several factors seem to have contributed (Steadman and Green 1996). The first is the 'GCSE effect'. The old O level exams were designed to be taken by only a minority of children. To fail at their pass mark meant a student left with no qualifications. GCSE was meant to be more all-inclusive. Most children were meant to take the exam at some level. Pupils could pass at the old O level standard or gain lower grades. More of the work was practical in nature. The result was that more children both took the exams and passed at good grades equivalent to the old O levels. This encouraged more children to stay on and take A level. At the same time the labour market was increasingly rewarding those who stayed on and was ceasing to offer jobs to those who had no qualifications. The social security rules also changed, denying the opportunity to draw benefit for those who left school at 16. Changes in the funding of higher education encouraged an expansion in places (see below). This is a complex story and it is not possible yet to disentangle fully the quantitative importance of each factor but there is evidence that all played some part.

Higher education

Targets were set in 1972 for higher education. It was hoped that about 22 per cent of the 18-year-old age group would enter higher education. In fact, the figure, which had been 13.7 per cent in 1970, fell to 12.6 per cent in 1980 and did not begin rising again until the mid-1980s. Reductions in access were partly caused by deliberate decisions by the Labour Government to reduce places in the colleges of education, which were producing too many teachers for the shrinking primary school age group, but, less forgivably, by the reductions in the number of university places funded by the next Government in the early 1980s at a time when the group of normal university age was increasing quite fast. Yet, it is also true that the demand from students was not rising at the expected level. The reasons seem to be a combination of deliberate Government policy and changing labour market factors. First, the Government began to erode the real value of the maintenance grant paid to students. It had been kept at much the same real level, with something of a dip in the mid-1970s, since the 1960s. Then both the full grant, and even more important the grant net of parental contributions, were allowed to fall steadily in real terms. In 1988/9 levels of maintenance in real terms had fallen by a third compared to 1980 (DES 1988). The direct private cost of going to university had risen. Indirect costs were rising too. Earnings of young people in their teens in the 1970s rose quite significantly, partly through trade union bargaining pressure and partly through labour market demand. The result was that the opportunity cost of going to university was rising too—the earnings young people would have to forgo to go to university or merely stay on at school. On top of this, in the 1970s the earnings advantage graduates received, over and above non-graduates, had eroded. The rapid expansion of graduate supply after the Robbins expansion of the 1960s reduced graduate wages relative to others just as the costs were rising (Pissarides 1982). However, by the mid-1980s these trends in the labour market began to go into reverse. The structure of industry and the service sector began to change fast in the 1980s. There was a growing demand for high skills from the expanding part of the economy and a collapse in the demand for lower skills. This was just the time when the Government was still cutting university places. For a while the rising costs of going to university dampened the demand but soon the growing gap between the supply and the demand for highly qualified people pushed up the rewards for those with higher qualifications again (Whitfield and Wilson 1991; Bennett *et al.* 1992; Schmitt 1993). The private rate of return rose and so did the demand from students to stay on longer at school. The Government changed course, encouraging an expansion in university places, thus removing the risk that had always attached to A level study—there might not be a college place available even after two years' study.

It is difficult to disentangle these interacting forces but all contributed to another remarkable change. Having stuck on a plateau for nearly a decade and a half, entry rates to higher education doubled in five years. The Government planned to achieve a 30 per cent participation rate by the end of the century (DES 1991). It was achieved by 1994/5. At that point the rising public spending consequences led the Government to check the expansion, holding universities to student quotas.

In Europe, notably in France, there has been an equivalent, indeed faster rate of expansion in higher education places. By comparison with America, however, the UK has caught up. Though it was once true that many more American children gained access to higher education, the percentage of the population going on to a *four-year* degree course in the States, roughly equivalent to our sixth form plus three years, has not risen in the past decade and more. The percentage going on to such degrees is now no more than that in the UK (Steedman *et al.* 1997).

So much for the more easily counted landmarks. None of this tells us whether children know any more! Have politicians' and the public's concern with basic standards produced any improvement in the achievements of children?

IV. Final outcomes

We have argued that governments, after 1976, gave greater weight to raising basic standards of achievement in schools and to the economic goals of education. Yet the difficulties we have in measuring the outcomes of such a policy shift are several.

First, there is a long time-lag to be expected. It took a decade to legislate a National Curriculum and it will take a further decade for it to be fully implemented. Only in 1995 did the first tests of 11-year-olds take place. We have no hard information on pupils' relative levels of achievement before and after the National Curriculum was introduced. It will take schools, publishers, children, and teachers some time to fully adapt to the new expectations. Certainly, the publication of national test results has focused a great deal of attention on standards. What impact that is having on schools compared to all the other influences at work is impossible to tell. Local experiments with a National Curriculum are a contradiction in terms.

Second, measuring changes in pupil performance over time is fraught with difficulty. We have already referred to the 'ceiling effect'. Moreover, as knowledge changes and as different kinds of knowledge become more important both in social life and the labour market, so teachers' emphasis and the curriculum will adapt. In the 1940s most children, those taught in secondary modern schools, were given a very restricted diet of the three Rs and woodwork and metalwork or domestic science. Since then the scope of the curriculum offered to the ordinary secondary school child has exploded—different sciences, geography, history, the environment, foreign languages, a variety of sports, music, travel. Even if children's reading capacity is no greater but they have a knowledge of science that their parents lacked, overall standards will have improved.

Third, subjects themselves have changed. Mathematics, as taught in schools, has changed greatly in the past thirty or more years. Simply asking pupils to take thirty-year-old maths papers may not be a very good test of their capacity.

Fourth, and an extension of the last point, if we are concerned to train pupils more effectively to perform better in the labour market, what kinds of skills does the labour market value? The Cockcroft Committee (DES 1982) was appointed because of press criticism and employers' complaints about the mathematical attainments of young workers. It turned out, on careful questioning, that employers had very few and vague complaints and that their own entrance tests had little relation to the tasks actually required of their employees. Pioneering work done at the National Institute of Social and Economic Research led by Professor Prais has pursued the question by comparing standards and types of education received by young workers in other countries. His most convincing point is that the English system is particularly deficient in equipping average and below-average students and in giving them basic standards of education and technical training as high as those of our European competitors (Prais 1995).

Finally, if changes in pupils' performance over time can be demonstrated they cannot necessarily be associated with schools. Social factors are known to be of overwhelming importance in explaining differences between schoolchildren's performance at school at any one time. We have already mentioned the influence of parenting. Other factors are at work, like poverty, family size, the influence of television and neighbourhood (CBO 1987). These could be having a far more important effect on pupils' performance than changes in schools. The issues are complex and controversial. They do illustrate the importance of social factors in explaining educational performance over time.

The same is true of labour markets. If young people are acting rationally they will not stay on at school if the financial costs of doing so are not matched by the future financial gain—at least not unless they gain great pleasure from education and are using it as a consumption good. In fact, British employers seem to reward those with vocational qualifications very poorly and even those with higher education are rewarded later in life and relatively less than in America (Bennett *et al.* 1992*a*, *b*, 1995). Those who value earnings now rather than in the future may rationally opt not to stay on at school. Blundell *et al.* (1995) show that employer-based training is particularly important in raising future earnings, especially for women. Staying-on rates and school-leaving performance are reflections not so much of the education system but of labour market conditions and wage policies. They may also reflect the fact that some of the most effective training is employer-based rather than gained in formal vocational qualifications.

Bearing in mind all these caveats, however, we now turn to examine what evidence there is on changes in the performance of schoolchildren over time and in comparison with other countries.

Basic standards in schools

Though there is a widely held popular view that basic standards have fallen in schools in recent years there is very little hard evidence. What there is relates mainly to mathematics and it is certainly not encouraging, especially since basic skills, and basic mathematical skills above all, turn out to be of crucial and growing importance in explaining wage differentials, according to some American evidence (Murnane *et al.* 1995). Being poor at maths means you will very likely be poor in a modern economy. It is not high-level maths that is important in this respect but basic maths—decimals, percentages, and recognizing geometrical figures.

There is still only one long-term follow-up study of basic standards achieved by school-children over a long period in the UK and that is in mathematics. As part of an International Study of Achievements in Mathematics a common test was set to 13-year-olds in England in 1964, in 1981, and in 1995. The study illustrates the difficulties we have mentioned. The teaching of mathematics had been transformed over the period in question. New tools and concepts were included in the syllabus which could not be compared with earlier ones. Other, more narrowly technical issues arose (Cresswell and Grubb 1987; Robitaille and Garden 1989). Since they turn out to be very important, readers are urged to refer to the original sources. Thirty-seven 'anchor' questions were selected from the 1964 survey and repeated in 1981. The response rate was less than 50 per cent in 1981 and the exam sat three months earlier than in 1964. The results, taken at face value, showed that the mean scores achieved were lower in 1981 than in 1964. The result was significant at the 5 per cent level. Fifty-two per cent of the items were answered correctly in 1964 and 43 per cent in 1981. Twenty-nine out of the 37 core questions were less well answered than 17 years earlier.

Some results of the 1995 survey were published in 1996 (Keys *et al.* 1996). They show a further, if small, relative decline, though there are still problems with comparability over time. There is a wealth of detail about different kinds of mathematical competence in this survey but on average it seems that English and Scottish 13-year-olds perform about as well as their counterparts in Germany, Denmark, Sweden, and the United States but less well than in Austria, Belgium, France, the Netherlands, and Switzerland. There was very little change in the relative positions of any of these rankings except France, which seems to have improved its position. The countries that are well ahead are those of the Far East—Singapore, Japan, Korea, and Hong Kong. Their position has not changed either! Britain's children were middling, as far as other English-speaking nations and our European neighbours were concerned, and remain middling.

Yet, when we turn to their capacities at science, the picture changes. English school-children outperform two-thirds of the countries in the survey with Japan, Singapore, and Korea still ahead, but not by much. No other English-speaking country outperformed English children and no major European nation's children did so. Moreover, the relative position of England in science had improved since the earlier studies. English children had pulled ahead of those in Switzerland and the Netherlands, who had previously been better, and drawn ahead of the Swedes, with whom we used to be equal. Similar results for 9-year-olds were published later (Harris *et al.* 1997). English children did moderately in maths and well at science. Once more, caveats are in order. Science syllabuses are more varied than maths. The international tests may have better reflected what English students are taught. But we should at least be careful not to condemn the whole English schooling system on the basis of the maths scores. The same schools produce these much better science results. We should do better to understand what factors may be affecting maths as a subject—perhaps, not least, the pride otherwise well-educated public figures profess in their mathematical ignorance!

A long-standing weakness of the British education system has been the particularly poor performance of low achievers. Secondary modern schools produced something like two to three times the numbers of low achievers in maths compared to France and Germany, while England produced nearly double the proportion of high achievers. Our failure with the very low achievers—nearly a quarter of all children—was only matched by the United States. Our secondary modern children were two years behind the German low achievers. (For a summary of these results see Prais 1995.) The depressing feature of the later international studies of mathematical attainment is that this picture is repeated even after the comprehensive revolution. Our most able, the top decile, performed as well as those in France and much better than the American students. The lowest achievers still do worse than their counterparts, again, except for the Americans. The high degree of inequality in achievements remained. This does begin to point to a possible interaction with the labour market. The highly unequal wage structures in the UK and the US may be giving strong signals to schoolchildren. The labour market will reward high achievers but many will end up in very low-paid jobs whatever they do. Green and Steedman (1997) argue that it is the considerable variation in the quality of teachers in US and UK schools in comparison to France and Germany that helps to explain the more varied performance of pupils. The differential achievements in core mathematical tasks in England compared to Germany and Switzerland suggests that the approach to teaching maths may have much more to do with the results than either the labour market or the structure of schooling. Sheer time spent on the subject matters. It is one of the few factors that has been correlated with differential achievement internationally (IAEP 1992). In France students taking the maths–physics and science–technology baccalaureates spend nine hours a week on maths in their final year, six the year before, and four the year before that. The overwhelming number of English maths students do single-subject maths for four to five hours a week for two years (London Mathematical Society 1995). All in all, it is surprising just how little we know about the reasons that lie behind the varied standards achieved by schoolchildren. The Assessment of Performance Unit, established by the Labour Government in 1974 to investigate these issues, was abolished by the Conservative Government as an economy measure.

Exam results

There is some dispute about how far the examination boards have managed to sustain constant standards over time for those taking A levels at 17 or GCSE/O levels at 15. There does seem to have been a significant improvement in results achieved after GCSE was introduced, as we noted above. But standards of examining cannot explain away the remarkable rise in

---

Table 3.5. ATTAINMENTS OF YOUNG PEOPLE AS A PERCENTAGE OF RELEVANT POPULATION

	1970/1	1975/6	1980/1	1985/6	1990/1	1993/4
GCE A levels or SCE H grades[a]						
% of 17-yr-olds[b] achieving 1 or						
more passes	16	15	15	16	22	22
GCSEs/O levels						
% of 15-yr-olds[b] achieving[c]						
1 or more higher grades[d]	42	53	55	58	69	70
1 or more other grades[e]	10	28	31	32	26	24
No graded results	44	18	14	12	5	6

[a] Two AS levels count as one A level pass. On a Great Britain basis up to and including 1990/1.
[b] Age at the start of the school year.
[c] Data before 1993/4 is only available on a school-leavers basis, while from 1993/4 it is only available in terms of all 15-year-olds. In order to make the figures consistent with the 1993/4 basis the numbers achieving O levels have been adjusted by including those who stayed on within the higher grade category.
[d] GCSE grades A–C or SCE grades 1–3 (O level grades A–C or CSE grade 1 prior to 1990/1).
[e] GCSE grades D–G or SCE grades 4–7 (O level grades D and E or CSE grades 2–5 prior to 1990/1).

Sources: DES (1995*b* and equivalents for earlier years); CSO (1996: table 3.6).

---

the percentage of the age group achieving good passes in these external exams. The DES has not helped by collecting the statistics on a different basis over time but our best attempt to put them on a comparable basis is set out in Table 3.5.

The percentage of 17-year-olds gaining one or more passes at A level has risen since the early 1970s but most rapidly since the mid-1980s as more young people stayed on for the reasons we discussed earlier. For those in school at 15 there has been a steady increase in the numbers gaining at least one higher grade at GCSE and in lower grades too. In 1970, before the school-leaving age was raised to 16 (in 1972) and before the majority of schools were comprehensive, 44 per cent of 15-year-olds left school with no graded results at all. By 1993 that figure had fallen to 6 per cent. School leaving results for boys and girls separately are shown in Annexe Table 3A.4.

Vocational training

It has long been argued that the UK's major weakness educationally has been its failure to provide good vocational training and that so few young people go that route. The case has been developed in a persuasive way by Prais and colleagues at the National Institute for Economic and Social Research (Prais 1995). Yet, in response to recessions, many employers reduced or ended their apprenticeship schemes. Partly in response, but mainly to soak up the growing numbers of unemployed young people, both parties in government rapidly expanded youth training schemes. The finance of general training has always posed a problem in a competitive labour market. It is not in the interests of an employer to give a general training to employees who may be attracted away by another employer. The cost of such training therefore falls on the young person in the form of lower wages (Becker 1964). If the young person cannot rely on parents for support his or her investment in education may be sub-optimal. Other countries try to solve the problem by compulsion—young people up to the age of 18 in Germany are normally expected to be in a job with some form of formal training or in full-time education/training, though not all are. The costs are shared by government and some form of training levy. This logic lay behind the Industrial Training Act of 1964 and the later creation of Industrial Training Boards. They could impose levies on employers to finance approved training schemes. The Employment and Training Act of 1973 created the Manpower Services Commission, which had the dual job of co-ordinating the work of the Training Boards and running the Employment Service and Job Centres. This latter function was handed back to the Department of Employment in 1987, which was then merged with the Department for Education in 1995. The Manpower Services Commission was abolished by the Conservative Government and local Training and Enterprise Councils set up to co-ordinate local training provision between local employers. The Government tried to rationalize the myriad of vocational qualifications. During our whole period, however, the number of people in the labour force with intermediate vocational qualifications, craft and technician level, actually fell while the numbers with university qualifications rose significantly. The contrast with Germany is striking. We have the same numbers of university-level qualified people in the population but less than half the proportion of vocationally qualified. In 1988/9 British trainees graduating in mechanical engineering at craft level numbered 2,400 while the number of Germans was 35,000 (Prais 1995). It is at the vocational Level 3 qualifications that Britain lags most dramatically behind her competitors such as France and Germany (Green and Steedman 1997). Yet simple expansion of the numbers of places on courses is not the answer. The opportunity cost of training is high in Britain and the rewards relatively poor. The private rates of return, future earnings gained compared to the cost of earnings lost in taking lower-level training, are so poor in the UK that young people's lack of interest in taking them is not surprising (Bennett *et al.* 1995).

Overall human capital content of the labour force

Despite the deficiencies at the craft level the overall human capital content of the labour force has increased substantially since 1974 (see Table 3.6).

Of those in their sixties only 5 per cent have a degree. Of those in their thirties nearly 14 per cent do.

In Table 3.7 we show the changes separately for men and women. It is women whose educational levels of achievement have increased most.

Table 3.6. HIGHEST QUALIFICATIONS ATTAINED BY POPULATION AGED 16–69, GREAT BRITAIN, 1994 (%)

Year of birth Age in 1994	Pre-1935 (60–69)	1935–44 (50–59)	1945–54 (40–49)	1955–64 (30–39)	1965–72 (22–29)	All (16–69)
Higher degree	0.6	1.0	1.5	1.8	0.8	1.1
First degree	4.3	6.2	9.1	11.9	11.8	8.3
Other post-A level	7.7	9.8	12.3	11.5	7.9	9.4
A level	2.4	5.2	10.1	14.3	19.1	12.2
O level/GCSE (5+)	10.1	9.9	12.0	13.9	18.0	14.1
CSE/O level 1–4	2.0	6.9	9.7	14.6	16.5	8.8
Commercial	5.5	5.4	4.8	3.1	2.7	4.0
CSE	n/a	0.1	1.5	7.1	7.5	3.7
Apprenticeship	6.5	5.2	3.2	1.0	0.6	2.8
Other	2.7	3.2	3.2	2.4	2.3	2.6
No qualifications	58.3	47.1	32.5	18.6	12.9	30.8

Source: Author's calculations from GHS raw data files.

Social and private rates of return to education

The fact that society has invested more in its human capital does not mean there are not limits at which such investments may become less rewarding than other forms of investment. What has been happening to the rate of return on that investment?

This is a controversial area. Ever since Gary Becker's (1964) pioneering work economists have thought of the additional earnings reaped by graduates and others who continue their

Table 3.7. HIGHEST LEVEL OF EDUCATION OF 16- TO 69-YEAR-OLDS IN 1974, 1979, 1985, 1990, AND 1994 BY SEX (%)

	1974		1979		1985		1990		1994	
	Men	Women	Men	Women	Men	Women	Men	Women	Men	Women
Degree	4.2	1.3	7.1	2.7	9.3	4.3	11.0	5.6	12.1	7.0
Other higher	5.1	5.2	6.5	6.3	8.6	7.8	10.4	8.4	10.6	8.4
A level	7.0	3.0	8.2	3.2	10.4	5.8	12.8	6.9	14.6	10.1
O level/GCSE	13.8	12.6	14.6	15.2	17.7	20.3	19.5	24.6	22.6	27.4
CSE/Apprenticeship	15.2	12.0	16.0	14.1	15.3	15.7	12.7	14.2	12.5	13.5
No qualifications	54.8	65.9	47.6	58.8	38.7	46.2	33.6	40.3	27.6	33.6

Source: Author's calculations from GHS raw data files.

education as a return on their investment in extended education. The costs of the extra education can be compared to the additional stream of lifetime earnings that is generated and the latter expressed as a rate of return produced by the former. This idea has widespread acceptance as at least a partial explanation of human behaviour. It can be seen as an individual's private rate of return from education. It is when the analogy is extended to society as a whole that the arguments begin. In a reasonably free labour market it may be assumed that employers are paying better-educated people more because they are that much more productive. Hence, why not take the extra earnings of graduates as a measure of society's economic or productive gain from the extra education? By analogy we can call this the social rate of return. But what if employers are paying more for more productive workers but are rewarding them not for what schools and colleges contributed to their skills but because colleges have rather successfully sorted out the inherently better-motivated, harder-working people? This is the 'filtering thesis' or 'signalling theory' and was developed in the 1970s (Arrow 1973; Taubman and Wales 1973; Stiglitz 1975). No economist has been able convincingly to disentangle these two equally plausible hypotheses. Clearly both effects are likely to be going on simultaneously but, if so, it does mean that attempts to calculate *social* rates of return have major theoretical problems. The DfEE have nevertheless tried to calculate them from time to time—most recently in 1997 as evidence to the Dearing Committee on the Future Funding of Higher Education. They reviewed more recent US evidence that earnings differentials may be a good proxy for the real productivity gains from education as well as quoting this author's more cautious view (Bennett *et al.* 1992*a*). In Britain the social class of parents continues to have a powerful influence on the future earnings of their children, reducing the rates of return the middle class gain from higher education. They would have relatively good job opportunities anyway. This suggests that, in Britain at least, educational signalling may be playing an important function, especially for lower-class children. The DfEE thus show caution and present their estimates of the social rate of return assuming that either 60 per cent or 80 per cent of the earnings differentials of the more educated population can indeed be attributed to education—the 'Alpha factor'. The overall results use lifetime income profiles from the General Household Survey and education costs from 1993 and earlier years (see Table 3.8).

We can see that the social rate of return on women's education is higher than men's but that if we assume only 60 per cent of the educated's earnings differentials are the result of education rather than ability, that rate of return for men and women together at 7 per cent is only just ahead of what the Treasury consider the minimum appropriate return on any public investment. If we turn to the historical trend data which are produced for men only there has been a remarkable stability and some upward movement in these rates. On closer inspection, however, this owes quite a lot to the decline in unit *costs* of education over the same period rather than increasing income differentials. If unit teaching costs in higher education had remained at the levels of the early 1980s the social rates of return would be below 6 per cent, i.e. there would have been no upward movement. If universities continue to take

Table 3.8. RATES OF RETURN TO EDUCATION

a. Social rates of return, entrants of all ages, 1993

	Alpha = 0.6	Alpha = 0.8
Men	6	8
Women	7	10
All	7	9

b. Social rates of return, 18-year-old male entrants

	Alpha = 0.6	Alpha = 0.8
1984/5 and 1986	6	7
1985–7	6	7
1986/7 and 1989	7	8
1987 and 1989/90	7	9
1989/90 and 1991	7	9
1992–4	7	9

c. Private rates of return, 18-year-old male entrants

	Alpha = 0.6	Alpha = 0.8
1984–7	18	21
1989–91	13	15
1991	11.5	13

Sources: private communication; also see Dearing Committee 1997, i, Report No. 7.

the same number of students, projections of demand in the economy for graduates suggest a decline in the rate of return. Temporarily, at least, the supply of graduates may have outpaced the demand in the economy. The whole concept of a social rate of return measured in this way is, however, profoundly unsatisfactory. It sounds as if it is measuring the social spillover benefits of education for the wider economy. The methodology used does not attempt to do this. It relies on individuals' earnings. Attempts to estimate future trends in earnings are notoriously unreliable.

Earnings of graduates in comparison to non-graduates are, however, a good guide to the demand for places. These have begun to fall quite sharply (Table 3.8). We do not yet have figures showing the long-term effect on earnings differentials given by employers to the products of the 'new' higher education. Part of that change has not only been a reduction in the teaching costs per student and with it probably standards of teaching and environmental comfort: more of the costs of taking a degree have fallen on students. The maintenance grant has been allowed to decline in real terms and students have had to take out loans and work their way through college. This suggests that private rates of return may go on falling. A more optimistic analysis is given by the Dearing Committee (1997).

So far we have been entirely concerned with the overall outcomes of education, not with its distribution. Issues of equality of opportunity once dominated debates about education. What has happened to these equity considerations in the period since 1974?

Equity considerations

By area A weak definition of equality of opportunity is that children in different areas of the country should have access to schools with the same levels of resources. A stronger definition is that areas with children needing more attention or having greater needs should get more resources. Since it is more difficult to attract an equally talented group of teachers to schools that face very difficult problems this would on its own justify rewarding those staff more to attract them to such schools. Some combination of these ideas underlies the additional educational needs component in the local authority funding formula. The importance of that element in the grant was reduced following a review by the Department for Education in 1993 (West *et al.* 1995). We have no ready way to measure spending in relation to needs but we can measure the variance in spending levels between schools in different local authority areas. Government policy had been to ensure more even spending ever since the 1940s through local grant allocations, building approvals and, for a period, teacher quotas. These were abolished in 1976. Between 1959/60 and 1971/2 variations between local school spending had been reduced quite substantially (see Table 3.9). The coefficient of variation in spending fell from 12.39 to 7.88.

From 1974 new education authorities with new boundaries took power but have since remained essentially unchanged except for the demise of the Inner London Education Authority (ILEA). From then on the picture is reversed. The coefficient of variation between average local education authority primary school spending grew from a figure of 9.2 to 19.1. This result is not as unambiguous as we should like since the definition of primary school includes some middle schools 'deemed primary'. The inclusion of nursery schools after 1990 also muddies the picture.

Achievement and Ethnicity One of the more encouraging results of the last twenty years has been the steady improvement in the performance of ethnic minority children. We saw that the attainments of black children and those of children of new British citizens more generally, had been a matter for concern at the beginning of our period. The ILEA literacy survey (ILEA 1981) showed that black children in London had low reading attainment at 8 and that it remained low at 16. There were also worries about the performance of Bangladeshi children and some other groups. The Swann Report (DES 1985) summarized the research and showed that the relative performance of various groups had improved between 1978/9 and

Howard Glennerster

1981/2. The percentage of students of Caribbean origin gaining five or more higher grades at CSE and O level had risen from 3 to 6 per cent in the period and the A level numbers had also nearly doubled. The ILEA Research and Statistics Branch compared the performance of children from ethnic groups between 1976 and 1985. Each ethnic group's performance improved. Smith and Tomlinson (1989) showed that ethnic minority children scored lower on maths and reading at ages 7 to 11 but that the gap narrowed later. Subsequent research has confirmed these findings. Sammons (1995) followed a cohort of London schoolchildren over a nine-year period. Ethnic group, language at home, gender, and socio-economic background were important between the ages of 7 and 11. Girls, students from non-manual class

Table 3.9. VARIATIONS IN AVERAGE LOCAL EDUCATION AUTHORITY SPENDING PER PUPIL, ENGLAND AND WALES

	All authorities outside London	All authorities in England and Wales including London	
	All schools	Primary[a]	Secondary[b]
Coefficient of variation in net institutional expenditure per pupil			
1959/60	12.39		
1965/6	7.92		
1971/2	7.88		
1974/5		9.20[c]	8.83
1980/1		12.90	11.30
1985/6		12.10	12.90
1990/1	10.00	16.50	16.30
1993/4	9.92	19.10	14.60
Standard deviation in pupil–teacher ratios			
1974/5		1.61	1.14
1980/1		1.61	0.96
1985/6		1.75	1.07
1990/1		1.67	1.03
1993/4[d]		1.80	1.07

[a] The primary category includes primary schools and middle schools deemed primary (as defined in CIPFA 1995). The primary category for the years 1990-1 and 1993-4 also includes nursery schools.
[b] The secondary school category includes secondary schools and middle schools deemed secondary (as defined in CIPFA 1995).
[c] 1974/5 has 11 missing returns from LEAS. The effect of missing out these same authorities in 1980/1 was to increase the coefficient by 0.2 and the standard deviation by 0.03.
[d] The pupil–teacher ratio is defined in CIPFA (1995) as 'pupils per qualified teachers within schools, using full time equivalent'.

Sources: Figures for 1959/60–1971/2 from Foster *et al.* (1980); other figures from author's calculations from raw data in CIPFA (1995: cols. 35, 38, 217, 231, 245, and equivalents for earlier years).

families, and those not on low incomes went on improving. More striking, through secondary school those from the ethnic groups went on catching up.

Asian students were found to obtain significantly better GCSE performance scores (a difference for Asian students equivalent to an extra Grade A GCSE pass) while the performance of those of Caribbean background was not significantly different from their English, Scottish and Welsh peers. This represents a reversal of patterns identified during the junior school period. (Sammons 1995: 479)

Indeed, in terms of relative progress in secondary school the ethnic minorities *all* outperformed the host community. This was especially true compared to male working-class students. Other work is confirming these findings.

Our analysis of the qualifications of the whole population (aged 16–69) is less encouraging because it is of an older generation and includes the parents of these more successful children. But there too, progress in the catching-up of the whole ethnic minority population is clear (see Table 3.10). The absence of coding for these categories in the General Household Survey beyond 1990 prevents us extending the analysis, as with social class, below.

Gender In a similar way the relative and absolute performance levels of girls have improved. Boys in 1980/1 obtained better A level results than girls. By 1993/4 this had been reversed. Girls had always done well at GCSE. They still do but they have drawn ahead (see Table 3.7 above and Annexe Table 3A.4).

The new National Curriculum assessment tests also enable us to compare the performance of boys and girls, even if they have not been going long enough to compare over time. The proportion of boys and girls reaching the 'expected' standards in science in 1994 was almost exactly the same at about two-thirds. Girls slightly outperformed boys in maths—63 per cent getting the expected level compared to 60 per cent. But in English the gap was very wide. Again two-thirds of girls reached the expected level but only 49 per cent of boys (CSO 1996).

Social class As schooling has lengthened the almost complete dominance of these upper levels of education by the upper classes has been relaxed. Through this century, the proportionate improvements in access to higher education have been achieved by the working class from a very low base. The biggest *absolute* increases in numbers going to university have been gained by the upper middle classes (Halsey *et al.* 1980). However, frequently quoted statistics show that the share of university places taken by the manual and especially the unskilled manual groups have not changed or have even declined in recent decades. But there is a major flaw in these crude figures. The social composition of the population has been changing. There are more families in the non-manual group and far fewer in the manual group. Stability in the shares of each going to university would imply a relative improvement in the achievements of children from manual groups. Similarly, the unskilled manual group may form a low percentage of students but there are far fewer people in that position to start with

Table 3.10. COUNTRY OF ORIGIN AND EDUCATIONAL QUALIFICATIONS, GREAT BRITAIN, 1985 AND 1990 (%)

| Educational level | Father from | | | | | | | | | | | | | |
| | UK | | Europe or North America | | Elsewhere | | White | | Non-white | | All (16 years and older) | |
	1985	1990	1985	1990	1985	1990	1985	1990	1985	1990	1985	1990
Degree	6.6	8.2	8.5	7.4	7.5	9.1	6.7	8.1	6.1	8.1	6.7	8.1
Higher qualification	8.1	9.4	10.4	7.4	8.2	10.1	8.2	9.4	7.8	8.7	8.2	9.3
A level	8.0	9.7	6.3	8.2	8.4	12.1	7.9	9.6	6.3	11.7	7.9	9.7
O level	19.3	22.7	14.6	17.5	17.9	17.9	19.1	22.3	16.8	19.7	19.1	22.2
CSE/Apprenticeship	15.0	12.5	16.8	20.6	24.5	23.3	15.2	13.2	25.8	21.5	15.5	13.5
No qualifications	43.0	37.5	43.3	38.9	33.6	27.4	42.8	37.4	37.1	30.3	42.7	37.1
n	14,542	13,485	796	767	682	780	15,442	14,373	523	641	15,965	15,014

Source: Author's calculations from GHS raw data files.

(Hellevik and Ringen 1995). The point is exactly the one Illsley and Le Grand (1987) made about the Black Report's findings on social class and mortality (see Chapter 4 of this book). There has been a lot of controversy about how exactly to measure trends in access over time to take this and other factors into account and some very complex statistical procedures have been used. One solution comparable to that adopted by Illsley and Le Grand is to use an indicator like that which economists use to measure the overall inequality in incomes—the Gini coefficient (another would be variations in the probability that you would have been able to enter the next level of education up from the one you were in depending on the class of your parents). Hellevick and Ringen (1995) discuss these alternatives and show that although the service class have maintained a relatively favourable position in entering higher education, the overall inequality in educational achievement measured by the Gini coefficient has more than halved in the 1960s cohort of births compared to the pre-war cohort born in the 1930s. The results reported in the last edition of this volume (Hills 1990: tables 3.14 and 3A.8) are consistent with that finding as is the data in Dearing (1997), Report 6. The updated figures are shown in Table 3.11 and Annexe Table 3A.5.

Since the General Household Survey has ceased to code social class, 1990 figures are the latest we have in our series. These figures do confirm the trends evident in the previous edition. The GHS gives us the percentage of the population aged 16–69 who have achieved different qualifications by the highest level achieved. It also gives us the occupation and from that the social class, traditionally categorized, of the individuals' parents. We can calculate the number of people with parents of each class gaining a given highest level of qualification and then compare that with the number of people in that social class in the relevant population. If a third of the managerial-class population has degrees and a third of the population has degrees the equivalence ratio is one. If two-thirds of the managerial class have degrees then the ratio is two—those with managerial-class parents are twice as likely to have degrees as the rest of the population. We compute this ratio, essentially similar to what Glass (1954) did in his original LSE social mobility study, and show the results in Table 3.11. Figures moving towards one show a movement to equality of achievement.

From Table 3.11 we can see that in 1974 there were 2.7 times the number of degree holders with professional and managerial parents as you would expect if their number matched their presence in the population. At A level the ratio was nearly two to one, while at O level the favourable ratio was down to only 1.4. The semi- and unskilled class ratios were the mirror image, showing under-representation. That under-representation has persisted but what is interesting and encouraging is that all the ratios have tended to move nearer to one. A strikingly greater degree of educational equality of achievement has been secured over the past twenty years. At degree level the ratio has fallen from 2.7 for professional- and managerial-class-born people to 1.8. The chances of having a degree if you had parents in that class were nearly three times the average; now they are less than twice. Most striking, the numbers gaining O levels or GCSEs as their highest qualification is roughly equal in all classes. Notice we are dealing with a very broad age range here from 16 to 69, so the results are not just about

Table 3.11. HIGHEST LEVEL OF QUALIFICATIONS GAINED, 16- TO 69-YEAR-OLDS, BY SOCIAL CLASS OF FATHER, GREAT BRITAIN (EQUAL PROPORTIONATE ACHIEVEMENT = 1.0)

Highest qualification	Ratio of achievers to their social class representation in the population			
	Professional and managerial	Intermediate non-manual	Skilled manual	Semi-skilled and unskilled manual
Degree				
1974	2.7	1.7	0.5	0.2
1985	2.1	1.6	0.5	0.4
1990	1.8	1.7	0.6	0.4
Post-A level				
1974	1.9	1.5	0.8	0.5
1985	1.4	1.4	0.9	0.6
1990	1.3	1.4	0.9	0.7
A level				
1974	1.8	1.5	0.8	0.5
1985	1.5	1.3	0.8	0.8
1990	1.5	1.3	0.8	0.6
O level/GCSE				
1974	1.4	2.1	0.7	0.6
1985	1.2	1.3	0.9	0.8
1990	1.0	1.1	1.0	0.8

Source: Author's calculations from GHS raw data files.

schooling but reflect the fact that those without O levels from school have been acquiring them later in life, mostly in their twenties and thirties. The figures so far have concentrated on the adult population as a whole or at least those aged 16–69 for which we have the relevant information. If we concentrate on the younger age group from 16–24 and look not at qualifications but at years of post-school education a similar narrowing can be seen. In 1974 those with professional parents had ten times the length of post-school education as those in the unskilled parent group. That difference had fallen to seven times in 1990—not as big a narrowing, but one that is still evident (see Table 3.12). In the 1990s, however, the rapid expansion of higher education has disproportionately benefited the higher-income groups, reversing earlier equalization. This has been especially true of the 18–24 age group, counteracted, in part, by the access of lower-income groups at a mature age (Sefton 1997).

Table 3.12. YEARS OF POST-SCHOOL EDUCATION RECEIVED BY
16- TO 24-YEAR-OLDS, GREAT BRITAIN, 1974, 1985, AND 1990

Father's social class	Ratio of share of extra years received to share of population[a]		
	1974	1985	1990
Professional	3.0	2.8	2.2
Managerial	2.4	1.6	1.5
Intermediate	1.0	1.5	1.3
Skilled manual	0.8	0.8	0.7
Semi-skilled	0.5	0.4	0.4
Unskilled	0.3	0.3	0.3

[a] Equal shares = 1.0.

Source: Author's calculations from GHS raw data files.

Poverty Social class is not as sensitive an indicator as poverty. Here we do not have good comparable figures of the achievements of poor children over time but we do know that poverty has increased sharply in our period (see Chapter 7). We also know, from an analysis undertaken by OFSTED for the Roman Catholic bishops, that schools with more poor children in them do far worse than others in exam performance (see Table 3.13).

Table 3.13. FREE SCHOOL MEALS AND GCSE RESULTS, ALL STATE
SECONDARY SCHOOLS 1985

Pupils with Free School Meals (%)	Number of schools	5 or more GCSE grades A–C (%)	5 or more GCSE grades A–G (%)
0–10	987	58.04	94.58
10–20	894	41.95	89.52
20–30	453	30.07	83.63
30–40	231	25.24	78.87
40–50	169	22.16	75.47
50–60	98	19.77	72.96
over 60	74	18.25	69.99

Source: Department for Catholic Education (1997).

International comparisons

How do these trends compare to those in other countries? Mills *et al.* (1996) compare trends in Sweden, Germany, and Britain. They concentrate on the extreme case of the chances of a child from an unskilled manual home progressing through the system as far as university. They develop a logit model of frequencies that measures movements between opportunity categories in a way that can be compared over time and between countries. In all three countries they find a slow attenuation of class differences. There is a trend to greater equality but a very slow one—greatest in Sweden, then Germany and then Britain. In all three we see a long-run decline in gender differences. They conclude:

The major differences emerge at the end of the lower secondary school. At this point Germany is much more successful at keeping children from working class homes within the educational system. This enables a significant proportion to enter higher vocational and technical training. In comparison the British educational system looks like a particularly leaky sieve, which neither retains working class children for university nor higher technical study (Mills *et al.* 1996).

It must be said that this pre-dates the expansion of staying-on in the 1990s.

The impact of comprehensive reorganization

We saw that one of the early statutes passed by the Labour Government in 1976 was to enforce comprehensive education. Though compulsion was removed by the next Conservative Government, over 85 per cent of English state school pupils were in comprehensive schools by 1986, 99 per cent of Welsh children, and 96 per cent of those in Scotland—most had become comprehensive before 1976 and most of those in Mrs Thatcher's period as Secretary of State for Education in the early 1970s. Even so, 85 per cent left a lot of children that were not in such schools and one study concluded that only one in three local authorities had by that time gone fully comprehensive (Gray *et al.* 1984).

The aim had been to improve the performance of those children who had previously followed such a limited curriculum and achieved such little success in secondary modern schools while giving wider opportunities to more able children in larger schools that were able to offer a wider curriculum. What impact did the reform have?

This has provoked sharp differences of opinion; see, for example, two whole issues of two academic journals in the same year (*Journal of the Royal Statistical Society*, Series A, 147:4 (1984) and *Oxford Review of Education*, 10:1 (1984)).

Gray, Jesson, and Jones compared the exam results of those local areas that went comprehensive with those that did not or not to the same extent. They conclude that they 'could find no overall trend to suggest that once differences in social composition have been taken into account, LEAs which had retained selection to a greater or lesser extent achieved better results than those that were fully comprehensive' (Gray *et al.* 1984: 45). A study in Scotland had richer material (Gray *et al.* 1982). This was a large survey of school-leavers in 1975/6. Their experience coincided with Scotland's move to abolish selection. It was possible to compare the achievements of those in comprehensive, mixed, and selective areas. The results showed that, overall, pupils from the uncreamed comprehensive areas did better in examinations than those in the selective areas, including those with highly selective schools equivalent to the old direct-grant grammar schools which had been abolished in England by the Labour Government. Those lower down the ability or achievement scale at 11 did much better in the comprehensive system. The top-ability children did slightly better in the selective system. These results were very similar to the results of a very careful study in Sweden in the 1960s (see a summary in the Public Schools Commission Report (DES 1970)). The uncreamed comprehensives had less class differentiation and less truancy. Heath (1984) used the British Election Survey to investigate the exam performance of those in the sample—not the best source but one that could be adapted to throw some light on the issue. He compared two cohorts—those who were between 31 and 45 in 1979 and had experienced the old system, and those aged 18 to 30, products of the new or partially new system. Overall the numbers gaining CSE and O levels rose sharply, A levels less so. Of the increase, comprehensives contributed 17 per cent more qualified leavers, secondary moderns 7 per cent, and grammar schools 7 per cent. Certainly the big increase in qualified school-leavers has happened under the comprehensive system. Under the old pattern in the 1960s access to the full range of academic secondary education was denied to 80 per cent of the population—it was rationed. The coming of the comprehensive school and the raising of the school-leaving age in the 1970s removed that rationing restriction. Most children could complete a full secondary education and take GCSE for the first time. As we have seen they did so in increasing numbers. These two measures essentially paved the way for the transformation in the school-leaving qualifications we saw earlier.

More recent research underpins this interpretation. 'Peer group effects', as economists and sociologists like to call them, do appear to be very important—who you are educated with is more important than additional resources in affecting your performance. A reanalysis of those children born in one week of 1958 (Robertson and Symons 1995) shows that those who have been educated with able and motivated others tend to do better. But peer groups can have negative as well as positive effects. Concentrating the least able together can pull down their results. Overall, Robertson and Symons suggest, the positive effects of mixing ability groups outweigh the negative. There are decreasing returns to selectivity for the able and large returns to mixing for the least able. Society at large benefits from mixed-school communities and teaching. Yet, for individual parents of able children the incentive, in any system where they have a choice, is to capture even a small peer group effect for their own child and to seek to avoid the contamination effect of the less able or lower-class child. This poses a real political and social choice dilemma for society. International research bears out the importance of peer group effects (Henderson *et al.* 1978; Rutter 1979; Hanushek 1986; Dynarsky *et al.* 1989; Duncan 1994). A majority of European and successful Asian countries—

France, Sweden, Norway, Denmark, Italy, Spain, Singapore, and Japan—have moved to comprehensive systems, have made them work, and show no signs of wanting to reverse that trend. A system that concentrates low achievers and those with low parental aspirations together is likely further to depress the achievements of those children markedly. The stock of human capital in that economy is affected. Moreover, for girls who come from poor homes and whose performance at school declines consistently there is a much-increased likelihood of early pregnancy and single parenthood (Kiernan 1995).

The move to encourage more selection and competitive choices of school may lead to 'cream skimming' and could end up depressing schoolchildren's achievements overall, working in the opposite direction to the other reforms in the 1988 Education Reform Act.

Choice and diversity and the 1988 Education Reform Act

The Conservative Government consistently tried to widen the range of schools on offer to parents—grant-maintained schools, city technology colleges, and more grammar schools. But in each case the numbers were small. Five per cent of schools became grant-maintained and 5 per cent remained grammar schools, with the two overlapping. Only a handful of city technology colleges were created—fifteen—and only 35,000 assisted places were available in independent schools. So considerable was the devolution of budgetary control to local authority schools that those opting out gained very little extra by way of independence. Nor was the curriculum in the city technology colleges that different (Whitty *et al.* 1993). Nevertheless, schools have felt themselves to be in a more competitive environment and to be concerned about how their potential parents will view their offerings and exam results. This may produce two kinds of response in theory—one is to improve the productive efficiency of the school, the other is to select easier or better students to teach (Glennerster 1991). There is some evidence of both happening (West and Pennell forthcoming). Grant-maintained schools and others seem to be applying more subtle ways of screening children. If the previous research quoted is correct this could have counter-productive effects for those excluded.

Unfortunately, for reasons we have discussed already it is not yet possible to identify results from the National Curriculum or the devolved budgets to schools. The results of the tests are not readily compared over time and have only just begun on a full national scale. There have been improvements in GCSE results since 1989 but, as we saw, this improvement began in the mid-1970s. Gray and Jesson (1996) do suggest an acceleration in grades achieved that was partly prompted by the publication of league tables. More pupils were entered for more subjects. Bell (1995) suggests there may even have been a decline for those at the bottom. Some schools may have given up on the least able, who they do not think will get results. In reality no clear picture has yet emerged. It will be many years before we can begin to piece together the results of this major Act, just as it has been a long time for the results of the reforms of the 1960s to show through.

V. In Brief

The basic trends in education spending and outcomes therefore turn out to tell a very interesting story—one that is almost the mirror image of that in the United States. The UK has barely increased the real resources available to education in a twenty-year period, if we take the price index of education costs as our deflator, and for much of the period there was a cut in the share of the gross domestic product that government spent on education. To some extent this has been offset by a reduced population of primary school children for part of the period. Yet, over the same period, the output of the education system grew, in terms of educational qualifications received by school-leavers and the range of subjects taken to gain these qualifications. There was continued evidence of poor mathematical skills compared to some other countries but, on the other hand, of good performance in science and signs of improvement relative to other countries. Moreover, there was a marked improvement in the standards achieved by girls compared to boys and of ethnic minority children compared to the white population—indeed in many cases they were outperforming the white population—and there was a catching up in the performance of those from less favoured socio-economic groups. How can we explain this paradox?

First, the changes of the much-maligned 1960s do seem to be part of the explanation. The old 11-plus system had put a ceiling on the achievements of four-fifths of the population, who were not able to take school-leaving qualifications equivalent to those in grammar schools. Entry to higher education was extremely restricted even for those who went to grammar school. The removal of the 11-plus broke that ceiling and gradually the aspirations of those who had been excluded grew. It took a generation finally to free ordinary people from the belief that they had no right to higher education or to take school-leaving qualifications, but gradually it happened. In this sense the UK caught up with the United States a hundred years late. The most important additional pull factor was the big change that overtook the economy. The economy was demanding much higher levels of qualification and punishing those without them more harshly. With the unnatural barriers to school performance removed, these demand-pull factors had a chance to work as never before. They resulted in more qualifications being gained by more of the population and by more women and those from minority ethnic groups. So we can lay the good news, not at the door of the spending restrictions of the 1980s, but at the removal of the barriers to education in the 1960s and 1970s, at the big labour market changes of the 1980s, and at the reforms of the 1990s—the National Curriculum and the devolved responsibilities to schools. But there is bad news too. Expansion in higher education was bought at a price of declining resources and variable quality. Other countries' basic standards of achievement in schools, especially for the less able, and especially in practical and vocational training, continued to outstrip ours. Competition between schools for good pupils could be leading back to the selectivity of the past, with all its consequences.

Howard Glennerster

Summary

- A change of emphasis was evident in the policy goals of government: there was
  - greater emphasis on basic standards of achievement;
  - greater emphasis on economic relevance and training;
  - less emphasis on equity and more on choice and diversity in schooling;
  - pressure to contain spending;
  - a growing emphasis on private finance for higher education.
- Education was accorded less priority in a tightened public spending strategy.
  - Education's share of public spending fell, as did the share of the Gross Domestic Product devoted to education financed from the public purse. It fell from 6.5 per cent in 1975/6 to 4.7 per cent at its lowest point in 1988/9, recovering to 5.1 in 1995/6.
  - The volume of resources for state education fell after 1976, rising again only slowly in the 1990s. Demography came to the rescue.
  - Over twenty years the real volume of resources devoted to each primary child rose by a little over a half. The comparable figure for secondary school children was a quarter.
  - Private educational spending has grown faster than public spending, largely replacing the cuts in the share of the GDP met from public funds. By 1995/6 it formed 0.9 per cent of the GDP—nearly a threefold increase in its share over 1973—and £6 billion in total.
- Cuts in resources from the Government affected the achievement of policy goals—the expansion of pre-school provision to all 3- and 4-year-olds was not achieved and nor was the building and improvement programme for schools set in the 1970s.
  - Average class sizes remained little changed and 8 per cent of secondary classes and a third of primary classes remained over thirty in 1995/6 (England).
  - There has been a growth in the range of forms of governance under which schools operate—opted-out schools, city technology colleges—and greater statutory parental rights to choice of school. Real practical choices for parents have remained limited, especially outside large cities and for those with very limited time and means.
  - The goal of a third of the age group going on to higher education was achieved in less than five years. The impact on the quality of the education received is disputed but could be serious.
- Final outcomes:
  - Standards of maths attainment remained relatively poor. Britain ranked in the middle of an ordering of advanced countries.
  - Yet English schools did well in science results at 9 and 13. These children outperformed those in most European and other English-speaking countries.

- Comprehensive education, however, seems to have been associated with rising aspirations and achievements for the average child.
- While the most able children continued to do well in international comparisons the spread of achievement remained much wider than in other countries.
- There remains a striking link between child poverty and school performance.
- On the other hand girls' exam performance has overtaken that of boys at both GCSE and A level.
- Children from ethnic minorities have been catching up with or surpassing the performance of white pupils.
- Britain produces far fewer young people with craft training than our competitors.
- But the percentage of 17-year-olds gaining one or more passes at A level has doubled since the early 1970s.
- Entry to higher education remains class-biased but there has been an equalizing in achievement by those from different social groups at every level.
- Over time there has been a substantial transformation in the human capital content of the working population, with far fewer holding no kind of qualification.

The results of the educational changes of the 1980s and 1990s will take a long time to come to harvest, for good or ill, just as did the changes of the 1960s and 1970s.

ANNEXE

Table 3A.1. NET PUBLIC EDUCATION EXPENDITURE, UNITED KINGDOM

	1973/4	1974/5	1975/6	1976/7	1977/8	1978/9	1979/80	1980/1	1981/2	1982/3
Current										
Primary[c]	5475	6566	6687	6595	6204	6207	6076	6277	6229	6122
Secondary	6484	7817	8025	8050	7726	7849	7599	8020	8192	8185
Special	630	749	801	837	826	891	900	961	989	1002
Higher, Further[d]	5914	6410	6375	6343	6029	6025	6060	6400	6300	6434
Other	989	975	1012	1045	1061	1026	1068	1119	1093	1105
Total	19492	22516	22901	22869	21847	21998	21702	22778	22803	22847
Education-related										
Health and welfare[e]	311	29	38	38	38	40	41	31	34	40
Meals and Milk	1316	1607	1641	1720	1445	1407	1305	1040	949	920
Youth Service	262	278	309	302	290	306	312	321	334	355
Transport	350	377	426	444	437	466	466	467	462	467
Miscellaneous	41	0	0	0	6	6	6	6	6	7
VAT[f]	186	302	287	277	316	346	545	649	579	662
Total[g]	2466	2593	2703	2781	2532	2570	2675	2514	2363	2451
Total current	21958	25110	25604	25650	24379	24568	24377	25292	25166	25298
Capital[h]										
Primary[c]	1247	922	801	677	434	369	356	391	277	243
Secondary	1594	1341	1149	1015	876	716	604	595	460	441
Special	135	129	149	132	76	45	47	57	44	38
Higher, Further	1029	866	845	743	529	478	519	538	450	476
Other	26	161	171	148	113	78	79	72	57	62
Education-related	311	245	248	232	179	138	141	125	105	95
Total Capital	4341	3663	3364	2947	2207	1824	1745	1777	1393	1355
Grants[i]	1232	1267	1352	1309	1249	1331	1364	1399	1417	1433
Total net	27531	30040	30320	29906	27834	27723	27487	28468	27977	28087
Net expenditure as										
% of public spending	13.3	13.0	13.1	13.2	13.1	12.3	11.9	12.1	11.7	11.5
% of GDP[j]	5.8	6.4	6.5	6.2	5.6	5.4	5.2	5.6	5.5	5.4

[a] Provisional data.
[b] Provisional data for England only, grossed up by author to provide UK figure.
[c] Includes nursery education.
[d] Includes public authorities' payment of tuition fees.
[e] From 1 April 1974 expenditure on the school health service is included in the NHS.
[f] VAT paid by local authorities.
[g] Aggregate of education-related categories as above.
[h] Includes loan charges, but excludes additional adjustment to allow for capital consumption made for National Accounts purposes.
[i] Refers to all mandatory and discretionary maintenance awards for further and higher education (including student loans from 1990/1 and support for residence costs in teacher training), plus grants for school uniforms etc.
[j] Adjusted before 1990 to remove the distortion caused by the abolition of domestic rates.

Sources: DfEE (1997b: annexe Bii); HM Treasury (1997: Table 8); ONS (1997d: table 3.2 and equivalents for earlier years).

(£ MILLION AT 1995/6 PRICES, ADJUSTED BY GDP DEFLATOR)

1983/4	1984/5	1985/6	1986/7	1987/8	1988/9	1989/90	1990/91	1991/2	1992/3	1993/4ᵃ	1994/5ᵃ	1995/6ᵇ
6081	5969	6026	6546	6949	7229	7565	7683	8114	8891	9093	9327	9411
8253	8149	8078	8624	8778	8847	8776	8502	8717	8994	9002	9103	9074
1029	1042	1064	1123	1190	1221	1295	1334	1393	1458	1483	1488	1492
6639	6610	6563	7002	7191	7196	7404	7606	7714	8072	8331	8915	9016
1158	1171	1174	1345	1319	1387	1530	1576	1524	1079	972	1006	1009
23159	22941	22904	24640	25427	25880	26660	26700	27463	28494	28882	29839	30002
44	48	54	62	84	73	95	162	224	282	361	368	369
916	885	848	863	801	644	624	602	622	173	156	151	150
369	381	381	326	360	381	421	414	403	423	412	411	410
463	451	445	448	442	427	430	468	495	450	464	498	497
7	9	9	8	9	14	22	2	3	8	10	32	32
706	747	760	533	523	548	585	587	654	650	606	655	657
2505	2522	2498	2240	2220	2088	2177	2234	2401	1987	2010	2116	2115
25664	25462	25402	26880	27647	27968	28837	28934	29864	30481	30892	31955	32117
259	253	274	289	281	338	403	420	421	407	428	530	491
410	353	356	289	312	268	510	554	561	563	513	579	537
35	23	26	36	16	45	49	43	40	34	32	38	35
497	441	359	573	489	484	570	523	587	560	627	630	660
63	57	54	15	47	30	52	46	37	26	13	46	43
95	94	92	37	31	34	41	31	22	19	24	26	24
1360	1222	1162	1239	1177	1200	1625	1617	1667	1609	1636	1849	1791
1489	1457	1363	1274	1235	1273	1235	1259	1589	1890	2059	2235	2172
28513	28141	27927	29393	30059	30441	31697	31810	33120	33980	34587	36039	36079
11.5	11.1	11.1	11.6	11.8	12.3	12.3	12.3	12.5	12.1	12.0	12.2	11.9
5.3	5.1	4.9	4.9	4.8	4.7	4.8	4.8	5.1	5.2	5.2	5.2	5.1

Table 3A.2. NET PUBLIC EDUCATION EXPENDITURE, UNITED KINGDOM (£ MILLION AT 1995/6 PRICES, ADJUSTED BY OWN-PRICE DEFLATOR)[a]

	1973/4	1974/5	1975/6	1976/7	1977/8	1978/9	1979/80	1980/1	1981/2	1982/3	1983/4	1984/5	1985/6	1986/7	1987/8	1988/9	1989/90	1990/91	1991/2	1992/3	1993/4[c]	1994/5[b]	1995/6[c]
Current																							
Primary[d]	6974	7138	7310	7413	7483	7629	7781	7455	7273	7168	7103	7003	7060	7329	7538	7735	8128	8221	8463	8875	9155	9313	9411
Secondary	8285	8523	8798	9077	9348	9680	9760	9556	9595	9609	9671	9586	9482	9666	9541	9481	9444	9108	9103	8979	9064	9089	9074
Special	803	816	878	942	999	1097	1153	1143	1157	1175	1203	1224	1247	1258	1292	1307	1393	1428	1454	1455	1493	1486	1492
Higher, Further and Adult education[e]	7464	7334	7367	7192	7289	7414	7794	7728	7283	7401	7613	7593	7549	7725	7624	7606	7898	8127	7958	8135	8768	8905	9016
Other	1244	1226	1273	1314	1335	1291	1342	1338	1284	1301	1361	1382	1383	1514	1439	1492	1653	1695	1598	1082	984	1009	1009
Total	24771	25037	25626	25939	26453	27111	27831	27219	26592	26655	26951	26788	26721	27492	27434	27621	28516	28578	28575	28527	29465	29802	30002
Education-related																							
Health and welfare[f]	398	31	41	44	47	49	52	54	53	59	62	65	69	73	91	103	126	198	251	292	366	369	369
Meals and Milk	1686	1756	1805	1945	1754	1738	1681	1243	1116	1084	1076	1045	1000	972	874	693	674	647	653	174	157	151	150
Youth Service	336	305	341	341	352	378	401	383	393	418	434	450	449	367	393	410	455	503	423	424	416	413	410
Transport	450	411	468	499	530	577	600	559	542	551	544	533	525	504	483	460	465	503	519	451	469	500	497
Miscellaneous	52	0	0	0	8	8	8	7	7	9	9	10	10	9	10	15	24	2	3	8	11	32	32
VAT[g]	189	331	316	313	383	427	701	776	680	780	830	882	896	600	571	590	632	631	686	690	612	657	657
Total	3112	2835	2972	3143	3073	3176	3443	3022	2791	2900	2955	2984	2949	2524	2422	2271	2375	2427	2534	2040	2031	2123	2115
Total current	27882	27872	28598	29082	29526	30288	31274	30242	29383	29555	29906	29772	29669	30016	29856	29893	30891	31006	31110	30567	31496	31925	32117
Capital[h]																							
Primary[d]	1595	1008	882	765	525	458	458	467	325	286	305	299	323	325	307	364	435	451	441	415	432	532	491
Secondary	2044	1467	1263	1149	1063	885	779	711	541	520	482	417	420	325	341	289	551	596	588	560	518	581	537
Special	173	142	166	150	93	57	59	68	52	45	41	28	31	40	18	48	53	46	42	35	33	38	35
Higher, Further and Adult education	1106	880	866	774	578	521	594	606	500	531	546	488	387	607	510	509	596	552	609	573	643	637	660
Other	34	176	189	168	137	96	103	86	67	72	74	67	64	17	51	33	56	49	38	26	13	46	43
Education-related[i]	398	266	272	261	217	171	181	149	124	112	112	111	109	42	34	37	44	34	23	19	24	26	24
Total Capital	5351	3940	3636	3268	2613	2187	2174	2088	1609	1567	1561	1410	1333	1356	1259	1279	1736	1728	1741	1626	1663	1860	1791
Grants[j]	1188	1266	1362	1283	1199	1315	1386	1424	1415	1412	1468	1436	1337	1245	1222	1243	1197	1204	1525	1818	2070	2231	2172
Total net	34420	33078	33596	33632	33339	33790	34834	33753	32406	32533	32936	32619	32340	32618	32336	32415	33824	33937	34376	34010	35228	36016	36079

[a] Own-price deflator is the CIPFA education price deflator, except for higher education, where the CVCP higher education price index is used. Grants are adjusted by the Retail Prices Index.
[b] Provisional data.
[c] Provisional data for England only, grossed up by author to provide UK figure.
[d] Includes nursery education.
[e] Includes public authorities' payment of tuition fees.
[f] From 1 April 1974 expenditure on the school health service is included in the NHS.
[g] VAT paid by local authorities.
[h] Includes loan charges, but excludes additional adjustment to allow for capital consumption made for National Accounts purposes.
[i] Aggregate of education-related categories as above.
[j] Refers to all mandatory and discretionary maintenance awards for further and higher education (including student loans from 1990/1 and support for residence costs in teacher training), plus grants for school uniforms etc.

Sources: As for table 3A.1, with price indices as above.

Table 3A.3. CURRENT EDUCATION SPENDING PER PUPIL[a]

£ per pupil, real terms (1995/6 prices, adjusted by GDP deflator)

	1973/4	1974/5	1975/6	1976/7	1977/8	1978/9	1979/80	1980/1	1981/2	1982/3	1983/4	1984/5	1985/6	1986/7	1987/8	1988/9	1989/90	1990/91	1991/2	1992/3	1993/4	1994/5	1995/6
Primary	902	1084	1117	1118	1078	1110	1129	1221	1249	1269	1303	1295	1316	1423	1502	1545	1591	1576	1649	1784	1797	1819	1808
Secondary	1402	1646	1648	1612	1514	1515	1450	1528	1567	1581	1616	1635	1664	1837	1935	2030	2098	2120	2211	2301	2292	2303	2271
Post-school	997	1028	994	948	864	919	959	940	876	843	869	866	844	858	860	846	823	778	717	692	617	631	622

Index numbers with 1973/4 = 100

	1973/4	1974/5	1975/6	1976/7	1977/8	1978/9	1979/80	1980/1	1981/2	1982/3	1983/4	1984/5	1985/6	1986/7	1987/8	1988/9	1989/90	1990/91	1991/2	1992/3	1993/4	1994/5	1995/6
Primary	100	120	124	124	120	123	125	135	139	141	145	144	146	158	167	171	176	175	183	198	199	202	201
Secondary	100	117	118	115	108	108	103	109	112	113	115	117	119	131	138	145	150	151	158	164	164	164	162
Post-school	100	103	100	95	87	92	96	94	88	85	87	87	85	86	86	85	83	78	72	69	62	63	62

£ per pupil, volume terms (1995/6 prices, adjusted by own-price deflator)

	1973/4	1974/5	1975/6	1976/7	1977/8	1978/9	1979/80	1980/1	1981/2	1982/3	1983/4	1984/5	1985/6	1986/7	1987/8	1988/9	1989/90	1990/91	1991/2	1992/3	1993/4	1994/5	1995/6
Primary	1149	1179	1221	1257	1300	1364	1445	1450	1459	1485	1522	1519	1541	1593	1629	1654	1710	1687	1719	1780	1810	1816	1808
Secondary	1791	1794	1807	1817	1832	1869	1862	1821	1835	1857	1893	1924	1953	2059	2103	2176	2258	2271	2309	2297	2308	2300	2271
Post-school	1207	1151	1123	1050	1008	1091	1186	1103	987	945	971	969	946	930	903	884	857	819	731	692	644	630	622

Index numbers with 1973/4 = 100

	1973/4	1974/5	1975/6	1976/7	1977/8	1978/9	1979/80	1980/1	1981/2	1982/3	1983/4	1984/5	1985/6	1986/7	1987/8	1988/9	1989/90	1990/91	1991/2	1992/3	1993/4	1994/5	1995/6
Primary	100	103	106	109	113	119	126	126	127	129	133	132	134	139	142	144	149	147	150	155	158	158	157
Secondary	100	100	101	101	102	104	104	102	102	104	106	107	109	115	117	121	126	127	129	128	129	128	127
Post-school	100	95	93	87	84	90	98	91	82	78	80	80	78	77	75	73	71	68	61	57	53	52	52

[a] Includes transfers to students in higher, further, and adult education, but excludes education-related and special schools current expenditure.

Sources: Table 3A.1 and DES (1997: tables 15 and 19).

Table 3A.4. SCHOOL-LEAVING QUALIFICATIONS BY SEX

	Males		Females	
% with qualifications higher than	1980/1	1993/4	1980/1	1993/4
3 or more A levels	10	14	8	15
1 or more A levels	16	21	15	23
5 or more GCSE grades A–C	24	39	26	48
1 or more GCSE grades A–C	50	64	55	75
1 or more GCSE grades A–G	87	91	90	93

Source: CSO (1996: table 3.6).

Table 3A.5. HIGHEST EDUCATIONAL LEVEL ACHIEVED, 16- TO 69-YEAR-OLDS, BY FATHER'S SOCIO-ECONOMIC GROUP (%)

	Professional (I)	Managerial (II)	Intermediate (III[1])	Skilled manual (III[2])	Semi-skilled (IV)	Unskilled (V)
1990						
Degree	27.2	14.3	15.5	5.3	3.9	1.9
Other higher	12.4	12.5	13.7	8.8	7.0	4.8
A level	22.4	17.8	16.5	10.7	7.5	6.2
O level	25.4	29.8	31.1	28.5	23.9	22.1
CSE etc.	6.8	12.1	9.2	15.2	15.1	13.6
No qualifications	5.9	13.5	14.0	31.5	42.5	51.4
1985						
Degree	28.8	13.3	12.4	4.1	3.1	2.2
Other higher	13.5	13.0	13.4	7.9	5.4	4.0
A level	20.0	14.8	14.3	8.9	7.2	7.4
O level	22.9	29.4	30.9	23.1	21.3	14.5
CSE etc.	7.3	13.0	13.0	17.9	17.3	14.0
No qualifications	7.6	16.4	16.0	38.1	45.7	57.8
1974						
Degree	16.7	5.5	4.4	1.3	0.6	0.7
Other higher	14.2	8.8	7.3	3.8	2.4	2.0
A level	14.8	8.5	8.5	3.8	2.7	2.3
O level	27.3	15.8	26.9	9.5	7.9	5.5
CSE etc.	13.6	15.3	15.4	14.1	11.2	10.2
No qualifications	13.3	45.9	37.5	67.5	75.2	79.3

Source: Author's calculations from GHS raw data files.

4 The National Health Service: Crisis, Change, or Continuity?

Julian Le Grand and Polly Vizard

I F THE British welfare state has a jewel in its crown, it is the National Health Service (NHS). Popular at home, attracting both admiration and hostility abroad, it is a permanent focus of political and media attention. As Rudolf Klein (1983) has put it, there is a 'rhetoric of crisis' that permeates all discussions of the NHS. In consequence government policies towards the NHS have become central to political controversies concerning the welfare state, with politicians vying with each other to reassure the electorate that the NHS is safe in their hands. In this chapter we address some of these policies, beginning with their aims and evolution since 1974 (Section I) and the resources devoted to them (Section II). Section III discusses the 'outputs' of the NHS, interpreted here as its performance relative to policy goals concerning efficiency and equity. Section IV considers health outcomes, concentrating on mortality and self-reported morbidity. The chapter's principal conclusions are summarized in Section V.

I. Goals and policies

Governments rarely have clearly defined, consistent policy goals, as we have seen in earlier chapters. Perhaps, in consequence, they rarely have consistent, well-defined policies. However, the NHS may be something of an exception to the first of these generalizations at least. There was specification of policy goals by both Governments during our period, as we shall now see.

75

Goals

The ultimate aim of policies directed towards health care has to be the promotion of health itself. More specifically, it is difficult to imagine a health care system that did not have as its principal goal that of effecting an improvement in the health of the individuals who use the system. The very name of the National Health Service implies a prime concern with health: it is not, after all, called the National Health Care Service or even the National Medical Service. However obvious the overriding priority of health itself may appear, it seems worth emphasizing, for it is too often ignored in the controversies that engulf the NHS.

It is also obvious, but also often ignored, that health care is not the only factor that affects health. Improvements in nutrition, in sanitation, and in environmental quality have historically proved to be of far greater importance in affecting the nation's health than have advances in medical care (McKeown 1976). Much current medical care is of unproven effectiveness; some may actually be harmful. Hence any assessment of health care policies over a period has to be aware of the danger of ascribing changes in individuals' health wholly, or even in large part, to those policies.

In most policy documents there is at least a genuflection in the direction of health as a policy objective. For instance, the original White Paper on the creation of a national health service described the 'real need' for the service as 'being to bring the country's full resources to bear upon reducing ill-health and promoting good health in all its citizens' (Ministry of Health 1944: 1). The Royal Commission on the National Health Service listed first among seven aims for the NHS that it should 'encourage and assist individuals to remain healthy' (1979: 9). A recent statement of goals by the National Health Service Executive (NHSE) emphasizes the importance of improving the nation's health (NHSE 1996: 3).

Most of these statements can be interpreted as reflecting a concern about the average or mean level of health. The Labour Government of 1974 to 1979 was concerned also about variations around that mean; that is, inequalities in health. So, for instance, David Ennals, Secretary of State for Health from 1976 to 1979, drew attention to the importance of 'narrowing the gap in health standards between different social classes' (Black Report 1980: 1). In contrast, one of the first acts of the Conservative Government when it took office in 1979 was to try to limit the circulation of the report of the working party on the subject that had been set up by David Ennals (Black Report 1980). Subsequent Conservative administrations remained quite unconcerned with health inequalities until, stung by criticism of their omission from the *Health of the Nation* initiative, the Major Government also established a working party on the topic that reported in 1995 (DoH 1995b); subsequently, the Department of Health was encouraged to launch a research programme in the area. The Labour Government elected in May 1997 looks set to make inequalities in health a priority.

However, most statements concerning policy objectives during the period under review have concerned health care more than health: indeed, specifically the forms of health care provided under the NHS. The 1974 Labour Government had a variety of aims for the NHS.

These included both quality goals, such as providing 'a broad range of services to a high standard' (Royal Commission on the National Health Service 1979: 9) and equity goals, such as providing 'equality of access' (ibid.) or 'equality of opportunity of access to health care for people at equal risk' (DHSS 1976a: 7). The Conservative Government's goals appeared regularly in its expenditure plans for the NHS; so, for instance, in the last of these it stated the Department of Health's overall aim to be 'to improve the health and well-being of the people of England, and to secure the provision of high quality health and social care for those who need it' (DoH 1997d: 3).

Perhaps the clearest statement of the goals of the NHS can be found in the NHSE report already mentioned. These are:

- **equity**: improving the health of the population as a whole, and reducing variations in health status by targeting resources where needs are greatest;
- **efficiency**: providing patients with treatment and care which is both clinically effective and a good use of taxpayers' money; and
- **responsiveness**: meeting the needs of individual patients and ensuring that the NHS changes appropriately as those needs change, and as medical and health care knowledge advances. (NHSE 1996: 3)

Some of these are slightly confused; for instance, equity is a concept relating to distributional issues, not with issues that relate to the population as a whole, such as improving its health. However, they are probably sufficiently general to serve as a benchmark for subsequent governments, as well as for analyses of the kind to be undertaken in this chapter. In subsequent sections we examine—as best we can, given the limitations of the data available—how far these goals have been achieved.

The evolution of policy: Labour, 1974–1979

The Labour Government elected in February 1974, and re-elected in October of that year, was seen by many of its supporters as having the opportunity to make the radical reforms that had eluded the 1964–70 administration. However, this opportunity, if such it was, was not exploited in the case of health. Some of the changes, such as the decision to phase out private beds in NHS hospitals, or the taxing as an employee benefit at all levels of remuneration medical insurance paid for by the employer, represented a definite reversal of policy, but others reflected the interests of the previous Conservative Government.

This was particularly the case with two out of the three principal concerns of policy during the period: the reallocation of resources to the relatively deprived regions, and also reallocation to the so-called 'Cinderella' or priority services for the elderly, the mentally ill, and the mentally handicapped (the third was pay-beds in NHS hospitals). In 1976 the Resource Allocation Working Party (RAWP) recommended the adoption of a new formula for allocating NHS resources between the regions (DHSS 1976). The principal innovation was the inclusion of measures of need (chiefly demographic factors and mortality rates) among the factors used to determine the allocation of funds. The effect of this was to divert resources that would otherwise have gone to regions that, relative to need, were well-endowed (primarily London and other South-Eastern regions) to poorly endowed ones (most of the rest of the country). Despite some obvious problems (such as the omission of morbidity as an indicator of need, the existence of extensive areas of deprivation even within the wealthier regions, and the neglect of inequalities other than geographical ones), the operation of RAWP during the period was quite successful, managing a measure of redistribution between regions (Le Grand *et al*. 1990: 116–20).

The attempt to reallocate resources to the Cinderella services met with more mixed success (ibid. 112–15). Perhaps part of the reason for the mixed performance in this area was the Government's preoccupation with the third major issue of the period: that of the removal of private beds from NHS hospitals. Despite the bitterness of the struggle (Klein 1995: 106–12) the success of this too was limited, reducing the number of pay-beds in England by just over a quarter (ibid. 112).

One of the by-products of the eventual compromise over pay-beds was the setting up of a Royal Commission to examine the overall state of the NHS. This reported in 1979, and provided, in the words of one commentator, 'an overwhelming—though not uncritical—endorsement of the NHS's achievements' (Klein 1995: 121). It was the last such endorsement the NHS would receive for some time. Another important inquiry initiated in this period was a response to one of the criticisms of RAWP: that it concentrated too heavily on regional differences, and did not address possibly more fundamental inequalities, particularly those associated with social class and income. In 1977 a Working Party was set up under the chairmanship of Sir Douglas Black to investigate these 'social' inequalities in health. However, it did not produce its report (Black Report 1980) until after the Conservative Government had taken office and its conclusions did not fit in with the philosophy of the new Government. Only a few copies were printed by the Government; however, the report became more widely available with the eventual publication of several commercial editions (such as Townsend *et al*. 1992).

The evolution of policy: the Conservatives, 1979–1987

The Conservative Government that took office in 1979 was initially not very different from its Labour predecessors with respect to the NHS. The 1979 Conservative manifesto stated 'we do not intend to reduce resources going to the National Health Service'. The 1983 manifesto was not quite so explicit in terms of overall resources going to the NHS, but made a number of specific spending commitments (notably, to hospital building and maintenance, to the priority services, and to the underprovided regions); and the 1987 manifesto made commitments to nurses, prevention, community care, management, and modernization, all within a general commitment to 'continue to improve the service'. None made any reference to large-scale reorganization of the service, although the 1983 manifesto did 'welcome the growth in private health insurance in recent years'.

It is therefore not surprising that in its earlier years the policy interventions in the health field by the Conservative Government were in large part a continuation of earlier concerns. There were two major organizational changes, both in the name of efficiency. The 1982 reorganization removed one tier of administration; and the changes following the Griffiths Report (National Health Service Management Inquiry, 1983) increased the role of professional management. Prescription, dental, and ophthalmic charges were raised. Some catering and cleaning services were contracted out; and there were measures to stimulate the private medical sector, through abolition of the Health Services Board that had regulated its activities, through changes in consultants' contracts that increased the opportunities for private practice, and through the restoration of exemption of employer-provided medical insurance from tax for employees below a certain level of remuneration. But overall the most striking feature of Conservative policy towards the NHS under the first two Thatcher administrations was its apparent continuity with the past.

The evolution of policy: the Conservatives, 1989–1997

However, in the late 1980s there was a dramatic change. In these years, there were a number of major developments, of which the most prominent were the publication of the White Paper *Working for Patients* (DoH 1989a) and the introduction of the internal or 'quasi'-market; the introduction of the Patient's Charter (DoH 1991); and the publication of the White Paper *The Health of the Nation* (DoH 1992).

We begin with *Working for Patients* and the internal market. From its inception in 1948 until the late 1980s the British National Health Service was essentially a command-and-control bureaucracy. Most hospital facilities were owned and operated by the state, who was also the employer of all the staff who worked there, including all physicians and nurses. GPs were a partial exception, being nominally self-employed; however, even they contracted almost exclusively with the state for the provision of their services.

The system had many merits. Since consultants were not paid on a fee-for-service basis, there was little incentive to overtreat patients. Indeed the incentive structure, if anything, was the reverse; consultants, being paid on a salary basis, had an incentive to reduce workload by undertreatment, especially since long waiting lists tended to increase the demand for private medical care often supplied by those same consultants. In consequence the system was less subject than fee-for-service systems to supplier-induced demand at the patient level. It was also what might be termed 'macro'-efficient, absorbing a relatively small proportion of the Gross National Product as compared with the health services of other countries, while providing a comprehensive service that was not notably inferior in quality to those elsewhere.

In other respects, however, the system was less satisfactory. It was generally considered to be 'micro-inefficient' (Enthoven 1985). The combination of clinical freedom and the absence of costing mechanisms within the system led to resources being used in a manner that bore little relation to their cost-effectiveness. It was locked inflexibly into historically determined patterns of care, and (in common with most other countries' health services) it was too dependent on hospital-based, technologically intensive services (Kirkup and Donaldson 1994). There were long waiting times (sometimes over two years) for relatively simple procedures, such as those associated with hip replacements, cataracts, and hernias (Frankel and West 1993). And the system was widely regarded as unresponsive and as restricting patient choice, with the professionals who worked within it apparently often more concerned with the pursuit of their own interests than with those of the people they were supposed to be serving.

By 1988, many of these concerns had become pressing. When they were combined with one of the perennial resource crises of the National Health Service, as they were in that year, the pressure on the politicians to 'do something' became almost irresistible (Lawson 1992: chap. 49). *Working for Patients* set out the Government's proposals for change, and these were incorporated into legislation in the National Health Service and Community Care Act of 1990.

Given its genesis in the middle of a NHS funding crisis and given the ideology of the Government that produced it, the White Paper was an astonishing document, both in what it included and what it excluded. It contained virtually no proposals for increased resources; and, with the exception of the introduction of tax relief for private health insurance for the elderly, it contained no proposals for expanding the role of private funding for health care. Instead the NHS would, in the words of Margaret Thatcher's foreword to the White Paper, 'continue to be available to all, regardless of income, and to be financed mainly out of general taxation'. At least as far as the level and sources of funding were concerned, continuity of policy was to be maintained.

So there was to be little change on the finance side of the NHS. However, the document was radical on the delivery side. An internal or quasi-market in health services was to be introduced, with the purchaser being separated from the provider of health services and with the introduction of competition between providers.

There were to be two kinds of purchaser. One was the old District Health Authority, which was allocated a budget to purchase secondary care based on the size and characteristics of the district's population. The other was the GP fundholder: GP practices with patient lists of over 11,000 who volunteered for the scheme were to be given a budget from which to purchase a more limited range of secondary care (mostly various forms of elective surgery) on behalf of their patients.

On the provider side, hospitals and the providers of other services were to become independent 'trusts': non-profit organizations, still nominally within the National Health Service, but with certain freedoms of action concerning pay, skill mix, and service delivery. These providers would contract with purchasers (of both kinds) to provide health care services.

The White Paper, virtually in its entirety, was translated into legislation in the National Health Service and Community Care Act of 1990, and implemented in April 1991. The organizational split between purchaser and provider was achieved with surprisingly little difficulty, and almost all health care providers became independent trusts. This was facilitated by the fact that many hospitals had historically been independent of central government; in some ways the reforms were returning them to their pre-1948 status. Various other aspects of the White Paper, not directly concerned with the internal market, were also introduced in the Act and also implemented relatively smoothly, including capital charges and a system of medical audit.

However, the changes were not costless. One of the most obvious costs was a sharp growth in the number of people involved in management and administration. The number of administrative and clerical staff increased by 15 per cent from 1990 to 1995 and of general and senior managers by 133 per cent—although the latter was affected by a reclassification of staff from other pay scales, such as senior nurses involved in management tasks (DoH 1996e). A preliminary estimate of the proportion of NHS expenditure on administration suggests that it rose from around 8 per cent before the reforms to around 11 per cent currently (Kings Fund 1997).

One of the most striking developments since 1991 has been the growth of GP fundholding. By April 1996, 50 per cent of all GPs were fundholders, covering 52 per cent of the population (NHSE 1996: 6). The scheme has been steadily extended since its inception. In 1993, practices of 7,000 patients were allowed to become fundholders and the range of services that could be purchased extended to cover community nursing and other community services, such as chiropody, dietetics, and physiotherapy. In 1995, practices with 5,000 patients were allowed to become fundholders. Even more significantly, two further 'tiers' of fundholding were introduced. One tier was 'below' the standard scheme, with practices of only 3,000 patients being allowed to hold budgets for their employed staff, drugs, and community services only. This was introduced partly in response to the perceived difficulty in recruiting further fundholders, to allow potential recruits to dip their toes in the water before committing themselves to the full scheme. The other new tier was 'above' the standard scheme, with a number of practices being given budgets large enough to purchase *all* hospital and community services. There were around 80 such sites; they were treated as experimental, and the Department of Health funded a large-scale evaluation of their performance by an independent team led by the Kings Fund.

Overall, the reforms were—and remain—highly controversial. There have been many criticisms (see, for instance, Paton 1992); and some attempts to evaluate aspects of them have been made (Le Grand and Bartlett 1993; Glennerster *et al.* 1994; Robinson and Le Grand 1994). But as yet an agreed verdict on their success or failure has yet to be given. We comment further on this below.

The Patient's Charter was introduced in 1991. It set out ten rights to care that patients could expect and seven national standards of care that the Government wanted achieved. Seven out of the ten rights in the Charter existed already. They included the right to receive treatment on the basis of need, regardless of the ability to pay, and the right to be registered with a GP. In addition, three new rights were created. First, patients should have access to detailed information on local health services, including quality standards and maximum waiting times. Second, all patients should be guaranteed admissions for all treatments within two years from the date of being placed on a waiting list. Third, complaints about NHS services should be properly investigated.

The national standards included standards for ambulance services (that an emergency ambulance should arrive within 14 minutes in an urban area and 19 minutes in a rural area); for appointments procedures at outpatient clinics (all patients to be given a specific appointment time and to be seen within 30 minutes of it); and for accident and emergency attendances (patients to be seen immediately and their need for treatment assessed).

The introduction of the Charter was an interesting development, especially when viewed in the context of the internal market. Like the market, it was an instrument for making the NHS more responsive to the needs and wants of its users; but it was a quite different kind of instrument that derived from a quite different tradition. The market was supposed to make providers more responsive through competition; if purchasers were dissatisfied with the service they were receiving from a particular provider they could threaten to take their business elsewhere, thus giving an incentive to the provider to improve its performance. The Charter, on the other hand, was a top-down management tool, symbolically aimed at the new consumerism, but designed to enhance performance by managerial directive. It would have been just as much at home in the old command-and-control NHS as in the new quasi-market one—indeed, if anything, more so.

In principle, few would disagree with the rights and standards embodied in the Charter. Moreover, anecdotal evidence suggests that its introduction has had a significant impact (there have not yet been any systematic studies of its overall effect that we know of). Health managers are taking the standards seriously, especially the numerical ones, and activities directed at trying to meet the relevant targets appear to be taking up a considerable portion of managers' time, especially those concerned with waiting times. Again, we return to this below.

But there are difficulties. Some of the rights are regarded as largely cosmetic: for example, the naming of nurses responsible for each patient. Other problems arise from its top-down nature referred to above. The 'rights' given to patients are not legal ones and their implementation cannot be pursued through the courts. Instead patients are basically dependent on managers for their fulfilment (although, in theory, if patients feel they have been denied their rights, they can take it up with the Chief Executive of the NHS). Additionally, there is a worry that managers will focus on the numerical targets and that the less quantifiable aspects of care will be neglected. Further, numerical targets can lead to distortions in their own terms (Baggott 1994: 197).

One of the ways in which the Patient's Charter targets and other aims are monitored is by the annual NHS Comparative Performance Tables, also a recent innovation. These show how hospitals and ambulance services are performing against some of the Patient's Charter standards and against other standards introduced by the Government. The performance indicators include: the waiting times in outpatient units and for accident and emergency services; the numbers of cancelled operations; the proportions of day-case surgery for hernia, arthroscopy, cataract, and lacarosocopy; the percentage of patients admitted for treatment within three months for general surgery, urology, trauma and orthopaedics, ear, nose, and throat, ophthalmology, oral surgery, plastic surgery, and gynaecology; and the proportion of ambulances arriving within the Patient's Charter limits.

These were published for the first time in June 1994. They received much attention in the national press, with league tables of hospitals being compiled. Although immensely controversial when they first appeared, they now are generally considered to be a useful addition to the information available to purchasers and patients.

There are now proposals to extend the scheme to include performance indicators covering post-operative mortality rates by hospitals: and a pilot scheme of this kind is already in operation in Scotland. This will be an important development, since it will be one of the first attempts to monitor an aspect of the 'outcome' of the NHS: the impact it has on patients' health. On the other hand it too has an obvious potential for creating problems: notably, the incentive it gives for a hospital to refuse to accept difficult cases in case they drag down its success rate in terms of post-operative mortality.

The importance of improving health, as distinct from improving health services, was recognized by the Conservative Government in the 1990s, which began to develop a much broader strategy for public health. This was expressed in a White Paper, *The Health of the Nation* (DoH 1992). This selected five target areas for action: cancer, heart disease and stroke, mental illness, HIV/AIDS and sexual health, and accidents. These were chosen on the basis that they contained major public health risks, that policy was relatively underdeveloped in the areas concerned, and that there was sufficient knowledge concerning risk factors, etc. to permit an evidence-based strategy to be developed. In each area, targets were set for reductions in death rates and in behaviours known to be risk factors for the disease concerned.

The strategy was to be implemented in a number of ways. At central government level, an interdepartmental Cabinet committee was set up to oversee the implementation of the strategy. Health authorities were supposed to monitor the health of their populations and to plan services in relation to needs. Regional co-ordinators were appointed to ensure the dissemination of good practice. The NHS Executive established 'focus' groups for each area; and a number of measures were announced which aimed at improving the information base.

The idea of setting specific health targets and of having some kind of overall strategy for achieving these was derived from the World Health Organization's (WHO) *Health for All* initiative, as developed by the WHO European Regional Office (WHO 1985). But the UK has probably taken these ideas further than anywhere else; and the initiative was widely recognized as imaginative and innovative.

It nonetheless had its critics (Baggott 1994: 258–9). First, there were concerns about the usefulness of crude targets. They focused attention on what can be measured, downgrading problems that may be just as serious but cannot be quantified. Second, the strategy was vague as to exactly how the targets were to be achieved. In fact many of them were in areas where policy was not known to be particularly effective; also, in several areas there were trends already operating in the right direction, without any assistance from policy. Hence there was a suspicion that the Government may have selected the targets at least partly on the basis that they will be achieved anyway, with the politicians concerned taking the credit. Third, the model was a medical one, relating more to the prevention of disease than the promotion of health. Fourth, it was not clear how the strategy was related to the internal market. Although purchasers were given the task of pursuing *The Health of the Nation* targets, it was not clear precisely how they were going to do it when their budgets were primarily taken up with maintaining existing curative and caring services, and when, in any case, there was a problem in finding the appropriate tools. Finally, and most controversially, the strategy said nothing about inequalities in health between different social groups and regions.

In response to the criticism concerning inequalities in health, the Government set up a departmental committee to look at the issue. This reported in 1995 (DoH 1995*b*) and recommended that purchasers draw up plans to identify and tackle health variations and to evaluate interventions. The report was followed by NHS Executive guidelines reinforcing the need for health authorities to target resources where needs were greatest.

All this does not bring to an end the catalogue of changes that were introduced in this remarkable decade. Two others stand out: the Private Finance Initiative (PFI) and the Primary Care White Papers. The PFI was an attempt to overcome the constraints on investment in health services imposed by the Treasury, with its concern for the Public Sector Borrowing Requirement. Under the scheme, private consortia would raise the finance to construct certain facilities and to operate them under contract to health service providers. All services except clinical ones could be provided in this way. However, the scheme, mired in complexity, has been quite unsuccessful, being largely confined to small projects involving information and management technology; at the time of writing, not a single major acute hospital scheme has been confirmed.

The Primary Care White Papers (DoH 1996*a, d*) went some way towards rectifying the obsession with secondary care that had dominated the Conservative Government's (and indeed its Labour predecessor's) agenda for health for so long. They introduced the possibility of providing primary care in a different way from the standard self-employed GP, encouraging experimentation with pilots involving salaried GPs, the merger of primary care budgets with other budgets, and so on.

Another issue that troubled the latter days of the Conservative administration was that of rationing—or, as it was often euphemistically termed, priority setting. Although some form of implicit rationing had always been a feature of the service (New and Le Grand 1996), the fact that the service could not provide all the possible treatments available to everyone who needed them became increasingly apparent in the early 1990s. Despite government instructions to impose no blanket bans, certain health authorities devised lists of procedures that they would not fund, including most notably *in vitro* fertilization (IVF); long-term hospital beds for geriatric care were closed down, leaving the people concerned to seek means-tested care from elsewhere; and, almost unnoticed, charges for services such as adult dental care began to rise to a point at which the service concerned could no longer really be considered to be part of a National Health Service free at the point of use.

Overall, the Conservative strategy with respect to the NHS since 1988 had three distinct stages. First, through the Griffiths changes, they tried to make the management of the system more efficient through the introduction of private sector management techniques and styles. Second, as the relentless resource pressure continued and it became increasingly apparent that improved management on its own was not enough to squeeze more services out of limited resources, they tried to encourage efficiency through the introduction of competition via an internal market (Glennerster and Le Grand 1995). Third, apparently lacking conviction that even these measures would be sufficient, they introduced top-down management tools as well: hospital league tables, the Patient's Charter, and the targets of *The Health of the Nation*. These changes were so large in scope that it will probably always be impossible to say unequivocally that they have succeeded or failed. However, in subsequent sections, we utilize such statistical information as is available to shed some light on the performance of these policies, as well as on those of the preceding administrations.

II. Trends in expenditure on health care

The bulk of public discussion of expenditure on health care concerns central government expenditure on the NHS. This is indeed by far the largest component of total expenditure on health care, and we begin by examining it in some detail. However, it is not the only one. Even within the services provided by the NHS, patients are charged for prescriptions and for ophthalmic and dental care, charges that have for long been a subject of political controversy. In addition NHS patients may face implicit costs in using the service, arising from the time spent travelling to NHS facilities and the costs of waiting for services to be delivered to them. Thus there are costs of the NHS that are paid for by patients as well those that are met by the Government; these are also discussed below.

Health care services are provided by the private sector as well as the public sector in the UK. The relationship between these two sectors has often been the subject of government policy, and it is in this area that there has perhaps been the sharpest difference between Conservative and Labour Governments. The private sector has been encouraged to grow under the Conservatives, and we end this section with a discussion of this growth.

Government expenditure in real terms

The first step in analysing the trends in central government expenditure is to deflate figures in current prices by a measure of inflation. There are a number of ways of doing this, and the

Julian Le Grand and Polly Vizard

statistics are sensitive to the choice made. We begin by using a general measure of the rate of inflation: the GDP price deflator. Using this deflator provides a measure of the resources devoted to the NHS in terms of the 'opportunity cost' of those resources: their value had they been spent elsewhere in the economy. We call this total real NHS expenditure and it is shown in index form in the first column of Table 4.1. Under Labour (1973/4 to 1978/9) there was an annual growth rate of 5.3 per cent; whereas under the Conservatives (1978/9 to 1995/6) the annual growth rate was 3.3 per cent. The annual rate of increase differed between the successive Conservative administrations: 2.9 per cent from 1978/9 to 1982/3, 2.3 per cent from 1982/3 to 1986/7, 4.3 per cent from 1986/7 to 1991/2, and 4.2 per cent from 1991/2 until 1995/6.

Table 4.1. GROWTH IN NHS EXPENDITURE AND GDP

	Real NHS expenditure (1973/4 = 100)	Volume NHS expenditure (1973/4 = 100)	Real GDP[a] (1973/4 = 100)	Real NHS expenditure as % of real GDP[a]
1973/4	100.00	100.00	100.00	3.87
1974/5	120.07	109.43	99.44	4.67
1975/6	128.04	118.55	98.85	5.01
1976/6	129.10	117.64	101.76	4.91
1977/8	125.37	117.22	104.52	4.64
1978/9	127.94	120.53	107.61	4.60
1979/80	128.59	121.76	110.70	4.49
1980/1	141.30	125.07	107.14	5.10
1981/2	143.00	126.89	106.54	5.19
1982/3	144.84	126.71	109.29	5.12
1983/4	147.86	130.11	113.46	5.04
1984/5	149.52	128.55	115.85	4.99
1985/6	151.41	130.37	120.28	4.87
1986/7	160.01	134.11	125.99	4.91
1987/8	167.23	135.59	132.21	4.89
1988/9	173.14	137.16	137.95	4.85
1989/90	175.46	139.34	140.32	4.84
1990/1	181.22	142.24	139.75	5.01
1991/2	194.25	150.98	137.11	5.48
1992/3	207.45	154.56	137.46	5.84
1993/4	212.12	151.65	140.83	5.82
1994/5	223.07	160.59	146.40	5.89
1995/6	221.92	162.00	149.42	5.74

[a] An adjusted series for money GDP is used in the calculations for years up to 1989/90. This has been constructed to remove the distortion caused by the abolition of domestic rates.

Sources: Real expenditure: Table 4A.1; volume expenditure: Table 4A.2; real GDP: calculated from HM Treasury (1997: table 3.1).

In the 1970s and early 1980s, the pattern of real government expenditure on the NHS reflected the electoral cycle. The Labour victory in 1974 was followed by sharp increases in rates of growth, of 20.1 per cent in 1974/5 and 6.6 per cent in 1975/6. These increases in the growth rate were rapidly reversed following the economic crisis of 1976, and low and negative growth rates of 0.8 per cent and −2.9 per cent in 1976/7 and 1977/8 respectively were only partly compensated for by a 2.1 per cent resumption in growth in 1978/9 (as the election approached). The Conservative victory in the 1979 election was followed by a small 0.5 per cent increase in growth in 1979/80 and a sharp 9.9 per cent increase in 1980/1. Again, these increases in the growth rate of expenditure were reversed as the election grew more distant, falling back to 1.2 per cent in 1981/2 and 1.3 per cent in 1982/3.

In the mid-1980s, the pattern of real government expenditure on the NHS seemed to have changed slightly. Unusually, growth rates increased only marginally following the 1983 election to 2.1 per cent in 1983/4 and 1.1 per cent in 1984/5, and remained depressed at 1.3 per cent in 1985/6. The average annual rate of growth of real expenditure on the NHS was only 1.4 per cent between 1981/2 and 1985/6, compared with an average rate of 3.3 per cent over the Conservative period as a whole.

However, this change did not endure. By the late 1980s, growth rates had resumed their tendency to reflect the electoral cycle, with relatively high rates of growth of real expenditure around the time of the 1987 general election, of 5.7 per cent in 1986/7, and, following the third Conservative victory in 1987, of 4.5 per cent in 1987/8. Real expenditure on the NHS fell to mid-term lows of 3.5 per cent in 1988/9, 1.3 per cent in 1989/90, and 3.3 per cent in 1990/1, before accelerating around the time of the 1992 election, to 7.2 per cent in 1991/2 and, following the fourth consecutive Conservative victory in 1992, to 6.8 per cent in 1992/3. During the fourth Conservative administration, growth rates dipped in 1993/4 to 2.3 per cent, but, unusually for the mid-term of an electoral cycle, real expenditure rose sharply in 1994/5, by 5.2 per cent. This increase in the growth rate was partially offset by a negative growth rate of −0.5 per cent in 1995/6. However, real expenditure on health (as defined in HM Treasury 1997: table 3.3) was estimated to have grown again, by 1.8 per cent, in 1996/7.

An alternative way of looking at these figures is to examine the share of total national resources, as measured by GDP, devoted to the NHS. The relevant percentages are given in the fourth column of Table 4.1. Under Labour (1973/4–1978/9), real government expenditure on the NHS as a percentage of GDP increased by 0.7 percentage points to 4.6 per cent. Under the Conservatives (1978/9–1995/6), it increased by a further 1.1 percentage points, to 5.7 per cent. The increase in real expenditure as a share of GDP under the Conservatives comprised a rise of 0.5 percentage points during the first Conservative administration, a 0.2 percentage point *fall* during the second, a 0.6 percentage point rise during the third, and a 0.3 percentage point rise during the fourth.

Julian Le Grand and Polly Vizard

Government expenditure in volume terms

One explanation for the 'hump-shaped' time path in increases in government real expenditure on the NHS lies in the large pay awards that the Governments concerned have apparently felt it was necessary to grant or to promise to health service workers during election periods. For instance, qualified nurses received pay increases of 21.5 per cent in 1974/5 and of 12.5 per cent in 1980/1 (Trinder 1987). The latter were a part of the Clegg award to nurses that was promised by Labour and paid for by the Conservatives after the 1979 election. Although there was no comparable award at the time of the 1983 election (perhaps because the Clegg awards had been implemented relatively recently), there were increases in the election years of 1987/8 and 1991/2: at 14.9 per cent and 6.5 per cent respectively, these were considerably greater than in the non-election years in the period (Trinder 1997: table 10).

These above-average wage increases show that it is possible for input prices to change in the health service sector at different rates from those in the rest of the economy. As a result, real expenditure as we have defined it may not be a good measure of the actual volume of health care services provided by the NHS. In order to strip out the effects of greater-than-average increases in the cost of inputs in the NHS, and to focus on changes in the volume of NHS output, we need to use a deflator specifically constructed for the NHS. A number of deflators are available for this purpose. We have chosen an NHS deflator derived from the UK National Income Accounts which covers the whole of our period. A volume index based on this deflator is given in the second column of Table 4.1.

The evidence from these estimates suggests that a significant component of the sharp rates of growth of real expenditure under both Labour and the Conservatives is indeed attributable to increases in input costs. For instance, increases in the growth of real expenditure of 20.1 per cent in 1974/5, 9.9 per cent in 1980/1, 5.7 per cent in 1986/7, and 6.8 per cent in 1992/3 correspond to much lower rates of growth of volume expenditure, of 9.4 per cent, 2.7 per cent, 2.9 per cent, and 2.4 per cent respectively. The tendency of expenditure to increase around election times is less marked for volume expenditure than for real expenditure throughout the period, possibly suggesting that politicians see at least as many votes in raising existing health sector workers' pay as in actually increasing the volume of resources going into the NHS.

Nevertheless, the statistics suggest that increases in the volume of NHS output did contribute to the expenditure rises. Under Labour (1973/4–1978/9), there was an average annual increase in volume of 3.9 per cent. In contrast, under the Conservatives (1978/9–1995/6), there was an average annual rate of growth of 1.8 per cent. This breaks down into average annual growth rates during the four Conservative administrations of 1.6 per cent, 1.1 per cent, 2.5 per cent, and 2.7 per cent respectively.

Both the real and volume expenditure statistics reveal a degree of continuity in the patterns of government expenditure on the NHS under both Labour and Conservative Governments. Generally speaking, the growth of expenditure has assumed a cyclical pattern, increasing around the time of general elections, and dipping in the electoral mid-term. This pattern is true for both measures of expenditure, although it is more pronounced for real expenditure than for volume expenditure.

Nevertheless, significant differences between Labour and the Conservatives can be identified. The average annual growth rate under Labour (5.3 per cent real and 3.9 per cent volume) was significantly higher than under the Conservatives (3.3 per cent real and 1.8 per cent volume). Moreover, the statistics also reveal differences between the various Conservative administrations, with the rates of both real and volume growth being significantly lower between 1978/9 and 1986/7 than between 1986/7 and 1995/6.

Composition of government expenditure

The proportions of expenditure devoted to current and capital spending are given in Table 4.2. It is apparent that the relative share of current expenditure in total expenditure increased during the period from 90.5 per cent of total government expenditure on the NHS in 1973/4 to 99.2 per cent in 1995/6. The share of capital expenditure declined by a corresponding amount over the period as a whole. The share of capital expenditure in total expenditure fell under Labour, then regained some of its lost ground during the first two Conservative administrations, only to decline even more sharply after 1985/6. By the end of our period, the share of capital expenditure in total expenditure had fallen to an extraordinary low of 0.8 per cent; this in part reflected the difficulties of initiating capital projects arising from the operations (or lack of them) of the Private Finance Initiative. (These figures do not correspond directly to those reported by the Department of Health (1997d: table 2.1); see Vizard 1997 for a discussion of this issue.)

Table 4.3 shows hospital and community health services' (HCHS) expenditure broken down by programme for 1984/5 and 1994/5. There was an increase over that decade in the proportion of spending on acute services and (very slightly) those with learning disabilities, and a slight fall in the proportion spent on maternity, elderly, and mental illness services.

Too much should not be made of these changes since there were some differences in definition of the categories. However, it is noteworthy that this contrasts with the period from 1974 to 1984, when there was some attempt to switch a small amount of hospital resources away from acute services and into more community-oriented or priority services (Le Grand *et al*. 1990: 112–15). The difference may reflect a relative neglect of the so-called priority groups in the later period, or their de-institutionalization, as geriatric wards and large mental hospitals were closed. If the latter, then the key question is whether local authority community-based services stepped in as hospital services were cut back—an issue addressed in Chapter 6.

Table 4.2. COMPOSITION OF TOTAL REAL NHS EXPENDITURE (%, YEARS ENDING 31 MARCH)

	Current expenditure				Total current expenditure	Capital expenditure
	HCHS, FHS[a]	Admin	Patients' payments	Other services[b]		
1973/4	87.9	3.0	−3.5	3.1	90.5	9.5
1974/5	88.4	3.8	−2.7	3.1	92.6	7.4
1975/6	88.3	3.9	−2.0	2.5	92.6	7.4
1976/7	88.5	3.9	−2.1	3.0	93.2	6.8
1977/8	89.4	3.9	−2.1	2.9	94.1	5.9
1978/9	89.4	3.8	−2.0	2.9	94.1	5.9
1979/80	89.5	4.0	−2.2	3.0	94.3	5.7
1980/1	90.0	3.8	−2.4	2.9	94.2	5.8
1981/2	90.5	3.6	−2.6	2.3	93.7	6.3
1982/3	91.3	3.4	−2.8	2.2	94.0	6.0
1983/4	92.0	2.9	−3.0	2.3	94.2	5.8
1984/5	91.8	2.9	−3.0	2.2	93.9	6.1
1985/6	91.4	2.7	−2.8	2.4	93.7	6.3
1986/7	90.0	2.9	−3.0	3.9	93.9	6.1
1987/8	90.4	3.0	−3.1	4.0	94.2	5.8
1988/9	91.5	3.0	−3.6	3.5	94.3	5.7
1989/90	88.7	3.4	−4.0	3.6	91.7	8.3
1990/1	90.6	3.5	−4.3	3.6	93.4	6.6
1991/2	91.3	3.5	−4.0	3.6	94.4	5.6
1992/3	90.9	3.6	−3.6	4.6	95.4	4.6
1993/4	95.5	na	−3.0	5.2	97.6	2.4
1994/5	94.5	na	−2.3	6.4	98.7	1.3
1995/6	94.6	na	−2.3	6.8	99.2	0.8

[a] HCHS: Hospital and Community Health Services; FHS: Family Health Services.
[b] Other central services and departmental administration.

Source: Table 4A.1.

Need, demand, and resources

Thus both Governments increased the resources going into the NHS. But did they increase them enough? Was the growth in resources sufficient to keep pace with the growth in the need or the demand for health care?

The concept of need for health services is a contested one and has been defined in a wide variety of different ways. Here we use a simple definition of need based on the demographic structure of the population constructed by the Department of Health. This is given for the years 1982/3–1995/6 (comparable values for earlier years are not available) in the third

Table 4.3. DISTRIBUTION OF HOSPITAL AND COMMUNITY HEALTH SERVICES EXPENDITURE BY PROGRAMME

Programme	Percentage of expenditure	
	1984/5	1994/5
Acute	45.9	49.0
Maternity	5.8	4.4
Elderly	13.0	11.8
Learning disability	5.1	5.2
Mental illness	11.3	10.7
Other community	5.4	7.3
Other	13.5	11.6
Total	100	100

Source: House of Commons Health Committee (1996: 31).

column of Table 4.4, together with the index of volume expenditures rebased to 1982/3. The needs index shows the annual percentage increase in the volume of resources needed to maintain current levels of HCHS services to different populations. The 'current levels' estimates are based on 1993/4 cross-sectional utilization data: that is, the DoH estimate of what the likely resource consequences would be for a population with a higher proportion of, say, over-75s than in 1993/4, but with the 1993/4 age-specific rates of utilization by over-75s and other age groups.

This methodology is somewhat crude, since it is not possible to be sure that current patterns of utilization reflect relative need, and this uncertainty increases the further we move from the base year (1993/4). However, according to these estimates, the rising population and changing age/sex structure has impacted on the need for HCHS quite gradually, with the resource requirement needed to maintain the use of services increasing at an average rate of 0.7 percentage points between 1982/3 and 1995/6. This figure is less than the average rate of growth of government volume expenditure on the NHS during this period, which was 1.8 per cent per year.

Various authors have challenged the validity of measures of need for the services provided by the NHS based on demographic variables alone. Although the DoH measures take account of the differential use of NHS services by different age and sex groups, they have been criticized for failing to take account of social and economic determinants of health needs and for being insensitive to the higher than average rates of ill-health that might arise among specific population groups. Attempts have been made to incorporate a broader range of indicators into measures of need, including mortality data and a range of socio-economic variables thought to be highly correlated with the incidence of ill-health (see Brennan and

Table 4.4. TRENDS IN PERSONAL INCOME, NHS VOLUME EXPENDITURE, AND DEMOGRAPHIC PRESSURE

	Growth of NHS volume expenditure (1981/2 = 100)	Growth of total personal income[a] (1981/2 = 100)	Growth of demographic pressure[b] (1981/2 = 100)
1981/2	100.00	100.00	100.00
1982/3	99.86	100.64	100.47
1983/4	102.54	103.76	101.10
1984/5	101.30	107.05	101.82
1985/6	102.74	110.82	102.85
1986/7	105.68	115.22	103.63
1987/8	106.85	120.06	104.63
1988/9	108.09	126.84	105.55
1989/90	109.81	131.90	106.39
1990/1	112.10	137.00	107.24
1991/2	118.98	134.78	107.92
1992/3	121.81	136.61	108.59
1993/4	119.52	137.72	109.16
1994/5	126.56	141.24	109.83
1995/6	127.67	146.06	110.40

[a] Total personal income (before tax, and before providing for depreciation and stock appreciation) deflated using implied consumers' expenditure deflator.

[b] Annual percentage increase in volume resources needed to maintain current levels of service to different populations. Based on 1993/4 expenditure patterns.

Sources: NHS volume expenditure: Table 4.1; total personal income: ONS (1996e: table 1.6 and 1997e, table 2.5); implied consumers' expenditure deflator: ONS, personal communication; demographic pressure index: DoH, personal communication.

Carr-Hill 1996). However, as yet no time series of indicators of this kind that would be of use for our purpose have been constructed.

In addition there may have been increases in costs due to the introduction of new medical technologies, although the latter might also be expected to be accompanied by increases in the quality of services provided. In the 1980s it was suggested that additional spending of 0.5 per cent per year was necessary on account of medical advance (letter from Mr B. Hayhoe to the Chairman of the Institute of Health Services Management, 28 Jan. 1986); if this were added on to the average growth rate in the demographic index of need over the period, it would increase that rate to 1.2 per cent a year, still below that of volume NHS expenditures (1.8 per cent).

The demand for health services is also difficult to define and to measure. Here, we adopt a concept of demand based on the tastes, perceptions, and expectations of the population. Since these variables are difficult to observe directly, we associate changes in gross personal income with changes in the demand for services provided by the NHS.

An index of the growth in personal income from 1982/3 to 1995/6 is given in the second column of Table 4.4. All the indices in Table 4.4—volume expenditures, needs, and income—are also illustrated in Fig. 4.1. It is apparent that, while the growth in volume expenditure has more than matched the growth in needs over time, it has been significantly less than the growth in income. If the income elasticity of demand for health services is one or greater than one (and there is controversy about this: see Kanavos and Mossialos 1997), then demand has been rising faster than supply. This may go some way to explaining the widespread perception that, despite the rise in real resources going into the service, the NHS was seriously underfunded during this period.

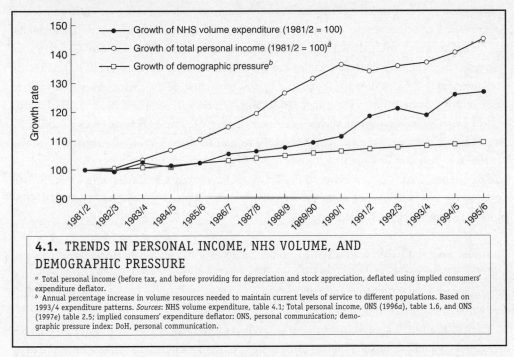

4.1. TRENDS IN PERSONAL INCOME, NHS VOLUME, AND DEMOGRAPHIC PRESSURE

[a] Total personal income (before tax, and before providing for depreciation and stock appreciation, deflated using implied consumers' expenditure deflator.
[b] Annual percentage increase in volume resources needed to maintain current levels of service to different populations. Based on 1993/4 expenditure patterns. *Sources*: NHS volume expenditure, table 4.1; Total personal income, ONS (1996a), table 1.6, and ONS (1997e) table 2.5; implied consumers' expenditure deflator: ONS, personal communication; demographic pressure index: DoH, personal communication.

Of course none of this tells us whether the NHS actually *was* underfunded. To begin with, we do not know whether at the baseline position for our data (1982/3) there was underfunding or overfunding; hence we cannot say whether there has been a movement towards a greater degree of underfunding or towards a lesser degree of overfunding. Also, these indicators of need and demand are extremely crude; more sophisticated ones would be needed before any more definite statement could be made. However, the movements in income do suggest that demand, at least, was increasing at a faster rate than supply, and therefore that the pressures on the NHS over the period were also steadily increasing. (For useful discussions of the historical debate concerning the underfunding or overfunding of the NHS, see Klein 1995: 98–9; for discussions of the present situation, see Dixon *et al.* 1997, and Harrison *et al.* 1997*a, b*.)

Moreover, judging from the Conservative Government plans for spending as given in HM Treasury (1997), to which the new Labour Government at the time of writing intends to adhere, it appears that no Government will be willing to make the effort, in terms of total spending, to restore even the 1982/3 balance between the growth of supply of health care services provided by the NHS on the one hand, and the growth of demand for those services on the other. A perceived 'crisis' of underfunding is therefore likely to continue.

Private expenditure on health care

Private expenditure plays a significant role both within the NHS (for instance, patients' charges and pay-beds) and in the financing of privately supplied health care. The policies of Labour and Conservative Governments towards both of these categories of private expenditure were more at odds than their policies in any other area. The Labour Government restricted the role of private finance within the NHS, allowing charges to fall in real terms and attempting to eliminate pay-beds, and opposing the use of tax concessions to stimulate demand for private medical insurance (PMI) and for privately supplied health care. In contrast, Conservative Governments have pursued a policy of relating private costs to ability to pay. Patients' charges have risen substantially in real terms (although exemptions for the elderly and those on low income have broadened) and pay-beds have been encouraged. In addition, successive Conservative administrations have used tax concessions to stimulate demand for PMI and to encourage growth of privately supplied health care. These developments are now discussed in more detail.

Charges The National Health Service makes charges for certain pharmaceutical, dental, and ophthalmic services. Although the amount of revenue raised is relatively small, patients' payments are highly political, and Labour and Conservative Governments have differed radically on their policies in this area.

The 1974 to 1979 Labour Government was reluctant to raise charges. Prescription charges remained constant in nominal terms at 20 pence per item. Charges for ophthalmic and dental services were increased once, in April 1977. The combination of constant or slowly increasing nominal charges and rapid inflation meant that charges fell in real terms. During the Labour Government, patients' charges for pharmaceutical, dental, and ophthalmic services fell in real terms by 30 per cent from £523 million to £368 million (1995/6 prices). As a proportion of NHS expenditures these charges fell from 2.9 per cent in 1973/4 to 1.6 per cent in 1978/9. The most dramatic decrease occurred in payments for pharmaceuticals, which more than halved (Table 4A.1).

The Conservative Government reversed these trends. Prescription charges were increased repeatedly under successive Conservative administrations. In April 1979, prescription charges stood at 20 pence per item. By April 1997, the charge reached £5.65 per item, representing a real increase of more than 1,000 per cent during the Conservative period in office. In addition, new dental treatment charges were introduced in April 1988, and charges for dental examinations were introduced in January 1989. Charges for sight tests were introduced in April 1989.

Despite these sharp increases in the real levels of patients' charges, the total amount of revenue raised from patients' charges was limited by other policy factors. For instance, the amount of revenue raised from charges for pharmaceutical services was limited by the fact that certain groups, such as those over retirement age and those on low income, were exempt from prescription charges. Whereas in 1979 the proportion of prescriptions which were exempt from charges in the UK was 65 per cent, by 1995 the figure for England had increased to 84 per cent. Moreover, prescription charges remained less than the cost of treatment. For example, in 1995 the average net ingredient cost of a prescription was £7.78, compared with prescription charges of £5.25 per item, and prescription charge revenue comprised only 7.5 per cent of the total value of pharmaceutical services (DoH 1996b; McGuigan 1997).

The amount of revenue raised from charges for ophthalmic services was also limited by other policy factors. Policy initiatives in 1985 and 1989 restricted NHS sight tests to certain priority groups: children, students aged under 19 in full-time education, adults on low incomes, and those with certain special medical needs. Because fewer people were using the service, total patients' payments for ophthalmic services fell sharply in real terms from £104 million in 1983/4 to £1 million in 1987/8 (at 1995/6 prices), and ceased to be identified as a separate category of patients' payments thereafter (Table 4A.1).

Despite these limiting factors, the amount of revenue raised from charges for pharmaceutical and dental services more than trebled in real terms during the period of Conservative government, increasing from £278 million in 1978/9 to £877 million in 1995/6. Patients' payments for pharmaceutical and dental services financed 2.2 per cent of NHS expenditures in 1995/6, compared with 1.2 per cent in 1978/9 (Table 4A.1).

Private care in the NHS Many NHS hospitals provide private care: that is, care paid for privately either by individuals themselves or by insurance companies. The physical capital, such as beds and other facilities, is provided by the NHS, which charges private patients for its use. The consultant seen by private patients will usually be employed concurrently in the NHS, either on a full- or part-time basis.

This mix of public and private care has also been viewed differently by Labour and Conservative Governments. The 1974 to 1979 Labour Government discouraged mixed public/private provision, attempting to phase out private beds in NHS hospitals. In contrast, consecutive Conservative administrations have initiated policy reforms which have encouraged the growth of private expenditure on publicly supplied health care. For instance, the conditions of employment for NHS consultants were changed to increase their incentive to undertake work in the private sector in 1981, while the 1988 Health and Medicines Act and the 1990 NHS and Community Care Act gave health authorities and NHS trusts the power and the incentives to compete with the private sector for private patient revenue. Whereas NHS units were previously restricted to recovering costs, these legislative measures empowered health authorities and NHS trusts to charge commercial prices with a view to making profits, and to carry on a wide range of commercial activities, including dealing in land (Laing and Buisson Ltd. 1996*a*: A69).

There are 3,000 authorized NHS pay-beds in the UK. However, data on the total number of NHS pay-beds has not been collected nationally since 1991, when health authorities ceased to be involved in the authorization of pay-beds. It is probable that any real competitive threat to the private sector comes not from increased use of pay-beds on ordinary NHS wards, but from new-style, dedicated NHS pay-bed units, which supply very similar services to the private sector. There were an estimated 77 such units in mid-1996, providing a total of 1,385 beds. The total number of private patients admitted for treatment in NHS hospitals increased from 81,000 in 1990/1 to 99,000 in 1994/5, with private outpatient attendances increasing from 148,000 to 151,000 during the same period (Laing and Buisson Ltd. 1996*a*: A83–85). Press reports suggested that the NHS had become the largest single supplier of private health care in the country.

The value of NHS private patient revenue is shown in Table 4.5. Despite the attempts of the Labour Government to phase out NHS pay-beds, the real value of NHS revenue from private patients increased in real terms by 114 per cent under Labour, from £84 million in 1973/4 to £96 million in 1978/9 (1995/6 prices). Under the Conservatives, this figure increased by an additional 230 per cent, to £210 million in 1995/6. Nevertheless, real NHS revenue from private patients' treatment as a proportion of real NHS expenditure has remained very small. This figure fell slightly under Labour, from 0.46 per cent in 1973/4 to 0.41 per cent in 1978/9, increasing to 0.52 per cent in 1995/6 under the Conservatives. (These trends are not reflected in the figures for receipts from hospital services given in Tables 4A.1 and 4A.2; see Vizard 1997 for a discussion of this issue.)

Private expenditure on private care An increasing number of patients are being cared for in private hospitals, some of which are run for profit. The number of beds available in registered nursing homes, private hospitals, and clinics grew at an average rate of around 13 per cent per year since 1980, rising to close on 190,000 in 1995/6. Of this total, 179,000 beds were available in nursing homes, and 11,000 beds were available in private hospitals and clinics (DoH 1996*f*). Therefore, although private nursing homes constitute the biggest market for privately supplied health care (as discussed in Chapter 6, its growth was in large part due to changes in the social security system), the private sector also makes a significant contribution to the provision of facilities for acute care and elective surgery.

The growth in the private health sector can be attributed to a number of factors. The growth of the private nursing home sector results mainly from demographic variables and from government policy, which has actively encouraged mixed health care (public finance, private supply) and private health care (private finance, private supply) to deliver nursing home services for the long-term care of the elderly, the mentally ill, and the mentally handicapped since 1984.

Table 4.5. NHS PRIVATE PATIENT REVENUE

	Real NHS income from private treatment[a] (£ million)
1973/4	84
1974/5	91
1975/6	94
1976/7	102
1977/8	100
1978/9	96
1979/80	95
1980/1	104
1981/2	111
1982/3	100
1983/4	106
1984/5	103
1985/6	107
1986/7	100
1987/8	107
1988/9	114
1989/90	127
1990/1	135
1991/2	166
1992/3	176
1993/4	184
1994/5	201
1995/6	210

[a] Deflated using adjusted GDP price deflator, 1995/6 = 100.

Sources: 1973/4 to 1992/3: Laing and Buisson Ltd. (1996a: table 2.7); 1993/4 to 1995/6: DoH (1995c, 1996g); GDP deflator: HM Treasury (1997: table 3.1).

The expansion of the private market for acute care and elective surgery has of course been heavily influenced by the growth of personal income and of PMI coverage during the 1980s. Laing and Buisson Ltd. (1996a: A69) estimated that in 1996 about 70 per cent of the private 'normally insurable' acute sector was funded by PMI (where normally insurable is defined to include acute medical/surgical and psychiatric treatment but to exclude fertility regulation, maternity, and screening, which are not usually covered by PMI policies). The remaining 30 per cent of revenue raised is from self-financing patients, about half of whom are British.

Demand for PMI has in turn been stimulated by government tax policy. Company purchases of PMI that meet certain conditions are not liable to tax. Various changes to personal tax law initiated by the Conservative Government during the 1980s also stimulated demand for PMI. The liability of people earning less than a certain threshold for tax on employer-paid PMI premiums was effectively eliminated. This threshold has been set at £8,500 per annum since 1979/80. In the late 1980s, demand for PMI was again boosted by a change in government tax policy. From 1989, relief has been available for individuals paying PMI premiums on contracts meeting specified conditions for people over the age of 60. Since 1989, the costs of this policy, in terms of revenue lost to the Exchequer, have escalated rapidly. The Exchequer cost of over-60 tax relief is estimated at £100 million in 1995/6, rising to £120 million in 1996/7 (HM Treasury 1996b: table 10). The new Labour Government elected in May 1997 has committed itself to abolishing this relief.

Partly in response to tax relief, demand for PMI boomed in the 1980s. There were 930,000 policy holders in the UK in 1970, corresponding to 2 million persons, or 3.6 per cent of the population, covered by PMI. Demand remained relatively low in the 1970s under Labour, and the number of policy holders grew relatively slowly, to 1.3 million in 1979. Under the Conservatives, however, the numbers of PMI policy holders grew rapidly, reaching 2.4 million in 1985 and 3.3 million in 1990, corresponding to 5.1 million and 6.6 million people covered by PMI respectively. Since 1990, however, the annual growth in the number of policy holders has remained flat, and in 1995 the number of PMI policy holders was 3.3 million, corresponding to 6.2 million persons, or 10.6 per cent of the population (Laing and Buisson Ltd. 1996a: table 3.1).

As would be expected, take-up of PMI varies significantly by socio-economic group. The only comprehensive data comes from the General Household Survey of 1987 and hence is now quite old. However, it showed that around a quarter of professionals, employers, and managers had private medical insurance compared with under 2 per cent of semi- and unskilled manual workers (OPCS 1989: table 4.11). A recent attempt to update these estimates concluded that this pattern had not changed much in the last ten years (Laing and Buisson Ltd. 1996a: P.A126).

It is easy to overestimate the importance of private medical care. Insurance schemes provide a service mainly in the area of elective surgery rather than emergency care or treatment for long-term chronic illnesses. So while, in 1987, 9 per cent of the population had private health insurance, benefits paid were less than 3 per cent of NHS expenditures (OHE 1987; CSO 1989). Despite increases in private expenditure on privately supplied medicine, the bulk of health care—care for the poor, the aged, and the chronically ill—is publicly financed, and is likely to remain so for the foreseeable future.

Private costs of using the NHS Even services provided free at the point of use impose costs on individuals who use them. These private costs of using the NHS include *monetary costs*, such as the cost of travelling to the GP or to a hospital, or the loss of wages due to time taken off work, and *time costs* of travelling or of waiting in the GP's surgery or for an operation. Both kinds of costs may be lower for certain groups of people—for example, people with cars or workers on a monthly salary; this could lead to social inequality in access to the NHS, discussed later in this chapter. In addition, the private costs of waiting may include welfare losses resulting from suffering and incapacity experienced while waiting, and a decline in the value of treatment as it is delayed.

Some of these costs are manifest most obviously in the phenomenon of waiting lists. The length of NHS waiting lists is thought to have an important impact on the demand for PMI. For instance, Besley *et al.* (1996: 14) estimated the demand for individually purchased PMI, and found that increases in long-term NHS waiting lists are positively and significantly associated with increases in PMI purchases. The authors predicted that if long-term waiting lists were to rise by one person per thousand, there would be a 1.9 per cent increase in the probability that an individual with average characteristics would buy private insurance, and a corresponding rise in the size of the proportion of insured individuals purchasing individual contracts from 7 per cent to 8.6 per cent. These results suggest that if long-term NHS waiting lists were to be eliminated, then this could put a significant brake on the demand for PMI, other things remaining constant. The fact that, as we shall see, there has actually been a significant drop in the size of long-term waiting lists since 1990 might therefore have contributed to the failure of PMI to grow since that time.

The observation that a person has an alternative to waiting for NHS treatment—that is, of jumping the queue by going private—provides a starting point for estimating the costs of waiting for NHS treatment. On the assumption that a person will only join the waiting list if the cost of waiting is less than the cost of going private, the cost of going private can be used as an upper limit on the cost to each person of waiting. Using this methodology, Cullis and Jones (1986) estimated aggregate NHS waiting costs at between 7 and 13 per cent of NHS expenditures. An alternative approach, used in Propper (1990), is the 'stated preference' methodology. Propper surveyed 1,360 people, chosen at random from the population. She presented each with a hypothetical choice between immediate treatment at a specified cost, or free treatment after a certain length of time. By presenting people with several such choices, she was able to estimate the cost of waiting. Using the same waiting list data as Cullis and Jones, she estimated the cost of waiting at around 2 per cent of total NHS expenditures.

Hospital waiting lists and the Patient's Charter Given costs of this magnitude, it is not surprising that hospital waiting lists have become an important political issue. The total number of people waiting to be admitted for in-patient treatment in NHS hospitals has been increasing steadily. In March 1981, a total of 628,333 people were waiting for ordinary admission for in-patient treatment in NHS hospitals. A decade later, in March 1991, this figure had increased to 729,100 (DoH, personal communication). Waiting lists have continued to grow in the 1990s. The number of people waiting for ordinary (in-patient) and day treatment combined rose from 948,200 in March 1991 to 1,071,100 in September 1994, falling back slightly to 1,061,600 in September 1996, and increasing to 1,164,400 in March 1997 (Table 4.6).

However, while waiting lists have been growing in length, *mean waiting times* have been falling in the 1990s. The Conservative Government was successful in eliminating the small

Table 4.6. PATIENTS WAITING FOR ADMISSION, BIANNUAL DATA FROM MARCH 1991 (ORDINARY ADMISSION AND DAY CASES COMBINED)

		Total number waiting (000s)	Months waiting (% of total)				No. of breaches of the 18-month Patients' Charter Standard	Patients treated from the waiting list per month[a] (000s)
			0–11	12–23	24+			
1988	September	900.1	75.6	14.2	10.2		—	212.6
1989	March	922.7	75.8	14.2	10.0		—	227.6
	September	929.1	76.5	14.0	9.5		—	224.0
1990	March	959.0	78.3	13.2	8.4		—	245.7
	September	957.5	78.8	13.8	7.4		—	228.3
1991	March	948.2	82.1	12.5	5.4		—	232.2
	September	947.8	83.6	11.8	4.6		—	243.7
1992	March	917.7	91.2	8.6	0.2		—	269.1
	September	939.7	91.4	8.5	0.1		—	258.3
1993	March	995.0	94.3	5.7	0.0		—	264.2
	September	1032.0	93.1	6.9	0.0		—	260.7
1994	March	1065.4	94.0	6.0	0.0		—	273.2
	September	1071.1	94.2	5.8	0.0		—	277.4
1995	March	1044.1	96.9	3.1	0.0		—	298.7
	September	1040.2	97.3	2.7	0.0		43	290.0
1996	March	1048.0	99.6	0.4	0.0		—	308.0
	September	1061.6	98.7	1.4	0.0		25	305.7
1997	March[b]	1164.4	97.3	2.7[c]	—		155	—

[a] Three-month average.
[b] Provisional figures.
[c] 12–17 months.

Source: DoH (1994b, 1996h, 1997a, c).

group of people waiting for very long periods of time for treatment, and people waiting for NHS treatment have, on average, been waiting for shorter periods of time. In September 1991, of the total number of people waiting for in-patient and day treatment, 11.8 per cent, corresponding to 111,840 people, had been waiting for between one year and two years, and 4.6 per cent, corresponding to 43,598 people, had been waiting for more than two years. The proportion of people waiting for between one and two years steadily declined to 5.8 per cent, corresponding to 62,124 people, in September 1994, and to 1.4 per cent, corresponding to 14,862 people, in September 1996. However, provisional figures point to a reversal of this trend in late 1996 and early 1997. The proportion of people waiting for between 12 and 17 months increased sharply to 2.7 per cent, corresponding to 31,160 people, in March 1997. Waiting times of more than two years were totally eliminated in March 1993, and had not reappeared by September 1996 (Table 4.6).

These shorter waiting times reflected a series of policy initiatives. A waiting list initiative introduced in 1986 was intended to reduce the time people wait for treatment. It was backed by a Waiting List Fund of £25 million for 1987/8 (£30 million for 1988/9), which was used by health authorities to provide, for example, extra operating sessions and beds, to bring forward medical appointments, to buy or make use of spare capacity in other NHS or non-NHS facilities (HM Treasury 1989). With the introduction of the Patient's Charter in 1991, national waiting list standards were introduced for certain specialities, and these were extended in April 1995, when a national maximum waiting time guarantee of 18 months to cover all admissions into hospitals was introduced. National waiting time standards for outpatients were also introduced in April 1995. According to these standards, nine out of ten people can expect to be seen within 13 weeks, and everyone should be seen within 26 weeks, of a written referral by a GP or dentist for outpatient treatment at an NHS hospital (DoH 1995a).

Judged by the Patient's Charter standards, the NHS performed quite well in 1995 and 1996. According to statistics provided by the Department of Health, of the total number of people waiting for ordinary (in-patient) and day treatment, only 43 people had been waiting for a period of more than 18 months in England at the end of September 1995 (DoH 1996h). One year later, in September 1996, this figure had fallen even further, to 25 (DoH 1997a). However, provisional figures suggest that the number of breaches of the 18-month standard jumped up to 123 in December 1996 (DoH 1997b) and to 155 in March 1997 (DoH 1997c).

Statistics on the number of people waiting for outpatient appointments became available in 1996, allowing outpatient performance to be monitored. In September 1996, 264,000 people waiting for outpatient treatment in England had not been seen within 13 weeks of referral, of whom 62,000 people had been waiting for 26 weeks or more (DoH 1996c). Given the existing Patient's Charter standards for outpatients, together with a promise of a tightening of these standards over time, significant improvements in these figures should be expected in the near future.

III. Outputs

The 'outputs' of the NHS are notoriously difficult to define. Here we do not intend to enter this debate, but instead confine ourselves to an assessment of the success of the NHS in terms of its ability to achieve the policy goals discussed earlier relating to efficiency, equity, and responsiveness.

Efficiency

A major priority of both the Labour and Conservative Governments has been the efficient use of resources within the NHS. One interpretation of efficiency concerns the relationship between activity and resources. If an increase in resources is accompanied by a more than proportionate increase in activity then a prima facie case could be made that there has been an increase in the efficiency with which resources are used, while if the increase in activity is less than proportionate, there has been a decrease.

Unfortunately the data are not available to enable us comprehensively to examine the relationship between all forms of health activity and expenditure over the whole of our period. However, Table 4.7 uses data supplied by the Department of Health to give a cost-weighted activity index for hospital and community health services from 1974/5 to 1995/6 and an index of expenditure on these services over the same period, deflated by a pay-and-prices index.

Two things are immediately apparent from the activity index series: that the index has increased every year and that the rate of increase rose sharply from 1991/2 onwards (after the internal market was introduced). The average annual rate of increase from 1974/5 to 1978/9 was 1.7 per cent; from 1979/80 to 1990/1, 2.2 per cent; and from 1991/2 to 1995/6, 4.1 per cent.

However, it is also apparent from the resources index series that this also rose every year and, again, more sharply after 1991/2. The average annual rate of increase for 1974/5 to 1978/9 was 1.9 per cent—faster than the rate in increase of activity and suggesting a *fall* in efficiency over that period. From 1979/80 to 1990/1, the annual rate of growth was 0.7 per cent, 1.4 percentage points less than the rate of growth of activity; and from 1991/2 to 1995/6 it was 2.1 per cent, 2 percentage points less than that for activity. So there was an increase in efficiency during both these periods, with that for the period after the introduction of the reforms being somewhat greater than that for the period before.

Thus, despite the increase in administrative costs mentioned above that followed the introduction of general management and the internal market, the overall effect does seem to have raised hospital and community services' activities by more than the additional spending. These changes, therefore, do appear to have contributed to an increase in overall efficiency.

Table 4.7. NHS EFFICIENCY HISTORY

	HCHS cost-weighted activity index	% increase over previous year	Expenditure adjusted for changes in input unit costs	% increase over previous year	Efficiency
1974/5	100.00		100.00		
1975/6	97.14	−2.86	100.80	0.80	−3.6
1976/7	103.10	6.14	101.88	1.07	5.0
1977/8	105.66	2.48	104.81	2.87	−0.4
1978/9	106.89	1.16	107.41	2.48	−1.3
1979/80	107.07	0.18	107.43	0.01	0.2
1980/1	113.23	5.75	108.25	0.76	4.9
1981/2	115.22	1.76	110.74	2.31	−0.5
1982/3	114.63	−0.52	110.89	0.13	−0.7
1983/4	120.96	5.53	111.73	0.75	4.7
1984/5	124.57	2.98	111.79	0.05	2.9
1985/6	127.90	2.67	112.00	0.19	2.5
1986/7	129.28	1.49	112.36	0.32	1.2
1987/8	131.92	1.63	113.22	0.76	0.9
1988/9	133.05	0.86	114.03	0.72	0.1
1989/90	135.98	2.20	116.02	1.74	0.5
1990/1	137.75	1.30	117.11	0.94	0.4
1991/2	144.95	5.23	120.16	2.60	2.6
1992/3	149.45	3.10	123.89	3.10	0.0
1993/4	155.41	3.99	125.86	1.59	2.4
1994/5	161.91	4.18	127.61	1.39	2.8
1995/6	168.19	3.88	129.85	1.76	2.1[a]
Average pre-reforms 1980/1 to 1989/90		2.4%		0.8%	1.6%
Average post-reforms (1991/2 to 1995/6)		4.1%		2.1%	1.95%

[a] Provisional figure.

Source: DoH, personal communication.

However, it should be remembered that activity is not health outcome. Arguably it is changes in health outcome attributable to changes in the NHS that should be measured if the efficiency consequences of these changes are to be properly assessed. Further, if activity estimates are being used as performance indicators (as they were during some of the period under review) then they encourage the units whose performance is being assessed to behave in ways that maximize activity as measured regardless of the impact on outcome. Hence all estimates that assess efficiency by relating activity to resources should be treated with a great deal of caution.

Equity by region

'Equity' is a heavily contested term (Le Grand 1991a). However, in the context of health care it is usually interpreted in two ways: as requiring equality of access and/or equality of treatment for equal need. In this subsection we consider equality of access by region, as indicated by the level of NHS resources in each region. In the next subsection, we consider the relationship between treatment and need for different social groups; and in the subsequent subsection we look briefly at a recent issue arising from the operation of the reforms: equity by purchaser.

In the previous version of this chapter, changes in the levels of NHS expenditure per head by region for the United Kingdom from 1974/5 to 1985/6 were examined, and it was concluded that there had been a fall in needs-adjusted inequality between regions (Le Grand *et al.* 1990: 116–20). Changes in expenditure definitions and in the regions themselves mean that it has not been possible to find directly comparable figures for the subsequent period. However, estimates of health expenditure in volume terms for the English regions alone from 1985/6 to 1994/5 have been constructed, and these are given in Table 4.8, together with the variance and coefficient of variation for each year to indicate the extent of inequality. Unfortunately the estimates are not adjusted for differences in 'needs' across the regions, and therefore the mere existence of inequality in spending between them does not necessarily indicate unequal access for equal need. However, the trends over time show a less reassuring picture than the earlier period, with inequality in spending apparently rising. Unless there was also a growing (and matching) inequality in need, this suggests that regional inequities may be increasing.

Health expenditures are dominated by hospital and community services and give relatively little weight to primary care. To rectify this, Table 4.9 shows the number of GPs per head for the same period; again they show a rise in inequality, as compared with a slight fall in the previous period (Le Grand *et al.* 1990: 119, table 4.10). Unless these changes were matched by corresponding changes in need, this again suggests that inequity is on the increase. In this context, it is worth noting that a recent study by Benzeval and Judge (1996) using some relatively sophisticated measures of need found continued inequalities in the distribution of GPs in relation to need.

Table 4.8. REAL CURRENT EXPENDITURE PER CAPITA, BY REGIONAL HEALTH AUTHORITY[a] £s

	1985/6	1986/7	1987/8	1988/9	1989/90	1990/1	1991/2	1992/3[b]	1993/4	1994/5[c]
England[d]	377.637	381.812	382.516	388.562	392.261	386.157	418.327	449.168	427.370	428.607
Northern	373.867	378.973	381.417	385.466	387.719	381.220	427.604	449.781	457.301	392.579
Yorkshire	360.743	364.076	364.107	364.904	367.412	363.746	372.269	426.580	398.529	438.683
Trent	337.885	345.327	349.123	352.994	356.090	349.393	407.218	418.377	402.622	401.395
East Anglia	333.971	339.231	341.897	351.509	354.641	352.420	431.275	398.571	295.159	376.700
North West Thames	388.041	391.212	386.868	400.242	404.864	389.824	443.216	490.828	540.529	386.823
North East Thames	451.387	454.119	447.931	459.841	464.146	459.032	455.921	512.290	494.854	583.551
South East Thames	414.367	413.669	410.123	419.850	421.612	415.636	445.485	480.742	453.060	395.951
South West Thames	380.973	385.302	405.395	412.299	419.157	400.626	411.857	481.096	442.250	510.263
Wessex	327.330	331.535	330.322	337.512	340.807	338.189	399.538	390.188	383.298	359.852
Oxford	301.784	304.189	305.939	312.532	316.703	314.251	395.750	368.893	341.234	371.519
South Western	352.511	355.712	353.804	357.891	361.124	358.420	290.189	422.183	408.183	453.216
West Midlands	349.080	354.303	355.915	358.309	365.857	362.916	436.274	416.486	389.599	399.531
Mersey	390.732	395.322	395.178	396.781	402.416	394.769	298.817	459.086	429.091	394.296
North Western	400.417	405.459	405.193	407.298	404.333	399.817	452.861	458.799	423.864	480.888
Coefficient of variation	0.103	0.100	0.097	0.098	0.097	0.093	0.125	0.091	0.140	0.143

[a] Deflated using NHS specific volume deflator.

[b] Prior to 1992/3, 'Diagnosis and Treatment' and 'Support Services' were included as categories of regional health authority expenditure. However, with the inception of NHS trusts and the corresponding decrease in the number of units directly managed by health authorities, the changed functions of health authorities to purchasers meant that these categories were no longer included in the 'current expenditure' total. The figures prior to 1992/3 are therefore not directly comparable with subsequent years.

[c] Based on estimated population figures.

[d] England total includes Special Health Authority expenditure.

Sources: Expenditure figures 1985/6 to 1993/4: DoH (1996b: table 7.5) for 1993/4 and equivalent tables for earlier years ('total revenue expenditure' category for the years 1985/6 to 1990/1: 'total expenditure' category for the years 1991/2 to 1994/5); expenditure figures 1994/5: DoH, personal communication; population figures: DoH (1996b: table 1.2) for 1994/5 and equivalent tables for earlier years; volume deflator: Table 4A.2.

Julian Le Grand and Polly Vizard

Table 4.9. NUMBER OF GENERAL MEDICAL PRACTITIONERS (GPs) PER 100,000 POPULATION[a]

	1975	1979	1984	1985	1986	1987	1988	1989	1990	1991	1992	1993	1994	1995
United Kingdom	48	51	54	55	56	56	57	58	59	59	60	59	61	61
England	47	50	52	53	55	55	56	56	57	58	58	57	59	59
Northern	45	48	49	50	52	53	54	55	55	56	57	56	61	62
Yorkshire	45	48	51	52	54	54	55	55	56	57	58	57	59	59
Trent	43	47	48	50	51	51	52	53	54	54	55	54	56	57
East Anglia	46	50	53	52	56	55	55	55	57	57	59	60	48	54
North West Thames	53	55	58	59	61	61	61	60	61	62	62	61	74	68
North East Thames	50	51	53	54	55	55	55	57	58	59	58	58	58	58
South East Thames	49	52	53	54	56	55	56	56	57	58	58	58	59	58
South West Thames	50	50	53	54	55	55	56	57	57	57	58	57	60	59
Wessex	47	50	53	54	56	56	57	57	57	58	58	57	57	58
Oxford	46	48	51	51	55	54	54	55	56	57	57	57	59	59
South Western	50	56	58	60	62	62	63	63	65	65	66	66	69	69
West Midlands	45	48	50	51	53	53	54	55	55	56	56	56	57	57
Mersey	44	49	52	52	54	55	55	56	56	57	57	56	58	58
North Western	44	47	51	51	53	53	54	54	55	55	55	55	53	53
Wales	49	52	55	56	59	59	60	61	62	62	63	63	64	63
Scotland	58	62	65	70	68	69	70	71	74	74	75	75	75	76
Northern Ireland[b]	49	49	60	60	59	59	61	62	62	63	64	63	60	61
Coefficient of variation	0.077	0.074	0.078	0.091	0.073	0.076	0.076	0.075	0.082	0.079	0.081	0.084	0.110	0.092

[a] Comprising restricted and unrestricted principals, assistants, and trainees.
[b] Comprising restricted and unrestricted principals and assistants.
Sources: OHE (1987); McGuigan (1997); coefficient of variation: authors' calculations.

Equity by social group

A major equity concern that received a good deal of attention over our period was the extent to which the NHS provided equal treatment for equal need between different social groups. A sizeable number of studies have explored this question, coming to mixed conclusions.

In one of the earliest, Le Grand (1978) used GHS data from the early 1970s on GP consultations, outpatient consultations, and in-patient days to construct estimates of total NHS expenditures per person reporting illness for different socio-economic groups. The results showed that the distribution favoured the better off, with, on an age-standardized basis, the families of professionals, employers, and managers receiving nearly 40 per cent more NHS expenditure per person ill than the families of semi- and unskilled manual workers. This reinforced earlier work by Forster (1976) and others who found a pro-rich gradient of use relative to need in the use of specific health sectors and services (see Le Grand 1982: 27–9).

However, similar analyses of the GHS data for later years by Collins and Klein (1980) and O'Donnell and Propper (1991a) came to rather different conclusions. (See Le Grand 1991b and O'Donnell and Propper 1991b for a detailed discussion of some of the differences between the studies.) O'Donnell and Propper found no evidence of a bias in favour of the better off, whether defined in terms of income or socio-economic group, indeed if anything rather the reverse. This finding was supported by a multivariant analysis of the determinants of GP consultations carried out by Evandrou *et al.* (1991) using GHS data from 1980. A further, more disaggregated analysis by Evandrou (1996a) found a pro-poor gradient for GP consultations in the surgery (which seems to have developed in the last few years: see Whitehead *et al.* 1997) and in in-patient use, but a pro-rich gradient for telephone GP consultations and outpatient use. In addition, many studies have found a pro-rich bias in the use of preventive and screening services (Benzeval *et al.* 1995: 102–4). In short, it appears that the question as to whether the NHS has achieved equity by special group depends to a large extent on which part of the service is the focus of interest.

There has also been some recent work on inequalities in the use of services relative to need by ethnic group (Smaje 1995; Smaje and Le Grand 1997). Here again the pattern is not straightforward. Overall, it appears that there is no gross inequity between ethnic groups in their use of health services relative to need, except for the Chinese population, who have strikingly low utilization patterns. However, certain other groups do make less use of certain services; for instance, South Asian and Caribbean groups make less use of in-patient and, particularly, outpatient services than their relative needs would indicate, even after controlling for possible confounding variables such as income. This suggests that, if there is inequity, it *may* appear at the referral stage; that is, people from minority ethnic groups may get referred on to secondary care less than their white counterparts with the same need. However, confirmation of this will have to await further research.

Equity by purchaser

A major equity issue that has arisen from the operation of the quasi-market reforms concerns the extent to which the treatment available to individuals differs between purchasers: health authorities or GP fundholders. In particular, there is undoubtedly some variation between health authorities concerning the treatments they will purchase (Klein *et al.* 1996). Such differences seem to be an inevitable consequence of the Conservative Government's policy of delegating such decisions to health authorities, although it is only fair to note that variations in the provision of different treatments almost certainly pre-date the purchaser/provider split.

An even more controversial issue concerns differences in waiting times between the patients of GP fundholders and those of health authorities. Rather surprisingly a report by the Audit Commission (1996b) found no indication of this. However, a more detailed investigation by Dowling (1977: 290–2) on waiting lists in West Sussex found strong evidence of differentials. If such differences do exist, then the crucial question is whether they arise because fundholders are better purchasers than health authorities, or because they are better funded; here the evidence is mixed with, for instance, Dixon *et al.* (1994) arguing that there was not fair funding between fundholders and health authorities, but Dowling finding no evidence of superior funding for fundholders in his study.

Finally, initial theoretical discussions of the quasi-market predicted that cream-skimming or adverse selection would become a major equity concern, especially for fundholders (Scheffler 1989; Le Grand and Bartlett 1993: chap. 2). That is, fundholders would have an incentive to turn away potentially expensive patients who applied to join their lists and get rid of the ones already on their list. However, little evidence of this has been found in practice (Glennerster *et al.* 1994). This was perhaps because the Government included as part of the scheme a provision that fundholders would not have to pay the costs of treatment over a certain limit per patient; this reduced the incentive for fundholders to cream-skim, but, of course, also reduced their incentive to economize on treatment for such patients.

Responsiveness

There are no readily available data on an aggregate level concerning the performance of the NHS with respect to the goal of enhancing its responsiveness to the needs and wants of its patients. However, it is possible to obtain some indication of its success in this respect from the annual survey of the public's attitudes to the NHS carried out by the British Social Attitudes Survey. Since 1983, this has asked questions relating to the level of general satisfaction with respect to the NHS, the level of satisfaction with respect to specific services, and attitudes towards increased public spending on the NHS.

A summary of the principal results of the Survey concerning attitudes to the NHS from 1983 to 1995 has been provided by Bryson (1995). This concluded that during the 1980s there

was a rise in general dissatisfaction with the NHS, with 46 per cent of the public expressing
dissatisfaction in 1989 compared with 26 per cent in 1983. In the early 1990s, there was a drop
in the proportion of dissatisfied to 38 per cent; however, this rose again in the next two years,
reaching 45 per cent in 1995. With respect to specific services, there was a high and fairly constant level of satisfaction with GPs (80 per cent in 1983, 79 per cent in 1995), but increasing
dissatisfaction with NHS dentists. There was a sharp rise in dissatisfaction with both in-
patient and outpatient care between 1983 and 1986, stability between 1986 and 1991, and
then a slight rise in the proportion expressing satisfaction with outpatient services and a significant fall in the proportion expressing satisfaction with in-patient services.

So far as attitudes towards public spending on the NHS are concerned, a large majority of
respondents have always named health as their top priority. However, the proportion
increased over the 1980s and fell during the early 1990s, but has now begun to rise again: the
same pattern as for the proportion expressing dissatisfaction with the NHS. There has also
been a significant increase in enthusiasm for raising taxation to pay for core welfare services
(including health), with 61 per cent saying that taxes should be increased and more should be
spent on welfare in 1995 compared with 32 per cent in 1983. However, as Bryson points out,
people were not asked in the surveys concerned if they themselves were prepared to pay the
extra taxes; and the fact that the parties proposing tax increases did not fare well in the general elections in our period does not inspire confidence that these results really reflect a will-
ingness personally to pay more. Mossialos (1997) in an analysis of citizens' views on health
care systems across Europe (where the UK's proportion of satisfied and very satisfied was
slightly under the average for the EU as a whole) found that the majority of those favouring
more spending on health care were opposed to raising taxes, preferring the Government
instead to spend less on other things.

There are obvious difficulties in interpreting the results with respect to the changes in the
levels of satisfaction and dissatisfaction with the NHS. Do they reflect changes in the NHS
itself, or in the consumerist culture outside the NHS? If the former, were the key factors the
NHS reforms, the Patient's Charter—or something more ephemeral such as a media-orches-
trated 'crisis in the NHS' scare? However, subject to these caveats, a possible interpretation
of the changes at least in the 1990s is that the reforms, the increase in resources associated
with them, and the waiting list initiatives did increase satisfaction at first; then a combination
of some of the deficiencies revealed by the operations of the Patient's Charter and hospital
league tables, coupled with a stricter control over resources, led to a rise in dissatisfaction in
the mid-1990s. But confirmation of this will have to wait until more data become available.

IV. Outcomes

As with outputs, the 'outcomes' of health policy are difficult to measure. Some relatively
sophisticated outcome measures are currently under development—notably the Quality-

Julian Le Grand and Polly Vizard

Adjusted Life-Year (QALY). However, these are not available on the kind of aggregate basis used here. There are a number of simpler outcome measures including mortality levels or rates, days off work and National Insurance incapacity certificates, and self-reported morbidity based on household interviews. The ones with data most readily available at an aggregate level are mortality (or life expectancy) and self-reported morbidity, and it is on these that we concentrate.

Mortality

Life expectancy rose significantly over the period. In 1970–2, it was 69 for males and 75.2 for females; by 1994, it was 74.5 for males and 79.7 for females. Interestingly, it *fell* in 1995 to 74.3 for males and 79.6 for females; however, similar small falls occurred in earlier years and did not significantly affect the general trend.

Although mortality rates fell overall, some forms of inequality continued to widen. This is illustrated by Table 4.10, which gives standardized mortality ratios (SMRs) by social class for men aged 15 to 64 for 1970–2, and for men aged 20 to 64 for 1979–80/1982–3 and 1991–3. (The SMR is a statistic designed to standardize for differences in the age structure of the social classes. It is the ratio of the observed number of deaths for men in the relevant age range and in a particular social class to the number that would have been expected if the age-specific death rates for England and Wales as a whole had applied to that group.) It is apparent that the gap between the social classes has widened, with the SMR for Social Class I increasing from nearly twice as much as that of Social Class V in 1970–2 to nearly three times as much in 1991–3.

Table 4.10. STANDARDIZED MORTALITY RATIOS, MALES 20–64 (ENGLAND AND WALES = 100)

Social class		1970–2[a]	1979–80 1982–3	1991–3
I	Professional	77	66	66
II	Managerial	81	74	72
IIIN	Non-manual skilled	99	93	100
IIIM	Manual skilled	106	103	117
IV	Partly skilled	114	114	116
V	Unskilled	137	159	189

[a] Age group is 15–64.

Source: Drever *et al.* (1996).

This kind of social class analysis has a number of difficulties associated with it (detailed in Illsley and Le Grand 1987), particularly when comparisons over time are concerned. In particular, the fact that the size of the classes (and sometimes the classification scheme itself) can change significantly over time implies that like is not always being compared with like. Also, social class can only be confidently ascribed to males aged between 15 to 64; hence class analyses are mostly confined to deaths for that group, which is now a very small proportion of all deaths.

An approach that does not suffer from these problems, but which addresses a rather different question, is to examine population inequality (inequality between individuals) rather than social inequality (inequality between social groups). This involves choosing an indicator that can be attached to individuals rather than to groups, such as individuals' ages at death, and then examining trends in that indicator's mean and dispersion. Results employing this approach are provided in Table 4.11. Estimates are provided for males, females, and the total of males and females from 1974 to 1994. The data in Table 4.11 are calculated from standardized deaths, i.e. those that would have occurred at each age if the age distribution for each year had been the same; the procedure is designed to overcome the difficulty that observed changes in the distribution of age at death can be the product of changes in the age distribution itself.

Table 4.11 provides the mean and two measures of dispersion: the variance and the Gini coefficient. Each of these has different properties. Of particular importance, given the change in the mean over the period, one (the variance) is translation-independent (that is, independent of translation by a constant) and the other is scale-independent (independent of multiplication by a constant). Further discussion of the methodology involved can be found in Illsley and Le Grand (1987).

It is apparent from the table that two things have happened over the period: there has been a small rise in the mean age at death, and there has been a fall in the dispersion of age at death, as measured by either summary statistic. The latter is of particular interest since, as we have seen, it is one of the main contentions of the social class analysis that social inequalities in health as measured by differences in the mortality experiences of the social classes are getting wider rather than narrower. But it is important to note that it is quite possible for there to have been a fall in measures of inequality between individuals while there was an increase in the gaps between the social classes, if there has been a fall in inequality between individuals within each social class whose aggregate effect outweighs the widening between the classes. Also, as noted above, the social inequality measures only refer to a minority of deaths, whereas the population measures take account of all mortality.

Finally, it should be noted that there have been many analyses of differences in mortality by region (for instance, Britton 1990; Whitehead 1992). One of the most recent of these (Illsley and Le Grand 1993) found that there had been a substantial convergence in death rates for younger age groups from 1931 to 1987–9, but not for older ones. In particular, in younger

Julian Le Grand and Polly Vizard

Table 4.11. INEQUALITIES IN STANDARDIZED LIFE EXPECTANCY, ENGLAND AND WALES, 1974–95[a]

Year	Men and women			Men			Women		
	Mean	Var[b]	GINI	Mean	Var[b]	GINI	Mean	Var[b]	GINI
1974	70.41	301.3	0.125	67.24	300.8	0.130	73.63	281.1	0.114
1975	70.54	297.1	0.124	67.45	294.9	0.128	73.71	279.8	0.114
1976	70.84	288.3	0.122	67.69	288.5	0.127	74.05	268.3	0.111
1977	70.61	291.3	0.123	67.50	289.6	0.127	73.79	274.1	0.113
1978	70.48	296.3	0.124	67.42	293.3	0.128	73.63	281.1	0.114
1979	70.59	295.6	0.123	67.48	295.6	0.128	73.75	277.2	0.113
1980	70.60	295.3	0.123	67.55	293.0	0.128	73.72	280.4	0.114
1981	70.75	288.1	0.122	67.67	290.4	0.127	73.88	269.0	0.112
1982	70.84	280.5	0.120	67.82	282.9	0.125	73.88	262.4	0.110
1983	70.91	275.4	0.119	67.92	275.7	0.124	73.94	260.1	0.110
1984	70.86	274.0	0.119	67.87	275.4	0.124	71.77	235.2	0.109
1985	71.16	272.2	0.118	68.16	274.4	0.123	74.12	256.0	0.109
1986	71.06	275.0	0.119	68.03	278.9	0.124	74.08	257.0	0.109
1987	70.79	276.5	0.119	67.75	280.3	0.125	73.75	259.1	0.110
1988	70.90	276.6	0.119	67.79	281.9	0.125	73.91	257.4	0.110
1989	71.14	271.4	0.118	68.02	279.0	0.124	74.09	250.6	0.108
1990	70.99	272.1	0.118	67.85	280.4	0.125	74.00	250.3	0.108
1991	71.31	269.6	0.117	68.10	278.4	0.124	74.33	247.4	0.107
1992	71.35	259.8	0.115	68.41	268.5	0.122	74.18	239.6	0.106
1993	71.64	254.7	0.114	68.67	264.2	0.121	74.45	234.5	0.105
1994	71.53	256.7	0.114	68.55	268.3	0.122	74.33	234.7	0.105

[a] Calculated from standardized mortality data 1974–94, base year 1974.
[b] Variance calculated as the product of the square of the mean and the square of the coefficient of variation.

Source: Authors' calculations. Population data and mortality data for 1992 : OPCS (1994b: tables 1 and 3) and equivalent tables for previous years; population and mortality data for 1993 and 1994: ONS, personal communication.

age groups the historic North/South divide seemed to have disappeared; but it persists in older age groups.

Since mortality is heavily affected by factors other than curative health policy, it is difficult directly to link any changes we may observe with changes in policy. Because of the absence of a proper counterfactual hypothesis as to what would have happened to mortality in the absence of the relevant policy (or under different policies) we cannot draw any unequivocal conclusions from this concerning the effectiveness or otherwise of health policy over the period. However, trends in mortality inequalities have been used to criticize the performance of the National Health Service. Hence it is worth noting that the population inequality analyses suggest that there have been improvements in some key aspects of mortality outcomes, and therefore that criticism of the effectiveness of the welfare state based on the proposition that there has been a widespread deterioration in these respects has to be treated with some care.

Morbidity

The morbidity picture is rather different from that of mortality. Data from the General Household Survey on self-reported morbidity is summarized in Fig. 4.2. In the GHS, individuals are asked whether they suffer from any long-standing illness, whether that illness limits their activities in any way (chronic illness), and whether in the last two weeks they have had to cut down any of the things they usually do because of illness or injury (acute illness).

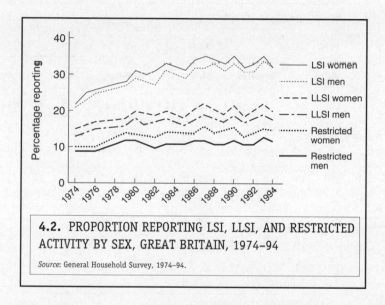

4.2. PROPORTION REPORTING LSI, LLSI, AND RESTRICTED ACTIVITY BY SEX, GREAT BRITAIN, 1974–94

Source: General Household Survey, 1974–94.

Fig. 4.2 shows trends in the percentage of people reporting chronic and acute illness over the period with which we are concerned. It is apparent that there is no fall in these kinds of morbidity paralleling the fall in mortality that we have observed. Indeed, if anything there was a rise in most forms of morbidity, although that is mostly confined to the period before 1984; since then they seem to have been relatively constant.

There are two possible explanations for the disparity. First, the population as a whole is ageing, which in so far as increasing age is correlated with increasing ill-health should lead to a rise in the latter (the mortality data were age-standardized, so this effect should not appear there). However, age-standardized rates of self-reported morbidity show the same pattern as the non-standardized rates (Dunnell 1997: 176, fig. 25.3). Second, people may be more willing to report illness today than in 1974, but the illness may be of a less significant kind (and in particular may have a lower impact on mortality).

Table 4.12 gives inequalities in morbidity by socio-economic group, again based on GHS data on self-reported chronic and acute sickness. As with the mortality data by social class, they show that people in the professional and managerial social classes are less likely to report long-standing or limiting long-standing illnesses, while manual workers and workers in the social services are more likely to report illnesses, as compared to the population as a whole. There are also differences between the top and the bottom groups in acute sickness, although these are much smaller.

Table 4.12. PREVALENCE OF LIMITED LONG-STANDING ILLNESS (LLI) AND ACUTE SICKNESS (AC) BY SOCIO-ECONOMIC GROUP

Socio-economic group	Percentage of group reporting											
	1974				1985				1994			
	Males		Females		Males		Females		Males		Females	
	LLI	AC	LLI	AC	LLI	AC	LLI	AC	LLI	AC	LLI	AC
Professionals	8	7	9	9	9	9	10	14	11	9	15	14
Employers and managers	11	8	12	9	13	9	15	11	15	12	14	14
Intermediate and junior non-manual	15	10	14	10	14	11	16	14	15	14	21	16
Skilled manual	13	10	12	10	18	11	17	15	22	13	20	15
Semi-skilled manual	15	10	20	11	21	11	24	16	24	13	25	17
Unskilled manual	23	11	23	12	23	12	30	18	23	14	31	17

Source: GHS, relevant years.

However, unlike for the social class mortality data, there is no obvious trend towards greater inequality over time. For instance, the absolute value of the gap between the professional and unskilled manual group for chronic illness has narrowed a little between 1974 and 1995 for males and widened very slightly for females, while for acute sickness it has remained virtually unchanged.

Finally, what of specific diseases and risk factors? As noted above, a major policy development during the period under review relating to health outcomes was *The Health of the Nation*. This focused on five areas—cancer, heart disease and stroke, mental illness, HIV/AIDS and sexual health, and accidents—identifying two kinds of target in each case. First, there were morbidity and mortality targets, setting out reductions in illness and death rates that were to be achieved in the key areas within a specific time-frame, starting from a 1990 baseline. So, for example, death rates in the under-65 age group for both coronary heart disease and stroke were to be reduced by 40 per cent by the year 2000; death rates from lung cancer in people under the age of 75 were to be reduced by at least 30 per cent in men and by at least 15 per cent in women by 2010; the death rates for accidents among children aged under 15 by at least 33 per cent by 2005.

The second set of targets were for risk factors aimed at tackling the cause of some of these illnesses. For instance, the consumption of cigarettes was to be reduced by 40 per cent by the year 2000; mean systolic blood pressure in the adult population to be reduced by at least 5mm Hg by 2005; the percentage of injecting drug-misusers who shared equipment to be reduced by three-quarters by 2000.

How has the strategy worked in practice? A report by the National Audit Office (1995) concluded that its achievements were patchy. As we have seen, good progress has been made on mortality itself, with falls in the numbers of deaths due to heart disease, strokes, and certain cancers; but there are rising levels of risk factors, notably obesity, alcohol drinking by women, and teenage smoking. In an analysis over a longer period, Dunnell (1997) found that, while overall cigarette smoking had reduced considerably since the 1970s, there has been little change among young men and women (16–24) during the last ten years; that alcohol consumption has been stable among men over the last decade, but has increased among women; and that there is no indication of any increase in rates of physical activity.

Overall, has there been an improvement in health outcomes over the period with which we are concerned? The picture is unclear. In terms of population mortality and life expectancy, the answer is unambiguously yes, both when the population mean and population inequalities are considered. However, social inequalities in mortality do seem to have widened, at least for men aged between 20 and 64. Also, average morbidity levels show no sign of falling; and there appears to be no significant change (in either direction) of social inequality in morbidity.

V. In brief

So, as the question in the title of this chapter asks, has the NHS over this period been subject to crisis, change, or continuity? The answer has to be no to crisis, but, paradoxically, yes to both change and continuity.

Despite the rhetoric of crisis and an apparently never-ending litany of doom-laden warnings, there have been no sharp turning points, and the NHS has shown a fairly continuous improvement over the period. There have been enormous changes in organizational structures, including the introduction of a highly controversial internal market. But, despite many predictions to the contrary, the NHS has not collapsed; its rate of activity has increased and, according to at least one indicator, its efficiency at producing those activities has increased. There is not significantly greater inequity in its delivery of services to social groups; indeed, if anything, such inequity that there was has diminished. Nor is there much sign yet of the private sector displacing the NHS as the principal provider of health care to the nation, or even to the wealthier parts of the nation. And, with respect to the wider issue of the health of the nation, most population mortality indicators have improved, both in terms of the average and in terms of inequality.

Of course the picture is not all so rosy. Morbidity figures have not shown the improvement that the mortality ones have. Social class inequalities in mortality for men aged 20–64 appear to have widened. Regional inequalities in NHS provision seem not to have diminished, at least in the last decade. Although spending on the NHS has risen more than demographic need factors alone would warrant, spending on the NHS (at least in volume terms) has risen significantly less than personal income, and public expectations, buoyed by technological advance, have not been fulfilled. Also, spending on the NHS is clearly characterized by an electoral cycle; this is probably unavoidable, but is nonetheless deplorable, being unrelated to any underlying changes in need or demand for health care and being quite destabilizing. The numbers of people on waiting lists have grown, and public dissatisfaction with the NHS, especially with in-patient services, has increased.

In the future, as incomes continue to grow, as the population ages and medical technology advances, there will be continued pressure on the NHS to do even more. The question for public policy is therefore whether increasing demand for health services is to be financed by taxation, or through a resumption in the growth of the private sector.

Despite all this, it is important to note that the NHS has coped with these kinds of pressures before; and—no doubt with a lot of noise—it will probably continue to do so. The experience of the period covered by this book suggests that what is necessary for the NHS to survive is the political will to support it. Despite the 1976 fiscal crisis, the 1974 to 1979 Labour Government did provide a faster growth rate of resources overall than did the subsequent Conservative administrations—although, if the cost-weighted activity index is to be believed, it may have used them rather less efficiently. During the early period of the succeeding Conservative Government, the rate of growth of expenditure on the NHS was particularly low. Nonetheless, resources going into the NHS increased under that Government overall, both in absolute terms and as a percentage of the national income. Thus, despite their ideological and other differences, both Labour and Conservative Governments gave political and economic support to the NHS. Changes in the organizational structure of the NHS in the 1980s and 1990s do not belie this essential policy continuity.

Further Reading

For useful overviews of the structure and state of the NHS see Ham (1992) and Baggott (1994), although they are getting somewhat dated. Klein (1995) provides an excellent analysis of the history and politics of the NHS since its beginnings; see also the chapters relating to health in Lowe (1993), Glennerster (1995), and Timmins (1995). Powell (1997) is an ambitious book-length attempt to evaluate the NHS, both in its own terms and with respect to outside criteria; it addresses many of the issues discussed here at much greater length. Glennerster *et al.* (1994) and Robinson and Le Grand (1994) provide some preliminary evidence on the success or otherwise of the NHS reforms.

Julian Le Grand and Polly Vizard

ANNEXE

Table 4A.1. NHS REAL EXPENDITURE, UNITED KINGDOM (£ MILLION AT 1995/6 PRICES,

	Fiscal years									
	1973/4[a]	1974/5	1975/6	1976/7	1977/8	1978/9	1979/80	1980/1	1981/2	1982/3
Current expenditure										
HCHS[b] and FHS	16110	19473	20721	20939	20553	20970	21105	23310	23721	24242
Administration[c]	555	844	906	928	887	889	936	976	937	900
Less payments										
Hospital services	−123	−108	−107	−121	−110	−102	−108	−124	−136	−133
Pharmaceutical	−187	−172	−116	−102	−90	−84	−126	−191	−211	−231
Dental	−219	−210	−159	−178	−203	−195	−200	−230	−261	−301
Ophthalmic	−116	−113	−90	−98	−90	−90	−85	−74	−75	−83
Total	−645	−602	−472	−500	−493	−470	−518	−618	−684	−747
Other (including departmental administration)	568	677	584	701	673	674	715	748	601	581
Total current expenditure	16587	20392	21738	22068	21620	22063	22238	24416	24575	24976
Capital expenditure	1748	1624	1738	1602	1367	1395	1338	1492	1644	1581
Total expenditure	18335	22016	23476	23670	22987	23458	23577	25909	26219	26557
GDP deflator	15.5	18.6	23.3	26.4	30	33.4	39	46.1	50.6	54.2

[a] Excluding £1,882.5 million of local authority health services expenditures at 1995/6 prices.
[b] Including the school meal service from April 1974, previously included in education.
[c] Administration costs are not separately identifiable from 1993/4.

Sources: Expenditure: ONS (1997a: table 3.3) for 1995/6, and equivalent tables for earlier years; GDP deflator: HM Treasury (1997: table 3.1).

ADJUSTED USING GDP DEFLATOR)

1983/4	1984/5	1985/6	1986/7	1987/8	1988/9	1989/90	1990/1	1991/2	1992/3	1993/4	1994/5	1995/6
24944	25170	25369	26408	27709	29037	28531	30090	32507	34581	37126	38665	38514
799	795	756	855	921	938	1099	1165	1252	1351	—	—	—
−136	−141	−146	−153	−156	−477	−523	−607	−604	−542	−384	−114	−42
−240	−250	−252	−315	−376	−278	−311	−294	−302	−319	−338	−351	−383
−339	−331	−358	−403	−426	−388	−437	−525	−534	−505	−459	−476	−494
−104	−87	−22	−2	−1	—	—	—	—	—	—	—	—
−818	−810	−779	−873	−959	−1143	−1271	−1426	−1440	−1366	−1182	−941	−919
624	597	677	1156	1211	1114	1150	1198	1295	1740	2005	2626	2780
25549	25751	26024	27546	28883	29946	29509	31027	33614	36306	37950	40350	40375
1563	1664	1737	1793	1780	1801	2662	2200	2003	1731	943	552	316
27111	27415	27761	29338	30662	31747	32171	33227	35617	38038	38892	40902	40691
56.7	59.5	62.8	64.7	68.1	72.7	77.8	84	89.4	93.1	95.8	97.5	100

Table 4A.2. NHS VOLUME EXPENDITURE, UNITED KINGDOM (£ MILLION AT 1995/6 PRICES,

	Fiscal years									
	1973/4[a]	1974/5	1975/6	1976/7	1977/8	1978/9	1979/80	1980/1	1981/2	1982/3
Current expenditure										
HCHS[b] and FHS	22068	24310	26281	26139	26327	27063	27378	28264	28836	29051
Administration[c]	760	1054	1149	1158	1136	1148	1214	1184	1139	1079
Less payments										
Hospital services	−168	−134	−136	−151	−141	−131	−140	−150	−166	−159
Pharmaceutical	−256	−215	−147	−128	−115	−108	−163	−231	−257	−276
Dental	−300	−262	−201	−222	−260	−251	−259	−279	−317	−360
Ophthalmic	−159	−141	−114	−123	−115	−116	−110	−89	−91	−99
Total	−884	−752	−599	−624	−632	−607	−672	−750	−831	−895
Other (including departmental administration)	778	846	740	875	862	869	928	907	730	696
Total current expenditure	22722	25458	27571	27548	27693	28474	28848	29606	29873	29931
Capital expenditure	2395	2027	2205	2000	1751	1801	1736	1810	1999	1895
Total expenditure	25118	27485	29776	29548	29444	30274	30584	31415	31872	31826

[a]   Excluding £1882.5 million of local authority health services expenditures at 1995/6 prices.
[b]   Including the school meal service from April 1974, previously included in education.
[c]   Administration costs are not separately identifiable from 1993/4.

Sources: Expenditure: ONS (1997a: table 3.3) for 1995/6, and equivalent tables for earlier years; deflator: calculated from data supplied by ONS, personal communication.

ADJUSTED USING BLUE BOOK DEFLATORS)

1983/4	1984/5	1985/6	1986/7	1987/8	1988/9	1989/90	1990/1	1991/2	1992/3	1993/4	1994/5	1995/6
30068	29643	29925	30320	30776	31510	31038	32355	34611	35295	36362	38130	38514
963	936	892	981	1023	1018	1196	1253	1333	1379	—	—	—
−164	−166	−173	−176	−173	−518	−569	−653	−643	−554	−376	−112	−42
−289	−295	−297	−362	−418	−302	−338	−316	−322	−326	−331	−346	−383
−408	−390	−423	−463	−473	−421	−475	−565	−568	−515	−450	−469	−494
−125	−103	−26	−2	−2	—	—	—	—	—	—	—	—
−986	−954	−918	−1003	−1065	−1240	−1383	−1534	−1533	−1394	−1157	−928	−919
753	703	798	1327	1346	1209	1251	1288	1379	1776	1964	2589	2780
30797	30328	30697	31626	32079	32497	32102	33362	35790	37055	37169	39792	40375
1884	1960	2049	2058	1977	1954	2896	2366	2133	1767	923	544	316
32681	32288	32746	33684	34056	34451	34998	35728	37923	38823	38092	40336	40691

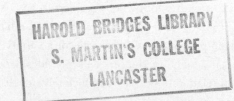

Housing: A Decent Home within the Reach of Every Family?

John Hills

I. Goals and policies

GOVERNMENT has never seen its role as being a universal provider or funder of housing in the same way as it has for education or health. One consequence of this is that policy goals in the sector have been pursued by less direct methods than in others. In terms of the matrix of provision and funding shown in Fig. 5.1, a much greater proportion of the sector's activity by value occurs in the private/private quadrant than for most of the other activities examined in this book.

Nonetheless, as the figure also shows, the public sector plays a substantial role in the housing market, both through provision of housing for which individuals pay rent and through a range of subsidies including Housing Benefit, subsidies to local authorities and housing associations, and tax expenditures for owner-occupiers. It has also played a substantial role regulating the housing market, both enforcing minimum standards and controlling private rents.

Housing has been part of the welfare state for a variety of reasons (Hills 1991: chap. 2). Because housing has a long life, the service it provides depends on a stock of assets whose size is very large in relation to the rate at which new investment can be made. Unlike most other commodities, the supply of housing is therefore very slow to adjust to changes in price. This can leave tenants open to exploitation by landlords in times of shortage, providing the rationale in the past for rent controls and security of tenure legislation. Another effect of the cost of housing in relation to current income is that capital market failure becomes important: purchasers may have difficulties in borrowing against their future incomes, particularly

	Public provision	Private provision
Public funding	Subsidies to council housing Housing Benefit for council rents	Housing Benefit for private rents Tax expenditures on owner-occupation Grants to housing associations Tax expenditures on private landlords Improvement grants
Private funding	Net rents paid by council tenants	Owner-occupiers' housing costs (net of tax expenditures) Net rents paid to private landlords and housing associations

5.1. HOUSING PROVISION AND FUNDING

where these are low and uncertain. Another kind of market failure stems from the externalities resulting from private housing consumption. The condition of one house affects its neighbours and, indeed, its whole neighbourhood. A private market is unlikely to allow for the 'spillover' effects of improvement in investment decisions. Historically, much housing policy has its origins in public health concerns—overcrowding and squalor breed disease for the whole population, not just for the residents affected.

Once a statutory floor is put to the quality of housing which the state permits, something has to be done for those whose incomes are too low to buy housing of that standard at unsubsidized prices. Combined with more general distributional concerns this has led to a series of interventions aimed at those with low incomes. Specific subsidies, primarily aimed at those on low incomes, have been given to keep down the rents of housing, while those on low incomes have also received housing benefits whose size has been directly tied to their spending on housing. This contrasts with the policy generally adopted in income support policies, under which benefits take the form of cash, which the recipient then uses to buy food, clothing, or whatever she chooses. There seem to be two reasons for this difference. First, housing is seen as a 'merit good' whose consumption by the poor society is readier to support (partly because of the externalities described above) than, say, the consumption of alcohol or tobacco. Secondly, the housing market has been so distorted in terms of the relationship between price and quality of service received that it has been seen as impossible (or very expensive) to give a standard allowance for housing as part of general cash benefits.

Beveridge (1942) was defeated by the 'problem of rent' in trying to set standard allowances, as was the DHSS in the 1980s:

Any such proposal would fail to take account of the very wide variations that exist in the cost of similar housing throughout the country. It would also fail to recognise that for a number of reasons many households on low incomes have unavoidably high housing costs in proportion to their disposable income. (DHSS 1985c: v)

A similarly pragmatic reason for continued intervention in the housing market is that everyone has adjusted their behaviour (and the prices they are prepared to pay) in the light of that intervention:

we certainly do not believe that the household budgets of millions of families—which have been planned in good faith in the reasonable expectation that present arrangements would broadly continue—should be overturned, in pursuit of some theoretical or academic dogma. (DoE 1977a: iv)

Further, if some people continue to receive concessions, equity suggests that others should too—if owner-occupiers have a favourable tax treatment, should not tenants receive comparable help, quite apart from any additional help that might be going to those on low incomes? From this observation come notions that tax and subsidy arrangements should start from the idea of 'tenure neutrality'.

Finally, housing policy has been seen as an instrument by which wider social aims can be achieved. Immediately after the war, the Government saw the private landlord as inherently incapable of providing housing on the scale which was required: by contrast, local authorities were 'plannable instruments' through which investment should be channelled. At the same time, it was hoped to promote social integration through developments which would house those of all incomes. Aneurin Bevan hoped that council housing would have 'the lovely feature of English and Welsh villages, where the doctor, the grocer, the butcher and the farm labourer all lived in the same street' (Foot 1975: 76). Policies like the Right to Buy had wider than just housing aims, including self-sufficiency, wider consumer choice, and the 'property-owning democracy'. In the 1990s housing policy has come to be seen increasingly as an arm of regeneration policy for low-income inner city areas and marginal estates, rather than as an end in itself.

The expression of policy aims

The phrase which gives this chapter its subtitle has recurred as the stated overall aim of housing policy in many official documents since the Second World War. The Heath Government's 1971 White Paper, *Fair Deal for Housing*, defined the goal of housing policy as 'a decent home for every family at a price within their means' (DoE 1971). Similarly, the Labour Government's 1977 Green Paper's opening sentence was that 'The Government believe that all families should be able to obtain a decent home at a price within their means'

(DoE 1977*a*: 1). Most recently, the overarching 'policy objective' of the Department of the Environment's housing programme set out in its 1997 *Annual Report* was 'To bring a decent home within the reach of every family' (DoE 1997*b*: 19). We explore later in this chapter what might be meant by the perhaps rather vague formulations of 'a decent home' and 'within their means' or, perhaps less ambitiously, 'within reach'.

However, after 1979 the promotion of owner-occupation became the dominant aim of policy. For instance, the Department of the Environment's part of the 1986 public expenditure White Paper baldly stated that 'The Government's leading housing policy aim is to encourage the widest opportunities for home ownership' (HM Treasury 1986: vol. ii, p. 142).

By the late 1980s, this exclusive emphasis had relaxed. The 1987 housing White Paper gave a much wider formulation of objectives, including reversing the decline of rented housing, and giving council tenants the right to transfer to other landlords as well as encouraging the growth of home ownership (DoE 1987: 1). By the time of the Conservative Government's last White Paper in 1995, three key aims were put forward: continued growth in *sustainable* home ownership (emphasis added); sustained revival in private renting; and continued provision of social housing (DoE 1996). Looking to the future, the Labour Party's successful manifesto for the 1997 election put forward similarly balanced objectives:

Most families want to own their own homes. We will also support efficiently run social and private rented sectors offering quality and choice. (Labour Party 1997: 25)

The shift of emphasis in the late 1980s appears partly to have been a result of the Conservative Government deciding that its main objective had been achieved by a rise in owner-occupation from 55 per cent of dwellings in Great Britain at the end of 1978 to 64 per cent ten years later (Table 5.11). It may also reflect a change in its perception of the universal applicability of that objective as the strains on marginal owner-occupiers grew at the end of the 1980s (see Section IV). Conversely, Labour had shifted away from its emphasis on council housing and initial resistance to the Right to Buy.

Policy: Labour Government, 1974–1979

Some of the 1974 Labour Government's first acts were direct reversals of its predecessor's policies. The 1972 Housing Finance Act's attempt to force local authorities to raise their rents to equal the 'fair rents' set by rent officers for regulated private tenants was abandoned. With increased subsidies, council rents were initially frozen in cash terms as part of the general 'Social Contract' anti-inflation policy and were subsequently increased by less than general inflation. By contrast, the Housing Finance Act's national scheme of income-related rent rebates (for council tenants) and rent allowances (for private tenants in unfurnished accommodation) remained in place, to be reformed into Housing Benefit in the 1980s.

Income tax deductibility of interest payments on personal borrowing was removed in 1974 *except* for housing, but a limit of £25,000 was put on the amount of a mortgage eligible for relief. This has only been raised in cash terms once, to £30,000 in 1983. In 1974, the limit only affected 0.1 per cent of new building society advances; by 1995, 73 per cent were above the limit (DoE 1997a: table 10.11).

The general policy shift towards renovation of the existing stock rather than clearance and redevelopment continued, a shift first signalled by the 1968 White Paper, *Old Houses into New Homes* (MHLG 1968). Housing Action Areas were introduced, giving a more intensive focus for area improvement than the General Improvement Areas introduced in 1969. The Housing Association Grant system was established, under which associations (non-profit organizations run by voluntary committees) could receive generous enough capital grants to allow them to break even while charging fair rents on newly rehabilitated or constructed property, setting in motion the continuing rise of this sector (counted as part of the private sector, but also as part of 'social' housing in combination with council housing).

Between 1969 and 1976 local authorities were free to decide how many new houses to build, subject to minimum, 'Parker Morris', standards and limits on costs (the 'Housing Costs Yardstick'). But after 1977/8, controls on local authority borrowing for capital spending were extended, including to the construction of new dwellings under the Housing Investment Programme (HIP) system (renovation spending was already controlled). This system was originally presented as 'a means of controlling public expenditure' which 'will increase local discretion by putting greater responsibility for deciding the right mix of investment on the local authorities' (DoE 1977a: 77). In the event, 'local discretion' did not figure prominently in the way the system operated (Leather 1983). As Table 5A.2 shows, gross capital spending on housing fell substantially after 1976.

The final lasting policy initiative of the period was the 1977 Housing (Homeless Persons) Act. Originally a (Liberal) Private Member's Bill, this placed a legal duty on local authorities to secure permanent housing for priority cases, such as families with children, pregnant women, 'vulnerable' individuals, or the elderly (with a local connection and not 'intentionally homeless'). These provisions remained intact until the Conservative's 1996 Housing Act, which changed the obligation on councils to provision of temporary accommodation only, with those classified as 'homeless' to join the normal waiting list for permanent homes.

Policy: Conservative Governments, 1979–1987

In looking at Conservative housing policy after 1979, it is striking that there were two waves of policy making. The first was in 1980, introducing the Right to Buy for local authority tenants and changing the system of subsidies to Housing Revenue Accounts and the general system of Rate Support Grant to authorities. The second came at the end of the 1980s.

Council house sales to sitting tenants had always been possible at the discretion of the authority (with discounts up to 30 per cent allowed between 1970 and 1974). The 1980 Housing Act gave public sector tenants of at least three years' standing the 'Right to Buy' the freehold of a house or the 125-year lease of a flat. Tenants were entitled to discounts of between

33 and 50 per cent on the market value of the property depending on the length of time they had been a tenant, up to a maximum of £25,000 (subsequently increased to a maximum of 70 per cent in some circumstances, and up to £50,000 in certain areas from 1989). The effect of the legislation has been far-reaching. By 1995 about 1.7 million tenants had exercised the Right to Buy, purchasing a quarter of the 1980 stock (Table 5A.3).

The 1980 Act introduced a new subsidy system for local authorities in England and Wales, allowing subsidy to be withdrawn from them on the *assumption* that they were increasing their rents in line with an annual 'rent guideline'. It was not compulsory to do so, avoiding the direct confrontation with recalcitrant councils like Clay Cross following the 1972 Housing Finance Act (Malpass 1989). Instead, the systems of Housing Subsidy and Rate Support Grant made it very expensive for them to choose not to increase rents (for instance by making 'Rate Fund Contributions' into their HRAs). In aggregate, rents rose substantially in real terms in the early 1980s (see Table 5.2), but central government's 'leverage' over rents declined as authorities fell out of subsidy altogether—only a quarter of English authorities still received Housing Subsidy by 1986/7.

As general subsidies were cut and rents increased, so Housing Benefit became more important. The system in place up until 1981/2 was essentially that established by the 1972 Housing Finance Act. In 1982/3 the system under which Supplementary Benefit (now Income Support) covered the housing costs of its recipients in full was amalgamated with the rent and rate rebate and rent allowance systems (which gave partial assistance to those not on Supplementary Benefit) to produce a combined 'Housing Benefit'. The main effects were administrative. Supplementary Benefit recipients no longer received cash with which to pay their rents. Instead, 'certificates' were sent by the DHSS to the local authorities, telling them to give full rebates. In effect, however, two separate systems remained (see Section IV). As Berthoud (1989) put it, 'Housing benefit . . . never looked like living up to its advance billing as a "comprehensive" solution. It was just the two old schemes tied together—with red tape.' The reform happened just as local authority rents rose by 50 per cent in real terms and unemployment was rising rapidly, both bringing many more tenants within the system councils had taken over.

Policy: Conservative Governments, 1987–1997

The second wave of Conservative policy reform was embodied in the provisions of the 1988 Housing Act and the 1989 Local Government and Housing Act, combined with the more fundamental reform of Housing Benefit in April 1988.

The 1988 Housing Act included two new mechanisms designed to reduce the importance of local authorities as direct providers of housing. Under 'Tenants' Choice', other landlords could bid to take over local authority housing - with tenants voting on whether this should go ahead. In the event, this has scarcely been used, although a group of tenants in Conservative-controlled Westminster did use its provisions to set up their own trust to 'continue council housing by other means'. Of much greater importance has been the use made by councils of rights which already existed to make 'voluntary transfers' to other landlords at their own discretion. Starting with Chiltern District Council in 1988, more than fifty councils have now transferred their entire stock, mainly to newly established 'transfer' housing associations built around the council's existing housing staff (Table 5A.4; see Gardiner and Hills 1992 and Mullins *et al.* 1993 for discussion of the early transfers).

Under the second new mechanism, central government established 'Housing Action Trusts' (HATs) to take over particular estates from councils. Despite promises of large investment in renovating their homes, tenants resisted the original HAT proposals as privatization. The six HATs eventually implemented came from local not central government initiatives and included the right of tenants to revert to the council as their landlord at the end of the renovation phase (see Karn 1993). A total of nearly £400 million was spent on them between 1991/2 and 1996/7, and spending is expected to total £1.1 billion over their ten-year lives (DoE 1997b: 67). Given that fewer than 20,000 homes are involved, the cost per unit has been huge, and the priority given to the scheme rapidly disappeared.

For most council housing, the effects of the 'new financial regime' from April 1990 were more important. The first key element was that Housing Revenue Accounts were 'ring-fenced': local authorities can no longer make discretionary transfers from their general funds into them (or, generally, vice versa). This leaves local authority housing departments looking much more like separate housing organizations than part of the council's general activities. Second, the general system of housing subsidies and the money paid to authorities for the parts of their rents covered by Housing Benefit were amalgamated into a single 'Housing Revenue Account Subsidy'. This is calculated as the cost of their rent rebates plus or minus an amount depending on the capital costs carried on the HRA and centrally determined rent and management and maintenance spending guidelines. In most cases this calculation implies that gross rents should be generating a surplus, which is then in effect used to cover part of the cost of Housing Benefit. By 1995/6 these deemed surpluses had reached over £1.1 billion (Table 5A.1).

From 1996/7, constraints on local authority rent-setting were tightened further, with the part of Housing Benefit costs resulting from any rent rise above the year's guideline increase deemed ineligible for subsidy. This implies that only about one-third of any additional rent increase would be available for extra spending for the typical council.

At the same time as these changes to revenue funding, controls on councils' capital spending were tightened further, and a number of loopholes which had evaded control were closed (Hills 1991: chaps. 5 and 6).

The system of grants to housing associations was also reformed from 1989. New association tenants are no longer entitled to fair rents, and their 'assured' rents are set by the association at the level needed to cover its costs within a less generous grant system. The percentage of capital costs covered by grant has fallen, first through reductions laid down each year by the Housing Corporation (or its equivalents in Wales and Scotland), and then in the mid-1990s as associations undercut each other in a competition for development funds. The balance of funding now comes from private borrowing, which counts outside the public spending total. Between 1988/9 and 1995/6, associations in Great Britain raised £5.4 billion of this 'private finance', and by 1995/6 it was paying for 38 per cent of gross association investment, that is, adding 60 per cent to the public investment (Wilcox 1996: table 54). The reform has achieved its aim of stretching public funds. The stronger incentives in the new system also appear to have produced greater cost-effectiveness. However, the smaller grants and the new requirement on associations to build up funds to cover future periodic major repairs (previously covered by grant) have meant higher rents (Fig. 5.7).

For private tenants, the 1980 Housing Act introduced new kinds of tenancy outside the 1965 'fair rent' regulations. These 'assured' and 'shorthold' tenancies never became significant numerically, but they paved the way for the large-scale changes of the 1988 Housing Act which made all new tenancies either assured or 'assured shorthold'. Rents for new private tenants were deregulated and are set by the market. The tenant retains some security of tenure, but only for a limited period in the case of shorthold tenancies. Fair rents remain for tenancies already covered by them, but their numbers are steadily falling, and fair rent levels have risen. In combination with the crisis in the owner-occupied housing market in the early 1990s (see Section IV), which meant some owners who were unable to sell their homes rented them, the deregulation of rents has led to a modest expansion of the private rented sector for the first time in eighty years (Table 5.11).

Tax concessions under the 'Business Expansion Scheme' (BES) were extended to new private lettings between 1988 and 1993, resulting in investment of £3.3 billion in the sector, covering about 80,000 dwellings (Crook et al. 1995). However, the concessions were very generous (tax relief covering about 44 per cent of the costs) and the lettings only had to be short-term (only 11,000 dwellings may remain in the sector at the end of the century) so this proved an expensive way of encouraging short-term market rent housing.

The Housing Benefit system was fundamentally reformed as part of the 'Fowler' reforms to social security in April 1988 (see Chapter 7). The new system brought the treatment of Income Support and other recipients into line. However, this extended the phenomenon that Housing Benefit changes pound for pound with any change in rent for all recipients (previously this was only true of Supplementary Benefit recipients). This sits rather oddly with deregulation of private rents. On the one hand, rents are being moved more towards 'market' levels, while on the other, the benefit system largely subverts any attempt to establish a functioning market. In the early 1990s the cost of Housing Benefit—particularly for association and private tenants—escalated rapidly (Tables 5.1 and 5.2). In reaction, a number of restrictions were introduced to the rents eligible for benefit. Limits which were related to local market rents were set to the rents taken into account, and from 1996 single people aged under 25 were limited to the rent of a room in shared accommodation. In one of its last moves before it lost the 1997 election, the Conservative Government proposed extending this last provision to all single people aged under 60, but the new Government decided not to do so.

For owners, there were two important changes. First, higher-rate mortgage relief was abolished in 1991, so all relief was at a single rate. This rate was then reduced to 20 per cent in 1994 and again to 15 per cent in 1995. With the £30,000 limit, the value of the relief is now closer to a lump sum subsidy to mortgagors (and therefore of most importance for relatively low-income mortgagors). At the same time other forms of saving received tax exemption (PEPs and TESSAs), while capital gains tax on other assets became less severe. Together these have reduced the relative advantages of owner-occupation compared to other ways of saving. Second, in reaction to the rapidly rising cost of paying the mortgage interest of Income Support recipients (Table 5A.1), from October 1995 new borrowers became ineligible for this assistance for the first nine months on Income Support. Instead they were encouraged to take out private insurance which would service the mortgage if they lost their job. However, the costs of these private policies were high, and in 1996 only about a fifth of new borrowers had taken them out, raising fears that more mortgagors would lose their homes if unemployment rose again (Burchardt and Hills 1997; Ford and Kempson 1997).

Finally, concern about the rising numbers sleeping rough, particularly in central London, led to the 'Rough Sleepers Initiative' from 1990, under which the DoE has supported increased immediate-access hostel places and other measures designed to help people into more permanent housing. The initiative has had some success in London (Randall and Brown 1993). Meanwhile similar problems have emerged in other cities and towns, to which the initiative was extended in April 1996.

Change and continuity in housing policy

Certain parts of housing policy have remained constant over the last twenty-five years. First, owner-occupiers have remained favoured by the tax system, despite recent restrictions to mortgage relief. The abolition of the taxation of owner-occupiers' 'imputed rents' under Schedule A of income tax in 1963 was not reversed by the 1964–70 Labour Government. Nor did that Government impose its new Capital Gains Tax on housing. When the tax-deductibility of interest payments on other forms of personal borrowing was removed in 1974, mortgage interest continued to receive tax relief, albeit subject to a limit which has become steadily tighter in real terms, and with the rate of relief cut back sharply as taxes in general were raised in the mid-1990s. The replacement of domestic rates with the Poll Tax in 1989 and 1990 removed a tax which was virtually the only offset to the tax advantages of housing as a whole. The Council Tax, which in turn replaced the Poll Tax from April 1993, is based on property values, but its structure means that only part of its effect is as a property tax (Hills and Sutherland 1991), and the amounts collected are less than with rates.

Second, there has been a continuing shift of emphasis since the late 1960s away from new local authority construction. The 'numbers game' of successive Governments vying with one another over who could achieve the largest number of new housing starts was abandoned, both in response to disillusion with some of the products of wide-scale clearance and redevelopment, and partly as the 'crude shortage' of dwellings disappeared (Table 5.9). Instead, there has been a steadily increasing emphasis on renovation of the existing stock.

What has changed more has been the balance between general subsidies designed to keep down rents for all local authority tenants and income-related housing benefits. While the national system of rent rebates and allowances introduced in 1972 was maintained by the 1974 Labour Government, its policies on rents and subsidies as a whole meant that the public expenditure cost of the rebate system did not increase—in sharp contrast to the experience since 1979. Housing Benefit now dominates government intervention in the housing market.

The Right to Buy marked a decisive change in the view of the role of local authorities as general providers of rented housing. With housing associations taking over as the main providers of new 'social' housing, and transfers of entire council stocks into the association sector, the role of councils as providers of housing continues to decline. Councils came to be seen as having more of an 'enabling' role. Changes like compulsory competitive tendering of their repair services from 1981 and management services from 1993, the shift to association provision, and more tenant involvement in management decisions were all part of the general 'quasi-market' reforms of the late 1980s (Chapter 8; Bramley 1993). While the new Labour Government announced in 1997 that it would relax constraints on council capital spending linked to previous receipts, the idea of further transfers to 'local housing companies' at arm's length from the council remains on the agenda (Wilcox et al. 1993).

But perhaps most clearly, 'housing' as an issue has moved down the political agenda. In the 1950s and 1960s political parties competed around housing policies and promises. In the 1997 general election campaign housing barely featured as an issue. Notwithstanding the discussion above, 'housing policy' *per se* hardly exists any more: it survives within the welfare state mainly as an adjunct of social security (through Housing Benefit) or as part of wider city regeneration policies, as for instance through the Single Regeneration Budget, which combines spending on a variety of areas, subsuming housing. As will be seen below, some of the fall in the salience of 'housing' in general as an issue may reflect the success in many respects of post-war policies.

II. Expenditure trends

The figures conventionally given for 'public spending on housing' are unsatisfactory in several ways. For instance, the amounts given in the Annual Reports of the Department of the Environment (DoE) include: current subsidies from central government to local authority Housing Revenue Accounts; *part* of the cost of Housing Benefit for local authority tenants (but none of the cost for other tenants); grants to private owners for improvement; capital expenditure by local authorities financed by loans from central government or the private sector; and outright grants to housing associations for capital development. Even in conventional accounting terms, the total of such items involves much adding together of apples and pears, with current spending added to capital items fully covered by borrowing and future debt repayment.

The conventional totals are net of receipts from rents (for current spending) and from sales of assets (for capital). While these net figures are of interest in terms of the new public resources which are being channelled into housing, they can—as explained below—be seriously misleading as a guide to how much is actually being spent on public housing. In addition, much of the cost of Housing Benefit—intimately related to the level of rents and hence to that of general subsidies—is counted as part of the social security programme (and the split between departments has varied over time), while the cost of tax expenditures on housing is excluded.

Fig. 5.2 brings together the main elements of public spending on housing on a consistent basis since 1973/4, including the total cost of Housing Benefit, and alongside that of mortgage interest relief. The figures are for the whole of the United Kingdom and at 1995/6 prices (cash spending adjusted by the GDP deflator). The net capital and net current figures are drawn from successive DoE Annual Reports for England and from other sources for Wales, Scotland, and Northern Ireland. Figures for 1973/4 to 1975/6 are adjusted from information originally given in 'survey price' (volume) terms. Housing Benefit totals are on a consistent basis for the whole period, giving the gross cost of payments relating to the rent of public and private tenants receiving Housing Benefit and its predecessors (including the rents covered by Supplementary Benefit—now Income Support—up to 1982/3).

The trends shown by Fig. 5.2 and in more detail in Table 5.1 and Annexe Table 5A.1 are clear. Public spending on housing and Housing Benefit taken together fell by 40 per cent in real terms between 1976/7 and 1981/2. During the rest of the 1980s the total was constant in real terms, but since then it has increased again, driven by rapid growth in Housing Benefit. In relation to GDP, the total peaked in 1974/5 at 4.2 per cent, nearly 9 per cent of General Government Expenditure (GGE). By the end of the 1980s, it was down to 1.8 per cent of GDP and below 5 per cent of total government spending. Despite its recovery in real terms, the 1996/7 total represented half the share of national income that it had in 1974/5. More than any other public spending programme explored in this book, the housing programme has clearly been substantially cut since the 1970s.

Throughout the period up to 1989/90 the total of net current expenditure (mostly central or local government general subsidies to HRAs) and Housing Benefit remained constant at around £8 billion (1995/6 prices). As general subsidies were cut, the cost of Housing Benefit rose by an equivalent amount. Much of this was cause and effect. As general subsidies fell, council rents increased by nearly 50 per cent in real terms between 1979/80 and 1984/5 (Table 5.2). At the same time, the proportion of council tenants receiving Housing Benefit rose from 40 to over 60 per cent, the increased numbers partly resulting from the higher rents. What were then Supplementary Benefit recipients had the whole of these rent increases covered by benefit and other recipients had 60 per cent covered (under the pre-1988

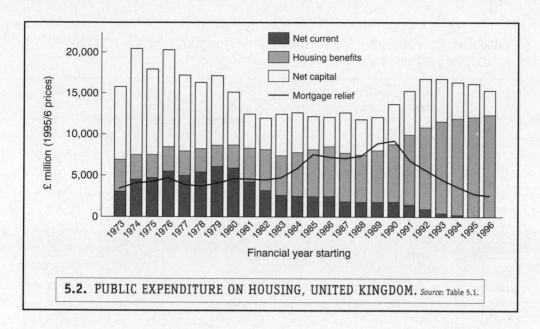

5.2. PUBLIC EXPENDITURE ON HOUSING, UNITED KINGDOM. *Source*: Table 5.1.

benefit formula). Almost half of the increased rents re-emerged immediately as higher Housing Benefit. Higher unemployment also meant greater numbers of benefit recipients. By 1984/5, the total number of tenants receiving Housing Benefit had jumped from 3.3 to 4.8 million. This increase happened despite a reduction in the inherent generosity of the benefit system (as measured by the relative value of the 'needs allowance' on which benefit levels depended).

In the 1990s the picture has changed. Net current spending has been eliminated. Indeed, by 1995/6 it was negative, as positive spending items and subsidies were more than offset by the surpluses which most local authorities were deemed to be making on their HRAs and contributing towards the cost of Housing Benefit (negative spending in this presentation, but netted out from part of benefit spending in current government presentations). But the growth in Housing Benefit has been far greater than this saving. It doubled in real terms between 1989/90 and 1995/6, again linked to a further real rise in local authority rents (by more than a third between 1989/90 and 1994/5). However, the factor really pushing up costs was the tripling of the real cost of benefits to housing association and private tenants, which had overtaken benefits to council tenants by the end of the period. This reflected some growth in the size of these sectors as well as the recession, but also rising rents following deregulation of the private sector and cuts in subsidies to housing associations. Looking at spending on Housing Benefit for private and association tenants also receiving Income Support, Evans (1996c: table 6) found that about two-thirds of the increased cost between 1989 and 1993 resulted from increased numbers, one-third from higher rents. However, by late 1996 the numbers of private tenants receiving Housing Benefit seemed to have peaked and were falling, perhaps reflecting some of the restrictions which had been introduced.

Table 5.1. REAL NET PUBLIC EXPENDITURE ON HOUSING, UNITED KINGDOM
(£ BILLION AT 1995/6 PRICES)

	Net current[a]	Net capital	Housing benefits[b]	Total public spending	Mortgage interest relief	Public spending % of GDP[c]	% of GGE
1973/4	3.0	8.8	3.9	15.7	3.6	3.3	7.6
1974/5	4.5	12.9	3.0	20.4	4.1	4.3	8.8
1975/6	4.7	10.4	2.8	17.9	4.3	3.8	7.8
1976/7	5.5	11.8	2.9	20.3	4.7	4.2	9.0
1977/8	5.0	9.3	3.0	17.2	4.0	3.5	8.1
1978/9	5.4	8.1	2.8	16.3	3.7	3.2	7.3
1979/80	6.0	8.5	2.6	17.1	4.2	3.3	7.4
1980/1	5.9	6.5	2.8	15.1	4.7	3.0	6.4
1981/2	4.2	4.1	4.1	12.4	4.6	2.5	5.2
1982/3	3.2	3.8	4.9	11.9	4.5	2.3	4.9
1983/4	2.6	5.1	4.8	12.5	4.9	2.3	5.1
1984/5	2.5	4.9	5.3	12.7	6.0	2.3	5.0
1985/6	2.5	4.0	5.7	12.1	7.6	2.1	4.8
1986/7	2.5	3.6	6.0	12.1	7.2	2.0	4.7
1987/8	1.9	4.9	5.8	12.6	7.1	2.0	5.0
1988/9	1.8	4.3	5.7	11.9	7.4	1.8	4.8
1989/90	1.9	4.1	6.1	12.1	8.9	1.8	4.7
1990/1	1.9	4.8	7.0	13.6	9.2	2.1	5.3
1991/2	1.5	5.4	8.5	15.3	6.8	2.4	5.8
1992/3	1.0	5.9	9.9	16.8	5.6	2.6	6.0
1993/4	0.5	5.2	11.1	16.8	4.5	2.5	5.8
1994/5	0.3	4.5	11.7	16.5	3.6	2.4	5.6
1995/6	−0.1	4.0	12.2	16.1	2.8	2.3	5.3
1996/7	−0.1	3.0	12.4	15.3	2.6	2.1	5.1
Real growth rates (% per year)							
1973–9	12.1	−0.6	−6.4	1.4	2.6		
1979–89	−11.0	−7.1	9.0	−3.4	7.8		
1989–95	n/a	−0.3	12.1	4.8	−17.5		
1973–95	n/a	−3.5	5.4	0.1	−1.2		

[a] Notional HRA surpluses contributing to Housing Benefit treated as negative spending.
[b] Includes rents of Supplementary Benefit recipients before 1983, and Income Support payments of mortgage interest.
[c] GDP figures before 1990/1 adjusted for impact of abolition of domestic rates to give consistent trend.

Source: Table 5A.1.

Table 5.2. HOUSING BENEFIT: COST AND RECIPIENTS

	1973/4	1979/80	1984/5	1989/90	1994/5	1995/6
Cost of housing benefits (£ billion, 1995/6 prices)						
Local authority tenants (GB)	2.6	1.8	3.6	3.8	5.4	5.4
Other tenants (GB)	1.1	0.7	1.2	1.7	5.0	5.4
Income Support mortgage interest (UK)	n/a	0.1	0.4	0.5	1.1	1.1
Total (UK)	3.9	2.6	5.3	6.1	11.7	12.2
Recipients (GB, millions)						
Local authority tenants	2.3	2.6	3.7	2.9	3.0	2.9
Other tenants	0.7	0.7	1.1	1.0	1.7	1.9
Recipients as % of all local authority tenants (GB)						
On Income Support/ Supplementary Benefit	22	22	32	34	41	42
Not on Income Support/Supplementary Benefit	17	18	29	24	25	25
Real local authority rents Index (1973/4 = 100)	100	78	115	129	175	181

Sources: Table 5A.1; DoE (1977a: tables 11.1 and 11.3, and earlier equivalents); Hills and Mullings (1990: table 5.2); Wilcox (1996: table 105).

The fall in the real value of net capital spending was even more dramatic. After 1976/7 the housing capital programme was a significant casualty of the cuts following the agreement with the International Monetary Fund. By 1986/7, real net capital spending was only 28 per cent of its 1974/5 level. As is discussed below, what happened to gross spending was somewhat different.

Alongside this, rising numbers of owner-occupiers and higher house prices and interest rates, offset to some extent by falling income tax rates, led the cost of mortgage interest relief to grow steadily from £3.6 billion in 1973/4 to its peak of over £9 billion (1995/6 prices) in 1990/1 (whether mortgage interest relief is an appropriate measure of the advantages of owner-occupation is discussed below). Since then its cost has fallen by more than two-thirds as interest rates and real house prices have fallen, the rate of relief has been cut to 15 per cent, and the £30,000 limit on the amount eligible for relief has fallen in real terms. The rise and fall in its cost has mirrored changes in the public spending items. As a result, the overall total of spending and tax relief has stayed within the band of £18–22 billion for most of the period. What has changed has been the composition of the items affecting the Exchequer, not the total.

Current spending

The bulk of current public spending on housing used to be made up of central government ('Exchequer') subsidies to local authority or new town HRAs and—until they were outlawed in 1990/1–Rate Fund Contributions made from local authorities' general funds to their HRAs. The relationship between these items and the total of current spending and income on local authority HRAs is shown in Table 5.3 and Fig. 5.3.

The dramatic fall in housing subsidies after 1979 does not correspond to a similar fall in the total amount spent on the management and maintenance of local authority housing. In fact, this grew continuously over the period. Real spending per unit, allowing for changes in the size of the stock, increased by 140 per cent between 1974 and 1995, or by 4.3 per cent per year, with faster growth after 1979 than before it.

Table 5.3. LOCAL AUTHORITY HOUSING REVENUE ACCOUNT, UNITED KINGDOM

	Spending		Income			
	Management and maintenance	Debt charges	Gross rents[a]	Rate Fund contributions	Housing subsidies	Total (including other)
Real spending (£ billion at 1995/6 prices)						
1974	2.7	6.7	5.7	0.9	2.9	9.7
1979	3.5	6.8	5.2	1.0	3.8	10.4
1984	4.2	4.5	6.7	1.1	0.7	9.2
1989	4.5	3.7	6.7	0.6	0.9	9.0
1994	4.7	3.1	8.1	—	0.8	9.5
1995	4.9	3.0	8.2	—	0.8	9.6
Index of real spending and income per unit (1974 = 100)						
1974	100	100	100	100	100	100
1979	119	93	84	103	118	98
1984	156	68	118	120	25	94
1989	190	62	134	83	34	104
1994	225	58	184	—	33	125
1995	240	58	190	—	35	129
Growth rates of real spending and income per unit						
1974–79	3.6	−1.5	−3.5	0.6	3.4	−0.3
1979–89	4.8	−4.0	4.8	−2.2	−11.8	0.6
1989–95	3.9	−1.0	6.1	n/a	0.4	3.7
1974–95	4.3	−2.6	3.1	n/a	−4.9	1.2

[a] Including rent rebates.

Sources: ONS (1996b: table 8.5); DoE (1997a: table 9.3, and equivalents for earlier years).

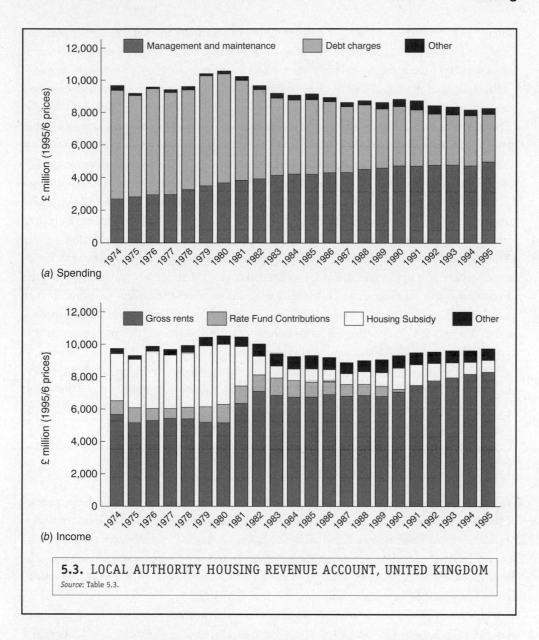

5.3. LOCAL AUTHORITY HOUSING REVENUE ACCOUNT, UNITED KINGDOM
Source: Table 5.3.

Ideally, it would be useful to relate this real growth to changes in the relative costs of providing management and maintenance to give an indication of the growth in the volume of services. Unfortunately a suitable index is not available, but these costs mainly depend on earnings growth, of manual workers for actual repairs and of white-collar workers for other elements of the service. With average earnings (for men working full-time) growing by an average of 1.5 per cent per year relative to the GDP deflator over the whole 1974–95 period (and earnings growing more slowly for manual workers), it is clear that spending on management and maintenance per unit also grew substantially in volume terms (although some of this may have been lost in overhead costs which were not reduced as stocks became smaller, rather than resulting in improved services to tenants).

This has been made possible by a combination of higher rents and lower debt-servicing costs. Debt servicing rose between 1974 and 1979, but since then has fallen back substantially. Spending per unit was 38 per cent lower in 1989 than in 1974 and has continued to fall (Table 5.3). Local authority housing as a whole has been in the position of an owner-occupier with a mortgage, whose mortgage payments fall in real terms as a result of inflation more quickly than they rise as a result of new borrowing. This has been particularly marked since 1979 as a result of the tightening restraints imposed on new local authority borrowing by central government. Total subsidies (including the old Rate Fund Contributions) fell by £4 billion between 1979 and 1994, virtually the same amount as the real fall in debt servicing. Lower subsidy could be justified on the grounds that greater help was needed when the real cost of servicing debt was at its highest, but less is needed now (that is, greater subsidy was needed to cope with the 'front loading' problem). However, government policy has gone further than this. Deemed surpluses of over £1 billion are now being channelled from HRAs in England and Wales into supporting Housing Benefit costs (Table 5A.1). The remaining debt is also being carried by a smaller number of units.

With higher management and maintenance spending, subsidy withdrawal, and then the extraction of assumed surpluses, rents have had to rise. Gross rents collected per unit were 40 per cent higher in 1984 than in 1979 and had more than doubled by 1994 (in real terms, adjusted by GDP deflator).

Capital spending

With capital spending, one has to make a distinction between what is actually spent on public provision and the way in which it is financed. It is also important to note the switch which has occurred between new building and renovation of the existing public sector stock. Fig. 5.4 and Table 5A.2 show what has happened to gross and net public capital spending and to the components of the former in England since 1976/7 (figures on a wider basis and for the period before 1976/7 are not readily available in this form).

As discussed above, net capital spending has collapsed for the UK as a whole, and this was even faster in England by itself. By 1988/9 net capital spending in England had fallen to a tenth of its 1976/7 real level. From being 4.2 per cent of UK General Government Expenditure and 1.9 per cent of GDP in 1976/7, the English total had fallen to a mere 0.4 per cent of GGE and less than 0.2 per cent of GDP by 1988/9. The fall in the gross total is less dramatic, although the 44 per cent real drop over the same period would be startling in most other contexts. Since 1988/9, the net total has recovered somewhat, but after a jump in 1989/90 in advance of the new financial regime for local authority housing, the gross total has fallen back to only two-thirds of its mid-1980s plateau, and only a third of its 1976/7 peak.

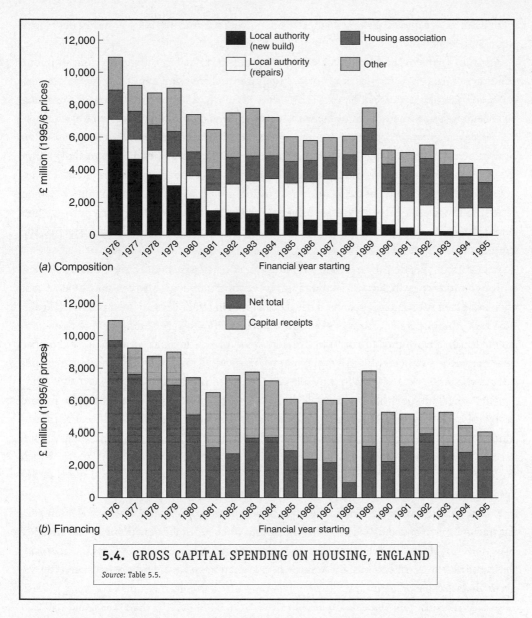

5.4. GROSS CAPITAL SPENDING ON HOUSING, ENGLAND

Source: Table 5.5.

The reason for the difference between net and gross spending lies, of course, in what has happened to capital receipts. These quadrupled in real terms between 1976/7 and 1988/9 as properties were sold under the Right to Buy, reaching a maximum of over £5 billion. After 1989, however, the rate of Right to Buy sales fell steeply (Table 5A.3) and real house prices fell, taking receipts down to only £1.5 billion in 1995/6, despite receipts from Large-Scale Voluntary Transfers (Table 5A.4).

To complicate the picture further, part of the difference between income and current spending figures on HRAs shown in Fig. 5.3 is accounted for by 'revenue contributions to capital outlays', capital spending financed from current income. By 1995/6 this totalled more than £800 million.

Again in terms of the framework of Fig. 5.1, the simple fall in the net amount of public funding of new provision masks a more complicated picture, with a much slower fall in capital resources devoted to public provision as a whole, but a larger proportion of this being financed by the proceeds from transferring existing provision to the private sector via sales.

Within the gross total, particular components have fared very differently. Real spending on new local authority building fell continuously over the period, and had been virtually eliminated by the end. However, the position of local authorities looks very different if one takes account of spending on the renovation of existing council housing. This trebled between 1976/7 and its peak in 1989/90 (as authorities spent in advance of tighter controls), and despite the subsequent fall was still higher in 1995/6 than it had been at the start of the period.

Real capital spending channelled via housing associations, mainly for housing to rent (through either 'new build' or rehabilitation of existing buildings) also fell until 1985/6, but then increased substantially, reaching nearly £3 billion in 1992/3 before being cut back again. The new funding system after 1988 meant that associations were adding private finance to public funding from the Housing Corporation and local authorities, reaching £1 billion per year between 1993/4 and 1995/6 (Wilcox 1996: table 54). This was adding more than 60 per cent to the public total shown in the tables by the end of the period.

The 'other' category has had a more variable history. This covers support for the private sector or home ownership schemes (including—in the figures in Fig. 5.4—local authority lending to finance the Right to Buy in the early 1980s, which caused an equivalent capital receipt). The most important part of this spending has been on improvement grants, which increased rapidly during the 'boom' in grants between 1981/2 and 1983/4 (Table 5.6) but subsequently fell back.

A final perspective on the public spending figures is given by Table 5.4, which gives indices for the volume of spending, adjusted by the output price index for new public sector housing (this does not allow for the effects of changes in land costs). Construction costs for new public sector housing rose less rapidly over the period than prices as a whole as measured by the GDP deflator, particularly after 1989/90, when they actually remained constant in cash terms. As a result, capital spending in volume terms fell less rapidly than real spending. Taking the period 1976/7 to 1986/7, the total volume of gross capital spending fell by 37 per cent, compared to the 47 per cent fall in real terms. By the end, the volume of gross spending was half that at the start, compared to only 38 per cent in real terms. Part of the fall in spending has thus been offset by favourable price movements.

Within the total, allowing for construction costs rather than general inflation suggests that spending on housing associations was still higher at the end of the period than it had been at the start and that local authority capital repairs were 75 per cent greater in volume terms.

Table 5.4. INDICES OF VOLUME OF CAPITAL SPENDING ON HOUSING, ENGLAND (ADJUSTED BY PUBLIC HOUSING OUTPUT PRICE INDEX; 1976/7 = 100)

	Local authority		Housing association	Other	Total gross spending
	New build	Capital repairs			
1976/7	100	100	100	100	100
1977/8	83	102	101	82	89
1978/9	69	129	93	105	87
1979/80	55	153	90	137	88
1980/1	39	116	85	114	70
1981/2	27	99	77	124	62
1982/3	26	154	103	150	77
1983/4	26	179	98	161	81
1984/5	26	191	91	129	76
1985/6	23	191	87	86	65
1986/7	19	215	88	69	63
1987/8	19	233	88	67	65
1988/9	21	232	81	64	64
1989/90	23	326	99	68	80
1990/1	13	182	110	49	56
1991/2	11	164	150	55	60
1992/3	5	182	224	55	71
1993/4	7	203	192	65	71
1994/5	3	178	151	59	58
1995/6	2	175	119	52	51

Source: Table 5.5, with price index from DoE (1997a: table A, and earlier equivalents).

III. Outputs

The previous subsection looked at the volume of public capital spending on housing. Table 5.5 shows the most straightforward measure of the output from this spending, the numbers of new dwellings being completed each year. In line with the figures for the volume of spending, it shows local authority and new town completions rising to a peak of 146,000 in 1975 and then collapsing to less than 2,000 across the whole of Great Britain in 1995. Housing association completions of new dwellings rose rapidly between 1973 and 1977, reaching a maximum of over 25,000, fell back again, but rose to a peak of nearly 40,000 in 1995. Since 1991 associations have been completing more new dwellings than have local authorities, but total public and social new housing completions remained between 30,000 and 40,000 from 1985

Table 5.5. NEW HOUSING COMPLETIONS, GREAT BRITAIN (000s)

	Local authority and new town	Central government	Housing associations	Total public and social	Private	Total
1973	96.6	2.0	8.9	107.5	186.6	294.1
1975	145.6	1.9	14.7	162.3	150.8	313.0
1977	135.6	1.8	25.1	162.5	140.8	303.3
1979	85.0	1.1	17.8	104.0	140.5	244.5
1981	65.2	0.3	19.3	84.8	114.9	199.7
1983	34.8	0.2	16.1	51.2	147.8	199.0
1985	27.1	0.1	13.1	40.2	156.5	196.7
1987	19.3	0.7	12.6	32.6	183.8	216.4
1989	16.9	0.7	13.9	31.5	179.6	211.1
1991	10.2	0.1	20.0	30.3	154.0	184.3
1993	2.5	—	35.3	37.9	140.7	178.6
1995	1.9	—	38.5	40.4	149.6	190.0

Source: DoE (1997*a*: table 6.1, and equivalents for earlier years).

to 1995, compared to more than four times this in the mid-1970s. The pattern of private sector completions has also fluctuated, with more rapid building when real house prices were high, as in the early 1970s and late 1980s.

This resulted in total completions averaging around 300,000 each year between 1973 and 1977, then falling to stabilize at or just below 200,000 since the early 1980s. The composition change was, of course, dramatic—the public and social sector was responsible for more than half of completions in the mid-1970s, but for only a fifth in the first half of the 1990s.

As stressed above, however, new building only represents a part of the picture. During the period there was a significant switch towards renovation and rehabilitation to improve the standards of existing dwellings. Some measures of this are given in Table 5.6.

Housing association rehabilitations mostly represent additions to the numbers of dwellings in that sector (mainly at the expense of the private rented sector). Spending per unit rehabilitated, £28,600 in England in 1994 (DoE 1997*a*: table 7.1), is substantial. Taking housing association new build and rehabilitation completions together, the total peaked at nearly 45,000 units in 1977, fell back to 26,000 in 1987, but reached nearly 50,000 in 1995.

The figures shown for local authority renovations (which do not add to their stock numbers) in Table 5.6 account for only part of their total spending on capital repairs. The notable features are the rapid fall in numbers between 1973 and 1975—capital controls were applied to local authority renovation spending in advance of general controls—but rapid growth

Table 5.6. PUBLICLY FUNDED HOUSING RENOVATIONS, GREAT BRITAIN (000s)

	Local authority[a] and new towns	Housing association	Grants to private owners
1973	188.1	3.4	199.6
1975	61.8	5.1	102.2
1977	94.0	19.6	71.0
1979	110.8	20.1	80.2
1981	79.0	13.8	94.1
1983	127.0	18.0	292.6
1985	151.3	13.4	199.9
1987	235.8	13.1	158.7
1989	255.9	15.0	136.7
1991	258.2	8.4	118.2
1993	362.5	7.8	118.0
1995	400.6	8.4[b]	126.7

[a] Figures for 1977–83 omit Wales.
[b] 1994 figure.

Sources: DoE (1997*a*: table 7.7, and equivalents for earlier years).

from 1981 to 400,000 units per year—more than a tenth of the stock—by the end of the period.

From 200,000 in 1973 (and a peak of 245,000 in 1974), the total of private grants dropped to below 100,000 between 1976 and 1981. The numbers then jumped in the 'grants boom' to reach 300,000 in 1983 and 1984, before falling back again, stabilizing above 100,000 per year. Average spending per dwelling varies greatly with the kind of work, for instance averaging about £5,500 in 1995 for 17,000 renovation grants in Scotland (still under the 1985 legislation) but around £11,000 for the 40,000 mandatory renovation grants in England and Wales (under the 1989 system; DoE 1997*a*: tables 7.2 and 7.3). Given the additional resources expected to come from those with the means to do so, some of the renovations represent substantial amounts of improvement work.

Tax expenditures

This is not the place to go into the argument about what precisely represents the true tax advantage of owner-occupation (see Hills 1991: chaps. 11 and 12 for detailed discussion). The conventional use of mortgage interest tax relief (as in Table 5.1) implicitly takes a benchmark of the tax treatment of other forms of consumer spending, for which interest has not been tax deductible since 1974.

Alternatively, if the tax treatment of private landlords is taken as the benchmark, it is the lack of taxation of owner-occupiers' capital gains or imputed rents (the value of living in their own homes rent-free) which represents the true tax expenditure, not the cost of mortgage tax relief. The value of the tax expenditure measured this way would also be substantial—£9.6 billion in 1989/90 adjusted to 1995/6 prices (assuming that the combination of the two gives owner-occupiers an untaxed real return of 3.5 per cent on the trend capital value of their dwellings; Hills 1991: 208). This advantage will have been reduced a little by subsequent cuts in income tax rates, but is much higher than the conventional figures given for mortgage interest relief. This kind of hypothetical cost does not allow for the way in which house prices—and capital gains—would be lower if such taxation really was imposed.

The lack of VAT on housing could also be taken as a tax expenditure (on all housing, not just owner-occupied housing) but the partly property-based council tax (or domestic rates before their abolition) could be taken as an offset to these tax advantages.

Whichever choice of benchmark one takes, the value given for tax expenditures on owner-occupiers will not be any lower than the simple total of mortgage tax relief, and will not have fallen as rapidly in recent years as that total.

Private spending

A substantial part of housing activity occurs as a result of either private funding or private provision. Indications of the scale of this are given in Tables 5.7 and 5.8. Table 5.7 shows consumers' expenditure on housing as defined for the national accounts. This includes official estimates of owner-occupiers' 'imputed rents', rather than mortgage interest payments, and also includes items like net local authority rates and sewerage and water charges. Rents are shown gross, before allowing for rent rebates and allowances. There is a break in the series after 1989, as the Poll Tax and Council Tax are classed as taxes on expenditure, unlike (net) domestic rates, which were counted as spending on housing.

A measure of the relative scale of public and private funding can be derived by comparison with various items shown in Table 5.1. For tenants, the total of net current public spending (mostly subsidies to tenants) and Housing Benefit remained constant at around £8 billion (in 1995/6 prices) between 1973/4 and 1988/9, since when it has risen to reach £12 billion by 1995/6. Between 1974 and 1991, the total amount paid by tenants in rent (netting off Housing Benefit) fluctuated around £6 billion, rising to £7 billion in 1995/6. In other words, public funding covered rather more than half of current expenses connected with rented housing for most of the period, but now covers more than 60 per cent of the total.

For owner-occupiers, the Office for National Statistics figures for imputed rents, maintenance, and other costs rose from under £20 billion (at 1995/6 prices) in 1973 to nearly £50 billion by 1995. This real rise of 150 per cent compares with an increase in the number of owner-occupiers of about 55 per cent over the period, giving a real increase of 65 per cent per owner-occupier. By comparison, the cost of mortgage interest tax relief and mortgage inter-

Table 5.7. CONSUMERS' EXPENDITURE ON HOUSING, UNITED KINGDOM (£ BILLION AT 1995/6 PRICES)

	Owner-occupiers		Other rents (gross)	Rates (net), sewerage, and water[a]	Total housing[a]	Total as % of consumers' expenditure[a]
	Imputed rents	Maintenance, etc.				
1973	13.7	5.6	10.0	8.6	37.8	12.7
1975	15.2	5.7	8.9	8.6	38.5	13.4
1977	15.7	5.4	8.9	8.9	39.0	13.3
1979	17.2	5.9	8.9	9.1	41.0	13.1
1981	18.0	6.2	9.9	10.6	44.7	14.7
1983	19.7	7.0	11.3	11.1	49.0	15.1
1985	20.4	8.3	11.3	11.6	51.6	15.0
1987	22.4	10.3	12.0	13.4	58.0	15.0
1989	25.2	11.5	12.1	14.4	63.1	15.0
1991	30.2	11.3	14.6	3.5	59.6	14.4
1993	33.4	11.8	17.9	4.0	67.0	15.7
1995	37.9	11.5	19.3	4.4	73.1	16.2

[a] Domestic rates abolished in Scotland from 1989 and England and Wales from 1990. The community charge is not classed as part of consumers' expenditure.

Sources: ONS (1996*b*: table 4.7, and earlier equivalents); prices adjusted by GDP deflator from ONS (1996*a*: table 1.1).

est paid with Income Support rose from £3.6 billion in 1973/4 to £9.8 billion in 1990/1, falling back to £3.9 billion in 1995/6. If this is taken as a measure of the share of owner-occupiers' current expenses which are publicly funded, it rose from about 19 per cent to over 25 per cent in 1989 and 1990, but was down to 8 per cent at the end of the period. Public funding is thus proportionately much less important for owners than for tenants, and the disparity has grown in the 1990s.

Table 5.8 allows comparison of the relative importance of public and private sectors in construction. For new housing, the shift was dramatic. Between 1974 and 1978, nearly half of new housing was publicly funded; by 1995, only a quarter was (and in the late 1980s, the proportion was even lower). A similar breakdown is not available for repairs and maintenance before 1985, but from Tables 5.3 and 5A.2 it would appear that local authority current and capital repairs both increased rather more rapidly between 1974 and 1985 than the public and private total shown in Table 5.8. Overall, the public share of repair and maintenance spending has continued to rise over the period, although it remains the smaller part.

Total public and private housing construction and repair has fallen significantly as a share of GDP—from 4.8 per cent in 1974 to only 3.1 per cent by the 1990s. The 3.6 per cent

Table 5.8. CONSTRUCTION OUTPUT, GREAT BRITAIN

	New housing		Repairs and maintenance			All housing	Total (% of GDP)
	Public	Private	Public	Private	All		
Real spending on housing (£ billion at 1995/6 prices)[a]							
1974	6.2	8.1			8.3	22.5	4.8
1975	6.4	6.7			7.2	20.2	4.3
1976	6.7	6.7			6.7	20.2	4.2
1977	5.8	6.1			7.0	18.9	3.8
1978	5.3	7.2			7.8	20.2	4.0
1979	4.5	7.0			9.5	21.0	4.0
1980	3.8	5.7			9.9	19.4	3.8
1981	2.4	5.0			9.0	16.4	3.3
1982	1.9	5.3			9.1	16.4	3.2
1983	2.0	6.5			9.8	18.3	3.4
1984	1.8	6.4			10.5	18.7	3.4
1985	1.3	6.0	5.4	7.3	12.6	19.9	3.5
1986	1.2	7.1	5.5	7.8	13.3	21.6	3.7
1987	1.3	8.7	5.8	8.8	14.5	24.5	4.0
1988	1.2	10.7	6.1	9.7	15.9	27.7	4.3
1989	1.2	9.1	6.3	10.5	16.8	27.2	4.1
1990	1.1	6.9	6.5	10.2	16.7	24.8	3.7
1991	0.9	5.7	5.6	9.1	14.7	21.3	3.3
1992	1.3	5.2	5.4	8.2	13.6	20.2	3.1
1993	1.5	5.5	5.7	7.7	13.4	20.4	3.1
1994	1.7	5.9	6.1	8.0	14.2	21.8	3.2
1995	1.7	5.5	6.5	8.2	14.7	21.9	3.1
Volume index at 1995 prices (1974 = 100)[b]							
1974	100	100			100	100	
1975	111	88			92	96	
1976	124	95			93	102	
1977	113	92			101	101	
1978	103	107			113	108	
1979	80	96			126	103	
1980	64	74			124	90	
1981	43	68			121	81	
1982	37	80			134	88	
1983	40	102			149	102	
1984	38	103			163	107	
1985	28	96			196	114	
1986	24	112			202	121	
1987	26	138			224	139	
1988	24	161			232	149	
1989	23	130			234	139	
1990	22	103			242	132	

Table 5.8. *Continued*

	New housing		Repairs and maintenance		All	Total housing	(% of GDP)
	Public	Private	Public	Private	All		
1991	20	97			245	130	
1992	34	102			259	141	
1993	40	114			273	153	
1994	46	121			283	160	
1995	42	106			275	150	

a Real spending adjusted using GDP deflator.
b Volume indices based on construction price indices.

Sources: ONS (1996*a*); DoE (1997*a*: table 1.6, and earlier equivalents)

average for the period 1980–93 is lower than the equivalent figures for any of the other six major industrialized countries, which devoted between 4.2 per cent (USA) and 6.1 per cent (Japan) of GDP to investment in housing over the same period (Wilcox 1996: table 7).

IV. Outcomes: decent homes for all?

Households and dwellings

The most obvious measure of the outcome of housing policies is the relationship between the numbers of households and of dwellings available. Whereas there had been fewer dwellings than households after the war, new construction had eliminated the 'crude shortage' of dwellings in relation to households by the late 1960s.

Table 5.9 shows what has happened since 1971 in England and Wales. Between 1971 and 1981 the two million increase in the number of dwellings outstripped growth in the number of households, taking the crude surplus of dwellings over households towards one million (census definitions of a 'household' changed between 1971 and 1981, so the figures are not wholly comparable). After 1981 household formation accelerated and completions fell, so that by 1995 the crude surplus was much smaller than it had been in 1981, and only a little higher than in 1971.

Not all dwellings are in satisfactory condition. The table shows how many were estimated to be statutorily 'unfit', that is, so far defective on one or more specified grounds as to be unsuitable for occupation. For consistency, the old unfitness standard is used throughout the table. More houses fail the new standard (Table 5.15 below). A substantial number of dwellings still fall into this category, although there has been a reduction over the period. As

147

Table 5.9. HOUSEHOLDS AND DWELLINGS IN ENGLAND AND WALES (000s)

	1971 (April)	1981 (mid-year)	1991 (mid-year)	1995 (mid-year)
Households	16,779	18,053	20,343	21,193
Dwellings	17,024	19,020	20,891	21,519
Crude surplus	245	967	548	326
Unfit dwellings	1,364[a]	1,253	890[b]	n/a
Deficit allowing for unfit dwellings	1,119	286	342	n/a
'Concealed households'	426	179	175	167
Deficit allowing for concealed households	1,545	465	517	n/a

[a] Using 1973 estimate for Wales.
[b] Using DoE estimates of unfitness in 1991 on old standard in England and applying ratio between old and new standards to Welsh figures for 1993.

Sources: DoE (1993); DoE (1997a: tables 9.3 and 9.10, and earlier equivalents); DoE (1977b: tables I.1 and I.5).

a result, the number of households exceeds the number of fit dwellings. The deficit fell from over one million in 1971 to less than 300,000 in 1981, but had risen slightly by 1991. Unless the reduction in unfitness accelerated sharply after 1991, the deficit would have risen again by 1995. If unfitness was being reduced at the same rate as in the 1980s, the deficit of fit dwellings relative to households would have been rising by 15,000 to 20,000 units per year in the early 1990s.

The Department of the Environment also publishes estimates of the number of 'concealed households', that is families headed by married couples or lone parents who through choice or necessity do not set up their own household. These numbers fell from 1971 to 1981, but have since stabilized. Comparing the total number of households including 'concealed' ones with the number of fit dwellings, there was a deficit of more than 1.5 million in 1971, but which fell to under half a million by 1981. During the 1980s this deficit rose slightly, but in the 1990s the reduction in the crude surplus suggests that the final deficit is rising more quickly on this measure as well.

Even with the adjustments to give the final line of Table 5.9, problems remain with this kind of measure of deficit or surplus. First, the rise in the number of households is to some extent an effect of the increase in the number of dwellings relaxing the constraint on new household formation: the number of households is not independent of the number of dwellings. Conversely, as the balance worsens, household formation may be inhibited, in which case the underlying position is now deteriorating faster than the table shows.

Second, there is no allowance for second homes in the figures. In England in 1994/5, there were about 215,000 of these (Green *et al*. 1996). Nor is there allowance for vacancies which occur while people move house. Each 1 per cent of the stock allowed for vacancies adds 200,000 to the estimated deficit. About 2.7 per cent of the English stock which was not unfit (under the new standard) was vacant in 1991 (DoE 1993). Third, the aggregate figures do not allow for differences in location of households and dwellings. Here the sources used in Table 5.9 show a variation in the crude surplus of dwellings over households in 1995 which ranged from 1.1 per cent in Yorkshire and Humberside and the South-East excluding London to over 5 per cent in Wales and Scotland. These figures do not, of course, say much about the location of dwellings in relation to where people would *like* to live.

Despite these shortcomings, the trends in Table 5.9 remain clear. Overall, dwelling provision in relation to the number of households is better than in the early 1970s, but was deteriorating in the early 1990s.

Homelessness

The figures shown in Table 5.10 present an apparent contradiction of this overall improvement since the 1970s. Between 1979 and 1992, the number of households accepted by local authorities in Great Britain for rehousing because they were statutorily homeless under the Housing (Homeless Persons) Act rose from 70,000 to 180,000, although it fell to 135,000 in 1995. The overall housing shortage may have changed little since 1981, but more families are 'homeless'.

Part of the explanation lies in the meaning of the statistics for homelessness. First, they relate to a *flow* of households rehoused during a year, not to the *stock* of households without a home at any one time. Second, homelessness has a statutory meaning here; it does not correspond to 'rooflessness' in the sense of being out in the streets (for which reliable statistics are scarce). The difference between the two works both ways. Single people do not qualify as being 'in priority need' under the 1977 Act, so those sleeping in cardboard boxes in London's street doorways are not part of the totals shown in the table. On the other hand, other groups can qualify as homeless on the grounds that they are threatened with entering one of the statutory categories within the next twenty-eight days. The distinction between homelessness in statutory terms and popular definition is illustrated by those classed as 'homeless at home'—the local authority accepts that they have a right to be rehoused as homeless, but they remain where they are, as preferable to alternatives like temporary bed-and-breakfast accommodation.

The homelessness figures give an index to the numbers entering local authority housing via a particular route, one which has risen steadily in importance relative to acceptances from the waiting list. But as Niner and others have argued,

it is important to note that the homeless and waiting list applicants are similar in many ways . . . it is possible to argue that it does not matter very much if local authorities can house no-one but the

Table 5.10. LOCAL AUTHORITY HOMELESSNESS ACCEPTANCES AND HOMELESS HOUSEHOLDS IN TEMPORARY ACCOMMODATION (000s)

	Homeless acceptances (Great Britain)	Households in temporary accommodation (England; end of year)			
		Bed and breakfast	Hostels[a]	Private sector leasing and other[b]	Total
1979	70	n/a	n/a	n/a	n/a
1980	76	1.3	3.4	n/a	4.7[c]
1981	84	1.5	3.3	n/a	4.8[c]
1982	90	1.6	3.5	4.2	9.3
1983	92	2.7	3.4	3.7	9.8
1984	98	3.7	4.0	4.6	12.3
1985	111	5.4	4.7	5.8	15.9
1986	122	9.0	4.6	7.2	20.8
1987	130	10.4	5.2	9.2	24.8
1988	136	11.0	6.2	12.9	30.1
1989	148	11.5	8.0	18.4	37.9
1990	172	11.1	9.0	25.1	45.3
1991	179	12.2	10.0	37.8	59.9
1992	179	7.6	10.8	44.6	63.1
1993	166	4.9	10.2	38.5	53.6
1994	155	4.1	9.7	31.8	45.6
1995	135	4.5	10.1	30.2	44.7

[a] Includes women's refuges.
[b] Includes short-life accommodation.
[c] Figures exclude short-life and other accommodation.

Source: Wilcox (1996: tables 83 and 84).

homeless, since council housing will still be serving essentially the same purpose as before. The major issue becomes one of fairness between applicants in roughly comparable circumstances, one of whom, either as a result of knowing the system or of genuine necessity becomes homeless, and one of whom does not. (Niner 1989: 98–9; see also Audit Commission 1989)

This is not to argue that many classified as homeless are not in desperate need, but it does mean that the trends shown in Table 5.10 have to be interpreted with a degree of caution. They partly show a change in the route by which people gain access to council housing as knowledge of the system and the priority given to homelessness cases spread, as well as giving an index of the pressure on local authority allocation systems.

Rooflessness

A national time series for the numbers literally roofless does not exist. Canter *et al.* (1989) found 753 people openly out on the streets or in stations in London on a cold night in April 1989, three times the equivalent figure found by a National Assistance Board survey in December 1965. The April 1989 figure did not include those in derelict buildings or covered basements. The authors suggest that the numbers sleeping rough fluctuate considerably: a pilot study in November 1988 had found 514 people at three central London locations, compared with 366 at the same places in April 1989. On a more extensive count, the April 1991 Census counted 1,197 people as sleeping rough in Greater London, and 2,852 throughout Great Britain (Wilcox 1996: table 88). Shelter, the housing charity, argued that many people had been missed by the enumerators, and that the true figure was still over 8,000 in 1993 (Shelter 1994). Monitoring of the DoE's Rough Sleepers Initiative suggest that the numbers sleeping rough in central London fell from 741 in April 1991 to 440 in March 1992 and 419 in November 1992 (Randall and Brown 1993; figures may be affected by seasonal fluctuations).

Temporary accommodation

A further index of the stress being experienced by the housing system—and by those it fails— is the number placed by local authorities in temporary accommodation (Table 5.10), of which, in the Audit Commission's words, 'Bed and breakfast (B&B) hotels usually offer the lowest standards at the highest costs' (Audit Commission 1989: 2). The number of households reported by local authorities in England as placed in bed and breakfast multiplied ninefold to 12,000 between the ends of 1980 and 1991, with the major rise occurring in the mid-1980s. Again, this indicator subsequently declined, to under 5,000 since 1993. Looking at temporary accommodation as a whole, including private sector leasing schemes (some run via housing associations), numbers rose from under 5,000 in the early 1980s to over 60,000 in 1992, falling back to 45,000 in 1995. While some temporary accommodation is of a high standard, its use gives another indicator of stress in the demands being placed on social housing. Looking at the trends in the table as a whole, it is clear that the stress reached its high point in 1990 and 1991, but the pressures had significantly receded by 1995.

Here again one has to be careful with interpretation of the trends. In some authorities a shortage of properties available for letting means that there is little alternative but the use of temporary accommodation. In others, better management of the stock and shorter intervals between properties falling vacant and being relet could eliminate the need for temporary solutions. Part of what has happened since 1990 is better use of the existing stock: local authority vacancy rates fell from 2.6 per cent in 1990 to 2.0 per cent in 1995, implying that a further 27,000 units were in use (GB figures; DoE 1997a: table 9.9).

Thirdly, forcing households accepted as homeless to go through bed and breakfast before permanent rehousing may be used as a rationing device:

several authorities also pointed out that B&B may deter applications and encourage households to seek alternative housing after they have been accepted if they are faced with long stays in hotels. (Audit Commission 1989: 21)

Whatever the qualification, it is clear that the policy objective to provide a decent home for all is not being met for a substantial, albeit now falling, number of households.

Housing tenure

People's tenure choice is not just a matter of government incentives: there are also psychic factors in owning one's own 'home' (Saunders 1990), and economic advantages from the occupant also being the beneficiary of improvements and good care of the property. Nonetheless, the 1980s policy objective of encouraging the growth of home ownership was more clearly successful (Table 5.11). From just over half of all dwellings at the end of 1973, the owner-occupied sector was two-thirds of the total twenty years later, with particularly rapid growth in the 1980s. This partly reflects the long-standing trend away from the private rented sector into much more favourably treated owner-occupation. This trend continued until 1988, after which the share of the private rented sector has crept up, reflecting deregulation of private rents and difficulties in the owner-occupied market.

Table 5.11. HOUSING TENURE, GREAT BRITAIN (STOCK OF DWELLINGS; END-OF-YEAR FIGURES)

	Number of dwellings (millions)	Percentage			
		Local authority/ new town	Owner-occupied	Housing association	Private rented and other
1973	19.4	30.5	52.3	17.2[a]	
1978	20.6	31.7	54.7	13.7[a]	
1983	21.4	28.1	58.8	2.3	10.7
1988	22.5	24.0	64.0	2.7	9.2
1993	23.5	20.1	66.5	3.7	9.8
1995	23.8	18.9	66.8	4.3	9.9

[a] Combines 'housing association' and 'private rented and other'.

Source: DoE (1997a: table 9.3, and equivalents for earlier years).

Since 1980 greater owner-occupation has also resulted from transfers out of the council sector. Whereas council housing accounted for nearly 32 per cent of the stock in Great Britain at the end of 1978, its share was below 19 per cent by the end of 1995. The impact of the Right to Buy can be seen in Table 5A.3. In the peak year of 1982, nearly a quarter of a million public sector dwellings were sold. In all, 2.2 million public sector dwellings were sold between 1979 and 1995, 1.7 million of them to sitting council tenants under the Right to Buy, representing a quarter of the 1980 council stock, and accounting for more than a third of the 4.6 million growth in the number of owner-occupied dwellings.

Another important tenure change has been the growing relative importance of housing associations within social housing. Their share of total stock rose from about 1.8 per cent in 1978 to 4.3 per cent in 1995, or from 5 to 19 per cent of social housing. This reflects not only the building trends shown in Table 5.5, and the effects of the Right to Buy, but also the impact of transfers from local authorities to (mostly newly formed) housing associations. The scale of these is summarized in Table 5A.4. Since 1988/9 more than fifty councils have transferred their entire stocks of more than 200,000 dwellings to associations, the equivalent of over 5 per cent of the starting council stock in England.

Polarization

Table 5.12 shows that this rapid change in tenure shares has been accompanied by dramatic changes in polarization between tenures in terms of income. In 1974 17 per cent of individuals in the top income quintile group and 33 per cent of those in the next group were local authority tenants. These proportions had changed little by 1979, but in 1994 only 2 per cent of the top quintile group and 7 per cent of the next group were local authority tenants. The Right to Buy had clearly been used extensively by tenants with the highest incomes. As a result, in 1994 92 per cent of the top group and 86 per cent of the next were owner-occupiers. Meanwhile the proportion of the bottom quintile group who were owner-occupiers fell from 44 per cent in 1979 to 34 per cent in 1994, while the proportion who were social tenants rose correspondingly from 45 per cent to 61 per cent in 1985, falling to 53 per cent in 1994. Although a part of this may be a result of the change in the definition of income used to classify the groups as a result of the 1982/3 Housing Benefit changes (see Chapter 1), it is clear that the rapid growth in owner-occupation has mostly occurred in the top three quintile groups. A smaller proportion of the poorest fifth were owner-occupiers in 1994 than in 1974 (although more of them were mortgagors).

Correspondingly, the social sector has become increasingly residualized. To look at the General Houshold Survey figures in a different way, while 51 per cent of individuals in local authority housing were in the bottom two quintile groups in 1979, the proportion had risen to 76 per cent in 1994. Only 2 per cent of local authority tenants were in the top income quintile group in 1994, compared to 11 per cent in 1979. The figures for housing associations are similar, with an even bigger change in the share of occupants in the top fifth, down from 17 per cent in 1979 to 1 per cent in 1994. By 1995/6 only 28 per cent of heads of council tenant households in England were working, compared to 66 per cent of owner-occupiers (DoE

Table 5.12. INCOME QUINTILE GROUPS ANALYSED BY TENURE COMPOSITION, GREAT BRITAIN (% OF INDIVIDUALS)

Quintile groups	Owners with mortgage	Outright owners	Local authority tenants	Housing association tenants	Other
1974					
Bottom	16	23	43	1.3	18
2	24	16	44	1.7	15
3	33	15	37	1.6	13
4	40	15	33	1.4	11
Top	49	21	17	1.0	12
All	32	18	35	1.4	14
1979					
Bottom	24	20	43	1.6	11
2	22	20	45	1.4	12
3	40	14	36	1.6	9
4	47	14	30	1.5	8
Top	56	15	19	1.4	9
All	38	17	35	1.5	10
1985					
Bottom	13	16	57	3.9	10
2	24	23	40	3.0	10
3	48	17	26	1.7	8
4	63	15	14	1.2	7
Top	73	17	5	0.5	6
All	44	18	28	2.1	9
1990					
Bottom	21	13	52	5.9	8
2	28	23	38	3.1	8
3	53	21	17	2.6	7
4	66	18	8	1.6	7
Top	77	16	2	0.6	5
All	49	18	23	2.8	7
1994					
Bottom	23	11	45	7.6	14
2	29	26	33	4.5	9
3	53	22	15	3.2	6
4	67	19	7	1.4	6
Top	78	14	2	0.2	6
All	50	18	20	3.4	8

Source: Author's calculations from GHS raw data files.

1997*a*: table 12.13). On some of the worst-affected estates, unemployment of working-age adults is over three times the national average (Power and Tunstall 1995).

Burrows suggests that if anything the pattern of new entrants to social housing will be worsening this trend (Burrows 1997: table 5.2). Slightly more new entrants to English social housing in 1993/4 were employed than those who already were tenants: 30 per cent compared to 28 per cent. However, existing tenants were much older, with 39 per cent retired. Of the new tenants 65 per cent were unemployed or unable to work despite being of working age, compared to 33 per cent of the existing tenants. While the proportion of new council tenants in work stayed around one-third for the whole period from 1984 to 1995/6, there was a major change for new association tenants, with the proportion of new tenants in work falling from 52 per cent in 1984 to only 27 per cent in 1995/6 (figures derived from *Survey of English Housing* data).

The post-war aim of a range of groups being housed by local authorities has most decidedly been abandoned (see Hills 1995*a*: chap. 6 and Giles *et al.* 1996 for discussion of the implications of this).

Tenure and ethnicity

By contrast, ethnic minority groups are somewhat less concentrated in particular tenures. Overall, owner-occupation increased in England from 61 to 67 per cent between 1984 and 1994/5. For all ethnic minority groups it rose from 52 to 58 per cent, and for West Indians from 35 to 47 per cent. Conversely, the proportion in social housing fell from 28 to 23 per cent overall, and for ethnic minorities as a whole from 33 to 29 per cent. For West Indians the fall was from 57 to 44 per cent (Green *et al.* 1996: tables A1.17 and A1.18).

Lettings

It is tempting to see the effects of the Right to Buy combined with the rapid fall in new local authority completions as causing a drop in the supply of local authority housing and therefore the rise in homelessness acceptances. The situation is more complicated, however. The key variable is the number of lettings which authorities can make. If someone who would not otherwise have moved out of the sector for several years purchases under the Right to Buy, there will be no immediate change in the number of new lettings the authority can make. New completions are only part of the supply of new lettings—authorities can also relet property whose tenants move elsewhere or die. This last factor makes the age structure of local authority tenants shown in Table 5.13 of some significance. The percentage of household heads and of all individuals housed by local authorities aged 65 or over rose steadily between 1974 and 1990, although the proportions had fallen back again by 1994.

While the supply of lettings from new completions more than halved in England between 1976/7 and 1984/5 (Kleinman 1988), the number of relets of existing properties rose. As a

John Hills

Table 5.13. AGE PROFILE OF LOCAL AUTHORITY TENANTS

	1974	1979	1985	1990	1994
			% of households		
Age of household head					
Up to 44	32	31	31	35	39
45–64	40	37	34	26	26
65–74	17[a]	20	20	39	35
75 and over	11[a]	13	15		
			% of individuals		
Age of individuals					
Under 16	29.3	24.8	22.4	25.6	29.8
16–64	58.3	59.7	58.7	52.7	51.3
65 and over	12.4	15.5	18.9	21.7	18.9

[a] Estimated.

Sources: Households: published GHS (OPCS 1977, 1981, 1987, 1992, 1996); individuals: author's calculations from GHS raw data files.

result, the total number of lettings to new tenants was constant at around 270,000 between 1976/7 and 1980/1, falling to 240,000 in 1984/5. Since then the number of local authority lettings to new tenants has remained constant, but the number of new housing association lettings has grown substantially (Table 5.14). As a result, *more* new tenants were gaining access

Table 5.14. LETTINGS TO NEW TENANTS BY SOCIAL LANDLORDS

	1979/80	1984/5	1989/90	1994/5
Local authorities (000s)				
England	275	240	229	239
Wales	14[a]	15	11	13
Scotland	n/a	46	47	40
Northern Ireland[b]	12	12	11	10
Housing associations (000s)				
England	42	49	60	111
% of new lettings to homeless households (England)				
Local authority	15	19	28	31
Housing association	n/a	n/a	n/a	23

[a] 1980/1 figure.
[b] Allocations to 'priority groups', which excludes transfers.

Source: Wilcox (1996: tables 90a, 90b, 95, 96, and 97).

to social housing in England in 1994/5 than in 1979/80, despite the shrinking size of the stock and disappearance of new council houses. However, the access route has changed, with 31 per cent of new lettings being to homeless households in 1994/5, compared to 15 per cent in 1979/80.

The situation also varies by region. New local authority lettings were 21 per cent lower in 1994/5 than in 1979/80 in London, the South-East, and the South-West, but 6 per cent or less down in the northern regions of England and in Wales (Wilcox 1996: tables 90*a* and 95).

The physical condition of the stock: House Condition Survey results

So far in this section we have looked at housing conditions in terms of simple numbers of dwellings available. House Condition Surveys give some information about the quality of that stock. Results from the English surveys are summarized in Table 5.15. Successive surveys have used different methods to decide whether dwellings are unsatisfactory and to gross up the sample survey results to the whole stock. In particular, a new, stricter 'unfitness' standard has been used since 1986. For comparability, unfitness estimates are shown on both

---

Table 5.15. UNSATISFACTORY HOUSING CONDITIONS, ENGLAND

	Unfit (old standard)	Unfit (new standard)	Lacking one or more amenities	In serious disrepair[a]	Unsatisfactory in one of these respects[b]
Numbers of dwellings (000s)					
1971	1,216	n/a	2,815	864	3,184
1976	1,162	n/a	1,531	859	2,223
1981	1,116	n/a	910	1,049	2,006
1986[c]	1,053	1,662	543	1,113	1,690
1991	808	1,498	205	n/a	n/a
Percentage of dwellings					
1971	7.5	n/a	17.4	5.4	19.7
1976	6.8	n/a	8.9	5.0	13.0
1981	6.2	n/a	5.0	5.8	11.1
1986[c]	5.6	8.8	2.9	5.9	9.0
1991	4.1	7.6	1.0	n/a	n/a

[a] Requiring repairs costing more than £7,000 at 1981 prices.
[b] Using old unfitness standard.
[c] On basis consistent with earlier years. On basis consistent with 1991 figures, 910,000 dwellings were unfit (4.8% of the stock) and 463,000 lacked amenities (2.5%).

Sources: 1971–81 from DoE (1982: tables B, H, J, K, and N); 1986 from DoE (1988: table 9.1 and figure 5.1); 1991 from DoE (1993: para. 13.25 and table A5.2).

bases. In addition, the estimates shown for 1986 are those calculated on the same basis as the previous surveys, which give the best guide to trends since 1971. The DoE's 'preferred' estimates for 1986 show a somewhat better position in that year.

There has been rapid progress in reducing the number of dwellings lacking one or more of the standard amenities (bath or shower, kitchen sink, wash handbasin with hot and cold water to each, and an indoor WC). Between 1971 and 1991, the number fell by 93 per cent and the proportion of dwellings affected fell from 17.4 per cent to 1 per cent. Similar figures show only 0.6 per cent of dwellings in Scotland in 1991 lacking amenities, but 5.4 per cent in Wales in 1993, down from 20.9 per cent in 1973 but up from 4.1 per cent in 1986 (Welsh Office 1982, 1988; Leather and Morrison 1997). Clearance, rehabilitation, and mandatory improvement grants to provide missing amenities have had a major effect.

Eliminating unfit dwellings has been slower. From an original total of more than 1.2 million in England in 1971, the number dropped by only about 20,000 each year until 1991. With the stock itself increasing, the proportion affected fell from 7.5 per cent to 4.1 per cent over the same period on the old definition. On the new definition, 7.6 per cent of English dwellings were still unfit in 1991, although this was also down from 1986. In Wales, 13.4 per cent of dwellings were unfit on the new standard in 1993, and 4.7 per cent of Scottish dwellings were 'below tolerable standard' in 1991 (Leather and Morrison 1997: table 3.1).

Trends in disrepair are harder to establish because of changing definitions. The number of dwellings in what was classed as 'serious disrepair' (requiring repairs costing more than £7,000 at 1981 prices) increased between 1971 and 1981. On a comparable basis, the DoE suggests that there was a slight improvement in the position between 1981 and 1986, although the 1986 figures are worse than those originally published for 1981. However, by the 1991 survey, only about 2 per cent of the stock required repairs costing more than £12,000 (roughly equivalent to the £7,000 at 1981 prices giving serious disrepair ; DoE 1993: fig. 6.1). This suggests a significant fall in disrepair between 1986 and 1991. On a comparable basis, average repairs required to the stock fell by 24 per cent between 1986 and 1991 (DoE 1993: para. 6.26).

Many of the same dwellings are affected by more than one of these defects. As a result the total which is unsatisfactory in one or more of these three respects is smaller than that given by simply adding the three categories together. This proportion more than halved between 1971 and 1986, from nearly 20 per cent to 9 per cent.

Table 5A.5 gives a breakdown of these results by tenure. The worst conditions are concentrated in the private rented sector (and amongst vacant dwellings), with a quarter of private rented dwellings classed as in the worst tenth of the whole stock in both 1986 and 1991. Over time, all tenures experienced a fall in the proportion lacking amenities, but the proportions of owner-occupied and local authority dwellings in serious disrepair increased between 1971 and 1986, and the proportion of the council stock classed as unfit also increased throughout the period. The shift in the relative balance between the tenures meant that overall unfitness declined nonetheless (especially if one excludes unoccupied dwellings) and that disrepair increased only slightly over this period.

Table 5.16 shows which households were in the worst tenth of dwellings in 1986 and 1991 analysed by income and tenure. Overall, there was some improvement in the relative housing conditions of the poorest group, driven by improvements for the poorest owners and council tenants, although over 40 per cent of private tenants in the poorest income group were in the worst tenth of dwellings, a higher proportion than in 1986. Relative conditions also deteriorated for poor housing association tenants. The relative improvement for the poorest income group overall continues a finding from the 1986 survey, which also found the greatest relative improvements in conditions (on different definitions) for the poorest income group (DoE 1988: table A9.5). On these figures, not only were conditions improving over the 1980s, but they were also doing so most rapidly for those on the lowest incomes. This contrasts with findings from the General Household Survey discussed below.

On a different dimension of inequality, race, narrowing of differentials is less evident from the English House Condition Surveys. The proportion of households where the head was born outside Europe who were in unfit dwellings was twice that for heads born in the UK in both 1976 and 1986 (DoE 1983: table D.2.7, 1988: table 6.2). Similarly, in 1991 7.2 per cent of white heads of household were in unfit dwellings, but 9.9 per cent of Asian and 14.9 per cent of black heads (Leather and Morrison 1997: table A5.9). The proportions who were in dwellings in 'poor repair' in 1986 were 20.3 per cent for those with the head born outside Europe, against 12.5 per cent for those with the head born in the UK, a higher disparity than

Table 5.16. HOUSEHOLDS IN WORST TENTH OF DWELLINGS IN ENGLAND BY INCOME GROUP AND TENURE, 1986 AND 1991

Income group	Owner-occupiers	Local authority	Housing association	Private rented	All
1986					
Lowest	16.9	11.0	7.2	38.7	16.8
Second	10.2	9.6	15.4	27.9	11.6
Third	5.3	4.5	n/a	21.8	6.1
Highest	2.9	11.3	n/a	35.3	4.8
All[a]	7.2	9.4	8.2	32.5	10.0
1991					
Lowest	11.3	9.1	12.0	43.7	14.4
Second	9.3	8.4	9.3	28.9	11.0
Third	7.3	7.3	5.9	19.0	8.3
Highest	4.6	2.0	5.6	28.0	5.7
All[a]	7.4	8.4	10.2	31.5	10.0

[a] Figures are for households with income information and so totals differ from those in Table 5A.5.

Source: DoE (1993: tables 11.24, 11.25, 11.26, and 11.27).

for the 1976 survey's category of 'in need of rehabilitation'. In the 1991 survey 19.0 per cent of white heads, but 28.5 per cent of black and 32.2 per cent of Asian heads, were in dwellings requiring repairs of £1,000 or more. Asian households are also far more likely to be over-crowded relative to the official bedroom standard than others—nearly a quarter of them being over the standard, compared to 2 per cent of white and 10 per cent of black households (DoE 1993: table A4.10).

The quality of the stock: General Household Survey results

Further indications of whether people do have a 'decent' home can be derived from the General Household Survey (GHS) and are shown in Tables 5.17–19. Table 5.17 shows what proportion of individuals (adults and children) do not have sole use of an inside WC and of a bath, Table 5.18 what proportion live in households where there are one or more people per room, and Table 5.19 the proportion living without central heating. The latter category illustrates a general problem with looking at subjective concepts like a 'decent home' over time. In 1974 most individuals lived in dwellings without central heating. By 1994 only 14 per cent lacked it, making it a more plausible indicator of low housing quality than it was twenty years ago.

The tables give breakdowns by five classifications—tenure, socio-economic group, age, income, and birthplace of household head. It should be borne in mind that the GHS only covers those living in private households—excluding those in institutions or literally roofless.

Lack of amenities Table 5.17 broadly confirms the House Condition Survey results, given that these results refer to dwellings, many of which are vacant if unsatisfactory, and to a slightly wider range of amenities. Between 1974 and 1990 (the series was discontinued after this) the proportion of individuals without sole use of a bath or an inside WC fell from 11 per cent to 1.1 per cent. The proportionate decline in percentages affected was roughly uniform across tenures, although 9 per cent of those in 'other' tenures (mainly private rented) still lacked sole use of amenities in 1990. Looked at by socio-economic group (for adults only), differentials decreased slightly in magnitude. Interestingly, the same was not true by income group, where four times the proportion of the bottom income group lacked amenities as in the top group in 1985 and 1990, a larger ratio than in 1974 or 1979 (although the absolute improvement for the bottom group was much larger). Looking at birthplace, adults born outside Europe and North America were much more likely to lack amenities than the average in all four years. The proportionate differential between those born outside the UK and the average stayed much the same (implying once more a more rapid absolute improvement for the disadvantaged group).

Density of occupation Table 5.18 shows how many people lived at a density of one or more persons per room (including kitchens but excluding bathrooms and lavatories). This measure

Table 5.17. MISSING AMENITIES (EITHER WITHOUT SOLE USE OF INSIDE WC OR WITHOUT SOLE USE OF BATH), GREAT BRITAIN (% OF INDIVIDUALS)[a]

By tenure

	Owner with mortgage	Outright owner	Local authority	Housing association	Other	All (including missing categories)
1974	3.4	13.5	6.4	10.0	36.0	11.0
1979	1.3	6.4	3.7	8.8	24.8	5.5
1985	0.7	2.7	1.1	2.2	10.7	2.0
1990	0.3	1.0	0.6	1.6	8.8	1.1

By socio-economic group (adults only)

	I	II	III	IV	V	VI
1974	5.1	5.6	9.0	12.7	15.8	19.1
1979	3.7	2.9	4.1	7.1	8.2	10.1
1985	1.8	0.8	1.8	2.0	3.1	2.8
1990	0.7	0.5	1.0	1.5	1.6	1.7

By age

	Under 16	16–64	65 and over
1974	8.5	10.4	18.3
1979	3.2	5.1	10.9
1985	1.2	1.8	3.7
1990	0.4	1.2	1.8

By income quintile group

	Bottom	2	3	4	Top
1974	18.2	13.4	8.5	8.0	7.3
1979	7.8	7.9	3.8	3.3	4.1
1985	4.0	2.8	1.5	1.0	1.0
1990	2.1	1.1	1.0	0.9	0.5

By birthplace (adults only)

	UK	Europe or North America	Elsewhere	All
1974	11.4	16.9	23.4	11.9
1979	6.0	8.5	10.7	6.2
1985	2.0	4.8	3.6	2.2
1990	1.3	1.2	2.8	1.3

[a] Series discontinued after 1990 as proportions were so low.

Source: Author's calculations from GHS raw data files.

has no statutory force, but is a convenient, if crude, measure of the living conditions of different groups which is available for all five years. It does not allow for any difference in needs per person between, say, a single adult and a couple with children.

Most of these figures for the proportions of individuals living in crowded conditions are necessarily higher than the corresponding figures for the proportions of households affected. The number of individuals affected seems in many ways a preferable measure of the problem. However, results by socio-economic group and birthplace are only available for all five years for adults. Because households with children are much more likely to be crowded, a smaller proportion of adults than of all individuals are affected in each year. The effects of this can be gauged from the results for all individuals shown in parentheses for 1994.

Over the period 1974 to 1990, the proportion of individuals affected fell in each tenure, and by 45 per cent overall. The greatest improvements were for tenants, who had started with the worst conditions. However, between 1990 and 1994 the proportion of individuals in crowded conditions increased for all categories except mortgagors. More of each of the tenant groups were crowded in 1995 than had been in 1985. Again, while the class gradient changed little between 1974 and 1994, the ratio between those affected in the bottom and top income quintiles increased sharply after 1979. Despite its poor starting position, the proportion of the bottom quintile group who were crowded rose between 1979 and 1994 (from 24.7 to 25.7 per cent) while it fell for individuals as a whole (from 17.3 per cent to 13.2 per cent). As one would expect, those over 65 lived in much less crowded conditions, while children were much more likely to live at high densities. High densities affected those born outside Europe and North America quite disproportionately, with the proportionate disadvantage increasing (but with a larger absolute improvement).

Central heating Table 5.19 shows that the proportions of individuals without central heating fell by three-quarters between 1974 and 1994. The decline was proportionately somewhat slower for council and private tenants, the two lowest socio-economic groups, and the two lowest income groups. All categories improved substantially in absolute terms. By contrast with the two other indicators of housing quality, birthplace made little difference to the presence of central heating in 1974, and the position of those born outside Europe and North America actually improved more rapidly than the average after 1979.

Housing conditions overall Putting the results of the three tables together, overall housing conditions improved greatly over the period, apart from the increase in crowding between 1990 and 1994. By and large this improvement affected all groups in proportion to the scale of their original problems, so that absolute differentials between the percentage of each group affected in each group declined, but proportionate differentials remained roughly the same. The main exception to this pattern is the experience of the poorest income quintile after 1979, where crowding increased in contrast to the overall improvement, and missing amenities in 1990 and lack of central heating in 1994 were twice and 1.6 times the average

Table 5.18. CROWDED CONDITIONS (1.0 OR MORE PERSONS PER ROOM), GREAT BRITAIN (% OF INDIVIDUALS)

By tenure

	Owner with mortgage	Outright owner	Local authority	Housing association	Other	All (including missing categories)
1974	16.6	7.4	35.1	33.2	23.4	22.2
1979	13.2	6.2	27.1	29.5	15.4	17.3
1985	10.7	5.2	24.0	20.1	10.0	13.3
1990	11.4	2.6	22.1	18.0	9.4	12.4
1994	11.3	3.6	25.2	22.4	15.7	13.2

By socio-economic group (adults only)

	I	II	III	IV	V	VI
1974	5.6	8.6	12.4	18.8	19.0	18.1
1979	3.6	6.5	9.1	15.0	15.7	14.8
1985	3.9	4.6	6.9	11.3	12.3	12.4
1990	3.8	3.2	6.3	10.4	10.7	10.9
1994	3.6	4.7	6.4	10.8	11.4	10.8
(1994[a]	5.6	9.0	8.1	19.2	16.9	16.5)

By age

	Under 16	16–64	65 and over
1974	40.8	18.6	2.2
1979	32.0	15.2	1.1
1985	26.8	11.3	1.1
1990	26.1	10.1	1.1
1994	27.9	10.8	1.1

By income quintile group

	Bottom	2	3	4	Top
1974	30.2	34.8	26.0	15.3	5.2
1979	24.7	22.3	25.5	14.2	4.4
1985	22.3	16.0	15.3	7.8	2.4
1990	20.4	17.7	16.7	5.2	1.7
1994	25.7	16.6	14.5	6.7	2.3

By birthplace (adults only)

	UK	Europe or North America	Elsewhere	All
1974	14.5	26.4	34.3	15.3
1979	11.9	15.5	28.3	12.6
1985	8.8	11.9	22.5	9.4
1990	7.8	5.9	22.4	8.3
1994	8.1	8.9	21.4	8.8
(1994[b]	12.8	11.0	22.5	13.2)

[a] All individuals; children given social class of head of household.
[b] All individuals, including children.

Source: Author's calculations from GHS raw data files.

Table 5.19. ABSENCE OF CENTRAL HEATING (INCLUDING NIGHT STORAGE), GREAT BRITAIN (% OF INDIVIDUALS)

By tenure

	Owner with mortgage	Outright owner	Local authority	Housing association	Other	All (including missing categories)
1974	32.2	52.1	66.2	62.4	79.1	54.5
1979	23.3	41.0	54.0	45.4	71.1	42.1
1985	14.8	26.0	42.3	40.0	52.2	27.6
1990	10.8	18.2	29.3	20.9	36.7	18.5
1994	8.6	14.0	20.4	15.0	26.4	13.6

By socio-economic group (adults only)

	I	II	III	IV	V	VI
1974	26.5	36.0	47.5	62.8	67.2	72.8
1979	17.9	26.6	33.9	49.7	54.8	60.3
1985	11.9	16.7	23.2	33.2	37.2	41.6
1990	6.3	10.4	14.8	22.4	25.9	27.7
1994	6.0	8.0	11.0	16.5	19.0	22.5

By age

	Under 16	16–64	65 and over
1974	49.4	54.2	65.2
1979	37.0	41.2	54.5
1985	23.5	27.0	36.3
1990	17.6	17.3	24.2
1994	12.7	12.8	18.1

By income quintile group

	Bottom	2	3	4	Top
1974	69.5	63.3	56.1	46.7	38.5
1979	49.9	51.3	43.6	36.2	27.8
1985	44.5	36.7	26.9	19.7	14.0
1990	28.9	27.2	16.9	12.0	7.3
1994	21.6	19.8	12.6	9.0	4.9

By birthplace of household head (adults only)

	UK	Europe or North America	Elsewhere	All
1974	56.2	55.3	59.3	56.3
1979	43.6	40.1	48.0	43.7
1985	28.9	31.8	23.9	28.8
1990	20.5	19.6	16.8	20.4
1994	14.0	11.2	13.3	13.9

Source: Author's calculations from GHS raw data files.

respectively, a much greater disproportion than in 1979. The position of the poorest group relative to the population as a whole worsened in all three respects. This contrasts with the picture in Table 5.16, which showed a fall in the proportion of the lowest of the four income groups living in the tenth of properties in worst repair.

The standard of service received by tenants

So far this section has concentrated on physical standards of housing. For most of the post-war period housing policy showed a similar bias. But for tenants, housing has another dimension—the repair and management service which they receive in return for their rent. As statistics and surveys tend to follow policy concerns, there is a lack of statistics on trends in standards of landlord services. This illustrates a general danger in using the statistics thrown up by the operation of policy to judge that policy—if an area has been neglected, it may be hard to gauge the extent of its problems. There have, however, been some recent surveys which have collected information about repair services and tenant satisfaction with them, although they do not allow an assessment of trends over time:

1. Asked whether they agreed with the general statement that 'councils give a poor standard of repairs and maintenance', 70 per cent of local authority tenants responding to the British Social Attitudes Survey in 1983 agreed, and much the same, 68 per cent, in 1985 (Jowell *et al.* 1986).
2. The 1986 English House Condition Survey found that 52 per cent of local authority tenants who had requested that repairs should be done had experienced at least some difficulty in getting them done, compared with only 16 per cent of housing association tenants and of private tenants (DoE 1988: table A7.10).
3. The University of Glasgow's Centre for Housing Research found that a third of local authority tenants sampled and 20 per cent of housing association tenants rated the service they received as unsatisfactory (CHR 1989: table 7.3; the kinds of areas covered by the two kinds of organization in the survey were not equivalent, so that the results are not truly comparable). 27 per cent of the local authority tenants in the sample said that they received poor value for the money they paid in rent, compared with 13 per cent of the housing association tenants.
4. The 1994/5 *Survey of English Housing* found that 28 per cent of local authority tenants were dissatisfied with their landlord's repairs and maintenance service, 17 per cent of them being 'very dissatisfied'. 19 per cent of private tenants and 17 per cent of housing association tenants were dissatisfied (Green *et al.* 1996: table A7.3).

Overall satisfaction with housing

All of the features discussed above feed into general feelings of satisfaction. A measure of whether people have a 'decent' home is whether they themselves are happy with it. The

Table 5.20. DISSATISFACTION WITH ACCOMMODATION, BY TENURE (% OF HOUSE-HOLDS DISSATISFIED)[a]

Coverage	Date of survey	All	Owner-occupiers	Local authority tenants	Housing association tenants	Other
England (NDHS)	1977	9	4	14	11	15
GB (GHS)	1978	11	6	16	17	17
GB (BSAS)	1983	9	4	19	21	
GB (BSAS)	1985	9	n/a	17	n/a	14
England (EHCS)	1991	5	3	11	7	13
England (SEH)	1994/5	7	4	14	10	12

[a] Options vary between surveys. Percentages include any expression of dissatisfaction.

Sources: DoE (1978); OPCS (1980); Jowell and Airey (1984); Jowell *et al.* (1986); DoE (1993); Green *et al.* (1996).

results of surveys which have explored this are shown in Table 5.20. This gives the proportions of household heads expressing some dissatisfaction with their accommodation. The phrasing of the question asked varied between surveys, so that they are not completely comparable.

The first feature to note is the low level of overall dissatisfaction, no more than one household in nine in any survey (and only one in twenty in the 1991 English House Condition Survey). Second, while there was no clear difference between the results of the surveys in the 1970s and 1980s, the two surveys in the 1990s do seem to show less dissatisfaction overall, although geographical coverage and questions asked varied, making it hard to be certain of trends. Housing standards may have improved in various ways as described above, but so have people's expectations. Consistently, council tenants express more dissatisfaction than other tenants, and tenants much more than owners. Much of the overall fall in dissatisfaction can be explained by the growing rate of owner-occupation. For instance, the 1977 and 1994/5 surveys, both in England, show dissatisfaction rates unchanged over the 17 years within both owner-occupied and council tenures, but a drop in dissatisfaction overall reflecting the composition change.

Tenure is not the only important variable, however. Satisfaction also depends on the type of house, with those living in flats expressing more dissatisfaction than those in houses. In the 1994/5 survey, 13 per cent of those living in purpose-built blocks of flats expressed dissatisfaction, compared to only 7 per cent for all households (Green *et al.* 1996: fig. 2.11). Specifically on maintenance of communal areas of purpose-built flats, 21 per cent of owners living in them expressed dissatisfaction, as well as 33 per cent of those in council blocks (ibid. table

2.25) Given that 35 per cent of the local authority stock, but only 6 per cent of the owner-occupied stock, consists of flats, this composition effect explains part of the differential in dissatisfaction between the two tenures shown in Table 5.20. However, analysis of the 1978 GHS suggested that controlling for dwelling type would reduce the differential in dissatisfaction between council and owner-occupied tenures, but only from 2.7 to 1 to 2.3 to 1 (Hills and Mullings 1990).

The various surveys also reveal clear differences in satisfaction by age and by ethnic group. In the case of the former, 20 per cent of household heads aged under 25 responding to the 1978 GHS expressed dissatisfaction, compared with only 8 per cent of those over 60. Similarly, in the 1994/5 survey, 12 per cent of household heads aged 16–29 were dissatisfied, but only 4 per cent of 65 or over (Green *et al*. 1996: table A2.21).

Meanwhile, in 1977, 17 per cent of those describing themselves as non-white expressed dissatisfaction, compared with 8 per cent of those describing themselves as white (DoE 1978: table 8). In 1991, non-white households were more dissatisfied with the state of repair of their dwelling than white households even where they were living in what was physically the best stock: 15 per cent compared to 5 per cent dissatisfied (DoE 1993: table 12.11). Within the worst stock 42 per cent of non-white and 36 per cent of white households were dissatisfied. Given that non-white households were 40 per cent more likely to be in the worst stock, overall dissatisfaction for non-white households must be much greater, although figures for this are not given in the survey.

Satisfaction with area and environment

Another, wider feature of whether people have a 'decent home' is the state of the area in which it is located. The physical standard and amenities of a council flat may be very good in themselves, but vandalism, graffiti, and litter may mean that its environment is squalid, although poor condition and poor environment can go together. In 1991 one-fifth of the dwellings in the worst condition were also in 'poor environments', and vice versa (DoE 1993: fig. 9.11).

Table 5.21 gives the results from the surveys that asked separately about dissatisfaction with area (in the 1978 GHS, the environment was a subsidiary reason for overall dissatisfaction with accommodation, which may contribute to the higher rate in this survey shown in Table 5.20). In all three cases more people are dissatisfied with the area in which they live than with their accommodation. Again, it is hard to discern a clear trend. While satisfaction with accommodation has grown overall, if anything more people were dissatisfied with their area in 1994/5 than in 1977, with an increase within each tenure (except for private tenants). In this case the clearest change is for housing association tenants, who are now expressing much more dissatisfaction with area than their (smaller number of) predecessors in 1977, and more than council tenants.

Hope and Hough (1988) showed a link between satisfaction with people's area and the risk

Table 5.21. DISSATISFACTION WITH AREA, BY TENURE (% OF HOUSEHOLDS DIS-SATISFIED)[a]

Coverage	Date of survey	All	Owner-occupiers	Local authority tenants	Housing association tenants	Other
England (NDHS)	1977	11	9	15	14	12
England (EHCS)	1991					
Neighbourhood		4	3	7	6	4
Immediate environment		7	4	13	9	10
England (SEH)	1994/5	13	10	17	21	12

[a] Any expression of dissatisfaction.

Sources: DoE (1978, 1993); Green *et al.* (1996).

of crimes like burglary and theft and 'incivilities' like drunks on the street, litter lying around, or teenagers hanging about. Using data from the 1984 British Crime Survey, they showed that a greater proportion of people living in 'low-risk' crime areas were 'very satisfied' with their area (46 per cent) than the national average, while those in medium- or high-risk areas were less likely to be very satisfied, the proportion falling to 24 per cent for 'multi-racial areas' and the 'poorest council estates'. In 1994/5, three-quarters of households said that crime was a problem in their area, 22 per cent saying it was a serious one (Green *et al.* 1996: fig. 3.10). Twenty-nine per cent of social tenants, and 35 per cent of those living in 'deprived areas' or in 'council estates or other low-income areas', thought crime was a serious problem in their area.

Summary

In many ways, the picture presented in this section has been one of success, with an increasing stock of dwellings, fewer of which are unfit or lack amenities and with a lower density of occupation. During the 1970s, the proportion of dwellings in serious disrepair increased, but repair standards improved between 1986 and 1991. Overall satisfaction levels appear to have improved between the 1970s and 1990s, suggesting that the improvement in standards at least matched expectations raised by higher incomes. By and large the improvement has benefited all classifications of the population. In these respects, and to the extent that policy has been responsible for the improvements, housing policy must be regarded as a success. The tenure shifts since 1973 (and particularly since 1979) also mean that the policy aim of promoting owner-occupation has been substantially achieved. As Whitehead says, it is easy to forget how much improvement there has been in housing conditions since the Second World War and equally how rapidly our housing aspirations have expanded to include many other attributes in addition to adequate shelter. (Whitehead 1997: 7)

Nonetheless, there are clearly problems. The stock is larger in relation to the number of households than it was in the 1970s, but the improvement seems to have gone into reverse by the 1990s. While the number of social housing lettings to new entrants has risen, many people still have problems in gaining access to housing, as witnessed by the statistics for homelessness acceptances and the numbers in unsatisfactory temporary accommodation, not to mention the numbers sleeping rough (although these problems seem to have peaked around 1990).

Not all groups have gained proportionately from improving conditions. In particular, it appears from the GHS that the housing conditions of those in the poorest fifth of the population fell behind the rest in various respects between 1979 and 1994, and crowding has actually increased. However, English House Condition Survey findings suggest that as far as repair standards are concerned, the poorest groups may have caught up somewhat between 1981 and 1991.

Perhaps most importantly, alongside physical improvements there has been a striking increase in social and economic polarization between tenures. As much social housing is located in particular areas and estates, this leads to geographical polarization. Dissatisfaction with one's area and environment has increased since the 1970s.

V. Outcomes: within the reach of every family?

Gross housing costs: Owner-occupiers

The most straightforward indicator of the cost of housing is the price at which owner-occupied houses are bought and sold. Real house prices and their ratio to average earnings (mean earnings of full-time men on adult rates) since 1974, taking the values in that year as 100, are shown in Fig. 5.5. The house price index used is for all dwellings on which building society advances have been completed, adjusted for changes in the mix of dwellings sold each year (DoE 1997a: table 10.8 and earlier equivalents). Table 5A.6 also shows these indicators each year since 1980.

For those buying houses, the price of the house they buy is only part of what determines monthly mortgage payments. These also depend on the proportion of the cost covered by the mortgage, the number of years over which repayment is made, and the interest rate (net of tax relief). Fig. 5.6 gives an impression of how these factors interacted, showing estimates of the mortgage outgoings of first-time buyers given their average borrowing each year, the interest rates applying at the end of each year, and basic rate tax relief (allowing for restrictions to the first £30,000 and in rates of relief in later years). The pattern differs in several ways

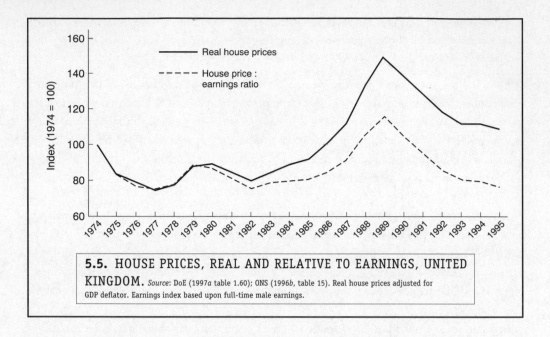

5.5. HOUSE PRICES, REAL AND RELATIVE TO EARNINGS, UNITED KINGDOM. *Source*: DoE (1997a table 1.60); ONS (1996b, table 15). Real house prices adjusted for GDP deflator. Earnings index based upon full-time male earnings.

from that shown in Fig. 5.5. In particular, it shows the effects of the coincidence of very high interest rates—15 per cent before tax relief at the ends of both 1979 and 1990—with the peaks in prices. It also reflects the effect of the extent to which owner-occupation has gone 'down-market': in 1974, the average income of first-time buyers (as reported to building societies and including that of a partner) was 30 per cent higher than average male earnings; by 1995 new mortgagors' average income was 5 per cent below average earnings. All of this compounded the strain on first-time buyers. At the 1990 peak, net payments took 28 per cent of their incomes. The results of this are discussed below.

Gross housing costs: Tenants

Fig. 5.7 shows trends in various rent indices in relation to average earnings. In comparing this with the costs of first-time buyers it should be remembered that, as a result of inflation, housing outgoings fall over time for most owner-occupiers (and they acquire an asset), but they do not for tenants. For local authority tenants the main feature of the graph is the substantial jump in rents relative to average earnings between 1980 and 1982, followed by a decline until 1988 as rents only rose in line with prices rather than earnings. After that, subsidy withdrawal under the new financial regime meant that rents had almost reached 10 per cent of average earnings by 1995.

By contrast, the fair rents set for housing association dwellings followed a much more stable path in relation to earnings from 1976 to 1990 (before which comparatively few rents were registered). Under the new grants system, fair rents for pre-1989 tenants have increased

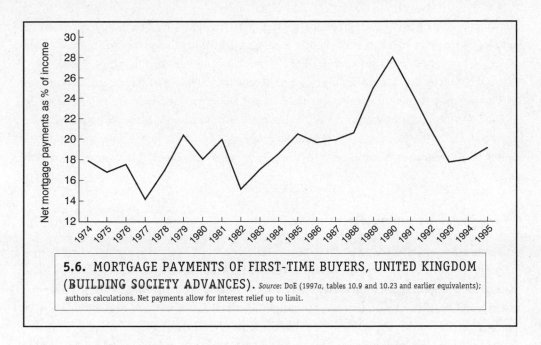

5.6. MORGAGE PAYMENTS OF FIRST-TIME BUYERS, UNITED KINGDOM (BUILDING SOCIETY ADVANCES). *Source*: DoE (1997a, tables 10.9 and 10.23 and earlier equivalents); authors calculations. Net payments allow for interest relief up to limit.

to over 11 per cent of average earnings, while the 'assured' rents for newer tenants were over 12 per cent of them.

Fair rents for private tenants with controlled tenancies followed a similar course to those for association tenants, but data are not available to show long-term trends in private market rents. The figure shows the average level set since 1989 by rent officers as representing private market rents for the purposes of calculating limits on Housing Benefit. This is not only higher than social rents, but has also risen rapidly to the equivalent of 17 per cent of average

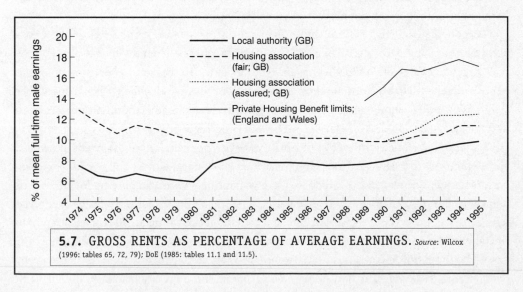

5.7. GROSS RENTS AS PERCENTAGE OF AVERAGE EARNINGS. *Source*: Wilcox (1996: tables 65, 72, 79); DoE (1985: tables 11.1 and 11.5).

earnings in 1995, almost as high as the mortgage payments of first-time buyers. As far as actual private rents are concerned, figures for England in 1995/6 show an average of £70 per week (19 per cent of average earnings). For uncontrolled rents alone, the average was £66 for assured tenancies and £91 for assured shorthold tenancies (DoE 1997a: fig. 11b).

The trends in relation to average earnings do not, of course, necessarily give a good guide to the relationship between rents and the incomes of those paying them, particularly in the period since 1979, when the dispersion of earnings has been widening. Tables 5.22 and 5.23 below show trends in payments after Housing Benefit in relation to net incomes within each tenure.

Housing Benefit

The net amount which households—particularly tenants—have to pay for their housing depends not only on their gross costs, but also on Housing Benefit. As discussed above, the cost of Housing Benefit has increased rapidly since 1980. This has primarily been a result of rising rents, combined with increased unemployment and a larger pensioner population. It has not been because the benefit system has become inherently more generous.

Before April 1988, the amount of benefit to which those not receiving Supplementary Benefit (now Income Support) were entitled hinged on the level of their incomes in relation to a 'needs allowance' for a family of each particular type. If income equalled the needs allowance, a rent rebate (for council tenants) or rent allowance (for private tenants) would be given, equalling 60 per cent of the gross rent. For those with lower incomes, this would be increased by an amount equal to the 'taper'—the means-test 'tax rate' on higher income—multiplied by the shortfall of gross income from the allowance. For those with incomes above the needs allowance, the rebate or allowance would equal 60 per cent of rent less a different taper multiplied by the excess.

The generosity of this system thus depended on two features, the level of the needs allowances and the steepness of the tapers (or marginal rates of benefit withdrawal as income rose). The real value of the needs allowances stayed at much the same level from 1977/8 to 1987/8. In relation to earnings the allowances therefore became steadily less generous. Other things being equal, someone whose income and gross rent remained constant in relation to average earnings would have seen a fall in benefit over the period.

The tapers remained constant until April 1983 at 25 per cent below the needs allowance and 17 per cent above it (as far as the rent element was concerned). At that point the system was reformed, one element of which was to give pensioners with incomes below the needs allowance a more generous taper of 50 per cent (so that benefit increased faster as income fell). This was, however, at the cost of benefit recipients above the needs allowance, for whom the taper was increased to 21 per cent, so that benefit was withdrawn more rapidly as income rose. The taper was increased repeatedly in later years until it had reached 33 per cent by April 1987.

After this the whole system was changed. The 1982/3 reforms had shifted the administration of benefit for the housing costs of Supplementary Benefit recipients from the DHSS to the local authorities. This group was entitled to benefit in respect of 100 per cent of rent and continued to receive 'certificated' benefit at this level after the change. Before 1982/3 rebates and Supplementary Benefit did not mesh together well. This led to what was known as the 'better-off problem', under which claimants like pensioners who could claim either rebates or Supplementary Benefit often chose the wrong one. After 1982/3, exacerbated by rising real rents, the same problem re-emerged in the form of an administrative horror known as Housing Benefit Supplement, a top-up payment needed to stop some Housing Benefit recipients falling below the minimum income which Supplementary Benefit was supposed to guarantee.

Part of the April 1988 reform was to change the Housing Benefit formula so that it meshed with the renamed Income Support system, payments being equal to 100 per cent of rent, less a new taper multiplied by the excess of a claimant's income over their Income Support rate. The new taper was based on net income (after allowing for tax, National Insurance Contributions, and any other benefits received). The taper was raised again to 65 per cent of net income in respect of the rent element of Housing Benefit.

The full effects of these changes between April 1982 and April 1995 are illustrated in Figs. 5.8 and 5.9. These compare the help given in respect of rent through the system as it was in April 1996 with the April 1982 system (on the assumption that the needs allowances in the earlier system would have been uprated in line with earnings growth, that is by about 147 per cent, which would have maintained generosity for someone whose earnings stayed constant relative to the average).

Fig. 5.8 shows how large a rebate would be received by a single person aged 25 or over towards a rent of £40 per week under the two systems. At the bottom, for this rent level, the 1982 system would have given 100 per cent assistance up to a somewhat higher earnings level than did the 1995 system. Thereafter, the tapers in the post-1988 system are much steeper than those which applied in 1982, and benefit runs out much more rapidly. In 1995, benefit would be lost altogether at *half* the 1982 level in relation to average earnings. The picture would look somewhat different in respect of the levels of help given for different rents or different household types, but the overall direction of change would be the same.

One of the consequences of this shift can be seen in Fig. 5.9. This shows the proportion which net rent (after Housing Benefit) would represent of net income (after tax and other benefits) at each income under the two systems. This ratio is sometimes used as a measure of the 'affordability' of rents after allowing for rebates, particularly in the debate over housing association rents. The difference between the two systems is dramatic. Under the uprated 1982 system, those with a gross rent of £40 per week would have been protected from paying much more than 20 per cent of their net income in rent after allowing for benefit; under the 1995 system, the ratio could exceed 35 per cent.

In effect, what has happened since 1982 is the following. Before then, a system of rebates

173

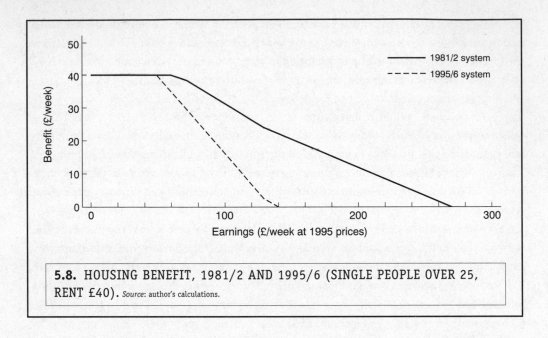

5.8. HOUSING BENEFIT, 1981/2 AND 1995/6 (SINGLE PEOPLE OVER 25, RENT £40). *Source*: author's calculations.

gave significant help to those whose incomes were some way above Supplementary Benefit. Now the Housing Benefit system does little more than ensure that no one's income falls below the total of their Income Support rate and their housing costs. The combined taper for rent and Council Tax—85 per cent on net income—is only marginally more generous than the 100 per cent taper which was embodied in the 'housing only' payments under the Sup-

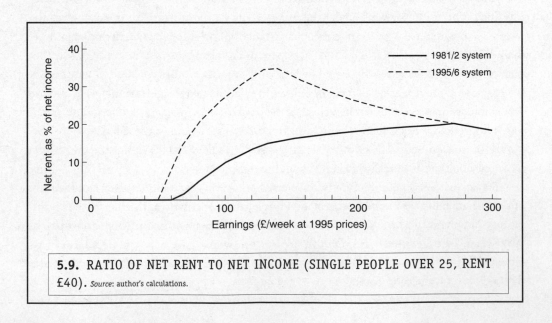

5.9. RATIO OF NET RENT TO NET INCOME (SINGLE PEOPLE OVER 25, RENT £40). *Source*: author's calculations.

plementary Benefit system until 1982. The old problem of which benefit would leave those with incomes just above their Supplementary Benefit scale rate 'better off' (see Donnison 1982: 184–93) has been solved—through the effective abolition of the old rent rebate system.

Net housing costs in relation to income

It is, of course, the level of net housing costs after allowing for benefits which is most important in determining whether people have found housing 'at a price within their means'. Unfortunately, the treatment of the housing costs of those on Supplementary Benefit before the 1982/3 reforms to Housing Benefit makes long-term comparisons difficult. Consistent figures are available since 1987, and Tables 5.22 and 5.23 compare net housing costs as a percentage of net incomes drawn from the 1987 and 1994/5 Family Expenditure Surveys. The costs included in the tables are rents net of Housing Benefit for tenants, and mortgage payments after interest relief for mortgagors.

In terms of overall averages, mortgagors were paying 14 per cent of net incomes in mortgage payments in 1987. After the traumatic rise and fall in costs around 1990 (see Table 5A.6), the proportion was down to 13 per cent in 1994/5 (having been as high as 19 per cent in 1990). By contrast, net rents for local authority and private tenants have risen as a share of net incomes despite the rising cost of Housing Benefit. For private tenants the averages are now significantly higher than that for mortgagors, and for council tenants the differential is much smaller than before, despite the fact that mortgagors are acquiring an asset.

As Table 5.22 shows, these ratios vary greatly within each tenure. Thanks to full Housing Benefit for the poorest tenants, 66 per cent of council tenants paid less than a tenth of their incomes in rent in 1987, and 60 per cent of them still did so in 1994/5. However, 15 per cent of council tenants, 19 per cent of association tenants, and more than 36 per cent of private tenants paid over a fifth of their incomes in net rents in 1994/5, all higher percentages than in 1987. By contrast a lower proportion, 20 per cent, of mortgagors paid out more than a fifth of net income in 1994/5 than in 1987 (although this proportion had reached 43 per cent in 1990).

As Table 5.23 shows, net housing costs generally fall with income for mortgagors, from over 40 per cent for the poorest ones to 10 per cent for the richest. For council tenants the proportion is at its highest, 13 per cent, for those with incomes in the middle of the ranges shown (although few tenants have incomes in the upper ranges).

Whether the percentages of income absorbed by housing costs in 1994/5 are still within 'people's means' or their 'reach' is a subjective judgement. What is clear is that costs are substantially higher in relation to incomes for tenants now than in 1979, both in terms of gross rents (Fig. 5.7) and net rents (Table 5.23).

For owner-occupiers, costs have followed an erratic course (Figs. 5.5 and 5.6). As costs rose in the 1980s an increasing number of mortgagors were pushed to the point where, for one reason or another, they ceased to be able to pay their mortgages. Table 5A.6 shows that the

John Hills

Table 5.22. RATIO OF NET HOUSING PAYMENTS TO DISPOSABLE INCOME BY TENURE, GREAT BRITAIN, 1987 AND 1994/5

Net payments as % of disposable income	% of tenure group in range				
	Mortgagors[a]	Tenants			
		Local authority	Housing association	Private unfurnished	Private furnished
1987					
Under 5	11	43	24	34	19
5–10	21	23	18	19	16
10–15	24	17	21	16	14
15–20	17	9	11	10	12
20–25	12	4	6	5	8
25 and over	15	3	20	16	32
Mean as % of income	14	8	12	10	18
1994/5					
Under 5	12	46	51	25	16
5–10	27	14	10	14	5
10–15	24	14	13	15	11
15–20	17	10	7	10	12
20–25	9	7	9	13	14
25 and over	11	8	10	23	41
Mean as % of income	13	10	11	16	25

[a] MIRAS recipients only in 1987.

Source: DoE (1997a: tables 12.9 and 12.10, and earlier equivalents).

number of mortgagors six months or more in arrears rose from 16,000 in 1980 to over 350,000 in 1992. Repossessions rose from 3,500 in 1980 to 75,000 in 1991. By 1991 12 per cent of all households accepted by local authorities as homeless, about 12,000, were in that position because of mortgage arrears (Wilcox 1996: table 86). While these numbers are not very large compared with the total number of mortgagors, the numbers in difficulty rose very rapidly between 1980 and the early 1990s. Cumulatively, 345,000 mortgagors were repossessed between 1990 and 1996, more than 3 per cent of all mortgagors. The numbers also represent only the tip of an iceberg of more general difficulties. As Table 5A.6 shows, by 1992 nearly 1.8 million mortgagors were in 'negative equity', with houses worth less than their outstanding mortgages. However, what can also be seen from the table is that the scale of the most severe problems had receded substantially by 1995 as real house prices and interest rates

Table 5.23. RATIO OF NET HOUSING PAYMENTS TO DISPOSABLE INCOME BY INCOME, GREAT BRITAIN, 1987 AND 1994/5

Range of disposable household income (£000/year)	Mortgagors: net mortgage payments as % of disposable income[a]	Local authority tenants: net rent as % of disposable income
1987		
Under 3	} 47	6
3–4		7
4–6	25	10
6–8	23	11
8–10	18	9
10–12	16	7
12–15	14	7
15–20	12	} 5
20 and over	10	
All incomes	14	8
1994/5		
Under 4	} 42	7
4–6		9
6–8	20	10
8–10	20	12
10–12	18	13
12–15	16	12
15–20	14	
20–25	12	} 8
25 and over	10	
All incomes	13	10

[a] MIRAS recipients only in 1987.

Source: DoE (1997a: tables 12.9 and 12.10; and earlier equivalents).

fell (and as the economy recovered from recession). Arrears, repossessions, and negative equity were all down by more than a third from their peak levels.

The balance between tenures: the economic cost of housing

One of the equity aims sometimes stated for housing policy is that of 'neutrality' between tenures. The costs of housing to owner-occupiers and tenants should in some way be equivalent. As discussed above, the cash outgoings of mortgagors and tenants are very different but comparing them requires some allowance for the asset purchase or saving aspect of owner-occupiers' costs. One way of approaching the problem is to observe that owner-occupiers pay for the management and maintenance of their own dwellings in full and also face the full effects of any depreciation of their property or the cost of remedying it (apart from some repair grants). If these elements are also deducted from the rents paid by tenants, what remains—in effect, the charge they have to pay for the capital tied up in the dwellings they occupy—can be compared with the 'capital cost of housing services' to owner-occupiers. Some calculations on this basis for council tenants are presented in detail in Hills (1991: table 13.1). This suggests that gross rents (including rebates) generated a gross rate of return on the capital value of the local authority stock in Great Britain in 1979/80 of only 2.5 per cent. By 1987/8 it had reached 3.2 per cent. The rent increases in relation to earnings described above would have raised this to about 4.2 per cent in 1995/6. Deducting management and maintenance costs gives a net return on capital of only 0.7 per cent in 1979/80, rising to 1.2 per cent in 1987/8 and about 1.9 per cent in 1995/6.

Making further adjustments for depreciation and the effects of capital gains (or anticipated real rent increases) gives a net yield to local authority landlords which rose from *minus* 0.4 per cent in 1979/80 to 0.6 per cent in 1987/8, and about 1.4 per cent in 1995/6. It is this yield which can be compared with the capital costs of owners.

With certain simplifying assumptions, the capital cost of housing services to owner-occupiers is given by the net interest rate they face less the return they might expect by way of capital gain. Over the 1979–88 period, end-year interest rates net of basic rate tax averaged 8.8 per cent. From mid-1979 to mid-1988 prices overall rose by 6.7 per cent per year. If one bases the long-run expected nominal capital gain on this figure plus a 1 per cent long-run real capital gain per year (as used in the calculations for council tenants above), the expected annual gain comes to 7.7 per cent per year. The net cost of housing services to owner-occupiers would then be 1.1 per cent of capital value, only just above the equivalent figure for local authority tenants calculated above for the mid-1980s.

In the subsequent period, from 1989–95, net interest rates averaged much the same, 8.7 per cent per year, but inflation was lower, generating a net capital cost of housing services of 3.5 per cent. By contrast, in the second half of the 1970s, high inflation implied that the figure was around *minus* 10 per cent, besides which the equivalent figure of just below zero for council tenants would look rather unfavourable!

These calculations are speculative and subject to wide margins of error. What they do suggest nonetheless is that there has been a major switch in the balance between the tenures. The evidence suggests that owners were in a much more favourable position than tenants in the inflationary conditions of the late 1970s. There may have been rough tenure neutrality in the mid-1980s. However, a decade later, although the net yield on capital generated by council rents had risen significantly, the equivalent cost to owners had risen faster, tilting the balance in favour of tenants.

These relative costs vary between individuals, of course. Allowing for the availability of assistance with rents for low-income tenants (including those not on Income Support), but the rising value of tax exemptions with income for owners, the overall pattern of costs and subsidies continues to push those with low incomes to be tenants, but those with high incomes to be owners.

The high cost of mortgages, arrears, repossessions, and negative equity in the late 1980s meant that, for these people at least, the policy aim of housing 'within reach' failed.

V. In Brief

- Housing policy *per se* is no longer a major political issue. In many ways it is now just an adjunct of social security and city regeneration strategies.
- Until the early 1990s tax concessions to owner-occupiers were maintained, and the sector remains favoured, despite recent restrictions on mortgage tax relief.
- Since 1979 there has been a dramatic shift from general subsidies for public housing towards higher rents and greater spending on Housing Benefit, also reflecting deregulation of private rents after 1988.
- There has been a steady shift since the mid-1970s from public capital spending on new dwellings towards renovation of existing ones. With the Right to Buy and other transfers, local authority provision has been falling since 1979.
- The total of net public spending on housing, Housing Benefit, and mortgage interest relief remained within the band of £18–22 billion (1995/6 prices) throughout most of the period (therefore falling in relation to GDP). What changed was its composition:
  - Cuts in current general subsidies were matched by increased Housing Benefit until the end of the 1980s, after which Housing Benefit costs rose more rapidly, particularly for private tenants.
  - Cuts in net capital spending were offset by the rising cost of mortgage interest relief until 1990/1. After this the cost of the relief fell while that of Housing Benefit rose.
- Despite falling general subsidies, real management and maintenance spending per council dwelling rose by more than 4 per cent annually throughout the period. This was possible as the real burden of debt payments fell and gross rents increased.
- Net public capital spending in England fell by 90 per cent between 1976/7 and 1988/9. However, during the 1980s much of the fall was offset by capital receipts, which meant that gross spending did not fall so fast. Allowing for changes in construction costs, the volume of gross capital spending in 1995/6 was half that in 1976/7.
- The 1980s aim of promoting owner-occupation was a visible success, its share of the stock in Great Britain rising from 52 per cent in 1973 to 67 per cent in 1995. However, high house prices, interest rates, and the recession led to a crisis in the early 1990s, with high mortgage arrears, repossessions, and negative equity.
- Tenures have become sharply polarized by income. By 1994 only 2 per cent of those

living in council housing were in the highest fifth by income, compared to 11 per cent in 1979; 76 per cent were in the poorest two-fifths in 1994, compared to 51 per cent in 1979.

- Since the 1970s there have been clear improvements in the overall number of dwellings in relation to households and their general physical standard:
  - The shortfall between fit dwellings and all households fell by over one million between 1971 and 1981. In the 1980s the shortfall increased slightly, but in the early 1990s it was rising by about 15,000 to 20,000 per year.
  - The proportion of people living without basic amenities or central heating fell dramatically between 1974 and 1994, as did the proportion living in crowded conditions until 1990, after which it rose. Problems of disrepair increased in the 1970s, but repair standards improved in the 1980s.
  - By and large, improving conditions benefited all socio-economic and income groups, except that the poorest fifth fell behind the rest in certain respects between 1979 and 1994.
  - Overall satisfaction levels improved between the 1970s and 1990s. Rising standards appear to have kept pace with expectations, although council tenants continue to be dissatisfied with repair services, and dissatisfaction with the neighbourhood appears to have worsened since the 1970s.
- Acute problems of access to housing grew in the 1980s, with rapid rises in homelessness acceptances, numbers in temporary accommodation, and people sleeping rough in city streets. All these problems seem to have peaked in the early 1990s and are now receding.
- Measured in most ways, housing has become more expensive in relation to incomes since the 1970s:
  - For tenants, gross rents have risen in relation to earnings, and potential assistance from Housing Benefit has become less generous for those with incomes above Income Support level. Net rents now absorb a higher proportion of tenants' incomes.
  - For owners costs have swung more wildly, peaking in 1989 and 1990. Mortgagors' net interest costs were lower in the mid-1990s than a decade before, but the economic cost of being an owner-occupier has risen.

Further Reading

The Joseph Rowntree Foundation's annual *Housing Review* (edited by Steve Wilcox) brings together a comprehensive selection of housing statistics and articles on contemporary issues. Statistical series can also be found in the Department of the Environment's annual volume of *Housing and Construction Statistics* and in the published results from the *Survey of English Housing* (e.g. Green *et al.* 1996).

More detailed discussion of housing finance issues can be found in Hills (1991) and Gibb and Munro (1991). Recent developments in housing policy are discussed in Malpass and Means (1993) and in Williams (1997).

ANNEXE

Table 5A.1. PUBLIC SPENDING ON HOUSING, UNITED KINGDOM (£ MILLION AT

	GB current spending				GB capital spending				
	General subsidies (including RFCs)	HRA surpluses	Other current	Net current (GB)	Gross capital (LA/NT)	Gross capital (HA)	Total gross capital	Capital receipts	Net capital
1973/4	2832	0	135	2968	9419	632	10052	1426	8626
1974/5	4188	0	215	4403	12446	1000	13446	801	12645
1975/6	4373	0	206	4579	10391	1386	11777	1639	10137
1976/7	4780	0	511	5292	10587	1917	12504	1152	11352
1977/8	4477	0	283	4760	8500	1883	10383	1427	8957
1978/9	4823	0	332	5156	7793	1707	9500	1722	7778
1979/80	5415	0	400	5815	7810	1715	9526	1333	8192
1980/1	5232	0	386	5618	5974	1690	7664	1479	6184
1981/2	3595	0	366	3960	4719	1557	6277	2387	3889
1982/3	2583	0	365	2948	5524	1978	7502	3950	3552
1983/4	2055	0	372	2427	6979	1815	8794	4046	4748
1984/5	1970	0	350	2319	6442	1661	8103	3590	4513
1985/6	1881	0	387	2268	5382	1559	6941	3309	3632
1986/7	1903	0	419	2321	5422	1577	6998	3748	3250
1987/8	1471	0	295	1767	7022	1878	8900	4372	4529
1988/9	1371	0	301	1673	8140	1790	9930	5939	3990
1989/90	1465	0	312	1778	7194	2197	9391	5542	3848
1990/1	1706	−252	326	1780	6067	2170	8237	3639	4598
1991/2	1364	−336	378	1406	5044	2752	7795	2658	5138
1992/3	1135	−556	363	942	4447	3607	8054	2383	5670
1993/4	904	−772	337	469	4901	2841	7742	2765	4977
1994/5	825	−957	384	251	3964	2409	6373	2098	4275
1995/6	669	−1114	357	−88	3608	2018	5626	1862	3764
1996/7	682	−1194	397	−115	3160	1836	4996	2279	2717

[a] Adjusted by GDP (market prices) deflator.
[b] Before 1983/4, figures show estimated rents of Supplementary Benefit recipients plus actual costs of rent rebates and allowances.
[c] Includes Option Mortgage Subsidy.

Sources: DSS (1997a: tables 1, 2, and 3, and earlier equivalents); HM Treasury (1997: table 3.1); Northern Ireland Office (1997: table 7.15, and earlier equivalents); Hills and Mullings (1990: table 5A.1); Newton (1991: table 46); Wilcox (1996: tables 56a, 57, 98, and 102); DoE (1997b: figures 2.a, 2.c, 2.e, 2.f, A1, and A5, and earlier equivalents); Scottish Office (1997: tables 3.2 and 3.4 and earlier equivalents); Welsh Office (1997: tables 7.0b, 7.04–7.10, and earlier equivalents).

1995/96 PRICES)[a]

Total Housing (GB)	Northern Ireland housing	Total Housing (UK)	Housing benefits[b]					Total UK public spending	Mortgage interest relief[c]	GDP (MP) deflator
			LA tenants (GB)	Other tenants (GB)	NI tenants	ISMI (UK)	Total benefits (UK)			
11594	277	11871	2619	1135	103	n/a	3858	15729	3613	15.5
17048	360	17409	1946	941	79	n/a	2966	20375	4140	18.6
14717	352	15069	1820	850	73	86	2829	17897	4309	13.3
16644	670	17314	1939	830	76	102	2947	20262	4659	16.4
13717	570	14287	1990	783	76	110	2960	17246	3973	30.0
12934	551	13485	1904	769	74	78	2825	16310	3743	33.4
14008	544	14551	1764	679	67	79	2590	17142	4203	39.0
11803	518	12321	1920	666	71	158	2815	15136	4746	46.1
7850	462	8312	2939	796	103	249	4087	12399	4569	50.6
6500	509	7009	3565	913	123	319	4920	11929	4531	54.2
7175	527	7702	3492	945	122	270	4829	12531	4924	56.7
6832	566	7398	3607	1155	129	375	5266	12664	6017	59.5
5900	551	6451	3656	1403	137	486	5682	12132	7564	62.8
5572	518	6090	3739	1539	142	553	5974	12063	7218	64.7
6295	495	6790	3680	1512	144	505	5841	12631	7122	68.1
5663	459	6122	3739	1451	144	404	5739	11861	7428	72.7
5626	344	5970	3779	1747	154	468	6148	12118	8869	77.8
6377	293	6670	4010	2118	160	675	6962	13632	9167	84.0
6544	285	6829	4550	2714	170	1079	8513	15342	6823	89.4
6612	280	6893	4959	3527	186	1247	9919	16812	5585	93.1
5446	247	5693	5245	4372	204	1293	11114	16807	4489	95.8
4526	232	4758	5381	4999	226	1102	11707	16465	3590	97.5
3676	246	3922	5440	5445	240	1052	12177	16099	2800	100.0
2602	242	2844	5499	5743	255	927	12423	15267	2634	102.5

Table 5A.2. REAL PUBLIC GROSS CAPITAL SPENDING ON HOUSING, ENGLAND (£ BILLION AT 1995/6 PRICES)

	Local authority		Housing association	Other[a]	Total gross spending	Capital receipts	Total net spending
	New build	Capital repairs					
1976/7	5.8	1.3	1.8	2.0	10.9	1.2	9.6
1977/8	4.6	1.2	1.7	1.6	9.2	1.6	7.6
1978/9	3.7	1.5	1.5	2.0	8.7	2.2	6.5
1979/80	3.0	1.9	1.5	2.6	9.0	2.1	6.9
1980/1	2.2	1.5	1.5	2.3	7.4	2.3	5.1
1981/2	1.5	1.2	1.3	2.4	6.5	3.5	3.0
1982/3	1.4	1.8	1.6	2.7	7.5	4.9	2.6
1983/4	1.3	2.0	1.5	2.9	7.8	4.1	3.6
1984/5	1.3	2.2	1.4	2.3	7.2	3.6	3.6
1985/6	1.1	2.1	1.3	1.5	6.0	3.2	2.9
1986/7	0.9	2.4	1.3	1.2	5.8	3.5	2.3
1987/8	0.9	2.6	1.3	1.2	6.0	3.9	2.1
1988/9	1.1	2.6	1.3	1.1	6.1	5.2	0.9
1989/90	1.2	3.8	1.6	1.2	7.8	4.7	3.1
1990/1	0.6	2.0	1.7	0.9	5.3	3.1	2.2
1991/2	0.5	1.7	2.1	0.9	5.1	2.0	3.1
1992/3	0.2	1.7	2.9	0.8	5.6	1.7	3.9
1993/4	0.3	1.8	2.3	0.9	5.3	2.1	3.1
1994/5	0.1	1.6	1.9	0.8	4.5	1.7	2.8
1995/6	0.1	1.7	1.6	0.8	4.1	1.5	2.5

[a] Other includes new town, home ownership, HATs, and local authority lending for house purchase (also counted as a capital receipt).

Sources: HM Treasury (1982: table 2.7); Wilcox (1996: table 56a).

Table 5A.3. SALES OF PUBLIC SECTOR DWELLINGS, GREAT
BRITAIN (000s)

	Total	Of which to sitting local authority tenants, including Right to Buy
1979	44	—
1980	92	—
1981	125	106
1982	240	210
1983	179	146
1984	135	110
1985	121	99
1986	116	95
1987	136	110
1988	193	167
1989	213	186
1990	155	128
1991	90	74
1992	84	65
1993	81	62
1994	81	66
1995	67	50
Total	2,152	1,674

Source: DoE (1997a: table 96, and earlier equivalents).

Table 5A.4. LARGE-SCALE TRANSFERS OF LOCAL AUTHORITY HOUSING

	Number of councils	Number of dwellings (000s)	Transfer price (£ million)	Price per dwelling (£)
1988/9	2	11.2	98.4	8800
1989/90	2	14.4	102.2	7100
1990/1	11	45.5	414.4	9100
1991/2	2	10.8	92.1	8500
1992/3	4	26.3	238.0	9000
1993/4	9	30.1	270.5	9000
1994/5	10[a]	40.2	403.0	10000
1995/6	12[a]	44.9	481.1	10700
Total	51	223.4	2099.7	9400

[a] Cherwell transferred its stock in two stages in 1994/5 and 1995/6. Two of the 1995/6 transfers are of only part of the council's stock.

Source: Wilcox (1996: table 62).

Table 5A.5. UNSATISFACTORY HOUSING CONDITIONS IN ENGLAND, BY TENURE (% OF DWELLINGS)

	Owner-occupiers	Local authority and new town	Housing association	Private rented	All (including vacant)
Unfit					
1971	4.2	1.5	21.7		7.5
1976	4.2	1.3	20.5		6.8
1981	4.7	1.3	17.7		6.2
1986 (old standard)	3.0	2.1	3.5	15.6	4.8
1986 (new standard)	6.6	6.8	4.9	25.4	8.8
1991	5.5	6.9	6.7	20.5	7.6
Lacking one or more amenities					
1971	11.2	11.1	40.3		17.4
1976	4.9	5.5	25.2		8.9
1981	3.3	2.8	13.5		5.0
1986	2.1	2.0	8.3		2.5[a]
1991	0.8	0.7	n/a	3.9	1.0
In serious disrepair					
1971	3.7	0.8	16.0		5.4
1976	3.9	1.0	15.6		5.0
1981	5.3	1.0	16.4		5.8
1986	7.4	2.2	17.1		5.9
Tenth of dwellings needing most repair					
1986	7.6	8.6	7.3	27.0	10
1991	7.5	8.5	5.2	25.6	10

[a] Preferred estimate for 1986.

Sources: DoE (1982); DoE (1988: fig. 9.3 and table 9.1); DoE (1993: fig. 8.13 and tables A5.2, A7.7, and A7.8).

Table 5A.6. INDICATORS OF STRESS IN OWNER-OCCUPIED HOUSING, UNITED KINGDOM

	Real house price index	House price-to-earnings ratio[a]	Mortgage interest rate (end of year; %)	Mortgage arrears over 6 months[b] (000s)	Repossessions during year (000s)	Households with negative equity[c] (000s)
1980	100	3.22	14.0	16	4	n/a
1981	95	3.01	15.0	22	5	n/a
1982	90	2.80	10.0	33	7	n/a
1983	96	2.94	11.0	37	8	n/a
1984	100	2.96	11.8	58	12	n/a
1985	103	3.00	13.5	70	19	n/a
1986	114	3.16	11.9	65	24	n/a
1987	126	3.42	11.6	71	26	n/a
1988	150	3.91	11.0	53	19	n/a
1989	169	4.31	13.6	81	16	230
1990	157	3.88	15.0	159	44	560
1991	145	3.55	12.7	275	76	780
1992	134	3.20	10.7	352	69	1770
1993	126	3.00	8.1	316	59	1390
1994	126	2.98	7.7	251	49	1270
1995	122	2.87	7.8	212	49	1160

[a] Using mix-adjusted index based on 1990 average prices and male full-time average weekly earnings in April each year.
[b] End-of-year.
[c] In fourth quarter.

Sources: ONS (1996*a*: table 1.1); ONS (1996*c*: table 15); Wilcox (1996: tables 42b, 45, and 46); Council of Mortgage Lenders (1997: table 25); DoE (1997*a*: tables 10.7, 10.8, and 10.25, and earlier equivalents).

6 The Personal Social Services

Maria Evandrou and Jane Falkingham

T HE PUBLIC image of the personal social services (PSS) has been that of a service composed of 'do-gooding' or altruistic social workers / care managers; their work or, more often, their inadequacies being highlighted by the media in times of 'crisis'. The recurrent waves of concern about child sexual abuse are a good example. This is an unrealistic as well as an unfair image. The PSS extend far beyond those which social workers alone provide; and those provided by social workers themselves are more complex than the narrow spectrum of activities highlighted by the popular press. The sector encapsulates a wide variety of services directed at a diverse range of client groups.

In this chapter we examine the effectiveness of the PSS in Britain since the early 1970s. We discuss the evolution of the PSS in relation to the goals and policies specified by the 1974–9 Labour and subsequent Conservative Governments. We survey the trends in public expenditure, looking at the resultant expansion and contraction of the different sectors and the impact on individuals using and 'in need of' the PSS. We explore the consequent outcomes of these trends and discuss their policy implications. Finally, we conclude with a summary of the major points, tracking the development and effectiveness of the PSS in the context of political, economic, and demographic change.

I. Goals and policies

The emergence of the personal social services

To understand the diverse nature of the PSS it is necessary to consider how such a disparate set of services came to be grouped together, dominated by a single department of local government. The very idea of a sector of statutory services called the 'personal social services' dates back no further than the mid-1960s, though the idea of a single 'family service' of a more restricted kind had been emerging for a decade before that. Prior to the formation of the Social Service Departments (SSDs) in England and Wales in 1971, services were provided by a wide variety of bodies. A diverse range of services had grown up over a century or more, supporting families and individuals who could not operate independently without help. Many of these services, such as those supporting individuals who were blind, or disabled, or elderly infirm, had begun as the work of voluntary organizations and gradually over time had become statutory responsibilities.

Separate from this group of supportive services for people living in the community was the provision for those who had ceased to be able to live without much more intensive residential care. In many cases, families could not provide such care themselves and were unable to purchase it. In these instances responsibility for such people rested with the state. In the nineteenth century this function had been performed by the Poor Law authorities and had been inherited by local authority welfare departments.

Distinct yet again were the powers the state had taken at the end of the nineteenth century to safeguard the interests of children without parents or who were neglected or cruelly treated by their parents—a function performed by Children's Departments prior to 1971.

This is not the place to attempt to describe the interplay of professional, bureaucratic, and party politics which produced the new SSDs in England and Wales, and Social Work Departments in Scotland (see Hall 1976; Cooper 1983). A chronology is outlined in Table 6.1. Suffice it to say that throughout the 1960s the social work profession had been fighting for recognition while the medical profession had been pressing for the creation of comprehensive health service agencies separate from local authorities. The reforms of the early 1970s gave both a part of what they wanted. In England and Wales, following the Seebohm Report (Home Office 1968), the statutory social work agency became the Social Services Department and in Scotland, following the Kilbrandon Report (Scottish Home and Health Department 1964), Social Work Departments were established, which retained responsibility for the probation services. Community health services were transferred to the National Health Service, under the new Health Authorities. The principle of professional demarcation is perhaps best illustrated by the medical social workers who practise in hospitals working closely with medical teams. They were transferred to the *employment* of SSDs after 1974.

It is important to note that in Northern Ireland, health and social care services remain combined. Due to the different nature of PSS in Northern Ireland, the differences in policies, and the difficulties in obtaining comparable disaggregated figures, Northern Ireland will not be explicitly discussed in this chapter. Expenditure from the province is, however, included in any UK figures presented. The structure of PSS in Scotland differs in turn from that in England and Wales, with the probation services being combined under the same authority as other juvenile services. Thus England and Wales will provide the main focus for the chapter, although not exclusively.

Table 6.1. CHRONOLOGY OF LEGISLATIVE CHANGES AND POLICY DOCUMENTS IN THE PERSONAL SOCIAL SERVICES

1964	Kilbrandon Report.
1968	Seebohm Report. Disabled Persons Act.
1969	Children and Young Persons' Act.
1970	Local Authority Social Services Act.
1971	Formation of the SSDs. CCETSW set up. CQSW established.
1973	Death of Maria Colwell and subsequent inquiry (East Sussex).
1976	*Priorities for the Health and Personal Social Services* published.
1977	*The Way Forward* published.
1978	Wolfenden Report, *The Future of Voluntary Organisations*.
1980	*Can Social Work Survive?* published (C. Brewer and J. Lait).
	Rules for board and lodging claims regulated by statute under parliamentary statutory instruments. Local limit imposed, i.e. private homes supported by social security payments.
1981	*Care in Action* (DHSS).
1982	Barclay Report, *Social Workers: Their Roles and Tasks*. Decentralization and patch system.
1983	DHSS transforms the Social Work Service (SWS) into the Social Work Inspectorate.
	Mental Health Act. New powers and responsibilities to 'approved social workers'.
1984	*Care in the Community* circular issued by DHSS. Aims to transfer long-stay hospital patients into the community.
	Registered Homes Act.
1985	Death of Jasmine Beckford (Brent).
	(Apr.) National limits on social security support for residential care introduced for each resident depending on type of incapacity and type of facility.
1986	The Disabled Persons' Act.
	The Mental Health Act.
	1986 Children's Act. Places more statutory duties on social workers. Stress on legal powers and court judgments.
1988	Wagner Report, *Residential Care: A Positive Choice*. Consumerism, choice, participation.
	Publication of the Cleveland Report regarding child abuse.
	Griffiths Report, *Community Care: An Agenda for Action*.
	Audit Commission Report, *Making a Reality of Community Care*.
1989	White Paper *Caring for People*.
	1989 Children's Act (implemented Oct. 1991). New and complex set of provisions for the protection of children by the courts.
1990	NHS and Community Care Act (fully implemented Apr. 1993). Greater responsibility placed with local authorities as 'enablers' rather than 'providers'. Service users' right to assessment and needs-led service. Care management and 'packages of care'.
1992	*The Health of the Nation: A Strategy for Health in England*.
1995	Disability Discrimination Act.
	Carers (Recognition and Services) Act, implemented Apr. 1996. Assessment for carers.
1996	Community Care Act (Direct Payments) Bill.
	Adoption Bill.
1997	White Paper *A New Partnership for Care in Old Age*.
	Community Care (Residential Charges) Bill.

Maria Evandrou and Jane Falkingham

Ultimate aims

The range of client groups served by the PSS is wide and objectives are necessarily varied. At one extreme there is the care and protection of children and work with the socially deviant, at the other the provision of support to elderly and disabled people. The potential values inherent in each are rather different. It is thus extremely difficult to identify one overarching goal that unifies the aim of the sector. The PSS are in part concerned with *social control*. Indeed the whole debate about the creation of the PSS began with concern about juvenile delinquency (Home Office 1959). On one level society could be said to be collectively concerned to protect its members from :

1. danger—e.g. from delinquents;
2. discomfort—e.g. mentally disordered behaviour we find embarrassing;
3. distress—e.g. seeing elderly people living in poverty and socially excluded.

For example, John Stuart Mill (1991 edn.: 14) argued that the state had a duty to protect minors (i.e. individuals in the making), who did not yet possess the capacity to look after themselves. Following from this kind of argument, the state takes on the role of collective protector of children against 'cruel' parents. This is not a public good in the normal sense, but the state is the only agency vested with the power to take children away from their parents.

More centrally, it can be argued that the PSS are concerned to protect those unable to participate fully as citizens in an unprotected competitive environment, for example individuals with mental illness, or with learning disabilities, or frail elderly persons who have never had the opportunity to earn resources for themselves or are not in a position to finance their social care in old age. In addition, there are individuals with physical disabilities who can live independently in the community with additional support in terms of physical help and care, as well as transport.

This goal may be summarised as the pursuit of fostering greater *social integration* amongst individuals or groups in society who would otherwise be marginalised or socially excluded. More specifically, it is to promote individual personal well-being in the face of a disabling condition. The dual aims of social integration and social control are summarised in the graph in Fig. 6.1.

The pursuit of social integration or inclusion for disabled groups in society involves fundamental issues of equity. Yet the PSS have largely been passed by in the debate on equality (though see Brown 1972). Equity is difficult to achieve, particularly when the availability of services is patchy, and when eligibility criteria, expenditure, and charging policies vary from local authority to local authority. In this chapter we investigate the extent to which these services are equally available to those from different income groups, and how far they have met the overarching aims of the PSS over time. How far the ultimate goals have been met by different Governments is not independent of the specific policy goals of those administrations. Below we summarise central government policy objectives for the period since 1974 and

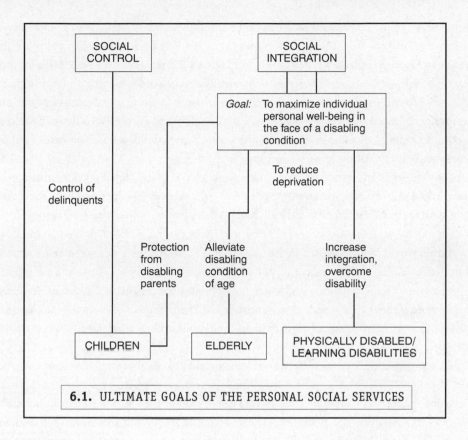

6.1. ULTIMATE GOALS OF THE PERSONAL SOCIAL SERVICES

distinguish those which have been common to both Labour and Conservative Governments from those on which the approach has differed.

Policy objectives

The 1970s and 1980s For most of the period since the Second World War, until the Thatcher administrations, there was cross-party support for all the major policy priorities pursued in the Personal Social Services. The reorganisation itself was supported by both major parties in Parliament.

A consistent and publicised aim throughout the 1970s and 1980s was that of fostering 'community care'. It was a much-affirmed, if ill-defined goal (Walker 1982b; Bulmer 1987) of both the 1974 Labour Government and successive Conservative administrations. However, its meaning has changed subtly over time. Initially the term meant, to many officials, no more than care outside NHS hospitals. The first public expenditure White Paper, following the creation of the SSDs, reflected the view that 'a major objective for local authority personal social services is to shift the balance of care from hospitals to the community where this is more appropriate' (HM Treasury 1971: 53).

In the wake of major political embarrassment at ill-treatment of patients in a number of long-stay institutions, Governments of both parties issued policy statements setting out a timescale for reducing places in such long-stay hospitals (DHSS 1971 and 1975) both for individuals with mental illness and those with learning disabilities (referred to at the time as mentally handicapped). In more recent years, the term has changed from meaning 'care in the community' to 'care *by* the community' and with this change has come a collapse in the consensus surrounding 'community care' as a policy aim. This is discussed further below, but for the time being let us continue with common policy aims.

All Governments attempted to shift more health and personal social service resources to the care of the priority groups, namely frail elderly people (over-75s), persons with mental illness or with learning disabilities, and individuals with physical impairments. The objectives set out in the 1974 Labour Government's *Priorities* Document (DHSS 1976*b*; see Chapter 4 of this volume) were largely repeated in the Conservative Government's equivalent document, *Care in Action* (DHSS 1981*a*), except in vaguer, non-quantified terms. The continuing priority for persons with mental illness and learning disabilities was reaffirmed in the White Paper *Caring for People* (DoH 1989*b*) and, more recently, with the inclusion of mental health as a key area in the Government's public health strategy, *The Health of the Nation* (DoH 1992; see Table 6.1).

A third common policy objective was not the product of deliberate policy planning, but rather a by-product of public concern about child neglect, heightened by the treatment of the issue by the media. In November 1973, a child in the care of East Sussex Council died as the result of ill-treatment by her stepfather. The girl's name was Maria Collwell. This case was subjected to a public inquiry and the report became the focus of great public interest and criticism of the new SSDs. The Collwell case was merely the first in a series of highly publicised tragedies. The adverse publicity which SSDs and social workers received meant that the priority accorded to work with children increased, leaving less time, especially of skilled staff, for other groups (Parton 1985). Throughout the 1970s and 1980s, the D(H)SS continued to issue advice on child abuse, and on the creation of 'at risk' registers. These concerns culminated in the 1989 Children's Act, which accorded greater rights to children than ever before. Implemented in October 1991, the Act emphasized two key themes: that children should be cared for within their own families where possible, and consulted in accordance with their age and understanding.

Finally, all administrations have been concerned to reduce public expenditure in general, and local authority expenditure in particular. If we take the range of activities undertaken by the new SSDs, their predecessors had spent the equivalent of 0.2 per cent of GDP in the 1950s. In the 1960s expenditure on PSS roughly doubled in volume terms, while in the period 1970–5 real spending doubled again (Ferlie and Judge 1981; Webb and Wistow 1982; Glennerster 1985). Thus just over 1.0 per cent of the GDP was devoted to these services in 1974. This pace of expansion was to slow significantly during the 1970s and early 1980s, only to pick up speed again in the 1990s.

If these themes were common, at least in principle, to both political parties, others were not. The 1974 Labour Government had set guidelines for social service provision and asked local authorities to submit plans for future development (DHSS 1976*b*; 1977*b*; Webb and Wistow 1986).

The Conservative Government gave up any attempt to set guidelines for local authority services (DHSS 1981*a*). Central direction and priority setting gave way to local choice, which was increasingly constrained by controls on local authority expenditure. This was exerted first through cash limits, then a grant formula that penalised high spenders. Within that formula there was a Grant-Related Expenditure figure which was in effect a target figure for social service spending for each authority in the country. Finally a rate cap was introduced to put a limit on the capacity of high-spending local authorities to raise rates to finance their services.

The other major break in policy continuity came after the 1979 election, when the new Government began to give increasing encouragement to the non-statutory sector (Wolfenden Committee 1978) and to extol the virtues of informal care by the family and neighbours. In the White Paper *Growing Older* it is clearly stated that

the primary sources of support and care for elderly people are informal and voluntary. These spring from the personal ties of kinship, friendship and neighbourhood. They are irreplaceable. It is the role of public authorities to sustain, and, where necessary, develop—but never to displace—such support and care. Care in the community must increasingly mean care by the community. (DHSS 1981*b*: para. 1.9)

This statement reflects a move by the Government to change the definition of community care. This philosophy was expounded more fully to the Conference of Directors of Social Services at Buxton on 27 September 1984. Norman Fowler (then Secretary of State for Social Services) rejected what he called the monopolistic approach, under which local authorities provided all the services (a situation which had never existed). Instead, he argued, drawing on the Seebohm Report, they should have 'an enabling role'.

There was rising dissatisfaction about the limited progress made in implementing community care policies in the 1980s. The 1980s represented a period of conflicting policy; that is, easy access to funding for institutional care via the social security system, yet limited funds for home care services via local social services departments due to an overall policy of restraining public spending. The Audit Commission report *Making a Reality of Community Care* (Audit Commission 1986*b*) identified the need for change, highlighting in particular the organisational fragmentation of service systems, the mismatch of resources to needs, and the 'perverse incentives' towards the growth of institutional care brought about by the system of funding (Challis and Traske 1997). In response, Sir Roy Griffiths was invited to 'review the way in which public funds are used to support community care policy and advise on the options for actions that would improve the use of the funds as a contribution to more effective community care' (DHSS 1988).

Maria Evandrou and Jane Falkingham

The Griffiths Report (DHSS 1988) recognised the importance of local authorities in promoting community care, but argued that rather than being the provider, SSDs' role should be redefined as a designer and co-ordinator of packages of care delivered by the care market. Local authorities, therefore, should assume a key *brokerage* role in the development of services, ensuring provision of appropriate and adequate care by a range of suppliers. In short, it recommended a more co-ordinated approach to the funding and management of community care, where the responsibility of needs assessment, funds allocation, and co-ordination of care lay firmly with the SSDs.

The 1990s: A break from the past The changes introduced in the White Paper *Caring for People* (DoH 1989b) affirmed many but not all the Griffiths recommendations, and were subsequently enacted in the 1990 NHS and Community Care Act. The community care reforms aimed to bring about the most far-reaching changes in the financing, organization, and delivery of social care services since the post-war welfare state (Wistow *et al.* 1996). These fundamental and complex changes were to be implemented over the long term, aiming for the next decade and beyond.

Six key objectives for community care were identified in *Caring for People*, covering the promotion of home care, carer support, needs assessment and care management, a mixed economy of care, a clear demarcation of responsibilities, and better value for money:

1. To promote the development of domiciliary, day, and respite services to enable people to live in their own homes wherever feasible and sensible.
2. To ensure that service providers make practical support for carers a high priority.
3. To make proper assessment of need and good case management the cornerstone of high-quality care provision.
4. To promote the development of a flourishing independent sector alongside the high-quality public services.
5. To clarify the responsibilities of agencies and so make it easier to hold them to account for their performance.
6. To secure better value for taxpayers' money by introducing a new funding structure for social care, where social security provisions should not provide any incentive in favour of residential and nursing home care.

A timetable of phased implementation over a period of two years, 1991–3, was outlined. The essence of the new community care policy meant that SSDs, as the lead agencies, would *assess* the needs of individuals, be *responsible* for deciding upon the 'mix' of services which would best suit those needs, and *monitor* and review the quality of services provided. To remove any 'perverse incentives', SSDs would become the sole source of funding for the social care of elderly people. SSDs were to produce integrated community care plans and arrange for the registration and inspection of all residential and nursing homes.

The Community Care reforms involved structural and organisational changes in five key areas:

1. integration of funding;
2. assessment and co-ordination of care;
3. mixed economy of care;
4. community care planning;
5. inspection and registration.

Integration of funding The new funding structure placed responsibility for the financial support of individuals entering residential care (public/private/voluntary) with the local authority. SSDs now assess individuals' need for such residential placements and are responsible for the funding of costs over and above social security entitlements. Such new arrangements do not apply to people in residential homes prior to April 1993, who continue under the previous system (that is, they are still paid for by social security). Social security funds spent on residential care were transferred to local authorities. A new specific grant to develop social care for seriously mentally ill people was also made available. This grant was ring-fenced for mental health projects; however, local authorities were expected to contribute financially to this too and agree the projects with the health authorities.

Assessment and co-ordination of care Local authority SSDs are now responsible, in collaboration with medical, nursing, and other interests, for assessing individual need, designing care arrangements, and securing their delivery within available resources. Assessment includes those seeking day care, domiciliary care, and publicly funded residential and nursing care. Care managers are appointed to assess and co-ordinate care for the most vulnerable.

A mixed economy of care was expected to develop, given that local authorities 'will be expected to show that they are making maximum use of the independent sector' (DoH 1989b: para 1.12). SSDs have been required to shed their position of monopoly provider, taking on the role of an 'enabling authority' where—by purchasing, contracting, and planning— SSDs would broker services, in part provide services, *and* create a care market (Challis and Traske 1997). How successful SSDs have been in creating and sustaining such a market is assessed in Section III below.

Inspection and registration Regulation is generally carried out by central government, and the new regulation powers assigned by the 1990 Act to the Department of Health have been operationalised by the Social Services Inspectorate. Local authority *inspection units* are now responsible for monitoring social services provided by public, private, or voluntary sectors. Inspection must be separate—'at arm's length'—from the local authority's management of

Maria Evandrou and Jane Falkingham

their own homes. Regulation can also be carried out through contracting, either through legally enforceable contracts between local authority purchasers and state/independent providers, or through less formalized financial transactions. Self-regulation by provider associations has been discussed as an alternative to the existing system. Policies which aim to bring about a more transparent, effective, and efficient regulatory system, rather than reducing regulatory requirements as an end in itself, need to be promoted (Day *et al.* 1996).

In summary, although there may have been common goals throughout our period of investigation, the means employed to achieve them and the final desired outcome have changed considerably. Throughout the time period there has been a steady shift away from a position where the policy focus was on centrally defined need and equality, with an emphasis on priority groups, targets, and planning, to one where the main concern is with public expenditure restraint and a shift in the balance of care provision between the state and the non-statutory sector. The implementation of the 1990 NHS and Community Care Act and also the 1989 Children's Act has led to the most fundamental changes in the organization and management of personal and social care since the creation of SSDs. The complexity of the recent community care reforms can be simplified in four core strategic *dimensions of policy change* (Wistow *et al.* 1996): a shift from institutional services to community services; from supply-led to needs-led services; from the public sector to the independent sector as the main provider; and from the NHS to local government as the player of the leading role.

To assess whether the different Governments have been successful in meeting such aims, both common and otherwise, it is necessary to develop a framework within which the effects of changes in policy over time can be identified. The framework should enable us to look at changes in total expenditure over time, as well as shifts in the balance of resources directed towards particular groups (such as children and elderly), and between types of care (such as residential and community). However, given the overwhelming importance attached by recent government policy to shift resources and provision between sectors, it is also necessary to examine the changing balance of care between the informal, independent, and statutory sectors. To do this we need to examine the 'mixed economy of care' and the role of the state within that economy.

The 'mixed economy of care'

If a broader conception of what we mean by social care is adopted, the traditional view that it is largely undertaken by statutory social care agencies is misleading. Increasingly it has come to be recognised that much of the care of individuals in need is, in fact, provided by the independent sector, and more importantly by families, particularly women (Finch and Groves 1983), although also by men (Arber and Gilbert 1989).

Non-statutory organisations have always played an important role in providing social care; children's homes and homes for the elderly being the obvious early examples. Both non-profit and for-profit organisations have continued to be major providers and from the 1960s

198

onwards, especially during the period under study, the range of work undertaken by such agencies has grown. The voluntary sector, defined here as comprising non-statutory, non-profit, private organizations, was analysed in what became the influential report of the Wolfenden Committee (1978). It charted the extent and changing nature of the sector and its important complementary role to both statutory services and families.

Throughout the post-war period organizations like Barnardo's, the National Children's Homes, and the National Society for the Prevention of Cruelty to Children (NSPCC) have been diversifying their approach to provide more services supporting and advising families rather than merely providing residential care. Other groups, such as MENCAP and SCOPE, are also working for people with mental illness and those with learning disabilities. They campaign on behalf of those groups but also provide less traditional services in sheltered staffed homes or workplaces. Furthermore, they offer support to carers.

Moreover, a combination of factors has led housing associations to move increasingly into the business of providing care as well as dwellings. In the 1970s and 1980s the NHS was being asked to provide more new non-hospital facilities for persons with mental health problems or learning disabilities (see Chapter 4). Whilst local authorities faced constraints, housing associations had a more relaxed subsidy system (see Chapter 5) and the Hostel Deficit Grant supported the extra costs of care when such groups moved into specially designed housing association accommodation. Moreover, their residents could draw DSS benefits, which they could not do in hospital. These incentives led the NHS to use housing associations as a source of new facilities for hospital residents.

These voluntary groups are not the only source of care outside the state sector. As Webb and Wistow (1987) observe, people turn most often to their immediate family for help. Care and tending, as Roy Parker (1981) called it, is usually undertaken by spouses or parents and usually by women for no financial reward (Finch and Groves 1980). Various benefits for the care of disabled dependants have been legislated in this period, such as the Invalid Care Allowance (surrounded by controversy even after its extension to married women carers in 1986). In a climate of public expenditure constraints the significance of such informal care has come to be more widely appreciated by politicians (Audit Commission 1986b). The more care that can be shifted from the public taxpayer to the private individual, the easier the pressures on the public spending total. This ideology tends to ignore private costs (financial, social, and health) met by the families concerned. We return to this theme below.

The private for-profit sector has also been increasing in size and importance. Since the 1960s there has been dramatic growth in privately funded residential care (Laing and Buisson Ltd. 1996b) and, to a lesser extent, domiciliary services (Midwinter 1986). There has also been a considerable increase in the number of local authority services 'contracted out' and supplied by non-statutory profit-making bodies, particularly post-1993, when local authorities shifted from the role of provider to that of purchaser (DoH 1996j).

Thus *provision* can be summarised as coming from four sources: the state, non-statutory voluntary organisations, non-statutory for-profit (or private) organizations, and the informal sector. Equally, finance or provision of resources for care (time in the case of the informal sector) can be seen as coming from both statutory and non-statutory sources. The economy of social care can be conceptualized in terms of the framework in Fig. 6.2.

Conceptually, the involvement of the state in social care is complex. Funding from the state for PSS comes not only from SSDs, but also, as we shall see, from the NHS and from the DSS. State activity ranges from the regulation and inspection of private provision, whether in homes for the elderly or childminder provision in people's own homes, through the direct provision of residential and day care services, to payments for services provided in the private sector. Such payments may buy services of a formal kind, like a place in a home, or be cash payments to carers. Private funding may either take the form of user charges levied by local authorities to help pay the costs of residential care or home helps, or constitute fees paid for the purchase of services from non-statutory sources. This could also be taken to extend to charitable donations and payments to friends and neighbours.

By far the greatest proportion of care is provided by the informal sector. This is also the most difficult activity to quantify in terms of finance, as the majority of the input constitutes time rather than money. Government survey data show that 16 per cent of adults in Britain provide care to children and adults who cannot look after themselves independently; that is, nearly one in six individuals (OPCS 1992). The policy implications are far-reaching and have gained greater urgency in the last ten years, particularly with the 1995 Carer's Recognition and Services Act. Attempts to put figures to the costs of informal care raise fundamental theoretical issues which we deal with later in the chapter.

Different Governments have put different emphases on the alternative elements in the matrix in Fig. 6.2. In the following sections we use the framework developed here and attempt to establish the changes in the balance of the mixed economy of social care over time. However, since the standard and availability of services *per se* is likely to be a function of the amount of resources devoted to them, we shall begin by examining the trends over time in total government expenditure on the PSS.

II. Expenditure trends

The post-war period witnessed a dramatic increase in spending on what are now the PSS. In 1955 the equivalent of today's PSS accounted for just 0.2 per cent of GNP, but by the early 1970s this had quintupled to about 1 per cent. Expenditure on the PSS grew at double the pace of growth for all social welfare (Gould and Roweth 1980), and the PSS expanded their share in total public expenditure from 0.6 per cent in 1955 to 1.9 per cent in 1975/6. In the first four years after the establishment of the new Social Service Departments in 1971, expenditure in constant prices increased by 74 per cent (Ferlie and Judge 1981). However, our period of study begins just as this 'golden age for spending' was about to come to an end.

Source of finance or resources		Provider			
		State	Voluntary	Private	Informal
State	Funder	Direct provision of local authority services, e.g. home helps; NHS community health	Purchase of residential and home care services through contracts with SSDs, e.g.WVS meals-on-wheels; GP commissioning of community services; DSS payments for residents in institutional care *(spans Voluntary and Private)*		ICA; payments by SSDs to foster parents
	Regulator	SSI	Regulation of private and voluntary homes, child/minders, day nurseries, etc. *(spans Voluntary and Private)*		
Voluntary			e.g. Age Concern day centres; MIND; Samaritans; counselling services	Sponsored places in private homes funded by charitable trusts, e.g. Drapers Charitable Fund	Respite care to carers
Private			Corporate donations to voluntary sector	Subsidized places in private homes; subsidized creches at the workplace	
Individual/family	From disability-related welfare benefits	User charges paid for out of benefits	User charges paid for out of benefits	Purchase of private home care using AA and other benefits	'Purchase' of informal care using AA and other benefits
	From own resources	User charges	User charges, e.g. contribution to lunch club meals	Fees for residential care homes; private home care; LTC insurance premiums	Opportunity cost to family, friends, and neighbours of time spent caring and resources given

6.2. THE MIXED ECONOMY OF SOCIAL CARE

Maria Evandrou and Jane Falkingham

Total expenditure

Table 6.2 shows the trend in total real expenditure on the PSS over the last two decades, from 1973/4 to 1995/6. As previously discussed, on 1 April 1993 local authorities took over responsibility from the Department of Social Security for the financing of places in independent residential care and nursing homes. In recognition of these new responsibilities total expenditure in the last three years, 1993/4 to 1995/6, has been increased by the Special Transitional Grant (STG). Over the entire period, real spending has more than doubled,

Table 6.2. REAL GOVERNMENT EXPENDITURE ON PERSONAL SOCIAL SERVICES FROM 1973/4 TO 1995/6, UNITED KINGDOM (£ MILLION AT 1995/6 PRICES)

Year	Expenditure	As % of GDP	Index of real spending (1973/4 = 100)
1973/4	3,574	0.8	100
1974/5	4,204	0.9	118
1975/6	4,700	1.0	131
1976/7	4,788	1.0	134
1977/8	4,163	0.8	116
1978/9	4,260	0.8	119
1979/80	4,577	0.9	128
1980/1	4,837	0.9	135
1981/2	4,783	1.0	134
1982/3	4,834	0.9	135
1983/4	4,989	0.9	140
1984/5	5,071	0.9	142
1985/6	5,537	1.0	155
1986/7	5,835	1.0	163
1987/8	5,645	0.9	158
1988/9	5,978	0.9	167
1989/90	6,269	0.9	175
1990/1	6,698	1.0	187
1991/2	6,982	1.1	195
1992/3	7,255	1.1	203
1993/4	7,823	1.2	219
1994/5	8,077	1.2	226
1995/6	8,849	1.2	248
Annualized growth rates (%)			
1973/4 to 1978/9	3.5		
1978/9 to 1987/8	3.1		
1987/8 to 1992/3	5.1		

Sources: ONS (1997*a*, table 3.1, and earlier versions); GDP deflator from HM Treasury (1997).

equivalent to an annual rate of growth of 4.2 per cent. If we exclude the period during which the STG boosted total expenditures, the growth rate drops to 3.8 per cent per annum (1973/4 to 1993/4). Expenditure on the PSS as a share of GDP has hovered around 1 per cent over the entire period.

The growth has not, however, been consistent over the entire period. Fig. 6.3 illustrates more clearly the changing fortunes of the PSS over time. There was a sharp rise in real spending during the first years of the new Wilson Government, but in 1977 real expenditure fell. It did not return to the 1976/7 level until 1980/1. Again, during the first years of the early Thatcher Governments there was a large injection of cash, following the 1979 and 1983 elections. However, in the intervening years, expenditure was almost stationary and actually fell slightly in 1981/2 and 1987/8. Since then, however, real expenditure has risen inexorably, growing at an average of 5.1 per cent per annum for the period 1987/8 to 1992/3.

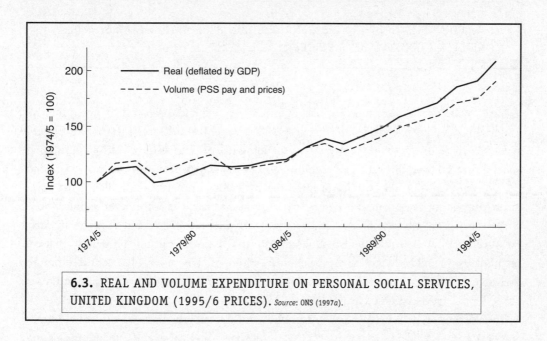

6.3. REAL AND VOLUME EXPENDITURE ON PERSONAL SOCIAL SERVICES, UNITED KINGDOM (1995/6 PRICES). *Source:* ONS (1997a).

The PSS, like the NHS, are a labour-intensive sector. To get a better idea of trends in the capacity to purchase increased levels of service provision in the PSS over time, we need therefore to take account of the change in actual prices met by local authorities both for social services staff and other inputs. Fig. 6.3 shows that volume total expenditure, that is after allowing for changes in PSS specific pay and prices, follows a similar path to real total expenditure on the PSS. The rate of growth in volume expenditure exceeded that of real expenditure in the late 1970s, reflecting rigorous enforcement of an incomes policy in the public sector. However, since 1985, expenditure on the PSS measured in volume terms has increased at a slower rate than if valued in real terms.

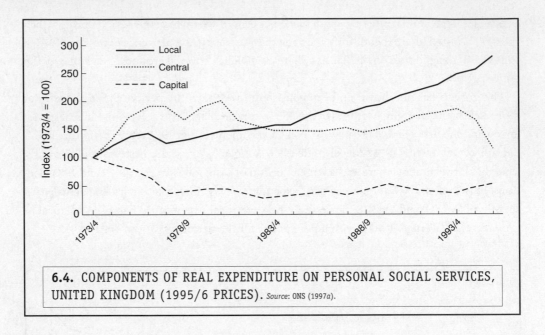

6.4. COMPONENTS OF REAL EXPENDITURE ON PERSONAL SOCIAL SERVICES, UNITED KINGDOM (1995/6 PRICES). *Source:* ONS (1997a).

Fig. 6.4 shows the trends in the components of real expenditure on PSS over time (the underlying data on real capital and current spending by central and local government are presented in Table 6A.1). All of the growth in spending has been in current rather than capital expenditure. In part, this reflects the shift in emphasis away from residential care to care in the community—the PSS capital programme providing primarily for building new and improving existing residential accommodation and day facilities for elderly people, those with learning or physical disabilities, persons with mental illness, and children in care. However, capital expenditure also suffered disproportionately during the period of fiscal restraint in the mid-1970s. Capital expenditure almost halved after 1976/7 and although there have been some periods of upward growth, most notably in the late 1980s and from 1993/4, it has never regained its pre-IMF level in real terms.

The current expenditure programme provides for the running costs of residential homes and day centres, for field social work, and for domiciliary support services, including aids and adaptations for physically handicapped persons. In Scotland it also covers probation and aftercare. Current expenditure by central government is largely in the form of grants for specific projects, and constitutes a small proportion of total expenditure. Central government spending rose rapidly during the first part of the Labour years, then fell and recovered up to 1980/81, after which it declined. Spending by central government was steady through the mid-1980s and fell dramatically after 1993, when the Community Care Act came into force, giving greater responsibilities to local authorities.

Spending by local authorities accounts for the majority of current expenditure on the PSS. Central government makes funds available to local authorities mainly through the Revenue

Support Grant (previously the Rate Support Grant). The amount allocated is based on a Standard Spending Assessment (SSA) which takes into account the demographic composition in each area, along with other need indicators. However, although central government exercises control through cash limits on the total Revenue Support Grant, the SSA merely provides guidance to local authorities on the level of expenditure that is considered appropriate, and it is up to each authority to decide how much to spend. During the 1970s total spending by SSDs largely followed central government plans. In fact, from 1976/7 to 1978/9 local authorities underspent planned expenditure on PSS by between 0.5 and 2 per cent (HM Treasury 1978, 1979a).

In the 1980s, however, the position was reversed. The new Conservative Government proposed radical reductions in PSS planned expenditure as part of an overall strategy to reduce total local authority spending. The public expenditure White Paper for 1980 indicated that current expenditure on PSS should be decreased by 6.7 per cent in volume terms in 1980/1. But during the fiscal restraint of the previous years many local authorities had already reduced their base as far as they were prepared to. Ferlie and Judge (1981) found that during this period SSDs on average only reduced expenditure by 2 per cent, overspending government targets by 4.7 per cent. The divergence between expenditure projections in successive White Papers and the actual spending levels of local authorities on PSS has persisted across the period. Most local authorities continue to spend more than the SSA and in 1995/6 the overspend averaged 7 per cent above the SSA (Audit Commission 1996a).

Joint finance and joint funding The continued growth in expenditure on PSS has in part been facilitated by the growth of joint finance projects resulting from collaboration between health and social services. Joint consultative committees were established in 1974 and joint care planning teams in 1976. Joint finance was introduced at the same time and was described by the then Secretary of State as 'collaboration money' (Castle 1975).

Health service provision for joint finance schemes with local authorities to develop community care grew by about 7 per cent per annum in real terms from 1978/9 to 1984/5 (HM Treasury 1986: 215) and such funds continued to increase by around 5 per cent a year between 1984/5 and 1994/5 (House of Commons Health Committee 1996: 29). In 1994/5 joint finance and funding schemes funded by district health authorities amounted to £211 million of gross expenditure. The provision of such financing has allowed SSDs to expand provision despite increasing constraints on local authority budgets. However, there are problems involved with joint finance pick-up. Growth is needed in SSD budgets to continue to finance projects or provision once joint finance has expired, and this growth will be in addition to that necessary to keep pace with demographic and other changes. Difficulties in determining the boundaries between health and social care have been sharpened by the introduction of purchaser–provider splits and increasingly local authorities see joint finance as a bribe to incur further expenditure (when the joint funding ends) to which they might not otherwise have agreed (Nocon 1994). It remains to be seen whether joint finance will continue to act 'as an ever increasing source of inescapable growth in PSS revenue budgets' (Webb and Wistow 1986: 38) into the next century.

Fees and charges: Client contributions for services It has been argued that another reason gross expenditure on the PSS has continued to grow is the increased use, and level, of charges for certain services over the last twenty years. The Association of Directors of Social Services reported to the House of Commons Social Services Committee in 1982 that 'local authorities who need to save money may well feel obliged to impose charges for services which were formerly free or to raise the level of those existing charges' (House of Commons Social Services Committee 1982: xlvi). Over the past fifteen years, the *choice* of local authorities whether to charge or not has all but become a *duty* to do so. In 1996, the Audit Commission noted that

The Government's view, confirmed in the Community Care White Paper *Caring for People* of 1989 and in its subsequent policy guidance, has consistently been that users who can pay for such services should be expected to do so, taking account of their ability to pay. (Audit Commission 1996a)

Local authorities have had the power to charge for residential care since the 1948 National Assistance Act, although local discretion in the level of charges was limited. Powers to charge for domiciliary and day care services are more recent, deriving largely from the 1983 Health and Social Services and Social Security Adjudications Act. This allows local authorities considerable discretion and has given rise to as many charging systems as there are local authorities (Audit Commission 1996a: 26). This has resulted in significant regional variations in charging, a point which we return to below.

Certainly the number of local authorities who charge for domiciliary services has increased over the last decade. In 1984/5, 78 per cent of metropolitan authorities and county councils charged for the provision of home helps (CIPFA 1985). By 1994/5 this had risen to 99 per cent (CIPFA 1996). What is not so clear, however, is whether the revenue raised from charging has risen significantly. Table 6.3 shows fees as a percentage of gross expenditure on the PSS in England. The figures for fees and charges include payments received from other local authorities for the purchase of services as well as payments made by people receiving services. No upward trend is visible in the total percentage, despite the main income-generating service, i.e. residential care, constituting a declining proportion of total PSS. It is interesting to note that it has been those services where contributions from *individual* users make up a high proportion of the total income from fees and charges that have experienced the greatest rise, most notably meals in the home.

Charging for domiciliary services raises a number of contentious issues. Most significantly, it has led some people to question whether they should continue with the services they receive (Chetwynd *et al.* 1996). There is also some confusion surrounding the principle of being charged, particularly where the service provided is one that can fall under the remit of either the NHS or PSS. Anomalies arise when health services remain free at the point of

Table 6.3. FEES AS A PERCENTAGE OF PERSONAL SOCIAL SERVICES EXPENDITURE, ENGLAND

	1983/4	1984/5	1985/6	1986/7	1987/8	1988/9	1989/90	1990/1	1991/2	1992/3	1993/4	1994/5
Children in residential care	9.6	9.3	9.0	8.7	7.8	7.5	6	3	2.5	3.8	4.2	3.4
Residential care for elderly and physically disabled	36.2	35.6	41.8	39.7	34.0	31.8	32	30	30.1	27.9	27.1	29.7
Other residential care	10.4	10.5	11.3	11.9	12.0	13.2	15	12.6	19.9	18.6	18.5	21.5
Home helps	7.0	7.2	7.5	6.9	5.9	5.6	5	6	6.5	6.7	7.9	6.8
Meals in the home	36.1	38.5	38.2	38.9	36.9	37.9	41	34	36.5	35.7	43.1	43.9
Day care	5.4	4.9	4.7	4.7	3.2	3.2	3	2	3.0	2.9	3.6	3.5
Other	1.6	1.3	1.3	1.5	1.5	1.5	2	2				
Total	13.8	13.5	14.9	15.3	12.3	11.4	11	10	11.0	10.2	11.1	14.1

Source: DoH (1996b and previous years).

delivery, while social services must be paid for; and it is difficult for individuals to understand the nuances of whether a bath is a 'social bath' or a medical one.

Regional variation in charging The discretionary framework for setting charges for non-residential services noted above has resulted in marked regional variations in charging policies and levels. Individuals living in similar circumstances can find themselves facing charges which vary markedly from SSD to SSD. In 1994/5 the standard charge for a meal at home for someone living in London varied from £1.60 in Hammersmith and Fulham to £1.05 in the City of London. Outside of London, there was even greater variation, with the cost ranging from £1.65 per meal in Dudley and in Kent, £1.25 in Clwyd, and 85p in Liverpool to only 35p in Derbyshire (CIPFA 1996).

As well as variations in levels of standard charges, there are also different approaches to assessing clients' 'ability to pay' that charge. There is no legal framework or guidance on how or whether to take users' savings or property into account when setting charges for non-residential services. As a result, a user on Income Support in one authority may pay more for home care services than someone with a substantial income or savings in a different authority. Furthermore, the net cost to authorities of care for people in their own homes is often considerably higher than the net cost of care in residential homes, even though the gross cost of care is the same (Audit Commission 1996a). Given the confusion surrounding the structure of charges for non-residential care, there is often a strong financial incentive for SSDs to place people in residential care, where the amount that clients are expected to contribute is set by statute, despite the fact that community care policy favours care at home when appropriate.

Expenditure by service sector Given the continued policy emphasis on community rather than residential care across the period, we might expect the different services under the umbrella of PSS to have fared rather differently in terms of the share of real expenditure devoted to them. Table 6.4 shows real net spending by local authorities on the different service sectors along with average annual growth rates. In 1987/8 there was a change in the manner in which expenditure was classified, basing it upon client group rather than service sector, so the figures are not directly comparable across time.

Expenditure on residential care grew rapidly in the 1970s but since 1978/9, growth in residential care expenditure has been outstripped by that directed towards 'day and community care' services. By 1992/3 day and community care services accounted for 38 per cent of net expenditure compared to 32 per cent for residential care. However, once fees and charges are taken into account, residential care still (but only just) accounts for the biggest share of gross expenditure on the PSS (39 per cent versus 38 per cent).

Expenditure by client group Real spending has increased for all client groups, but the growth has been most marked on services directed towards persons with mental illness,

Table 6.4. REAL NET EXPENDITURE BY LOCAL AUTHORITIES ON PERSONAL SOCIAL SERVICES BY SERVICE SECTOR, GREAT BRITAIN (£ MILLION AT 1995/6 PRICES)

Year	Fieldwork	Residential care	Day care	Community care	Miscellaneous	Total
1973/4	477	1430	316	715	29	2968
1974/5	639	1601	386	872	71	3568
1975/6	646	1839	416	897	71	3868
1976/7	684	2079	423	944	76	4207
1977/8	656	2069	423	927	98	4173
1978/9	659	2112	448	971	98	4288
1979/80	724	2204	449	988	101	4467
1980/1	778	2307	488	1007	112	4692
1981/2	784	2283	511	1024	119	4721
1982/3	796	2308	543	1075	123	4846
1983/4	830	2336	576	1154	135	5031
1984/5	850	2289	596	1175	144	5054
1985/6	859	2223	621	1223	146	5072
1986/7	916	2257	687	1343	144	5346
1987/8[a]	1515	1731	1877		58	5181
1988/9	1354	2002	2003		68	5426
1989/90	1442	1984	2144		105	5674
1990/1	1524	2065	2230		170	5989
1991/2	1603	2046	2304		194	6148
1992/3	1726	2025	2427		231	6408
Annualized growth rates (%)						
1973/4 to 1978/9	6.7	8.1	7.2	6.3	n/a	7.6
1978/9 to 1986/7	4.2	0.8	5.5	4.1	n/a	2.8
1987/8 to 1992/3	2.6	3.2	5.3[b]	5.3[b]	n/a	4.3

[a] In 1987/8 there was a change in the manner in which expenditure was classified, basing it upon client group rather than service sector. Fieldwork refers to all support services and is split as follows: 55% children, 25% elderly, 7% physically disabled (younger), 9% learning difficulties, 3% mentally ill, 1% other. Day care and community care are combined.
[b] Growth rate for day and community care services.

Sources: DHSS (1978: table 2.10, and equivalents for later years); Welsh Office (1979: table 2.10, and equivalents for later years); Scottish Office (1980: table 4.8, and equivalent for later years); GDP deflator from HM Treasury (1997).

where expenditure trebled in real terms between 1986/7 and 1994/5, and the younger physically disabled, where real expenditure doubled.

Fig. 6.5 shows the breakdown of PSS net current expenditure between the main client groups. Between 1978/9 and 1991/2 the proportion of PSS spending on children and elderly persons declined and the proportion of spending on people in all other client groups increased. This is the result both of the differential growth in spending on people with

Maria Evandrou and Jane Falkingham

Table 6.5a. REAL NET SPENDING ON PERSONAL SOCIAL SERVICES BY CLIENT GROUP, ENGLAND,1986/7 TO 1994/5 (1986/7 = 100)

	Children	Elderly	Younger physically disabled	Learning difficulties	Mental illness	Other
1986/7	100	100	100	100	100	100
1987/8	104.5	109.8	106.1	108.8	109.9	95.0
1988/9	113.1	115.6	96.5	107.9	97.3	131.4
1989/90	116.4	119.4	102.6	116.4	114.3	134.6
1990/1	123.3	123.0	106.0	127.7	122.8	139.4
1991/2	122.5	119.6	126.4	140.4	188.8	279.1
1992/3	126.7	119.8	148.0	147.0	225.9	218.4
1993/4	132.6	139.2	154.4	161.5	279.6	196.2
1994/5	139.4	164.3	203.4	170.5	322.5	265.4
(£ million in 1995/6 prices)	(1,946)	(2,975)	(484)	(870)	(319)	(86)
Annual growth rate, 1986/7–1994/5 (%)	4.2	6.4	9.3	6.9	15.8	13.0

Source: DoH (1966b and previous years).

Table 6.5b. ANNUALIZED RATES OF GROWTH IN REAL SPENDING BY CLIENT GROUP, 1974/5 TO 1994/5 (%)

	Children	Elderly	Other groups
1974/5 to 1978/9	2.6	6.8	5.7
1978/9 to 1984/5	1.6	2.2	5.3
1986/7 to 1994/5	4.2	6.4	9.1

Source: DoH (1996b and previous years).

mental illness and younger disabled, and of a shift away from more expensive residential care services towards community-based services, especially for children. Additionally, over this period there was a growing tendency for elderly people, who might otherwise have received social services from a local authority, to become resident in independent homes, often funded through the social security system. The transfer of responsibility for persons entering residential care to SSDs reversed this trend and by 1994/5 spending on elderly persons had regained its dominant share of total expenditure.

210

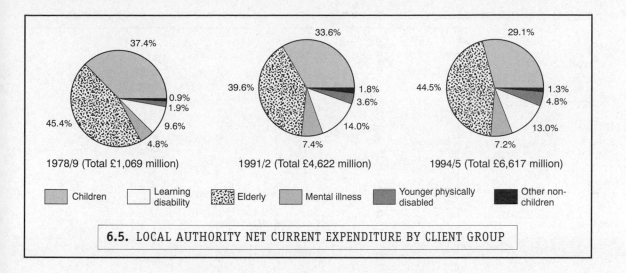

1978/9 (Total £1,069 million)   1991/2 (Total £4,622 million)   1994/5 (Total £6,617 million)

Children — Learning disability — Elderly — Mental illness — Younger physically disabled — Other non-children

6.5. LOCAL AUTHORITY NET CURRENT EXPENDITURE BY CLIENT GROUP

Expenditure and need

There is no doubt that the last twenty years have been a period of sustained growth in real spending on the PSS. And at face value it appears that expenditure on the PSS has grown at a pace that has outstripped need. For many years the DHSS argued that 2 per cent per annum growth in the real volume of spending was necessary for the PSS to meet demographic and other 'inescapable' increases in need. In the 1990s this figure has been revised downwards to around 1 per cent. In fact, as Table 6.2 shows, real growth averaged 4.2 per cent per year over the 22 years 1973/4 to 1995/6. Thus, growth in expenditure on the PSS appears to have not only kept pace with changes in need but to have exceeded it. Have these extra resources brought better-quality services or a greater quantity of services, or have services just been provided more inefficiently?

Service outputs Table 6.6 shows selected activity statistics for the period 1976/7 to 1994/5 drawn from the public expenditure White Papers. These figures provide us with an idea of what has been 'bought' by the growth in expenditure. Given positive rates of growth in both current and volume expenditure across the period one might expect this to be reflected in increases in service provision. However, there have been reductions in absolute levels of activity in a number of categories, most notably residential care for the elderly and for children 'in care'.

A number of alternative interpretations can be made when analysing the data in Table 6.6. On the surface the data could reflect the substitution of one mix of service provision for another, for example an increase in domiciliary support—home helps and meals—enabling more elderly persons to remain in the community, and this being reflected in a decrease in the elderly in residential accommodation. Alternatively they may indicate a fall in the target

Table 6.6. PERSONAL SOCIAL SERVICES ACTIVITY STATISTICS (000s)

	At 31 March																Annual % change
	1977	1979	1981	1983	1985	1987	1988	1989	1990	1991	1992	1993	1994	1995		
Residential care (sponsored residents)																*1977–94*
Elderly	117.0	117.1	117.2	115.5	110.0	104.7	100.8	97.3	90.8	84.6	75.1	68.7	89.0	102.4		–0.8
Physical and/or sensory disabilities[a]	10.3	10.0	9.8	9.0	8.0	6.9	6.3	6.2	6.5	6.8	6.3	6.2	6.5	7.2		–2.0
Mentally ill (local authority places)	4.4	4.9	4.4	4.3	3.9	3.6	4.6	4.7	4.4	4.5	4.4	4.1	3.8	3.7		–1.0
Learning disabilities[b] (local authority places)	12.0	13.7	15.3	16.7	16.9	17.1	16.8	16.9	16.9	16.7	16.3	15.5	14.5	13.6		+0.7
Children in residential care	36.0	32.8	29.7	22.1	16.1	14.3	13.3	12.0	11.5	10.6	8.7	7.2	6.8	6.3		–9.2
Day care (local authority places)																*1977–92*
Mixed client	10.7	12.3	13.9	15.7	17.0	17.4	17.4	17.5	18.3	17.8	17.2					+3.2
Elderly	15.3	18.9	20.7	21.1	21.8	21.9	21.9	23.3	24.5	27.0	25.9					+3.6
Places funded by local authority in sample week												139.1	147.6	176.4		
Physical and/or sensory[a] disabilities	10.3	10.2	9.6	9.1	8.7	9.0	9.0	8.8	8.5	8.5	9.2	n/a	n/a	n/a		–0.8
Places funded by local authority in sample week												53.1	51.9	53.5		

Mentally ill	4.3	5.3	5.7	6.4	6.7	7.1	5.8	6.1	6.4	7.0	7.8	n/a	n/a	n/a	+4.0
Places funded by local authority in sample week												39.8	45.3	50.5	
Learning disabilities[b]	38.9	42.1	43.6	46.6	48.8	51.2	51.8	53.0	54.2	55.9	56.7	n/a	n/a	n/a	+2.5
Places funded by local authority in sample week												139.1	259.2	268.8	
Domiciliary Services															*1977–94*
Home helps (wte staff)[c]	42.1	44.7	46.6	49.3	52.0	56.5	59.5	60	60	59	58	58	57	58	+1.8
Social work staff (wte)[d]	n/a	22.7	23.0	23.7	24.8	27.1	27	28	29	30	31	32	33	35	+2.7
Main meals (annual estimate in millions)	41.2	40.9	41.4	41.0	42.9	45.4	46.4	46.2	46.3	45.9	45.7				*1977–92*
Meals for a sample week in Sept./Oct.												776.7	768.4	794.1	+0.7

[a] Prior to 1987 refers to younger physically handicapped.
[b] Prior to 1987 refers to mentally handicapped.
[c] From 1989 domiciliary services staff (wte).
[d] Including team leaders/assistant team leaders and from 1994 care managers.

group, such as the total number of children in care over time. The figures, however, could also be interpreted to suggest that expenditure has failed to increase in line with rising unit costs, resulting in a fall in service output. Such activity statistics are limited in that they tell us about the *number* of people reached by the services but not about *frequency* of use or *quality* of care.

Activity statistics alone tell us little about whether the provision of services, allowed for by increasing real expenditure, has kept pace with need and changes in unit costs. Webb and Wistow (1986) suggest an alternative indicator, i.e. a constant level of service output per head of the relevant population, as a useful analytical baseline or yardstick. Throughout the last twenty years there has been a steady increase in the number of people who could be thought of as having a 'potential' need for social services. Most of this growth has been fuelled by changes in the age structure of the population. Fig. 6.6 shows the changes in size of different subgroups of the population over time. The number of people in England and Wales aged 85 and over has more than doubled in the last twenty years to 917,000 in 1994, while the population aged 75–84 has increased by a third to 2.64 million. Related to the increase in the elderly population has been a growth in the number of persons who are registered as blind, deaf, and 'severely handicapped' (Table 6.7). However, lower fertility in the 1970s meant that there were fewer children under 5 in the late 1970s and early 1980s. Below we go on to examine the changes in service output for each major client group and, as far as possible, relate this to changes in the size (and need) of that group.

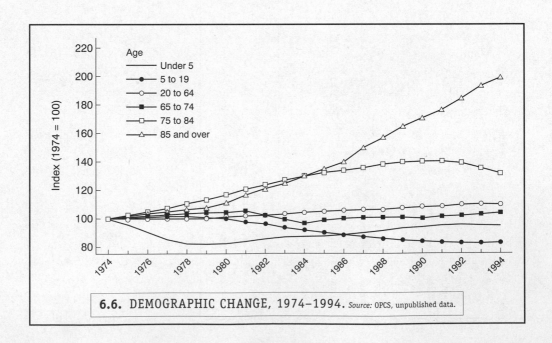

6.6. DEMOGRAPHIC CHANGE, 1974–1994. *Source:* OPCS, unpublished data.

Table 6.7. GROWTH IN POTENTIAL DEMAND FOR PERSONAL SOCIAL SERVICES, ENGLAND (000s OF PEOPLE)

	1975	1980	1986	1990	1994	Annual rate of increase (%)
'Very severely handicapped'[a]	15.6	56.5	76.1[b]	75.9	87.0[c]	10.0
Blind[a]	99.3	107.8	120.5	136.2[d]	149.7	2.2
Deaf[a]	25.6	29.6	34.1	37.9[e]	45.5[f]	2.9
Aged 85 and over	452	510	603	740	864	3.5
Children under 5	3,228	2,793	3,004	3,189	3,235	0.0
Children on the child protection register				43.6	34.9	−5.4
Children in care		95.3	67.3	60.5	49.0	−4.6

[a] Persons registered under section 29 of the National Assistance Act.
[b] Refers to 1987.
[c] Refers to 1993.
[d] Refers to 1991.
[e] Refers to 1989.
[f] Refers to 1995.
Source: DoH (1996b and previous years).

Has local authority provision kept up with 'demand'? Service outputs and client groups

Children Expenditure on children's services has risen in real terms by about 40 per cent since 1987/8 and accounts for around 29 per cent of net total expenditure on PSS. 'Social Services Authorities are required to admit to care any child under 17 who is in need of care, where the Authority considers it necessary to do so in the child's interest' (Audit Commission 1986a). It is their duty to keep the child in care until 18 where his/her welfare requires it. The authority's major objectives are the child's rehabilitation, and that the vast majority of children in care should eventually return to their own homes. The main policy objective is 'in developing forms of help which minimise the need to take the child away from the family' (DHSS 1976c: 64). This has remained the consistent goal throughout the period.

The 1989 Children's Act, which was implemented on 14 October 1991, radically altered the legislative framework for the provision of services to children. The intention of the Children's Act was to promote the use of accommodation as a family support service, and when a child has to live away from home to make voluntary arrangements with parents whenever possible. As a result of less interventionist policies in the early 1980s and the implementation of the Children's Act in 1991, the number of children in care has fallen (Fig. 6.7). Although the number of children in the population has also fallen, the number of children in

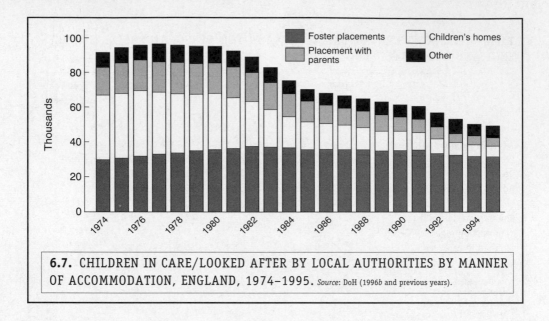

6.7. CHILDREN IN CARE/LOOKED AFTER BY LOCAL AUTHORITIES BY MANNER OF ACCOMMODATION, ENGLAND, 1974–1995. *Source:* DoH (1996*b* and previous years).

care has fallen even faster. In 1974 there were just under 90 children in care per 10,000 children under 18, but by 1995 this figure had dropped to just 44. This has been paralleled by a change in the manner in which children in care are looked after, with a reduction in the proportion in children's homes and a rise in foster placements (from 50 per cent in 1985 to 64 per cent in 1995). The data appear to support the idea that local authorities are working more closely with families to meet the needs of the children through greater preventative work.

Fig. 6.8 shows the trends in day care places for children under 5 between 1985 and 1995. The main growth in overall places has been provided by a rise in the number of registered childminders. In 1995 there were 97,100 registered childminders providing 373,600 places, compared to 58,390 childminders providing 126,847 places in 1985—equivalent to a growth rate in places of 11 per cent a year. Day nursery provision has also increased rapidly, trebling over the period 1985 to 1995 from 54,890 places in 1985 to 161,500 in 1995. All the growth has been in the independent sector, with places in registered nurseries increasing from 25,242 in 1985 to 139,300 in 1995 whilst places in local authority provided nurseries fell from 28,904 to 20,900 (DoH 1996*i*).

Table 6.8 gives us a better idea of what local authorities themselves are providing (and purchasing) in the way of day care for children. Since 1986, there has been a steady fall in the number of children on the registers of local authority day nurseries and this has only been offset in part by a rise in the number of children placed and paid for by local authorities in private and voluntary day nurseries. The Children's Act introduced registration of out-of-school clubs for 5- to 7-year-olds and in 1995 there were 22,400 children on the registers of such clubs run by local authorities (out of a total number of 44,600).

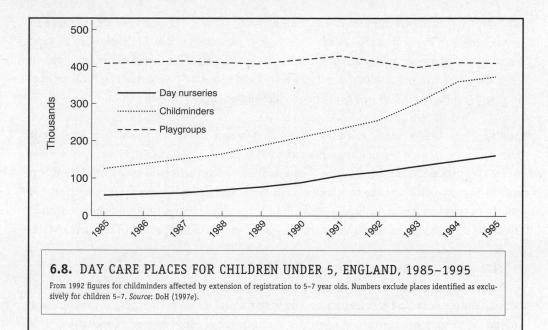

6.8. DAY CARE PLACES FOR CHILDREN UNDER 5, ENGLAND, 1985–1995

From 1992 figures for childminders affected by extension of registration to 5–7 year olds. Numbers exclude places identified as exclusively for children 5–7. *Source*: DoH (1997*e*).

Table 6.8. CHILDREN RECEIVING LOCAL AUTHORITY DAY CARE, 1985–1995

	Facilities provided by local authorities				Children placed and paid for by local authorities in private or voluntary day care facilities		
	Children on the register of			Children placed with local authority childminders	Day nurseries	Playgroups	With childminders
	Day nurseries	Playgroups	Out-of-school clubs				
1985	32911	3196			1567	9726	3006
1986	34917	3150			1788	11513	3884
1987	34709	3370			1825	12173	4984
1988	34398	3205			2084	11976	5107
1989	32585	2717			1823	11107	5738
1990	32413	2525			1788	11556	5492
1991	30302	2319			1970	11678	6916
1992	28400	1600	9200		2000	11100	6300
1993	27100	1600	11700	1100	1700	12200	4100
1994	29000	2300	12500	1700	2800	13600	5000
1995	27500	2300	22400	1400	2300	9300	4800

Source: DoH (1996*i*: table 8).

Maria Evandrou and Jane Falkingham

Comparing the total number of day care places shown in Fig. 6.8 with the number of places provided by local authorities in Table 6.8, it can be seen that the main role of local authorities with regard to day care for children is that of a *regulator* rather than a provider. In 1995, fewer than 15 per cent of day nursery places were paid for or provided by local authorities, and less than one-half of 1 per cent of childminder and playgroup places.

Elderly There are currently just under 12 million people in the UK population aged 60 or over. Older people are the major users of most PSS, and those aged over 75 are the heaviest users. This group has increased in size dramatically over our period of study, from 2.8 million in 1974 to 3.7 million in 1986 to 4.2 million in 1996. The general aim of policy is to enable elderly persons to maintain independent lives within the community, and thus the main emphasis of policy from all Governments has been on the development of domiciliary services.

SSDs provide a wide range of services for the elderly. There are no requirements for the level of service provided. However, they are under statutory obligation to provide 'adequate' home help services, and services for people with mental illness or learning or physical disabilities who may be elderly, and so to this extent there is some degree of regulation. It is important to note, however, that a recent judicial review of Gloucestershire County Council's decision to withdraw services from five service users held that SSDs did not have an absolute duty to meet the clients' needs (M. Richards 1996; Wistow 1997). Thus it appears that SSDs are not under statutory obligation to provide services to elderly persons even if they have been assessed by that SSD as being in need of such services.

Priorities for the health and social services (DHSS 1976b) quoted targets and guidelines for domiciliary service provision which were endorsed in 1977 in *The Way Forward* (DHSS 1977a): 12 home helps per 1,000 elderly (65 years plus) population, and 200 meals a week provided per 1,000 elderly. In general, these were not met. Table 6.9 shows selected service provision in absolute terms and per 1,000 elderly persons. (The data source used here, that is CIPFA 'Actuals', is different from that used to compile Table 6.6 and so the figures are not comparable. Coverage is for England and Wales although it should be pointed out that the returns from local authorities are not always complete.) In 1993, fifteen years after the targets were set, there were on average just over 7.5 full-time equivalent home helps per 1,000 persons aged 65 or over and around 100 meals provided for the same group, i.e. the level of provision has remained at approximately *half* of the target level. In recent years targets within PSS have been abandoned, with the level of provision based on needs assessment although, as mentioned above, there is no statutory obligation to provide a service once a person is assessed as being in need of it.

The number of meals provided has been fairly stable across the last twenty years, despite the fact that the population aged 75 and over has been increasing. Therefore, the annual number of meals provided per 1,000 people aged over 75 has actually fallen from 15,500 in

Table 6.9. PERSONAL SOCIAL SERVICES AND THE ELDERLY POPULATION: INDICES, ENGLAND AND WALES (1974 = 100)

	Number 1974	At 31 March 1974	1976	1978	1980	1982	1984	1986	1987	1988	1989	1990	1991	1992	1993	1994
Total elderly population (000s)																
aged 65 plus	6,929.2	100	102.7	105.6	108.3	108.9	107.9	111.9	113.6	114.5	115.4	115.9	117.3	117.8	118.2	118.4
aged 75 plus	2,468.2	100	104.5	109.9	115.8	121.7	128.3	133.4	137.1	139.9	142.8	144.7	146.7	146.8	145.6	144.2
Total elderly in residential care (000s)	113.9	100	107.4	110.0	110.9	109.3	105.1	100.1	98.1	94.6	91.4	85.4	79.6	70.6	64.8	83.0
per 1000 population aged 65 plus	16.4	100	104.8	104.2	102.4	100.3	97.4	89.5	86.3	82.3	79.0	73.3	67.9	60.0	54.9	70.1
per 1000 population aged 75 plus	46.1	100	103.0	100.1	95.8	89.8	81.9	75.0	71.5	67.6	64.0	59.0	54.3	48.1	44.5	26.6
Home helps (000s) (wte)	42.1	100	110.8	118.1	119.4	122.1	128.4	123.4	129.6	n/a	141.4	152.5	148.4	152.0	148.0	n/a
per 1000 population aged 65 plus	6.1	100	107.8	111.8	110.3	112.1	119.1	116.3	114.1	n/a	122.1	130.9	126.5	129.0	125.2	n/a
per 1000 population aged 75 plus	17.0	100	106.1	107.5	103.2	100.3	100.1	97.5	94.6	n/a	99.1	105.4	101.2	103.5	101.6	n/a
Meals (000s)	38,330	100	110.6	105.0	107.6	111.8	109.8	97.2	102.5	114.1	112.7	127.2	126.2	115.0	113.4	113.3
per 1000 population aged 65 plus	5,532	100	107.6	99.5	99.4	102.6	101.8	86.9	90.2	99.2	97.2	109.2	107.6	97.6	95.9	95.7
per 1000 population aged 75 plus	15,529	100	105.8	95.6	93.0	91.8	85.6	72.8	74.8	81.5	79.0	87.9	86.0	78.3	77.8	78.5

Source: DoH (1996b and previous years).

1974 to 12,200 in 1994. Fig. 6.9 shows that there has been a particularly sharp drop in the number of meals provided to elderly people from 1991. It has been suggested that this may reflect more targeting of services, with clients who might previously have received meals at home or in luncheon clubs using other services such as day centres (DoH 1997e). However, the General Household Survey shows that amongst elderly people living alone with mobility difficulties, i.e. those who require meals at home, the proportion in receipt of meals on wheels also fell (see Table 6.18 below).

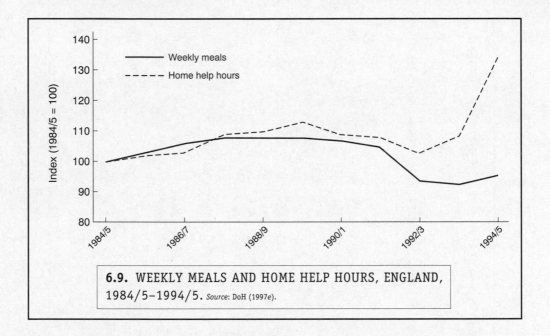

6.9. WEEKLY MEALS AND HOME HELP HOURS, ENGLAND, 1984/5–1994/5. *Source:* DoH (1997e).

There was a sharp rise in home help/care hours after 1992/3, following the implementation of the Community Care Act (Fig. 6.9). In 1994/5 the majority of home help/care contact hours were still provided by the local authorities themselves (80 per cent) although virtually all the growth shown in Fig. 6.9 was provided by expansion in the independent sector. In 1994/5 the voluntary and private sectors provided almost five times the number of contact hours that they had done in 1993/4.

Day care places for elderly clients have also increased, rising by 69 per cent from 15,300 in 1977 to 25,900 in 1992 (Table 6.6), while the population aged over 75 increased by only 40 per cent over the same period. The majority of day care places are provided by the local authority, although the size of the voluntary and private sector has been increasing in recent years. In 1995 the independent sector accounted for 18 per cent of places in day centres purchased or provided by local authorities compared with 10 per cent in 1992. However, although the absolute and relative number of places has increased, the proportion of the (larger) elderly population who report the use of a day centre has fallen from 5 per cent in 1985 to 3 per cent in 1994 (see Table 6.14 below).

Other local authority provided services for the elderly have also shown little or no increase over the period. From Table 6.9 it can be seen that the absolute level of SSD provision of residential care for the elderly (in local authority homes and sponsored places in private and voluntary homes) has fallen, despite an increase in the size of the 'target group'. When the two trends are taken together, the number of local authority sponsored residential care places per 1,000 aged 75 and over has more than halved between 1974 and 1993, from 46.1 per 1,000 to 20.5. In 1994 there is a marked upturn in the number of local authority sponsored residential care places as the 1990 Community Care Act comes into effect.

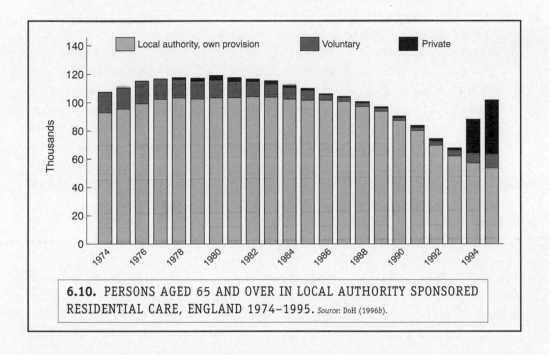

6.10. PERSONS AGED 65 AND OVER IN LOCAL AUTHORITY SPONSORED RESIDENTIAL CARE, ENGLAND 1974–1995. *Source:* DoH (1996*b*).

During the early 1980s the fall in local authority sponsored residential care places was largely due to a decline in local authority sponsored places in the voluntary and private sector, but from 1988 onwards places in local authority homes contracted sharply (see Fig. 6.10). After 1993, when local authorities became responsible for residential care previously covered by social security, local authority funded places rose dramatically, with all of the growth being in the voluntary and private sector. However, even by 1995/6 the number of total local authority sponsored residential care places for the elderly remained lower in absolute terms than in 1973/4, despite the fact that the population aged 75 and over increased by nearly 50 per cent across the period.

Maria Evandrou and Jane Falkingham

In summary:

- The volume of services for the elderly has increased, but local authority provided or purchased residential care places have not kept pace with demographic change.
- There has been a shift in emphasis from residential to community care, with more day places and home help hours.
- Use of the independent sector has grown markedly.

People with learning disabilities Around 3 to 4 people out of every 1,000 suffer from a severe learning disability (Felce *et al.* 1992). Many others have some degree of disability that necessitates support from SSDs. The majority of people with learning difficulties live within the community. Nine in every ten such children live at home, although the proportion falls with age and 60 per cent of 'severely mentally handicapped' adults receive institutional care (Audit Commission 1986*a*).

In 1971 the DHSS published a White Paper, *Better Services for the Mentally Handicapped*. This document identified a 'serious shortage of adult training centres and a great need for more trained staff'. It set targets for an increase in such training places to 74,500 and residential care places to 29,800, to be achieved over the next twenty years. Table 6.6 shows that there has been a rise in both the number of adult training places and residential care, although not sufficient to reach the targets set out in 1971. Day care places for people with learning difficulties rose from 38,900 to 56,700 between 1977 and 1992, an annual rate of increase of 2.5 per cent. Local authority *provided* residential care places increased up to the mid-1980s, remained steady during the late 1980s, and then fell from 1990. However, local authority *funded* places continued to rise, with an increase in places sponsored by local authorities in the voluntary and private sector (Fig. 6.11). Once again the impact of the 1990 Community Care Act is reflected in a rapid increase in supported residents post-1993, and in 1995 there were 22,700 people with learning difficulties supported by local authorities in residential and nursing care homes.

On the face of it, it appears that there has been an expansion of services for people with learning difficulties over the past twenty years. However, looking at changes in the volume of PSS presents only part of the picture. In line with the Government's policy on reducing institutional care, there has been a reduction in the number of hospital in-patients. The estimated number of in-patients under the care of a mental handicap specialist fell from 40,170 in 1983 to 11,400 in 1995 (House of Commons Health Committee 1996: table C7.1). Over roughly the same time period, the number of specialist community mental handicap nurses increased from 770 in 1984 to 2,020 in 1994.

Taking all of this together, it is not clear whether this represents a net increase or reduction in service provision to people with learning disabilities. Certainly the additional 7,100 local authority sponsored places in residential and nursing care homes between 1984 and 1995 are not sufficient to offset the fall in in-patients of nearly 29,000. Most of the in-patients

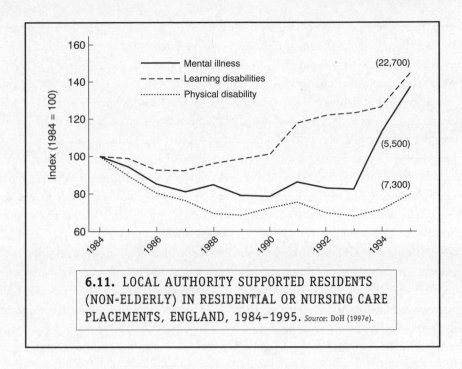

6.11. LOCAL AUTHORITY SUPPORTED RESIDENTS (NON-ELDERLY) IN RESIDENTIAL OR NURSING CARE PLACEMENTS, ENGLAND, 1984–1995. *Source*: DoH (1997e).

discharged have returned to the community. Day places and community nurses have risen but it is questionable if these rises are enough.

In summary:

- Day care places for people with learning difficulties rose from 38,900 to 56,700 between 1977 and 1992, an annual rate of increase of 2.5 per cent.
- There were an additional 7,100 local authority sponsored places in residential care— a rise of 46 per cent; but
- the number of in-patients with learning disabilities fell by 29,000 between 1984 and 1995.

People with mental illness In the 1975 White Paper *Better Services for the Mentally Ill* (DHSS 1975) it was estimated that five million people annually consulted GPs about mental health problems, and some 600,000 people receive specialist psychiatric care each year. These levels have increased as awareness of mental health problems in society in general has risen. Recently Golberg and Huxley estimated the annual incidence of mental health problems per 1,000 population in England, on a scale of severity, to be: 5.7 for people needing in-patient treatment, 23.5 for mental health service users, 101.5 for problems identified by GPs, 230 for GP attendances, and 260–315 for problems in the community (Audit Commission 1994). Thus on a narrow definition of people with mental illness as those with very serious

Maria Evandrou and Jane Falkingham

problems, just over 2 per cent of the population require specialised care, that is, approximately 1.3 million people in the UK. If more broadly defined, nearly a quarter of the population have attended a GP with problems related to mental health.

Mental health policy has changed over time. For many years specialist care was provided in large remote hospitals but, from around the time of the 1959 Mental Health Act, the aim has been to provide most people with a range of community services, supported by hospital care only when necessary. The 1983 Mental Health Act placed significant duties on SSDs for the appointment of social workers and for the provision of alternatives to psychiatric hospital care and the planning of post-hospital care. Recently mental health has been receiving renewed attention with its inclusion as a key priority in *The Health of the Nation*, and with growing public concern about the adequacy of community care after several highly publicised murder cases involving recently released mental health patients.

The provision of specific mental health services has until recently been a relatively small part of local authorities' work. This is due to the historical dominance of health service provision in this sector. The 1990 Community Care Act, however, has given local authorities a leading responsibility for assessing the social care needs of vulnerable people in the community and providing appropriate packages of care to support independent living. The Mental Illness Specific Grant (MISG) was introduced in 1991 to assist local authorities to expand social care provision for people with mental illness in collaboration with health authorities, GPs, and other agencies.

The main emphasis of policy has been to shift the care of the mentally ill from hospital in-patient care towards care in the community. The number of occupied hospital beds has fallen by 47.3 per cent since 1984/5 (House of Commons Health Committee 1996). Table 6.6 shows that local authority places in residential care, however, were fairly steady across the 1980s and decreased in the early 1990s. Not only did direct provision shrink but, as Fig. 6.11 shows, local authority sponsored places also fell up to 1993. This was largely the result of a greater proportion of people with mental illness living in private accommodation, supported by social security payments. The private sector is the largest provider of residential care for people with mental health problems. In 1995, the private sector accounted for over 55 per cent of all residents (supported and otherwise), with the voluntary sector and local authorities accounting for about 25 per cent and 20 per cent respectively (DoH 1997e; see also Fig. 6.17).

The number of community mental health nurses, funded by district health authorities, has more than doubled since 1984, from 1,880 in 1984 to 4,760 in 1994. Local authority day care places for the mentally ill have also expanded. In 1995/6 there were 53,000 day centre places provided or purchased by local authorities for people with mental illness during a particular week, compared to 39,800 in 1992/3, a rise of a third in three years. Therefore it appears that services to the mentally ill have improved although it must be remembered that it has been at a price. Spending by SSDs on persons with mental health problems has increased threefold in real terms between 1986/7 and 1994/5 (Table 6.5a).

In summary:

- After stagnating during the late 1980s, social care provision for people with mental illness has expanded in recent years as a result of the MISG.
- Day care places increased by a third between 1992/3 and 1995/6.
- Local authority sponsored residential care places rose by 67 per cent over the same period.
- This expansion in social care has been accompanied by a fall in in-patient care, with the number of occupied hospital beds almost halved since 1984/5.

People with physical disabilities Under section 29 of the National Assistance Act, local authorities are required to compile and maintain registers of 'persons who are blind, deaf or dumb and other persons who are substantially and permanently handicapped by illness, injury, or congenital deformity'. In 1993 there were 36,900 persons aged under 65 registered as very severely handicapped and a further 198,800 registered as severely or appreciably handicapped. This represents an increase of 34 per cent and 52 per cent respectively on the numbers of younger persons registered as disabled in 1981 (27,500 very severely and 130,600 severely or appreciably handicapped; DoH 1994a: 9). Registration of disablement with SSDs is voluntary and is not a condition for the provision of certain social services. The registers, therefore, do not necessarily measure the prevalence of physical disablement in the population. The OPCS Survey of Disability found that 14 per cent of all adults living in private households had at least one disability. Over 30 per cent of these were aged under 60 (Disability Alliance 1988).

There has been no direct policy statement concerning targets or levels of service provision to this group, as has been the case with persons with learning difficulties and the mentally ill. However, the 1986 Disabled Persons Act has given more positive responsibilities to local authorities for the care and welfare of persons with disability. SSD services to this group include sheltered employment, day care services, laundry and incontinence services, aids and adaptations, a range of domiciliary services, telephones and alarm systems, occupational therapy and concessionary fares, as well as assistance to voluntary organisations. Services are also provided by a range of other bodies such as the NHS, the Training Commission, housing authorities (especially with regard to sheltered housing), and local education authorities.

Expenditure on local government services for younger physically disabled persons has increased in real terms (Table 5.5a). However, this does not appear to have been accompanied by a growth in the provision of services. The 1976 *Priorities* document suggested that an additional 600 day places should be provided annually. This has not been the case. Table 6.6 shows that local authority day care places remained roughly constant through the earlier part of the period and declined slightly in the late 1980s, despite the rise in the number of persons registered by SSDs as disabled.

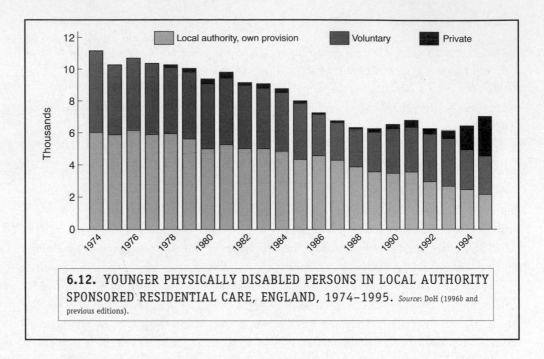

6.12. YOUNGER PHYSICALLY DISABLED PERSONS IN LOCAL AUTHORITY SPONSORED RESIDENTIAL CARE, ENGLAND, 1974–1995. *Source*: DoH (1996*b* and previous editions).

The number of younger physically disabled supported residents in residential care declined steadily across the period, although the numbers did rise significantly in 1994/5 (Table 6.6 and Fig. 6.12). The mix of provision has changed, with local authorities purchasing more places in the independent sector and providing fewer places themselves. Looking at *all* residential care for younger physically disabled, the main provider remains the voluntary sector.

In summary:

• There has been an increase in the number of younger persons registered with SSD as 'severely handicapped', from 27,500 to 36,900 between 1981 and 1993 (increase of 34 per cent). Over the same period, the number registered as 'severely or appreciably handicapped' has risen from 130,600 to 198,800 (a rise of 52 per cent).
• There has been a 40 per cent fall in the number of residential places for younger physically disabled persons between 1974 and 1994.
• There has been no corresponding increase in day care places.

To recap, although expenditure has increased on all client groups, higher spending has not necessarily been reflected in increased provision, especially when changes in the size of the group in need of services is taken into account. The mix of services has also shifted, from higher-cost residential care to lower-cost day and domiciliary care. To what extent therefore has the increased spending on PSS been efficient? Total expenditure has risen by around 4 per cent per annum over the last twenty years, but over the period to 1993, when the community care reforms began to be implemented, most of the measures of activity and service discussed above have tended to decline.

Increased expenditure: Value for money?

Fig. 6.13*a* shows that weekly unit costs for children in residential care (including children placed with foster parents) have risen significantly in the last decade. After taking account of the rise in prices met by local authorities for social services staff and other inputs, the unit costs for children in local authority homes increased by nearly 80 per cent, from just under £600 a week in 1984/5 to £1,060 in 1994/5 (in 1994/5 prices), while unit costs for children in foster homes nearly doubled, from £81 in 1984/5 to £156 in 1994/5 (at 1994/5 prices). Real unit costs for other client groups have also risen (Fig. 6.13*b*).

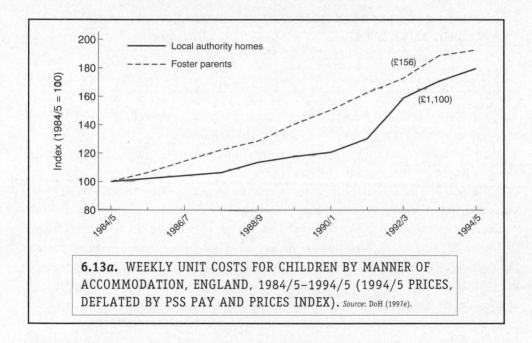

6.13*a*. WEEKLY UNIT COSTS FOR CHILDREN BY MANNER OF ACCOMMODATION, ENGLAND, 1984/5–1994/5 (1994/5 PRICES, DEFLATED BY PSS PAY AND PRICES INDEX). *Source:* DoH (1997e).

Higher unit costs can be explained by change in the client profile (greater dependency), an increase in the quality of service, a reduction in efficiency, or a combination of all of these factors.

Greater client dependency? As we saw in Fig. 6.7, the number of children in residential care has fallen over time, and now children are looked after away from home only when there are severe problems. Many children who in the past may have been placed in homes are now being fostered, whilst some who might in the past have been fostered are now being provided

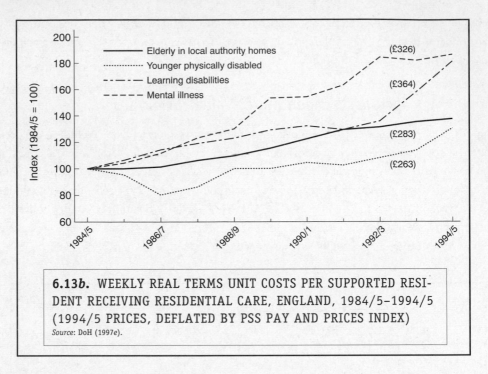

6.13b. WEEKLY REAL TERMS UNIT COSTS PER SUPPORTED RESI-
DENT RECEIVING RESIDENTIAL CARE, ENGLAND, 1984/5–1994/5
(1994/5 PRICES, DEFLATED BY PSS PAY AND PRICES INDEX)
Source: DoH (1997e).

with services in their own homes. It may be that the concentration of children requiring
more intensive support in each sector is associated with higher costs.

A similar case for a change in clientele, with an increase in more difficult or dependent
clients, can also be made for other sectors. The reduction in NHS provision for persons with
mental illness and learning or physical disabilities has increased pressure on community services. The shift towards community-based provision may increase the unit cost of each individual service without changing the combined cost of services. For example, those people
who would formerly have been the *least* dependent residents of geriatric hospitals are now
the *most* dependent residents of local authority homes, replacing the less dependent residents, who now become the most dependent clients of home care (Knapp 1987). However,
although there has been a shift to community care, Bebbington and Kelly (1995) argue that
there is limited research evidence that local authority services did indeed become targeted
on more difficult clients during the 1980s. And even if they did, it is not clear that the additional cost of caring for such clients is sufficient to explain all the higher costs.

Higher service quality? Expectations of quality have tended to increase across the period.
There has been a change in the skill mix of PSS personnel, with a rise in the proportion of
fully trained social workers (DoH 1997e). This has tended to increase staff costs and resulted
in higher unit costs. There have also been substantial increases in the ratio of staff to clients
in residential homes for the elderly (38 per cent from 1984/5 to 1994/5) and in maintained
children's homes (47 per cent) (DoH 1997e).

However, Bebbington and Kelly (1995) conclude that the rise in unit costs can only be partly accounted for by the general rise in input prices and changes in the circumstances of clients. Explanations must therefore lie in changes in quality or efficiency. In the absence of solid evidence pointing to a rise in quality, there appears to be a prima facie case that efficiency declined during the 1980s.

So far we have examined the trends in expenditure and service provision. It appears that both residential and domiciliary services have failed to keep pace with increases in the level of potential demand, especially amongst the younger physically disabled, and the elderly population. Below we go on to examine whether the trends in service outputs have been consistent with the strategy of community care and with the policy objective of 'protecting the most vulnerable' and enabling them to live independently within the community.

III. Outputs—extent, efficiency, and effectiveness

In this section we examine the extent to which policy aims and goals, other than general expenditure constraints, have been met by the different Governments over our period of study. For the purposes of presentation the policies of promoting 'community care' and a 'mixed economy of welfare' are addressed separately. However, they are not the outcome of separate policy decisions but rather are intimately interrelated.

Community care

As we have seen, 'community care' was an objective subscribed to by both Labour and Conservative Governments from the early 1960s on. Initially it was most frequently interpreted as meaning non-hospital care. The meaning of 'community care' has been refined over time and is now taken to mean non-residential care as opposed to just non-hospital care. In *Making a Reality of Community Care* it was stated that community care involves

the bringing of health services out of hospital settings into more local, domestic settings; and a change in balance between the provision of residential care and the provision of day and domiciliary services. (Audit Commission 1986b: para. 10(b))

Hence, it is necessary to look at both the balance between hospital and non-hospital care, i.e. between the health services and the social services, and at the balance of care within the social services between residential care and day care and other support services. Furthermore, recently the aim of community care has been seen increasingly to mean care *by* the community. The balance of care between the statutory sector and the private/voluntary and informal sectors is examined later.

Maria Evandrou and Jane Falkingham

The balance between health and social care One of the central aims of community care has been the reduction of the number of persons in long-stay hospital accommodation, particularly amongst persons with learning disabilities and mental health problems. Implicit in this is a shift in responsibility between the health services and the social services. Thus, although the focus of this chapter is on the PSS, we briefly look at the balance of spending between them and the health services.

The Audit Commission undertook a study to examine 'to what extent community care policies are being adopted in practice' (Audit Commission 1986b) and its report, as well as that of the National Audit Office (1987), drew attention to the relatively slow progress made towards these goals during the early 1980s. As we previously discussed, the 1990 Community Care Act gave local authorities a leading responsibility for assessing the social care needs of persons with mental health problems living in the community and the Mental Illness Specific Grant was introduced in 1991 to assist local authorities to expand social care provision for people with mental illness. Table 6.10 shows the balance of expenditure between health and social services for specific groups. There has been considerable movement between the two sectors, particularly during the 1990s. By 1994 nearly a third of all spending on people with learning disabilities was undertaken by local authority SSDs.

If we look at the level of hospital provision for these groups, the average number of beds occupied daily in mental illness hospitals and units in the UK fell by 47 per cent from 79,000 in 1984 to 42,000 in 1995, while the number of outpatient attendances increased by 13 per cent.

Table 6.10. BALANCE OF EXPENDITURE ON PERSONS WITH A LEARNING DISABILITY OR MENTAL ILLNESS, ENGLAND (%)

	1977	1985	1989	1994	Balance implied by 1971/5 White Paper target
Learning disability					
HCHS	73.8	64.5	63.6	61.2	44.2
PSS	26.2	35.5	36.4	38.8	55.8
Residential care	82.3	79.0	77.8	67.9	66.6
Community care*a*	17.7	21.0	22.2	32.1	33.4
Mental illness					
HCHS	97.0	95.5	96.2	94.4	87.0
PSS	3.0	4.5	3.8	5.6	13.0
Residential care	90.7	86.2	79.9	71.7	66.2
Community care*a*	9.3	13.8	20.0	28.3	33.8

a Community care includes HCHS outpatient and day patient expenditure as well as community and domiciliary services.

Sources: Figures for 1977 and 1985 from Audit Commission (1986b); figures for 1989 and 1994 from House of Commons Health Committee (1996: tables A4.1 and A4.2).

A similar pattern occurred for persons with learning disabilities. Daily occupied beds fell by 63 per cent while outpatient attendances increased more than twofold (Table 5.12; DoH 1996b). However, although in-patient beds have decreased the actual number of in-patient cases treated has increased as length of stay has been reduced. In 1995 74 per cent of all discharged patients with learning disabilities had been in hospital for under a week compared with 52 per cent of those discharged in 1983 (House of Commons Health Committee 1996: 119).

It could be argued that these overall trends reflect moves towards keeping the mentally ill and persons with learning disabilities living predominantly within the community, attending hospital when necessary and for respite care rather than for long stays. Parallel to these trends has been an increase in the number of persons living in local authority sponsored residential care for persons with mental health problems and learning disabilities, as seen above. There is, however, an obvious shortfall in the number of local authority places for the mentally ill when compared with the increase in discharge rate. In 1986, the Audit Commission expressed concern about where these people had gone (1986b: 17–18) and this concern was re-emphasized in 1994 in their review of mental health services, *Finding a Place* (Audit Commission 1994).

It is also open to question whether one form of institutional care has just been substituted for another or whether there really has been an increase in those living in the 'community'. We go on to look at the changing balance of care provided within the personal social services themselves.

The balance between residential and community care within the PSS If local authority expenditure on the PSS is broken down by service (Table 6.4) it can be seen that since the early 1980s spending on the community care services has grown at a faster rate than that on residential care and that the growth in expenditure on day care services has exceeded both of them.

The pattern of provision has changed over time. The activity statistics presented in Table 6.6, along with the other output data presented for each client group above, further confirm that the trend within PSS has been one of increased day care and support service provision. Fig. 6.6 showed the number of children in care by manner of accommodation. There is a clear trend toward reducing the proportion of children in care housed in residential homes, and increasing the proportion of those placed with foster parents. In 1995 nearly two-thirds of all children in local authority care were placed with foster parents compared with only a third in 1973. Local authority provided residential care has also fallen in absolute terms for the elderly and the younger physically disabled.

Table 6.11 presents data on some of the services which local authority SSDs provide or purchase for the disabled. Such services are thought to allow disabled persons to continue to live in their own homes within the community instead of having to enter institutionalised care. Many voluntary organisations also provide similar services for the disabled or supplement those financed by the local authority.

Maria Evandrou and Jane Falkingham

Table 6.11. LOCAL AUTHORITY SERVICES FOR PERSONS WITH DISABILITIES, ENGLAND (000s)

	At 31 March							
	1974	1976	1978	1980	1982	1984	1986	1987
Aids to households								
Telephone installations	21.8	14.8	14.0	12.9	9.4	14.5	14.5	14.8
Telephone attachments	1.1	1.6	2.1	1.4	1.6	2.9	3.7	3.8
Telephone rental	28.8	69.0	76.3	94.7	89.8	93.3	100.8	99.5
Television (supply)	2.5	1.6	1.2	0.7	0.3	0.4	0.7	0.8
Television licence	6.5	38.5	41.5	20.6	18.4	19.3	21.2	5.4
Radio (supply)	0.9	0.5	0.5	0.9	0.8	1.1	1.3	1.3
Other personal aids	142.5	191.2	219.3	245.9	278.6	345.6	394.8	448.1
Adaptations to property	19.1	22.9	303	31.7	34.0	49.3	60.0	76.4
People receiving assistance with holidays	89.8	101.4	87.0	84.5	67.2	63.0	53.1	56.6

Note: Figures not published beyond 1987.

Source: DoH (1996b and previous years).

It is clear that the provision of personal aids and adaptations to private properties has increased considerably over time. But, as we have seen, the number of disabled persons in the population has also risen. The growth in absolute terms of other services such as assisted telephone rentals has not been so marked, with the rate of growth slowing considerably post-1980; indeed provision of television licences showed an absolute decline from 1979. The number of persons receiving assistance with holidays, which may provide the only respite from care for informal carers, has also declined over the period for which data are available. Again these trends have occurred during a period of rapidly changing need (see Fig. 6.6). Thus, although there have been marked improvements in the provision of domiciliary care and other support services, from these trends and Table 6.9 it can be seen that they have been struggling to keep pace with changes in need. It is far from clear that levels of services have been sufficient to keep people in their own homes and thus *decrease* the size of the residential sector. In fact, if the total real government expenditure on the residential care sector for the elderly is examined, rather than just that from the PSS budget, we can see that there has been no decrease (see Table 6.12 below).

Has residential care decreased? We have seen that local authority and hospital residential care have been declining over the period. But this is only a partial picture of the total residential care sector. The total number of elderly persons living in residential accommodation in any sector between 1974 and 1995 in England increased by 72 per cent. Growth in resi-

232

dential care places for the elderly has outstripped the rise in the number of persons aged 75 and over and in 1994 there were 74 places per 1,000 persons aged 75 and over, compared to 60 in 1974, a rise of 25 per cent. There was also an increase in the number of places for persons with learning disabilities or with mental illness in residential accommodation, whilst there was a slight decline in overall places for the younger physically disabled. Figs. 6.14 to 6.17 map out these trends, distinguishing the development of the respective private, local authority, and voluntary sectors. Figs. 6.14 and 6.15 also distinguish between local authority sponsored places in the voluntary and private sectors and places in these sectors financed outside of SSDs' budgets.

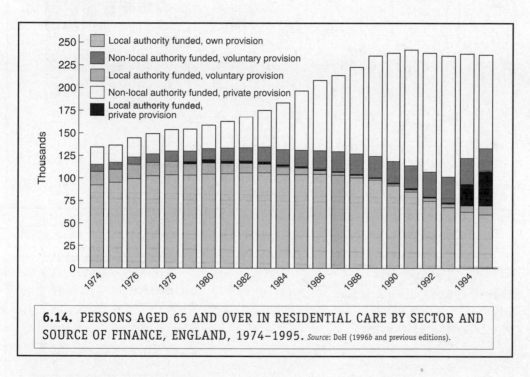

6.14. PERSONS AGED 65 AND OVER IN RESIDENTIAL CARE BY SECTOR AND SOURCE OF FINANCE, ENGLAND, 1974–1995. *Source*: DoH (1996*b* and previous editions).

What is striking is the marked growth in the private sector. For the elderly, in particular, local authority provision decreased alongside dramatic growth in the private sector from the mid-1980s onwards. This growth was fuelled by changes in social security legislation which allowed Income Support to persons in independent homes. By 1992/3 social security payments to elderly persons in residential and nursing homes amounted to nearly £2.5 billion (in 1994/5 prices) and accounted for nearly half of all public spending on institutional care of the elderly (Table 6.12). As discussed earlier, it is this dramatic growth in social security payments that prompted some of the changes enacted by the Community Care Act. Some have termed this growth in the provision of private residential care to the elderly as 'creeping privatisation' (Estrin and Perotin 1989) where similar patterns have been found in France with respect to residential care.

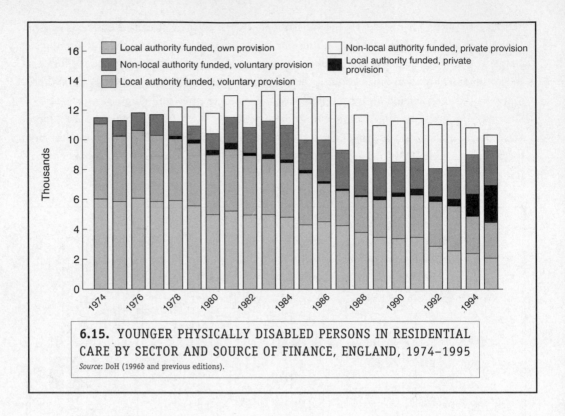

6.15. YOUNGER PHYSICALLY DISABLED PERSONS IN RESIDENTIAL CARE BY SECTOR AND SOURCE OF FINANCE, ENGLAND, 1974–1995

Source: DoH (1996*b* and previous editions).

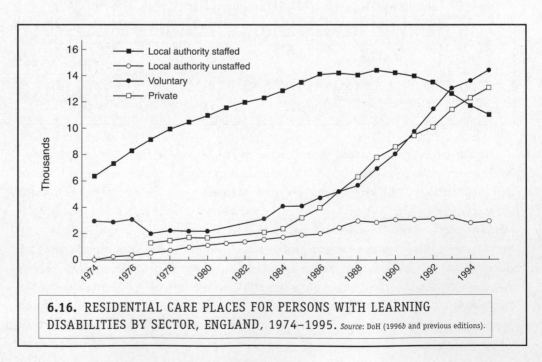

6.16. RESIDENTIAL CARE PLACES FOR PERSONS WITH LEARNING DISABILITIES BY SECTOR, ENGLAND, 1974–1995. *Source*: DoH (1996*b* and previous editions).

Growth rates have not been nearly as rapid for the younger physically disabled as for the elderly and this partly reflects the relatively low limits for social security funding compared to the much higher costs this group entails. However, as Figs. 6.16 and 6.17 show, there has been a rapid expansion in private residential care places for persons with learning disabilities and for those with mental illness, with growth again stemming from the early 1980s.

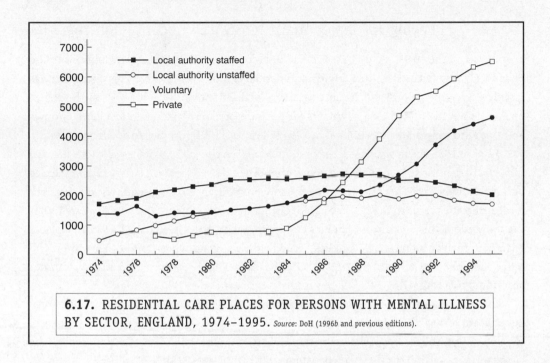

6.17. RESIDENTIAL CARE PLACES FOR PERSONS WITH MENTAL ILLNESS BY SECTOR, ENGLAND, 1974–1995. *Source*: DoH (1996*b* and previous editions).

The 1980s and 1990s have witnessed an increase in the total residential care sector. There appears to have been a shift from one pattern of residential care, based on hospitals, to an alternative, supported by Income Support payments—missing out community care altogether. How this has occurred, whether recent legislative changes have been successful in reversing this trend, and the implications for the balance of care provision between sectors are further examined below.

Changes in the mixed economy of welfare

At the beginning of this chapter in Fig. 6.2 we distinguished between the provision of care and its finance. Increasingly we have moved from a large reliance on services publicly financed and provided by SSDs to a pattern of services which remain largely publicly financed but are provided by a range of private bodies. The main vehicle for this change has been the social security system. One of the main planks of the Community Care Act was to reverse the situation whereby social security provisions created an incentive in favour of residential and nursing home care. To achieve this, local authorities became responsible for financing residential care places. A further objective of the new legislation is that local authorities are expected to make maximum use of the independent sector in the provision of services. Both of these have implications for the balance in the mixed economy of welfare. We assess the success of these goals below.

Paying for residential care: Social security and the STG

From 1948 on the social security system had discretion to make limited contributions to the board and lodging costs of those living in residential and nursing homes. This discretion was sternly exercised and only small sums were involved. As shown by Table 6.12, at the beginning of our study period DSS payments for the care of elderly people in residential homes amounted to only about £18 million at 1994/5 prices. This figure began to creep up in the 1970s but in 1980 the new social security regulations gave local DSS offices scope to meet in full the charges made by private and voluntary homes. This relaxation led to a faster pace of public funding of private care. The regulations were tightened on subsequent occasions but local authorities came to realize they could rely on the DSS to finance old people's care rather than provide it themselves and families began to realise that too. As local authority places became difficult to find many families turned to the private sector as another option and relied on the DSS to pay. By 1992/3 DSS payments to residential and nursing homes amounted to a staggering £2.5 billion (in 1994/5 prices).

Not only did local authorities' own provision fall, they also decreased the amount of residential care services bought in from the private and voluntary sector. There was no necessity to 'buy in' as they could rely upon the DSS to pay the bill. This ran counter to the Government's overall strategy of promoting contracting out (Baldwin *et al.* 1989).

Table 6.12. PUBLIC EXPENDITURE ON THE INSTITUTIONAL CARE OF ELDERLY PERSONS (£ MILLION AT 1994/5 PRICES)

	1977/8	1980/1	1985/6	1990/1	1992/3	1994/5
NHS geriatric beds	1,220	1,301	1,345	1,429	1,593	1,484
Local authority residential homes	956	1,037	1,059	1,076	957	1,736
Social security funding of residential and nursing homes	18	42	840	1,846	2,446	1,865
Total	2,195	2,380	3,244	4,351	4,996	5,085
Social security as % of total	0.8	1.8	25.9	42.4	48.9	36.7

Sources: Figures for 1977/8, 1980/1, and 1984/5 from Day and Klein (1987); figures for 1990/1 to 1994/5 derived from House of Commons Health Committee (1996: tables A4.1 and A.7).

A key feature of the 1990 Act was that local authorities became responsible for financing people in residential care in the independent sector. This took effect in 1993. The impact of this is clearly visible in Fig. 6.14 above. From 1993, there is a dramatic increase in the number of local authority sponsored places in the private and voluntary sectors. This rise is almost entirely matched by a corresponding fall in the number of places in the private sector which are 'independently' financed—overall there is no change in the total number of residential care places for the elderly. The additional places purchased by local authorities in the independent sector are not new places and what this amounts to is a shift in the financing of previously existing places.

Table 6.13. CHANGES IN SOURCES OF FINANCE FOR ELDERLY AND PHYSICALLY DISABLED RESIDENTS IN INDEPENDENT HOMES, GREAT BRITAIN 1986–1995

	1986	1988	1990	1991	1992	1993	1994	1995
Private payers[a]								
Residents (000s)	90	103	116	104	100	111	102	103
Share of total (%)	52	43	41	34	29	31	28	28
Income support[b]								
Residents (000s)	76	128	157	196	225	233	187	137
Share of total (%)	44	54	56	63	66	65	51	37
Local authority								
Residents (000s)	6	6	6	8	10	11	66	120
Share of total (%)	3	3	2	3	3	3	18	32
NHS								
Residents (000s)	2	2	2	2	4	6	9	13
Share of total (%)	1	1	1	1	1	2	2	3

[a] Excludes third-party top-ups.
[b] Fees wholly or partly paid by the social security system. From 1993 this includes those with Preserved Rights.

Source: Laing and Buisson Ltd. (1995, 1996b).

The explicit aim of policy was to shift responsibility for finance from social security to local authorities and the legislation has clearly been successful in achieving that. Table 6.13 shows that in 1992, 29 per cent of residents in the independent sector were paying wholly for themselves without receiving any public subsidy. Of the remaining 71 per cent the majority were in receipt of Income Support (66 per cent) and only 4 per cent were funded by local authorities or the NHS. In just three years, by 1995, only 37 per cent of residents in the independent sector were receiving Income Support while the proportion of residents funded by local authorities had risen to 32 per cent. The balance between the two main funding sources is changing rapidly as people in residential and nursing care with preserved rights under Income Support die (Joseph Rowntree Foundation 1996).

Central government has provided local authorities with additional finance through the Special Transitional Grant (STG) in order to achieve this. By 1997 the grant had been phased out and merely added on to local authorities' central government grant. One of the main concerns about the community care reforms has been whether the monies under the STG are sufficient for the local authorities to carry out their new responsibilities.

Other public funding of private provision: local authorities as 'enablers not providers'

As we have seen above, the buying in of residential care fell during the 1980s. So too did the purchase of other services by local authorities from the private and voluntary sector (Evandrou *et al.* 1990).

At the heart of the community care reforms was the creation of a care market. Under the terms of the *Caring for People* reforms, local authorities in England were required to spend 85 per cent of the STG on services in the independent sector. As a result local authorities have dramatically increased the use they make of voluntary and private sector providers both for residential care (as we saw in Figs. 6.14 and 6.15) and domiciliary care. In particular, there has been a tenfold increase in the proportion of all home help/care contact hours provided by the independent sector, from 2.4 per cent in 1992 to 29.2 per cent in 1995 (Table 6.14). The independent sector's largest proportionate contribution is in meals services—it provided 42 per cent of meals delivered to people's homes and 62 per cent of meals served at lunch clubs in 1995 (DoH 1996j). It is estimated that local authorities across the UK were contracting out home care to the value of over £150 million per annum in 1994 (Laing and Buisson Ltd. 1995).

Although these trends indicate a measure of success for the community care reforms in 'promoting the development of a flourishing independent sector' there remains a considerable degree of disquiet amongst independent home care providers concerning contracting arrangements between themselves and local authority purchasers. In a survey of UK Home Care Association members, three-quarters of providers felt that hourly rates of pay in the home care industry were 'too low' and just under a half reported that these levels 'inhibited' their ability to recruit suitable carers (Young and Wistow 1996). Other commentators have also voiced 'fears that the market changes put downward pressure on pay structures operated by homes and agencies' and that this has implications both for quality of services and for recruiting and retaining staff (Kenny and Edwards 1996).

Again, it remains to be seen what will happen to the balance of provision between sectors, and the volume of community care services more generally, after the ring-fencing of monies for community care under the STG ceases (see Audit Commission 1993).

Table 6.14. PROVISION OF LOCAL AUTHORITY FUNDED DOMICILIARY CARE SERVICES BY SECTOR, ENGLAND (000s)

	All sectors	Direct	Under contract using	
			voluntary sector	private sector
Contact hours of home help and home care				
1992	1,687.0 (100%)	1,647.8 (97.6%)	6.8	32.3
1993	1,780.0 (100%)	1,694.3 (95.2%)	16.1	70.4
1994	2,215.1 (100%)	1,787.0 (80.7%)	62.2	366.0
1995	2,384.1 (100%)	1,689.0 (70.8%)	76.6	618.5
Meals provided[a]				
1992	776.7 (100%)	468.6 (60.3%)	270.3	33.5
1993	768.4 (100%)	461.3 (60.0%)	262.1	39.4
1994	794.1 (100%)	443.7 (55.9%)	282.4	63.6
1995	814.8 (100%)	448.9 (55.1%)	283.8	77.2
Places at day centres				
1993	524.9 (100%)	465.7 (88.7%)	57.5	1.8
1994	569.3 (100%)	487.1 (85.6%)	78.3	3.8
1995	602.0 (100%)	496.5 (82.3%)	97.3	8.2

[a] All sectors total includes meals provided under contract from NHS, therefore figures do not sum to 100%.

Source: DoH (1996*j*: tables A1.1, A2.1, and A3.1).

Private resourcing

So far, we have examined the changing balance of public funding of both public and private (non-statutory) *provision*. As well as a shift in the pattern of provision of social services, there has also been a change in the overall sources of finance for care services, with an increasing share borne by individuals and families. Individuals have not only had to contribute towards the cost of local authority services through greater user charges, but as we shall see, they have also been buying more private care services as well as placing greater reliance on the informal sector.

Private resourcing of private provision From Fig. 6.8 it can be seen that the number of nursery and child care places provided by the private (registered nursery or registered childminders) and informal (volunteer-run playgroups) sectors have increased over time. However, there is no specific information available on the level of expenditure by families on such services. Research on the extent of private domiciliary services is also limited. A small-scale report based on 150 carers, carried out in the mid-1980s by the Centre for Policy on

Maria Evandrou and Jane Falkingham

Ageing (CPA), found the incidence to be very low (Midwinter 1986). This was confirmed with data from large national surveys: the 1980 General Household Survey (GHS) indicated that only 1 per cent of the elderly population paid for help with domestic tasks (OPCS 1982). However, there is evidence that paid care schemes have been increasing considerably over time (Leat and Gay 1987). In 1994, the GHS indicated that 7 per cent of the elderly population had paid for help with domestic tasks (OPCS 1996). Excluding local authority user charges, it is estimated that in 1995 individuals spent around £340 million on private home care and £85 million on aids and adaptations (Laing and Buisson Ltd. 1996b).

There are now a wide variety of 'paid' care schemes and services, and these cover a range of client groups. Distinctions are made between paid care provided in the client's home and that provided in the carer's home, and also between substitute care (i.e. paid carer 'standing in') and supplementary care (Leat and Gay 1987). Examples of such schemes include short-term respite paid care for the elderly, paid fostering of 'normal' children as well as those with learning or physical disabilities, and also 'difficult adolescents'. By far the largest amount of formal non-statutory provision (excluding residential care) and finance is provided by the charitable and voluntary, that is the non-profit, sector.

Voluntary Organisations and Charities Over the past two decades there has been a marked increase in the number, and income, of charities and voluntary organisations in Britain. In 1970 there were 76,000 registered charities, of which 65 per cent had an annual income of less than £100 per annum (CSO 1976). By 1994/5 there were 120,000 'general charities' with 'almost £12 billion in income, operating costs of almost £11 billion, net assets of £35 billion and contributing 0.6 per cent to GDP' (Hems and Passey 1996). One of the main reasons for this dramatic growth relates to the expanding role of organisations as service providers for government. The Charities Aid Foundation's annual survey of voluntary sector income from UK local authorities showed an increase of 12 per cent between 1992/3 and 1994/5 to a total of £1,271 million, of which £625 million was spent on social services (CAF 1996; see the growth in contracting in Table 6.14 above). In addition, a substantial proportion of charities and voluntary organisations provide services and support that operate in *parallel* with the PSS.

In 1995, of the top 500 fund-raising charities, 33 per cent of expenditure was directed to 'medicine and health' (with cancer research comprising just over a third of this, but services to blind, deaf, physically disabled, and mental health making up another a third) and 25 per cent to 'general welfare'. Thus it is estimated that around £1,180 million was expended on PSS-related activities in this sector. Some of this expenditure reflects local authority grant and fee income, but a significant proportion is in *addition* to spending on such local authority contracted services. Table 6.15 shows the expenditure of selected charities, and for 1995 income from central and local government grants and fees.

The highest expenditure is from those charities which support residential accommodation such as the Salvation Army and Barnardo's, although their range of activities extends far

Table 6.15. EXPENDITURE BY SELECTED CHARITIES (£ MILLION, CASH)

	1978/9	1985/6	1995	
			Expenditure	Central and local government fees and grants
Salvation Army	13.1	38.7	55.0	2.0
Barnardo's	14.9	36.0	76.5	33.6
SCOPE	13.9	35.7	57.3	33.0
Save the Children	5.8	46.1	91.8	22.1
Royal National Institute for the Blind	10.6	20.5	51.1	16.1
Guide Dogs for the Blind Association	n/a	9.9	34.9	—
National Society for the Prevention of Cruelty to Children	n/a	14.7	41.9	4.5
Children's Society	n/a	15.2	23.7	7.0
Help the Aged	5.8	11.5	37.5	0.3

Sources: 1978/9 figures from CSO (1980); 1985/6 figures from CSO (1988a); 1995 figures from CAF (1996).

beyond this. The non-statutory organisations have the freedom to develop more flexible approaches to care.

For example, the National Society for the Prevention of Cruelty to Children provides immediate help for children in need and supports a 24-hour national network of 'Child Protection Schemes' which respond to calls from families and the general public as well as from professional workers. In addition to the increase in the range of provision from charities, during the 1980s and 1990s a substantial network of voluntary advisory and counselling services has developed. There has been a rise in the number of enquiries across the board. The number of calls received by the Samaritans rose from 87,000 in 1971 to 393,000 in 1986 and 2.4 million in 1993, whilst the number of clients seen by Alcoholics Anonymous increased from 6,300 to 35,500 and then 47,000 over the same period (CSO 1988, 1995). In 1995/6 ChildLine counselled around 90,000 children, nearly four times as many as in 1986/7 (ONS 1997).

Another key development has been the advent of the National Lottery. By July 1996, the National Lotteries Charities Board had 'awarded £318 million to more than 4,000 organisations involved in worthy causes' and it is estimated that 'more than £800 million from the first full year of lottery sales will go to charities and voluntary organisation' (Sproat 1996). Of course, not all of these organisations will be concerned with welfare and service provision.

The last decade has also seen the emergence of the new phenomenon of charity appeals sponsored by television and radio, such as the 'Telethon'. The BBC 'Children in Need' trust

Maria Evandrou and Jane Falkingham

is now ranked by the Charities Aid Foundation as the sixth largest grant-making trust, with an income in 1994 of £17.2 million, more than some SSDs' budgets. Thus, it has become acceptable to 'supplement' services previously thought of as the preserve, or more centrally the statutory requirement, of public bodies with self-help, extending the ideology of the individual.

The informal care sector

The White Paper *Growing Older* (DHSS 1981c) stressed the primary importance of informal care for elderly persons and the importance of the 'personal ties of kinship and friendship'. There has been increased emphasis laid on the responsibility of the individual and a withdrawal from the idea of collective responsibility and provision. The informal care sector makes up by far the largest proportion of total care provision in private households.

Fig. 6.18 shows that amongst those aged 65 and over living in private households and in need of assistance with personal care or other daily living tasks, the overwhelming majority receive such support from the informal sector. The main source of support continues to be the family and friends/neighbours (Evandrou *et al.* 1986). As discussed above, a small but growing proportion reported relying upon privately paid support; in 1994/5, 12 per cent of elderly persons unable to carry out domestic tasks for themselves received support paid for privately, as compared with 1 per cent in 1980.

Sources of support reflect the living arrangements of elderly persons. Evidence from the 1994/5 GHS indicates that for the activities of walking, bathing, and domestic tasks, elderly

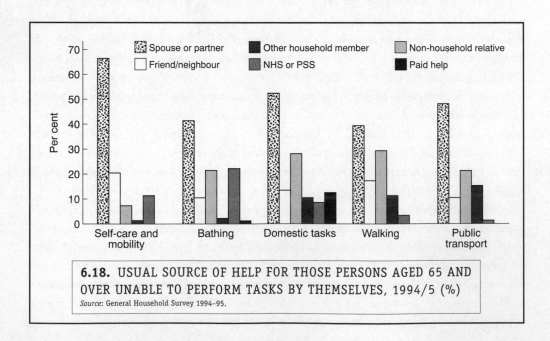

6.18. USUAL SOURCE OF HELP FOR THOSE PERSONS AGED 65 AND OVER UNABLE TO PERFORM TASKS BY THEMSELVES, 1994/5 (%)
Source: General Household Survey 1994–95.

people living only with their spouse are most likely to receive support from their spouse (87 per cent, 82 per cent, and 91 per cent respectively); elderly persons living alone are most likely to be supported by a relative living outside the household (67 per cent, 46 per cent, 59 per cent) and also by the NHS and personal social services (6 per cent, 45 per cent, 19 per cent); and amongst elderly people living in other household types, the main source of care is another household member or their spouse (OPCS 1996).

This constitutes the informal part of the private resourcing of private provision section of Fig. 6.2. The scale of this informal care provision for sick, incapacitated, or elderly persons is significant. Recent evidence from the GHS indicates that one adult in six provides such care, that is, 16 per cent of the population (OPCS 1992). The gender difference is small, 17 per cent of women compared to 14 per cent of men (Arber and Ginn 1995) although the type of caring work done differs between male and female carers: female carers are more likely to provide personal care, whereas male carers are more likely to provide support with physical tasks and practical support (Parker and Lawton 1994). Grossing up the figures nationally indicates that 1.7 million informal carers in Great Britain care for someone within their own home (excluding child-rearing) and another 1.7 million carers spend at least 20 hours per week providing care and support. Over one in ten of the 1990 GHS sample (i.e. 500,000 carers) reported providing both personal and physical care.

The financial implications of informal care have been costed by both academics and policy analysts (Netten 1991; Nuttall *et al.* 1993; Laing 1994; Richards 1996). Laing and Buisson Ltd. (1996b) estimate the cost of informal care work carried out in Britain in 1995 at £35 billion, assuming an average hourly cost of £7 (reflecting formal care rates). The amount spent by the Government for the whole of the PSS sector in 1994/5 (i.e. £6.8 billion) compares poorly with the cost of family support, at most constituting one-fifth (see Table 6.16). It is also important to note that this figure only deals with replacement costs of informal care, ignoring the opportunity costs of providing such support, which requires a more complex approach. An analysis by E. Richards (1996) endeavours to take into account the cost of carers' *waged* and also *unwaged* time, career costs, accommodation costs, and the costs of goods associated with care provision. The opportunity cost of such informal caring is estimated by Richards at about £17.7 billion for 1995, rising to £20.3 billion by the year 2031.

The economic and financial impact of caring may have short- and long-term effects, from reduced current disposable income to disrupted labour market histories, which result in the tragic legacy of lower earnings-related benefits and pensions in the carers' *own* old age.

Research using both the 1985 and 1990 GHS shows that carers' employment, earnings, hourly wage rates, and total income have been found to be significantly lower than their non-carer counterparts, standardizing on age, gender, and full-/part-time employment (Evandrou and Winter 1992). Multivariate analysis using the 1990 GHS indicates that informal caring has an independent negative effect on employment for both men and women (Evandrou 1995).

Few carers are eligible for Invalid Care Allowance (ICA), which was seen by some as an

Table 6.16. ESTIMATED EXPENDITURE ON COMMUNITY CARE, UNITED KINGDOM, 1994/5 (£ MILLION)

Source of finance/resources	Provider			
	State	Voluntary	Private	Informal
State				
NHS community health	£2,000[a]		£190 (NHS contracts)	
DSS			£2,200 (DSS residential allowance and preserved rights)	£90 (Independent Living Fund) £2,570 (Attendance Allowance) £3,000 (DLA) £530 (ICA) £100 (social fund community care grants) £260 (payments to foster parents)
Local authorities SSD	£5,440 (net, current)	£625 (grant and fee income to voluntary sector for community and residential care services)	£500 (private residential care)[b] £140 ('for profit home care)[b]	
Voluntary	n/a	£555		n/a
Private	n/a	£26 (corporate donations to voluntary sector)[c]	n/a	
Individual		£620 (user charges)	£2930 (fees for residential care)[d] £470 (private home care)[d] £160 (aids and adaptation)[d]	£17,700–£35,000[e]

Note: The figures in this table should be taken as indicative rather than as absolute.

[a] Estimates for UK, derived from GB figures.

[b] Informed estimate based on division between for-profit and not-for-profit organizations.

[c] Estimated as 25% of all corporate donations to voluntary sector.

[d] 1994, not 1994/5.

[e] £17.7 billion from Richards (1996), £35 billion from Laing and Buisson Ltd. (1996) valued at £7 an hour.

Sources: Laing and Buisson Ltd. (1995, 1996b); CAF (1996); DSS (1996a); DoH (1997e).

alternative 'wage for caring'. Set at £37.35 per week (as of April 1997) it is much lower than the basic pension and unemployment benefit, sadly failing to provide any kind of earnings replacement.

The extent to which carers can expect to recover their economic welfare over their lifetime is questionable. Research using dynamic micro-simulation modelling shows that the lifetime impact of caring on earnings and other income remains (Evandrou and Falkingham 1995). In particular, women with such caring responsibilities face lower lifetime earnings and pension income than women on average. The health consequences of caring, particularly where the dependent is physically and mentally impaired, have also been empirically documented (Evandrou 1996b).

The Carers (Recognition and Services) Act 1995 obliged local authorities to carry out separate assessments of carers when assessing individuals for service support. Whether this will result in higher levels of support for carers remains to be seen.

To conclude this section it is useful to return to our framework of the mixed economy of care presented in Fig. 6.2 and to try now to make some estimates of the amount of resources devoted to each cell. It is extremely difficult to get a clear view of total resources on community care as figures for different care sectors are calculated on different bases. Table 6.16 presents an educated 'guesstimate' of the relative contributions of different sectors in the mixed economy of care.

If we include a calculation for the replacement cost of informal care at £7 an hour, by far the largest contribution is the individual sector, totalling a staggering £35 billion (5 per cent of GDP). However, what is notable is that even if we *exclude* non-cash contributions, individuals and their families still spent around £4.2 billion on private care and contributions to statutory care services. This compares with around £7 billion spent by SSDs, £2.2 billion by the NHS, and £8.5 billion from the social security budget. The total *cash* cost of caring for the elderly and vulnerable groups in the community amounts to around £22 billion per annum.

Future directions

After several years of growth following the implementation of the community care reforms, with additional monies provided under the STG, levels of total local authority net current expenditures on PSS are expected to stabilise and remain constant in real terms (HM Treasury 1997). It is not clear what will happen after April 1998, when the monies under the STG cease to be ring-fenced for community care purposes. Options for alternative financing of long-term care have increasingly come under the spotlight, with the Joseph Rowntree Foundation Inquiry into the costs of continuing care highlighting the need for a National Care Insurance scheme (Joseph Rowntree Foundation 1996).

There is no doubt that the demand for social care and PSS will continue to increase into the twenty-first century. When the first 'baby boomers', represented by the five-year birth cohort 1946–50, reach retirement age in 2010, they will constitute one million more persons than the same age group (60–64) in 1995. Furthermore, when the 1960s baby boomers reach the same age in 2025, there will be over half a million *more* persons in that age group than in 2010 and 1.6 million more than in 1995 (Falkingham 1997). The demand pressures on the PSS in the early decades of the next millennium will be influenced by demographic changes, not only in terms of the numbers of elderly people but also with respect to changes in their living arrangements, with more divorce and 'solo' living, their health and degree of dependence, their financial resources, and the extent of isolation or social exclusion experienced as well as the availability of informal care (Evandrou 1997). The fact that the baby *boom* of the 1960s was followed by the baby *bust* of the 1970s is significant in this latter respect. In 1991 there were 84 persons aged 75 and over per 100 women aged 45–59. By 2031 it is expected that this ratio will rise to 125 and that by 2046 there will be a staggering 150 persons aged 75 and over per 100 women aged 45–59 (Evandrou and Falkingham 1997).

The ageing of black and minority ethnic communities has so far received very little attention. Progress by the social services agencies in the provision of appropriate support services for a multicultural society has been slow and uneven. In part this is due to the relatively small numbers of minority ethnic elderly today. However, one in fourteen of the 1960s baby boomers are from minority ethnic groups. Providing for a multiracial population in 2020 will be important.

In the 1990s generally the poor got poorer whilst the rich became richer (Rowntree Foundation 1995). The gap between the resourced and under-resourced is likely to be wider in 2020 and beyond. There will be fewer potential sources of informal support to rely upon when the baby boomers age. Those who have the financial resources will be in a position to purchase the social support necessary to remain in their own home for as long as possible. This may include aspects of 'smart housing' technology that facilitate independent living. However, the outlook for childless low-income elderly may well be bleak, forced to rely upon whatever services can be provided by the state and voluntary sectors. In the next section we look at issues of equity and whether persons across the income distribution are equally 'able' to purchase care.

IV. Outcomes

Equity and distributional issues of the personal social services

The discussion so far has focused on central government policy and expenditure trends, dealing more with the *macro* side of PSS. In this section, we confront issues of equity and analyse the distributional impact of PSS from the point of view of individual users, examining the *micro* side too. Data from selected years (1974, 1979, 1985, 1991, and 1994) of the General Household Survey were employed in order to unravel these issues.

The proportion of elderly persons in receipt of domiciliary care provided by the state sector is fairly small. The primary form of domiciliary care provided by local authority departments is home help services. In Britain, 8 per cent of elderly persons aged 65 years and over were reported in 1994 to have received local authority home help services in the previous month (Table 6.17). Even fewer, 3 per cent, received meals on wheels and 4 per cent attended an elderly day centre. It is interesting to note that there has been little change in these trends over time. Table 6.17 shows that between 1974 and 1980 the percentage of elderly persons reporting receipt of home help services rose by 2 per cent from 6.6 per cent to 8.8 per cent, but then remained virtually constant, hovering around 9 per cent for the whole of the next decade. Meals on wheels and community health services (e.g. health visitors, district nurses) provided similar levels of service over the whole time period, whilst there was a drop in the proportion reporting use of a day centre.

Thus, the proportion of the elderly in receipt of services has remained relatively constant over the last twenty years. This is despite the fact that there has been a change in the composition of the population aged 65 and over, with an increase in the proportion who are very

Table 6.17. USE OF PERSONAL SOCIAL SERVICES IN THE PREVIOUS MONTH AMONG PERSONS AGED 65 AND OVER BY SEX, GREAT BRITAIN, 1974–1994/5 (%)

	1974	1980	1985	1990/1	1994/5
Men					
Home help (local authority)		4	6	6	5
Home help (private)				4	5
Meals on wheels		2	2	2	2
Day centre		3	3	2	3
District nurse/health visitor		4	4	4	4
Women					
Home help (local authority)		12	12	11	10
Home help (private)				4	8
Meals on wheels		3	3	3	3
Day centre		7	7	4	4
District nurse/health visitor		8	8	7	7
Total					
Home help (local authority)	7	9	9	9	8
Home help (private)				4	7
Meals on wheels	3	2	2	3	3
Day centre	3	5	5	3	3
District nurse/health visitor	4	6	6	6	6

Note: the home help question changed in 1990/1.

Source: Authors' calculations from GHS raw data files for 1980, 1985, and 1994/5.

Maria Evandrou and Jane Falkingham

old and likely to be in greatest need of PSS. If we control for changes in dependency amongst the elderly population over time, a different picture begins to emerge. Table 6.18 shows the proportion of elderly persons who used a personal social service in the last month *amongst* those who were unable to walk out of doors unaided by household composition. There are several features to note. First, receipt of personal social services is markedly higher amongst those in need of support of daily living activities than for all elderly—indicating that services are generally targeted to those in greatest need. There appears to be a strong relationship between need for assistance with mobility and with self-care activities and visits from local authority home helps and the district nurse.

Table 6.18. USE OF PERSONAL SOCIAL SERVICES IN THE PREVIOUS MONTH AMONG PERSONS AGED 65 AND OVER BY FUNCTIONAL CAPACITY, GREAT BRITAIN, 1980–1994/5 (%)

	1980	1985	1994/5
Of all persons aged 65 and over			
Percentage unable to walk out of doors unaided	12	12	13
Home Help (local authority)			
Lives alone	62.3	55.3	45.1
Lives with others	14.9	16.5	15.1
Private domestic help			
Lives alone			19.2
Lives with others			6.0
Meals on wheels			
Lives alone	17.7	18.0	16.6
Lives with others	4.3	2.9	3.6
District nurse/health visitor			
Lives alone	33.1	30.4	29.7
Lives with others	24.4	18.0	17.7

Source: Authors' calculations from GHS raw data files for 1980, 1985, and 1994/5.

There is also, however, a strong relationship between the elderly person's living arrangements and receipt of PSS. Elderly people living alone are twice as likely to use a local authority home help or private domestic help as elderly people living with other household members. However, it is also worth pointing out that in 1994 one-third of elderly people residing alone and unable to manage bathing, showering, or washing had *not* been visited by either a local authority home help or a district nurse in the previous month (OPCS 1996: 150). Thus although services are targeted to those in greatest need there still appears to be a shortfall in provision.

Thirdly, and most importantly, there has been a marked decline in the proportion receiving PSS over time. Receipt of local authority home help amongst elderly persons living alone *and* unable to walk out of doors unaided has fallen from 62.3 per cent in 1980 to 55.3 per cent in 1985 and 45.1 per cent in 1994/5 (Table 6.18). At the same time private domestic help may have risen in response to this, although data are not available to confirm this. Proportions receiving a visit from a district nurse or health visitor in the last month have also fallen, from 33.1 per cent to 29.7 per cent between 1980 and 1994/5.

The proportion in receipt of home help services varies with the age, household composition, social class, and income of the elderly person as well as by dependency (Table 6.19). Use of home help services rises steadily with age, from 2 per cent of those aged 65–69 to 27 per cent of those aged 85 years or more.

There is some evidence that home help services are used more intensively by people at the lower end of the income distribution and by those in the manual social classes. Table 6.19 shows that when people are ranked by their household equivalent income, those elderly persons who were located in the bottom two-fifths of the income distribution were twice as likely to be in receipt of home help services in 1980 and 1985 than those in the top three-fifths. By 1994/5 the picture is more mixed, with those in the third quintile being most likely to receive home help services. However, a clear distinction between the top two quintiles and the bottom three remains. There is also a very clear gradient by social class.

Interestingly, there is also a marked difference in the receipt of private home help services in 1994/5 by class and income, with elderly persons in the top quintile of the income distribution (i.e. in the richest 20 per cent of the whole population and hence 'very well-off' pensioners) being *nine* times as likely to receive such services as those in the bottom quintile.

These figures are based on the relative position of the elderly person's income (in quintile groups) within the income distribution for the population as a whole. However, we also provide these trends using the elderly person's position within the income distribution for just the elderly population. This was felt to be of importance as the majority of elderly persons fall within the bottom two quintiles of the general income distribution. Looking solely at the relative position within the elderly population allows a more focused approach. Now the picture is less distinctively 'pro-poor' although right across the period those elderly people at the lower end of the income distribution (although not necessarily the bottom) are more likely to be in receipt of home help than those individuals at the top end. This trend occurs even after standardizing on the age of the elderly person, which takes into account a proxy for 'need'.

To recap, although there is some evidence of targeting PSS at the lower end of the income distribution, this has become weaker over time. Meanwhile people from higher occupational social classes and with higher equivalent family incomes are much more likely to purchase private home help services. Furthermore, although there is evidence that PSS are targeted at those most in need (in terms of ability to perform activities of daily living), again this has weakened over time as the proportion in receipt of local authority provided domiciliary services has fallen.

Maria Evandrou and Jane Falkingham

Table 6.19. USE OF HOME HELP SERVICES IN THE PREVIOUS MONTH AMONG PERSONS AGED 65 AND OVER BY SOCIO-ECONOMIC CHARACTERISTICS, GREAT BRITAIN, 1980–1994/5 (%)

	1980	1985	1994/5	
			Local authority	Private
AGE				
65–69	2	1	2	3
70–74	6	5	4	4
75–79	11	11	9	10
80–84	22	21	14	11
85 and over	31	35	27	16
All	9	9	8	7
SOCIAL CLASS				
I and II	5	6	5	14
IIIN	7	8	7	10
IIIM	8	8	7	2
IV and V	10	11	10	3
INCOME QUINTILE (total population)				
Bottom	9	13	6	3
2	12	10	8	5
3	3	5	10	6
4	4	4	2	11
Top	3	4	2	28
INCOME QUINTILE (pensioner population only)				
Bottom	8	12	7	3
2	11	16	9	4
3	13	7	8	5
4	9	7	11	7
Top	3	3	3	16
REGION				
North	10	10	9	6
South	8	9	5	9
Wales	11	9	11	2
Scotland	9	9	12	6
TENURE				
Owner-occupier	5	6	5	8
Local authority	13	14	12	3
Other	10	10	13	6

Source: Authors' calculations from GHS raw data files for 1980, 1985, and 1994/5.

Final outcomes in relation to ultimate aims

There is a difficulty in defining measures of outcome for the PSS. One possible way is to look at consumer satisfaction and whether 'the political market' has met rising expectations. However, to date the British Social Attitudes Survey has contained no questions on attitudes to or satisfaction with social services provision.

Another possible outcome measure would be in relation to the ultimate aims of PSS; namely to what extent the PSS have been successful in increasing social integration or alternatively reducing social isolation. Furthermore, how successful have SSDs been in exercising their role as agents of social control? The latter would be very difficult to measure.

A broad indicator reflecting the general level of social control in society is the level of crime. Acknowledging the problems of interpreting crime statistics, government data show that the number of notifiable offences recorded per 100 population tripled in England and Wales between 1971 and 1992, to just over one offence for every ten people (CSO 1995). Another indicator proposed to measure the extent of social control is the number of children taken into local authority care. The number of children in care nearly halved between 1976 and 1995 (Fig. 6.7 above).

There is the question of how one should interpret a change in these statistics. A decrease in the number of older children in care could be a sign that delinquency is decreasing and thus that social control has increased. However, the rise in crime statistics would indicate an opposing trend. Changes in the number of children in care alternatively could be taken to indicate that the social services are not being effective in reaching those children in need of care, and therefore decreasing social control. Similarly, rising recorded offences could indicate improved detection and thus greater social control.

Social integration may be defined in terms of 'contrasting those who have many community and family ties with those who are isolated' (Stark, 1987). The Health and Lifestyle Survey found that a low level of social integration, i.e. living alone and seeing relatives less than weekly, was associated with poor psycho-social health, especially for men (Swain, 1993). The reported frequency of social contact is only one indicator of social integration/isolation. It does not take account of the subjective feelings of the individual, irrespective of how frequent the level of contact is. Perceptions of a lack of social support have been found to be as important as, if not more important than, objective indicators of social contact, especially amongst women (Stark, 1987, Blaxter 1990). However, we feel it is still a useful measure and is also employed by others (Willmott, 1986) in their research. Trends in these measures are examined using data from the General Household Survey (Table 6.20).

Social isolation, as measured by the frequency of seeing relatives and friends, appears to have increased across time. Nearly a third of elderly persons saw someone every day in 1980 and 1985, but by 1994/5 this had dropped to a quarter. Conversely, whereas only one in eight saw relatives and friends less often than once a week in the 1980s, in 1994/5 this figure had risen to one in every five. Visits to and from relatives and friends have also declined.

Maria Evandrou and Jane Falkingham

Table 6.20. INDICATORS OF SOCIAL ISOLATION: FREQUENCY OF SOCIAL CONTACTS AND USE OF PUBLIC TRANSPORT AMONG PERSONS AGED 65 AND OVER, GREAT BRITAIN, 1980–1994/5 (%)

	1980	1985	1991	1994/5
Frequency of seeing relatives and friends				
Every day	32	33	25	25
2–3 times a week	29	29	27	29
Once a week	25	22	25	33
Subtotal	85	84	77	77
Once or twice a month	10	9	13	17
Less than once a month	2	4	8	4
Subtotal	12	13	21	20
Does not see relatives or friends	3	2	2	3
Uses public transport				
65–74	75	69	65	63
75 and over	58	52	53	53
All	69	62	60	58
Men	67	59	57	54
Women	70	65	63	62
Reasons for not using public transport				
All Elderly				
Uses household car	13	18	n/a	19
Uses other car	3	7	n/a	8
Ill health/disability	10	14	n/a	13
Public transport too inconvenient	2	4	n/a	5
Public transport too expensive	1	1	n/a	1
Other	3	1	n/a	1
Elderly aged 85 and over				
Uses household car	9	9	n/a	10
Uses other car	11	14	n/a	14
Ill health/disability	38	45	n/a	37
Public transport too inconvenient	1	7	n/a	9
Public transport too expensive	0	1	n/a	1
Other	9	4	n/a	1

Source: OPCS (1982, 1987, 1994*b*, 1996).

The use of public transport and private car are also indicative of the level of social isolation experienced by individuals in society. The percentage of elderly persons reporting that they have used public transport in the last month fell from 69 per cent in 1980 to 62 per cent in 1985 to 58 per cent in 1994/5. The level of use is related to age and gender, with younger elderly persons and elderly women being more likely to be users than their respective counterparts.

Use of public transport is related to access to private transport and to one's own health and locomotive ability. In fact, these were the two main reasons reported for not using public transport. Not surprisingly, the proportion of elderly persons reporting access to a household or other car as the main reason for not using public transport increased from 16 per cent to 27 per cent between 1980 and 1994/5.

V. In Brief

- The key trend since the early 1970s in the PSS has been the growth of private provision. This was under way prior to 1979 but intensified thereafter, first as a result of the perverse incentives provided by social security for financing places in private residential care in the 1980s, and later as part of the explicit policy goal of the 1990 community care reforms, changing the role of social service departments from that of 'provider' to 'purchaser and regulator'.
- Certain policies and practices were shared by both Conservative and Labour Governments during the 1970s and 1980s: first, a 'reactive' approach to child abuse cases; secondly, the tightening of public expenditure directed to the PSS; and thirdly, the shift to community/non-institutional care and priority groups.
- A policy of community care has been fostered by both Labour and Conservative Governments over the last two decades. However, the meaning attributed to it has changed. Initially it meant shifting the balance of care from hospitals to the community. More recently, it has been used in a way which reasserts individual and family responsibility.
- Total UK real expenditure on PSS has grown across the last two decades at an average of 4 per cent per annum from 1973/4 to 1995/6. The growth has not, however, been consistent over the entire period. Spending remained at about 0.9 per cent of GDP for much of the period, only rising to 1.2 per cent in 1993/4 after the implementation of the community care reforms.
- The rate of growth in volume expenditure exceeded that of real expenditure in the late 1970s, reflecting rigorous enforcement of an incomes policy in the public sector. However, since 1985, expenditure on the PSS measured in volume terms has increased at a slower rate than if valued in real terms.
- Growth in expenditure on PSS has been maintained despite Conservative Governments' planned local authority expenditure cuts, and greater constraints through cash limits and rate capping during the late 1980s. Much of the continued growth has been facilitated by joint finance and user charges. Increasingly local authorities are charging for services that have never previously been charged for and also raising the level of existing charges. Because of the discretionary nature of the level of charges for domiciliary care this has resulted in marked regional variations.
- The DoH, in its planning figures, argues that 1 per cent per annum growth in the real

volume of spending is required for the PSS to meet demographic increases in need. On this yardstick, growth in expenditure on the PSS appears to have not only kept pace with changes in need but to have exceeded it.

- But higher spending has not necessarily resulted in higher levels of service provision. There have been reductions in absolute levels of activity in a number of categories, most notably local authority residential care for elderly people and for children 'in care'. Domiciliary and other support services have increased but not at a sufficient rate to keep pace with a growing elderly population. For example, the annual number of meals provided per 1,000 people aged over 75 in England fell from 15,500 in 1974 to 12,200 in 1994.

- Unit costs have risen across the PSS. These increases can only be partly accounted for by the general rise in input prices and changes in the circumstances of clients, with greater levels of dependency. In the absence of solid evidence pointing to a rise in quality, there appears to be a prima facie case that efficiency within the PSS declined during the 1980s.

- Real spending has increased for all client groups, but the growth has been most marked in services directed towards people with mental illness, where expenditure trebled in real terms between 1986/7 and 1994/5, and the younger physically disabled, where real expenditure doubled.

- There has been a significant shift in the balance between health and social care with the contraction and closure of long-stay hospital accommodation, particularly amongst persons with learning disabilities and mental health problems. But it is far from clear whether the expansion of community care services has been sufficient to offset this fall in in-patient care.
  - The number of in-patients with learning disabilities fell by 29,000 between 1984 and 1995 whilst
  - there were an additional 7,100 local authority sponsored places in residential care.
  - Day care places for people with learning difficulties rose from 38,900 to 56,700 between 1977 and 1992, an annual rate of increase of 2.5 per cent.

- Spending on the community care services has grown at a faster rate than that on residential care and the growth in expenditure on day care services has exceeded both of them. Therefore, it appears that there has been a move away from residential care towards care within the community. However, local authority funded residential care is only part of the picture of the total residential care sector.

- The total number of elderly persons living in residential accommodation in any sector between 1974 and 1995 in England increased by 72 per cent. Virtually all of the growth has been in the private sector, stimulated by changes in the social security system.
  - By 1992/3 DSS payments to residential and nursing homes amounted to a staggering £2.5 billion (in 1994/5 prices).

- The balance of care has shifted from public provision and funding to provision by the independent sector and greater private funding through user charges, charitable spending, and the family. At the heart of the community care reforms was the creation of a care market. There is evidence that such a market is emerging but growth remains slow and uneven.
- The majority of social care is provided by the informal care sector. One adult in six provides such assistance (16 per cent). Grossing up the figures nationally indicates that 1.7 million informal carers in Great Britain care for someone within their own home (excluding child-rearing) and another 1.7 million carers spend at least 20 hours per week providing care and support.
- In terms of financial costs alone, the locus of social care provision by different sectors is clear.
  - Expenditure by the charitable sector constituted £555 million in 1994/5.
  - Social security expenditure on private residential care was £2.2 billion.
  - Statutory PSS net support cost £7 billion in 1994/5.
  - Individuals paid £620 million in user charges for local authority services and £3.6 billion in fees for services in the private sector.
  - Informal care provides care to the estimated value of between £17 billion and £35 billion.

Further Reading

DEPARTMENT OF HEALTH (1989), *Caring for People* (Cmd. 849), London: HMSO.

LEWIS, J., and GLENNERSTER, H. (1996), *Implementing the New Community Care*, Milton Keynes: Open University Press.

WISTOW, G., KNAPP, M., HARDY, B., and ALLAN, C. (1994), *Social Care in a Mixed Economy*, Milton Keynes: Open University Press.

———— ———— FORDER, J., and MANNING, R. (eds.) (1996), *Social Care Markets: Progress and Prospects*, Milton Keynes: Open University Press.

ANNEXE

Table 6A.1. REAL GOVERNMENT EXPENDITURE ON THE PERSONAL SOCIAL SERVICES, UNITED KINGDOM (£ MILLION AT 1995/6 PRICES)

Year	Local authority running expenses	Central government	Capital
1973/4	2,982	122	534
1974/5	3,584	162	476
1975/6	4,053	210	438
1976/7	4,209	232	357
1977/8	3,734	231	204
1978/9	3,872	203	217
1979/80	4,125	232	242
1980/1	4,360	244	248
1981/2	4,383	198	216
1982/3	4,496	188	162
1983/4	4,662	179	164
1984/5	4,718	179	184
1985/6	5,182	178	197
1986/7	5,438	179	217
1987/8	5,276	184	185
1988/9	5,579	175	224
1989/90	5,811	184	274
1990/1	6,233	194	270
1991/2	6,546	213	224
1992/3	6,835	217	203
1993/4	7,398	225	199
1994/5	7,631	202	244
1995/6	8,428	140	280

Sources: ONS (1997*a*: table 3.4, and earlier versions); GDP deflator from HM Treasury (1997).

7 Social Security: Dismantling the Pyramids?

Martin Evans

The Caliph of Cairo saw the Pyramids at Giza and ordered his engineers to dismantle them. They were an affront—monuments to pre-Islamic heathen civilization. Returning some months later he saw that the work of the engineers had had no discernible effect but, perversely, to one side was a huge and equally impressive pile of masonry and debris that had been taken from it

(based on Haag 1990)

The message that underlying growth in social security has exceeded, and will continue to exceed growth in the economy, is an uncomfortable one.

(DSS 1993: 2)

This chapter puts the significant changes in social security policy that have been attempted, and to some extent achieved, since 1974 in the context of changing demands for social security and changing social and economic circumstances.

There are four potential causes for increased spending.

- Explicit policy decisions: decisions about social security policy itself—about benefit levels and needs—lead to spending commitments. These have both immediate consequences for spending and leave a legacy for future policy makers to honour, amend, or reject.
- Other social and economic policy decisions: but social security spending is also, in part, the consequence of other policy actions, both on the welfare state and on the macro-economic management of the economy (see Chapter 2).
- Social and economic change: increased demands on the social security budget arise from social and economic changes beyond politicians' control. For instance, more elderly people require pensions for longer lives, and increased unemployment and a

changing labour market create more demands for support during unemployment and to supplement low earnings.

- Endogenous causes: social security may itself foster behaviour that leads to increased demands. Benefits and the income and capital tests that accompany them may have negative effects on the working and saving habits of the population.

What is social security? In the 1940s it was seen as a state-run method of income protection held in common for all citizens. Present usage is narrower and more functional. It covers all the cash transfers provided by the Department of Social Security. This definition thus ignores tax expenditures and allowances, private assurance, insurance, and pensions, and the informal transfers of cash and time that occur between kith and kin. This chapter ignores Housing Benefit, which is part of the social security budget but which is covered in Chapter 5. For Continental European readers, the British concept of social security is equivalent to most cash transfers under the heading of 'social protection'. It explicitly excludes health services and includes social assistance. For US readers British social security is equivalent to the sum of Federal retirement and disability insurance, supplementary security incomes for the elderly, 'welfare', and unemployment benefits.

I. Goals and policies

Barr (1993) outlines three social aims of state intervention in income distribution.

1. The relief of poverty: to protect a minimum income standard.
2. The protection of accustomed living standards: to ensure that no one has to face an unexpected and unacceptably large drop in their standard of living.
3. Smoothing out income over the life-cycle.

This theoretically clear division of aims is not matched by distinct programme responsibilities. They interact. Moreover, the balance between them and the responsibility of the state for each can differ over time and between countries. Take two contrasting policy models. In the first, priority is on the first aim, and the others are dealt with by private means: through savings, through personal insurance against unemployment and sickness, and through investment and personal and occupational pensions. In the second, the second and third aims are a priority and are met through state-run earnings-related social insurance. Poverty relief is a subsidiary task to catch those who fail to obtain sufficient social insurance coverage, and there is less scope for private provision. These two crude opposing models to some extent illustrate the difference between the Australian and Continental European models of social security, with the UK in between but, in the period of study after 1979, moving towards the Australian model.

The economic aims of policy include efficiency of operation and outcome efficiency. The

Meade Report (1978: 269) required that 'the design of benefits, and of the taxes necessary to finance them, should be such as to minimize any adverse effects on the incentive to work and save'. Administrative efficiency means that 'The whole system should be as simple, as easy to understand and as cheap to administer as possible' and that 'benefits from the system should be as little open to abuse as possible' (ibid.).

The aims of social security policy are not merely to be measured in income terms. Social and political participation may be seen as important civic virtues by a broad spectrum of political opinion. Social security maintains a standard of living that supports such inclusiveness (Townsend 1979; Mack and Lansley 1985). A growing tradition in Europe uses the phrase 'social exclusion' to emphasize the consequences of failure in this respect.

Policy under Labour, 1974–1979

Labour continued where they had left off in 1970 with an agenda based on universal coverage. They extended the scope of non-contributory and non-means-tested benefits, introducing child benefit and benefits for disabled people, and introducing a state earnings-related pension scheme. But they did not undo selective Conservative policies of the Heath Government: national rent rebates and allowances and Family Income Supplement (FIS), an in-work means-tested benefit for families with children.

Earnings-related social security contributions were introduced to improve the finance of social insurance in order to fund higher benefits and pay towards a new earnings-related pension scheme. For the first time, legislation gave a statutory basis for the indexation of benefits to protect pensioners against inflation. The new earnings-related pensions (SERPS) were introduced to supplement Beveridge's basic retirement pensions (Barr 1975). The scheme introduced contributory protection for interruptions in working lives to look after children or disabled people and SERPS pensions were based on an individual's twenty best years. These innovations were designed to improve the pension position of women and non-salaried workers.

Child Benefit was introduced as a non-contributory cash allowance for every child to replace the mix of child tax allowances and family allowances. The coverage of non-contributory benefits for disabled people and their carers was expanded, filling another gap left by Beveridge's social insurance plan. Mobility Allowance (MA) for those with difficulties in walking, Invalid Care Allowance (ICA) for carers, and a wider set of non-contributory disablement benefits were all introduced in 1976.

The combined effect was intended to reduce the role of means-tested assistance (in particular for pensioners). The emerging welfare rights lobby was critical of growing means-testing and the operation of Supplementary Benefit (SB) (McCarthy 1986). The Supplementary Benefits Commission (SBC) supported moves away from discretion towards a rights-based approach, and questioned SB's role in relationship to other policy, in particular housing benefits (Donnison 1982; Walker 1983).

Labour expanded universal provision in the name of equity and comprehensiveness in three ways. First, the revised social insurance scheme could ensure higher levels of benefit, but by becoming more flexible and redistributive social insurance became less and less like actuarial insurance, and increasingly like a tax-transfer scheme. Second, a more comprehensive set of non-contributory benefits tried to ensure that those who were penalized by a contributory system had coverage. Third, selective means-tested benefits would, it was hoped, be further reduced by improved universal coverage and was, in any case, set to become more rights-based.

The Conservatives under Margaret Thatcher, 1979–1990

The election of 1979 began a fundamental, if gradual, shift in policy. The major theme in 1980s policy development was to reduce the scope and costs of the public sector. In social security this drive to reduce spending had to counter the effects of increased unemployment and the maturation of Labour's pension plans, and the effect of their benefit uprating policy. Thatcher's Government had strong ideological ideas about the future shape of social security that saw a greater role for private provision, and deep concerns about the effect of social security on behaviour.

The first area of constraint was social insurance. The comprehensiveness and generosity of Labour's changes to social insurance were unpicked. Benefit indexation rules were changed so that they rose to match price increases only, *not* the higher wages and prices as under Labour. This change led to a steady fall in the value of basic retirement pension and other benefits relative to the earnings of those in the labour market—a change of considerable long-term significance to the budget and to income differentials. But at the same time, it is suggested that the relative fall in the value of basic rate pension will probably become unsustainable in the medium to long term for a future Government (Hills 1993).

Spending was less difficult in aggregate because deflationary economic policy increased unemployment. Numerous ways were found to lessen the entitlement of unemployed in order to improve work incentives and to lower claimant counts of unemployment (Atkinson and Micklewright 1989). Men over 60 were encouraged into economic inactivity by the removal of their requirement to sign on and by receiving higher levels of social assistance as a result. The earnings-related supplements for Unemployment Benefit (UB) and Sickness Benefits were abolished in 1982, and UB and basic rates of SB paid to unemployed people became taxable. The overall effect of these changes was cumulatively to bring about a major reduction in support for the unemployed, widen the gap between benefits and wages, and cut costs.

The Conservatives advocated targeting and a selective means-tested approach. Labour's review of SB was adopted on a revenue-neutral basis and hence lost most of its proposed progressivity. Discretion was replaced by legally binding regulations in 1980, and SB administration became more centralized with the dissolution of the SBC (Beltram 1984). In 1983 unified housing benefit was introduced and all responsibility for payment of all rent and rates bene-fits passed to local authorities. (For further details see Chapter 5.) However, those SB claimants who paid mortgage interest continued to have these costs paid by SB.

In 1984 a review of the whole social security system began under the then Secretary of State, Norman Fowler. This led to changes in means-tested benefits, pensions, and disability benefits. The overhaul of all means-tested provision introduced a new set of assistance scales and rules which would underpin all other means-tested provision through the newly named Income Support (IS). IS was simpler to administer because it categorized claimants accord-ing to broad types rather than assessing individual needs. FIS was improved in generosity to assist in lifting families off means-tested assistance and into work and renamed Family Credit (FC). The realignment of FC, IS, and housing benefits reduced the extreme poverty traps where over 100 per cent of extra income was taken at the margins of entitlement. The major-ity of one-off cash grants of social assistance were placed under a strict cash-limited budget ceiling and many grants were changed into loans in the newly named Social Fund. Child Benefit was frozen, tilting the balance from (non-means-tested) Child Benefit that was accused of being poorly targeted.

The changes were controversial at the time and coincided with the Government deliber-ately distancing itself from any recognition that social assistance represented a 'poverty' level of income (see below). Overall the changes only marginally relieved the impact of poverty traps (see Dilnot and Webb 1989).

The other priority was privatization. In 1983 Sickness Benefit for the majority of employ-ees was changed so that the sick were paid sickness benefits as a wage by the employer, who then recouped the money from reduced national insurance contributions. This Statutory Sick Pay (SSP) scheme paid for up to eight weeks of sickness (subsequently extended to 28 weeks) in a tax year, which covers the vast majority of health-related absences. The original intention had been fully to privatize sick pay, but the suggestion raised a storm of protest, notably from the insurance industry, which was reluctant to insure anyone except white-col-lar, salaried employees. (For an account of the pitfalls of attempts at reform, see Prest 1983.)

The Fowler Review Green Paper did produce one big proposal: the abolition of SERPS. SERPS, it was alleged, failed 'to take account of the very substantial financial debt [being handed] down to future generations' (DHSS 1985b: para. 1.1). This proposal aroused con-siderable opposition and was not implemented. But SERPS was amended to make it less gen-erous (in particular to women and those with low earnings and interrupted work histories). Private pension coverage was encouraged as an alternative by increasing tax rebates for those taking our private pensions while occupational pensions were made more transferable between employers. The response by the private pensions industry to the new financial encouragement for people to take out pensions was to oversell them. At least 400,000 people were wrongly advised to change to private schemes (in particular to change from employer-funded schemes) and proposals to compensate these cases are still awaited at the time of writing.

Martin Evans

The Conservatives under Major, 1990–1996

The Major years took forward the majority of Mrs Thatcher's agenda. The period began with some softening of her approach. Child Benefit was unfrozen and was changed so that it is paid at a higher rate for the first child in every family. As part of the abandonment of the Poll Tax, the requirement for claimants of IS to find 20 per cent of their local government tax bill from benefit was abandoned (it had been introduced by the Fowler reforms in 1988). The separate benefits for mobility and attendance were merged into a new Disabled Living Allowance (DLA) for all under 65. Three rates for care needs were recognized (instead of the previous two for Attendance Allowance) as well as a separate mobility component. Attendance Allowance (AA) remained unchanged for those over 65 (Gal 1997). In addition, an in-work benefit for disabled people, Disability Working Allowance (DWA), was introduced on the same lines as Family Credit.

However, for the most part, policy under John Major was concerned to trim a rising budget driven by high levels of unemployment, sickness, low wages, and a rise in divorce, separation, and single parenthood. First, as part of the community care changes, payments for residential care were removed from IS (see Chapter 6). Second, a range of measures was taken to control costs within the social security budget. Increased lone parenthood and the increasing bill for Income Support that this represented led to proposals to ensure that maintenance paid by fathers/ex-husbands was enforced. The Child Support Act allowed the DSS (by means of a new executive agency—the Child Support Agency) to initiate and take over responsibilities for maintenance from 1993. The formulae for calculating payments and apportioning income needs between the first and second families of separated fathers were set nationally and led to a great deal of criticism. The CSA has not performed to targets since 1993 and the legislation has had to be amended to reflect the problems encountered during implementation (Garnham and Knights 1994).

SSP was further privatized in 1991 and 1995 and all medium and large employers have now had their ability to recoup their SSP costs from social insurance payments removed, moving sickness benefits firmly into the private sector. Claims for long-term sickness benefit had grown sharply in the 1980s and 1990s, mostly due to increases in working-age sickness, some of which was linked to unemployment, and increased longevity of such claims (Lonsdale *et al.* 1993). This, in turn, led to increased spending on long-term invalidity benefit (IVB). A new Incapacity Benefit with a stricter test of incapacity for work was introduced in April 1995 and had no earnings-related components and, unlike IVB, was taxable.

The recession and rising unemployment in the early 1990s led to a further change in the treatment of the unemployed by social security policy. First, the costs of paying their mortgages were reduced. IS payments for mortgages were withdrawn for the first nine months of unemployment. Private insurance was encouraged to take over. Contributory Unemployment Benefit and means-tested Income Support for those who are signing on were joined into a single benefit, Jobseeker's Allowance, in 1996. This new benefit will have a contributory basis but only for the first six months of unemployment, after which it will be means-tested. Lower rates will be paid to the under-25s and a 'contract' between the claimant and benefit agency formalizes job-search and training criteria on top of establishing availability for work.

Overview

There have been fundamental changes in the administration of benefits. Social security is now the concern of a single department, separate from health. However, policy responsibilities have been separated from administration and several agencies now carry out the work of the DSS—the Benefits Agency, who pay benefits; the Contributions Agency, who collect social security contributions; the Child Support Agency, who enforce maintenance; and other, smaller agencies.

Social security changed from concerns about coverage in the 1970s to concerns about fiscal constraint and labour market incentives. Targeting, economic incentives, and efficiency became the central concerns of policy in the 1980s. Policy became largely reactive to respond to increased costs and yet also had to change to meet demands that arose from social and economic restructuring of society and adapt to mass long-term unemployment. Policy had to reinforce overall economic objectives: 'The social security system must be consistent with the Government's overall objectives for the economy' (DHSS 1985a: para. 1.12).

It is possible to talk of a paradigmatic shift in policy aims over the period of 1974 to 1997 covered in this chapter. But the history of British policy is more sophisticated and complex: universalism and selectivity have always existed side by side, as have concerns about efficiency and social solidarity. As the period ended, both Conservatives and Labour have considered increasing private provision of pensions onto individuals. Privatization of long-term care insurance and health income protection and other areas were being actively considered, despite evidence of their costs and consequences (Burchardt and Hills 1997). But there was also renewed concern about growing inequality and social exclusion. Three major enquiries have examined the prospects for welfare in the early twenty-first century and the potential to redress the growing costs of social inequality (Borrie 1994; Barclay 1995; Dahrendorf 1995). Particular emphasis was also being placed on the future relationship between paid work and benefits and of mechanisms to ensure movement from 'welfare to work'.

The issue of costs and affordability are at the core of calls for further reform. How have demands for and spending on social security changed?

II. Expenditure trends

Before examining the changes in social security spending it is necessary to consider the demands that were being made on it.

- Demographic change: for instance, the numbers of children and elderly people are indicators of demand for family allowances and retirement pensions respectively.
- Economic changes: economic growth and recession affect the numbers out of work and the work profile of those who are employed in terms of their hours, earnings, and job security.
- Social change: changes in mutual support and family relationships such as the levels of divorce and lone parenthood and the age of independent household formation and size of households affect demand for benefits. Socio-economic behavioural changes such as increasing early retirement, increasing levels of owner-occupation, and changing profiles of sickness, disability work, and caring all influence demand, though may, in their turn, be affected by the existence of social security benefits.

Demographic and economic demands

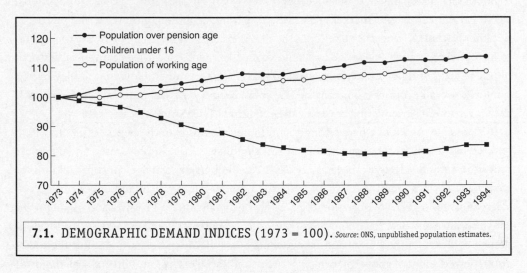

7.1. DEMOGRAPHIC DEMAND INDICES (1973 = 100). *Source:* ONS, unpublished population estimates.

Fig. 7.1 distinguishes three demographic demand indices: the numbers of people over retirement age, children under 16, and the remaining population of working age. Numbers of pensions have risen faster than those of working-age people, but not by much. The numbers of children have fallen significantly to 80 per cent of 1974 levels. These trends suggest that falling numbers of children and increased economic activity amongst non-pensioners could have mitigated problems in the crude dependency ratio (the ratio of working-age people to pensioners) over the period.

The potential demographic problems of funding social security were lessened by real growth in GDP but worsened by lower participation in the labour force. Fig. 7.2 shows that real GDP grew by almost 50 per cent but this growth was not linear. Three major recessions occurred: in the early 1970s, the early 1980s, and the early 1990s. Much higher levels of unemployment have accompanied real economic growth. The long-term trend in unemployment is a 360 per cent growth between 1973 and 1994. The total of unemployed has risen with each recession.

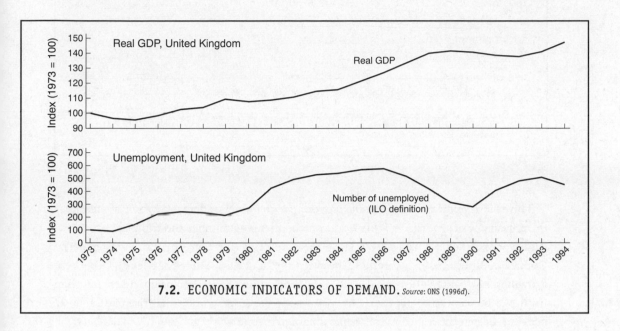

7.2. ECONOMIC INDICATORS OF DEMAND. *Source:* ONS (1996d).

Changing employment patterns

The composition of the workforce has changed dramatically since 1973. The overall work-force has grown by 9 per cent but this growth has not been even. Fig. 7.3 shows that the number of male employees has fallen by 20 per cent between 1973 and 1994, but numbers of women have increased by about the same proportion. However, the fastest growth has been in part-time employment (under 30 hours a week), where the number of women (the majority of part-time workers) and men have grown by about 60 per cent and 70 per cent respectively.

Employment has increasingly become part-time: in 1973 17 per cent of all employees were part-time, of whom 82 per cent were women. Since then there has been an increase in numbers of women working and an increase in the proportion of part-timers amongst women employees, from 36 per cent to 46 per cent. This increase in part-time work has also affected men: 5 per cent of male employees were part-time in 1973, but now it is 11 per cent, despite the 20 per cent fall in their total number. Growth for all employees was flat (−1 per cent) but increased 62 per cent for part-timers. While increasing male part-time work flattened the decrease in male employment, part-time work accounted for 93 per cent of the increase in women working between 1973 and 1994.

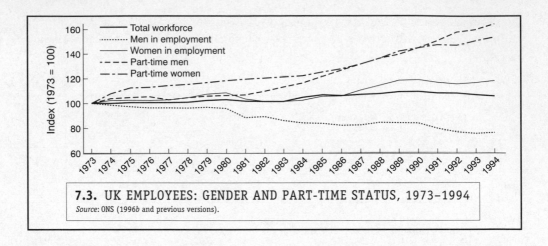

7.3. UK EMPLOYEES: GENDER AND PART-TIME STATUS, 1973–1994
Source: ONS (1996*b* and previous versions).

The other significant change in the labour force to influence demand for social security is the prevalence of low wages. Table 7.1 shows the changing number and composition of low-paid workers (defined using the relative measure of 68 per cent of mean earnings—The Council of Europe decency threshold) between 1979 and 1994. There has been an 18 per cent growth in low-paid full-time workers and the proportion of such low-paid workers has risen from 28.3 per cent to 37 per cent. Low pay among part-time workers has risen faster, by 42 per cent, despite a fairly constant proportion of part-time workers being low-paid, between 77 per cent and 78 per cent. Women were and remain more likely to be low-paid workers but this likelihood is declining for full-time women: from 58 per cent in 1979 to 50 per cent in 1994 and represented also by a 10 per cent fall in their number. For part-time women workers, then, between 77 per cent and 82 per cent were and remain low-paid between 1979 and 1994, and their numbers have increased by 24 per cent. But low pay is increasingly experienced by men. The number of full-time low-paid men has increased by 68 per cent and of part-time low-paid by 371 per cent. A growing proportion of male employees is low-paid: growing from 15 per cent to 30 per cent and from 62 per cent to 72 per cent of full- and part-time employees respectively.

Growing economic inactivity

In addition to growth in unemployment and low pay there has been a rise in economic inactivity among working-age people. The main reasons for economic inactivity are illness and disability, domestic work in the home (including caring for children and disabled adults), and early retirement. There was a rise in economic inactivity between 1981 and 1984, due to the recession, that increased the numbers of inactive men. In particular, male early retirement grew during this period. Over the longer period, there has been a gradual decline in the numbers of economically inactive women.

Table 7.1. LOW-PAID EMPLOYEES, 1979–1994

	Men			Women				All			
	full-time		part-time	full-time		part-time		full-time		part-time	
	n	million	n	% of all	n	% of all	n	% of all	n	% of all	n
1979	1.64	14.6	0.17	62.2	3.00	57.6	2.99	79.0	4.64	28.3	3.16
1982	1.83	17.7	0.46	63.9	2.75	55.6	3.04	80.5	4.58	30.0	3.50
1988	2.77	26.7	0.68	79.5	2.91	55.0	3.50	82.2	5.68	36.2	4.18
1994	2.76	29.9	0.80	72.2	2.71	49.7	3.70	76.6	5.47	37.0	4.50

Growth, 1979–1994 (%)

Low-paid full-time men	68
Low-paid part-time men	371
Low-paid full time women	−10
Low-paid part time women	24
All low-paid full time workers	18
All low-paid part time workers	42

Attributable growth in low-paid workers, 1979–1994

Men as % of growth in full-time low-paid	134 (women −34%)
Women as % of growth in part-time low-paid	53 (men −47%)

Source: Low Pay Unit (1995 and earlier versions).

Table 7.2 breaks down these trends by cause. The largest single change in cause of economic activity is a downward trend in numbers who are looking after their home and/or family. These represented almost 77 per cent of all economically inactive in 1981, but dropped, over the eleven years, to just over 50 per cent. Counterbalancing this decrease in home and family responsibility have been increases in the numbers of early retired and long-term sick and disabled people.

Table 7.2. ECONOMIC INACTIVITY OF ADULTS OF WORKING AGE, 1981–1991 (000s)

	1981		1986		1991		Increase, 1981–91 (%)
	n	%	n	%	n	%	
Long-term sick	548	9.5	1,085	16.3	1,321	22.4	141.1
Looking after home/family	4,449	76.9	3,455	52.0	2,963	50.2	−33.4
Retired	162	2.8	445	6.7	505	8.6	211.8
Discouraged workers	122	2.1	403	6.1	134	2.3	9.5
Other reasons	416	7.2	1,077	16.2	559	13.4	34.4
All economically inactive people	5,785	100	6,641	100	5,904	100	13.1

Note: Working age is 16 to 64 for men and 16 to 59 for women.

Source: Author's calculations from Labour Force Survey.

The growth in divorce and lone parenthood

Figure 7.4 shows indices for divorce rates, for divorce rates for couples with children, and for the number of lone-parent families. All have risen significantly, with the number of lone-parent families rising most. In the mid-1970s these trends rose at approximately the same rate, but there has been a growing differential acceleration in numbers of lone-parent families since the 1980s. This is partly due to the increased incidence of births outside marriage (Kiernan and Estaugh 1993), and in part due to longer periods of lone parenthood.

Measuring spending

As in other chapters real social security spending is measured by deflating cash spending by the GDP deflator. This answers the question, 'How did social security fare in the allocation of national resources?' A second question, 'How did the value of benefits change from the consumer's point of view?', is better answered by showing their changing real value deflated by the retail price index.

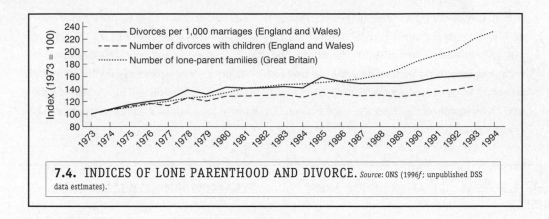

7.4. INDICES OF LONE PARENTHOOD AND DIVORCE. *Source:* ONS (1996*f*; unpublished DSS data estimates).

Problems of consistency are several. Changes in the benefit regimes have accompanied changes in the accounting status of some transfers. Statutory Sick Pay (SSP) and Statutory Maternity Pay (SMP), which are accounted for as negative revenue in the National Insurance Fund, are included as benefit spending here. A second set of adjustments amended SB totals to remove spending on rents, which are now classed as Housing Benefits, and to deduct payments towards mortgage interest in SB and IS, which are covered in Chapter 5.

A set of more difficult problems arises with the overlapping of tax expenditures in the role of social security and income maintenance. I follow the tradition that tax allowances are not part of social security spending but are shown separately. Consistency in the treatment of Child Benefit, which replaced a child tax allowance, necessitates that the value of these tax allowances be included for the earlier years. There is a further problem in that some social security benefits are tax-free and hence worth more in real terms. The range and number of benefits which are tax-free has diminished in recent years and no allowance is made for the effects of this change or to express expenditure consistently on this basis over time. The last problem is that some areas of private spending on social security, especially pensions, are given encouragement through tax discounts and allowances.

The broad picture

The balance of policy has moved away from social insurance to poverty relief and private provision. Is this move in policy discernible in spending outcomes? Table 7.3 shows that real spending on all social security has risen by 109 per cent since 1973/4, an average annual growth rate of 3.4 per cent. National Insurance had always been the largest single element of spending and remains so, mostly due to growing numbers of pensioners and the maturing of SERPS, but since 1973/4 has grown by 62 per cent, more slowly than total spending and than any other element of spending. However, as it has remained one of the largest components of spending, it also accounts for a very large proportion of overall growth: 37 per cent for the whole period. However, the most dramatic increase has been in spending on means-tested

Martin Evans

benefits, which has risen by 609 per cent since 1973/4, and accounts for 36 per cent of overall growth in spending. There is therefore substantial evidence of the move to means-testing, but such provision does not yet account for the majority of spending. Spending on non-contributory non-means-tested benefits has grown by 102 per cent, a slower aggregate rate than all social security, and accounts for 19 per cent of all increased spending. Higher administrative costs result partly from the move towards means-testing and account for 5 per cent of overall growth.

Table 7.3. REAL SOCIAL SECURITY SPENDING, UNITED KINGDOM (£ BILLION AT 1995/6 PRICES)[a]

	Insurance	Non-contributory	Means-tested	Administrative costs	Other	Total social security	
1973/4	25.1	8.0	2.5	1.7	1.5	38.7	
1979/80	31.1	9.3	4.3	2.0	2.8	49.4	
1984/5	35.6	10.4	10.7	2.7	2.1	61.3	
1989/90	36.1	10.1	10.1	3.1	2.0	61.4	
1990/91	36.1	10.9	10.7	3.2	2.2	63.1	
1991/2	39.2	12.1	12.9	3.4	2.3	69.8	
1992/3	39.9	13.4	15.9	3.7	2.5	75.4	
1993/4	41.2	14.8	17.0	4.0	2.7	79.7	
1994/5	40.7	15.2	17.4	3.8	2.8	79.9	
1995/6	40.6	16.2	17.6	3.6	2.8	80.8	
Growth 1973/4 to 1995/6 (%)							
Overall growth	62	102	609	115	90	109	
Average annual rate of growth	2.2	3.3	9.3	3.5	3.0		3.4
Contribution to overall growth	37	19	36	5	3		100

[a] Excluding Housing Benefit, mortgage interest payments from Supplementary Benefit and Income Support, and previous means-tested rent and rate support in Supplementary Benefit.

Source: Table 7A1.

Fig. 7.5 shows the proportion of all spending under each heading. The change in direction of delivery of social security, away from contributory social insurance towards means-tested delivery, is clear. Social insurance has fallen from nearly 65 per cent of all spending in 1973/4 to just under 50 per cent in 1994/5 while means-tested spending has risen from over 6 per cent to almost 23 per cent. Readers are reminded that these figures understate the role of means-testing because means-tested housing allowances are excluded here. (If housing allowances were included the proportions of means-tested expenditure (in Great Britain) would have risen from approximately 15 per cent to over 30 per cent over the same period.)

The lines in Fig. 7.5 begin to change direction most noticeably in the early 1980s and hence may confirm the previous discussion about a change in policy paradigms at the beginning of the Thatcher period. However, Fig. 7.5 also gives an indication of the effects of the underlying economic cycle and of the effects of the introduction of policy changes. For instance, the graph shows the rise in spending on contingency benefits in the late 1970s because of the introduction of child benefits. Similarly, the rise in expenditure on means-tested benefits also shows the fluctuations of the economic cycle from the early 1980s and 1990s. The rise in unemployment appears to have had a less dramatic effect on the proportion of spending on social insurance: there is a slight hump in the line around 1980/1 but the second depression of the early 1990s is characterized by declining proportions of social insurance and rising proportions spent on means-testing.

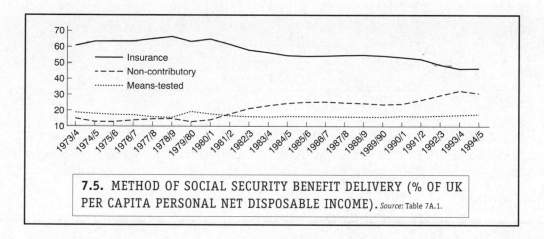

7.5. METHOD OF SOCIAL SECURITY BENEFIT DELIVERY (% OF UK PER CAPITA PERSONAL NET DISPOSABLE INCOME). *Source:* Table 7A.1.

Table 7.4 shows the different rates of growth for each of the major political policy periods: Labour (1973/4 to 1978/9), Thatcher (1979/80 to 1989/90), and Major (1990/1 to 1995/6). The problems with assessing outputs according to the political tenure of government are several. First, there is no equal distribution of cyclical effects, and some care must be taken in interpretation of results if the end years of analysis come in different stages of growth of recession. Second, the effects of policy change are not always immediate. One Government's changes are their successor's inheritance. Last, because the periods of each political regime differ, comparison is made on average rates of growth rather than aggregate growth totals.

The most significant difference between Labour and Thatcher is the changing pattern of spending. The Thatcher period saw means-testing responsible for 48 per cent of all increase in spending, whereas increased pensions and other social insurance accounted for 42 per cent. The roles of social insurance and means-testing were reversed. Major's tenure has been one of recession and slow recovery and hence annual growth in social security spending has been 5.1 per cent. Means-testing has grown fastest at 10.6 per cent per year, while social insurance spending has fallen to a 2.4 per cent annual growth rate. Major also presided over a

Table 7.4. GROWTH IN SOCIAL SECURITY SPENDING BY POLITICAL REGIME, UNITED KINGDOM (%)

	Insurance	Non-contributory	Means-tested	Total social security[a]
Growth under Labour, 1973/4 to 1978/9				
Average annual rate of growth	4.8	−1.6	13.4	4.8
Contribution to overall growth[a]	64.8	−6.0	21.9	100
Growth under Conservatives: Thatcher, 1979/80 to 1989/90				
Average annual rate of growth	1.5	0.8	8.9	2.4
Contribution to overall growth[a]	42.0	6.8	48.3	100
Growth under Conservatives: Major, 1990/91 to 1995/96				
Average annual rate of growth	2.4	8.2	10.6	5.1
Contribution to overall growth[a]	25.1	29.8	39.2	100

[a] Rows do not add to 100 because small areas of spending have been omitted.

Source: Table 7.A1.

growth in contingency-related non-contributory benefits due to the reinstatement of indexation of child benefit, and changes to disablement benefits. Overall, means-testing accounted for 39 per cent of all social security growth while social insurance and contingency benefits accounted for around 22 per cent and 30 per cent respectively.

Spending by claimant type

Table 7.5 breaks down expenditure according to claimant type, and thus can be related back to changes in demand. 'The elderly' are those over pensionable age, and since 1982 also include men aged 60 to 64. The 'sick and disabled' are those who claim any of the contributory sickness and invalidity benefits or who claim the non-contributory disablement, invalidity, and caring benefits and those who get means-tested benefits on similar grounds. The 'unemployed' are those who claim unemployment benefit or are receiving means-tested benefits and are registered as unemployed (readers are reminded that this definition has become more restrictive over time). 'Widows' are those claiming widows' benefits and/or a variety of death and war pensions. 'Families' are those claiming child benefit and one-parent benefit together with those families claiming means-tested benefits who do not fall into any other category, primarily lone parents. These definitions are not entirely consistent over time, although the series after 1988/9 is entirely consistent.

Spending on elderly people has grown by 93 per cent, and this growth accounts for 37 per cent of all increased social security spending. Expenditure on sick and disabled people has grown by 275 per cent, and such spending accounts for 32 per cent of all increased real spending. The largest and fastest-growing type of spending has been on unemployment, which has

Table 7.5. REAL SOCIAL SECURITY SPENDING BY CLAIMANT GROUP, GREAT BRITAIN (£ BILLION AT 1995/6 PRICES)

	Elderly	Sick/ disabled	Unemployed	Widows	Family	Total
1973/4	20.1	5.9	2.1	2.2	7.8	38.0
1979/80	26.1	7.2	3.8	1.9	10.6	49.6
1984/5	31.7	9.3	10.7	1.8	10.7	64.2
1989/90	32.2	12.2	5.7	1.6	11.1	62.8
1990/91	33.9	13.3	6.3	1.9	11.8	67.3
1991/2	35.5	15.1	8.5	2.1	13.0	74.3
1992/3	36.7	17.3	10.1	1.9	15.8	80.9
1993/4	38.2	19.9	10.2	1.9	15.8	86.0
1994/5	38.4	20.9	9.4	1.9	16.5	87.0
1995/6	38.8	22.0	8.6	2.1	17.2	88.7
Growth, 1973/4 to 1994/5 (%)						
Overall growth	93	275	320	—	121	133
Contribution to overall growth	36.8	31.9	13.0	—	18.6	100

Note: These figures include housing benefits but there is a discontinuity in treatment of housing costs and allowances before 1982 as the old rent allowance and rebate schemes are not included in the figures.

Source: DSS (1997a: table 5, and previous versions).

grown by 320 per cent, but this only accounts for 13 per cent of all increased spending. Spending on widowhood has remained fairly flat in real terms. Spending on family benefits grew by 121 per cent overall. This breakdown gives a clearer impression of the underlying causes of increased social security spending: first, increased economic inactivity due to retirement and sickness and disability; second, unemployment; and third, having children, with the presence of children being more often linked to low income (DHSS 1985a).

Programme spending

Pensions Table 7.6 shows the changing numbers of pensioners, and the changing composition and real value of their basic and additional pension entitlements (graduated pension, SERPS, assistance top-ups, and additional increments). The overall number of pensioners has grown by 29.6 per cent over the whole period. The average pension awarded has risen by 18.2 per cent in real terms. This is not, however, solely due to uprating policy on basic pensions but also reflects the changing profile of additional elements of pension paid over time. First, the percentage of pensioners receiving additional pension because they deferred retirement and earned additional increments has fallen from 26.8 per cent in 1974 to 13.7 per cent in 1994. This smaller percentage of increment holders has seen almost a doubling in the value of their additional pension (a 98.6 per cent increase). However, there are a growing percentage of pensioners who receive additional elements of pension from the old Conservative graduated and newer Labour SERPS schemes. Graduated pension receivers grew from one-third in 1974 to three-quarters in 1994 but the value of the extra pension was small, about £2 a week.

The contrast with SERPS is stark. While payments only began in 1979, by 1994 almost 42 per cent of pensioners had a SERPS element. The real value of these additional pensions had risen dramatically. This growth is better described in terms relative to the average total pension payment: 2 per cent in 1979 and 15 per cent in 1994. The proportion of pensioners who receive means-tested SB and IS in addition to their pension has as a consequence fallen, as shown in the final column.

These figures suggest that increasing pension expenditure is due to *both* maturing policy promises and increased demographic demand. The promise of more adequate pension provision is also shown by consistently declining proportions of pensioners requiring means-tested help for their living costs: a fall from 22.3 per cent in 1974 to 18.5 per cent in 1982, and a fall from 16.9 per cent in 1983 to 14.3 per cent in 1994. It is important to stress that this reduction, a successful outcome according to the aims of 1970s policy, is not solely the reflection of the influence of state pensions but also results in part from increasing receipt of private and occupation pensions paid in addition to state pension. The proportion of pensioners receiving assistance is also linked to the relative value of retirement pensions to assistance rates, which I discuss below.

How much of increased pension spending resulted from deliberate policy and how much from demographic demand? Table 7.7 shows that one-third (35 per cent) of increased spending is due to increasing numbers of pensioners, whilst two-thirds (65 per cent) is due to increases in the real value of pension payments. Almost 14 per cent of increased spending comes from maturing SERPS claims and the additional pension paid as a result. Graduated pension only accounts for 4.5 per cent of increased spending, and increases due to deferred retirement under 1 per cent.

An explanation in these terms is largely static, whereas pension expenditure is also strongly influenced by changes in the number of people born at different times as well as by their subsequent work histories and longevity. For instance, those who were between 65 and 69 in 1973 would have been born between 1904 and 1908. This birth cohort was far larger than the one born 21 years later, who were between 65 and 69 in 1994. A decline in the birth rate has not led to fewer potential pensioners because of increased rates of survival to pensionable age. Increased rates of survivorship are shared by men and women but women are increasing pension expenditure by having longer and more remunerative working lives which enable them to claim a pension in their own right. In addition the longer relative longevity of women means that higher numbers are also claiming pensions as widows on the basis of their dead husband's contribution record. The effects of these various factors are shown in Table 7.8 by splitting the pensioner population into age bands.

Table 7.6. STATE PENSIONS, GREAT BRITAIN, 1973–1994

	All NI pensioners		Pensioners with increments		Pensioners with graduated pension		Pensioners with net SERPS additional pension		Pensioners with Income Support/ Supplementary Benefit paid
	000s	average payment (1994/95 prices)	% of pensioners	average payment (1995 prices)	% of pensioners	average payment (1995 prices)	% of pensioners	average payment (1995 prices)	% of pensioners[a] (1973–1979 pre-housing benefit) (1985–1994 post-housing benefit)
1973	7824	£43.41	26.8	£2.87	33.0	£1.38	—	—	22.3
1978	8602	49.25	23.8	3.09	50.1	1.26	—	—	18.9
1979	8750	54.38	22.8	3.56	53.0	1.45	0.9	0.95	18.2
1985	9525	49.43	18.5	4.29	65.9	1.64	15.2	2.82	16.8
1989	9791	50.38	16.6	4.87	71.2	1.79	25.9	4.25	15.7
1990	9967	55.69	16.5	5.41	72.8	1.97	30.8	5.90	15.4
1991	10028	57.21	15.8	5.59	73.7	2.05	33.6	7.05	13.8
1992	10095	58.72	15.1	5.62	72.9	2.11	36.3	7.80	14.2
1993	10102	60.34	14.4	5.69	73.9	2.15	39.1	8.64	15.6
1994	10138	61.63	13.7	5.70	74.6	2.18	41.9	9.35	14.3
Growth 1973–94	29.6	18.2		98.6		58.0		884[b]	

[a] Those over pensionable age who receive NI pensions, hence differs from the 'elderly' category used in Table 7.5.

[b] Growth between 1979 and 1994 (effective growth from zero).

Source: DSS (1995a: tables B1.08, B1.10, B1.21, B1.23, and A2.23, and previous versions).

Table 7.7. EXPENDITURE ON RETIREMENT PENSIONS, 1973–1994

	% of real spending increase
Aggregate expenditure growth	
% growth attributable to increased pensioner population[a]	35
% growth attributable to increase in general pension levels[b]	65
Growth in pension levels due to additional pension elements	
% of growth attributable to payments of increments (due to deferred retirement)	0.7
% of growth attributable to payments of graduated pension	4.5
% of growth attributable to payments of SERPS	13.9

[a] Formula: ((1973 rates × 1994 population) − (1973 rates × 1973 population)) / total growth.
[b] Formula: ((1994 rates × 1994 population) − (1973 rates × 1994 population)) / total growth.

Source: Author's calculations from Table 7.7.

Unemployment Table 7.9 shows the growth of unemployed claimants and the response by the social security system. There has been over a 300 per cent increase over the whole period, but between 1973 and 1985 this was almost 390 per cent. Unemployment fell in the late 1980s and rose again in the early 1990s recession. By 1994, the final year shown here, unemployment was

Table 7.8. THE AGEING OF THE PENSIONER POPULATION: SURVIVORSHIP RATES AND GROWTH

	Total of actual pensioners (000s)		% of total growth, 1973–94	Notional 1994 totals adjusted to 1973 survival rates (000s)	Growth due to increased survival (%)
	1973	1994			
Aged 60–64	794	1056	11.9	849	24
Aged 65–69	2395	2434	1.8	1818	34
Aged 70–74	2067	2654	25.5	1877	41
Aged 75–79	1365	1666	13.1	1074	55
Aged 80–84	782	1312	22.9	797	65
Aged 85–89	325	696	16.2	379	83
Aged 90 and over	94	306	9.3	145	112
Total	7823	10124	100.0	6939	46

Note: No adjustment is made for differential survival due to marriage; adjustment relies on gender-based calculations: male survival for male pensioners and women survivors, and female survival for the remainder.

Source: Author's calculations from DSS (1995a: table B1.08, and previous versions).

falling again. Coverage by social insurance has declined. In the first instance there has been a growing proportion of unemployed people who have had no social insurance cover: 40 per cent were covered in the 1970s but only around 20 per cent in the 1990s. Secondly, the value of such cover has worsened with the withdrawal of earnings-related supplement (ERS) in the early 1980s. Means-tested assistance has taken over as the main form of income relief for unemployment. This is reflected in the growth in the proportion that receives it: from just under 50 per cent in the 1970s to around 70 per cent in the 1990s. The declining relative value of UB and its declining coverage mean that more of the unemployed rely solely on means-tested benefits. The effects of this on incentives to work are discussed below.

Long-term sickness

What underlies the huge growth in spending on long-term sickness? Table 7A.1 shows that spending on IVB grew by over 400 per cent between 1973/4 and 1994/5 (its final year of existence). Piachaud (1986) found strong correlation between worsening labour market conditions between 1971 and 1981 and older men redefining themselves as disabled and early retired. Lonsdale *et al.*'s survey of IVB claimants in the early 1990s found that three-quarters of long-term IVB claimants were in their fifties and sixties. In general, they found IVB claimants were 'a mainly, though not exclusively, static population, who have gradually lost touch with the labour market after claiming IVB for the first time and for whom IVB is a bridge from work to retirement' (Lonsdale *et al.* 1993: 58). A study of new claimants also found 80 per cent still on IVB after over a year (Erens and Ghate 1993).

Table 7.10 shows that long-term incapacity (i.e. of over six months) has risen by 363 per cent over the whole period. How much of this is due to 'early retirement' and retirement? Table 7.10 breaks down the older long-term claimants into three age bands. The first is those women aged between 40 and 49 and men aged 45 to 54 who are within 11 to 20 years of pension age. This age band has grown at about the same rate as overall long-term incapacity, 355 per cent, and has remained at around 22 to 23 per cent of all such claimants. The second is women aged 50 to 59 and men aged 55 to 64 who are within 10 years of their pensionable age. This age band was nearly 60 per cent of all claimants in 1973/4 but had fallen to just over 40 per cent by 1993/4, and has grown more slowly than overall claimant growth. The last is for claimants who are over pensionable age and the growth of this oldest age band has been dramatic, rising from around 5 per cent to nearly 17 per cent of all claimants. Turning to how much growth is explained by these age bands, the oldest account for nearly 19 per cent of all growth, the next eldest almost 36 per cent of growth, and the youngest age band almost 11 per cent. This leaves one-third of growth 'unexplained' for claimants younger than those described by these three age bands. Thus the argument that older workers are retiring early on IVB should not be overstated. First, there is a cohort effect that is difficult to establish from this cross-sectional evidence. Second, more evidence is needed on the age of inflows into IVB and subsequent duration.

Table 7.9. UNEMPLOYMENT AND SOCIAL SECURITY, GREAT BRITAIN, 1973–1994

	Unemployed (000s)	% unemployed with no unemployment benefit	Unemployment Benefit claimants			Supplementary Benefit/Income Support
			% of unemployed	% with earnings-related supplement	% with Supplementary Benefit or Income Support	% of unemployed with assistance
1973	621	37.8	40.9	15.9	7.7	45.6
1978	1283	39.8	41.0	15.9	8.8	48.6
1979	1105	42.2	40.9	16.0	7.8	50.0
1985	3038	55.8	30.1	—	7.1	62.9
1989	1649	60.5	22.9	—	6.1	66.6
1990	1433	63.8	20.9	—	3.3	67.1
1991	2048	59.2	27.1	—	5.0	64.2
1992	2546	61.4	26.2	—	4.9	66.3
1993	2759	64.0	23.9	—	4.2	68.2
1994	2551	67.8	20.5	—	4.5	72.2
Growth, 1974–94	311%					

Source: Author's calculations from DSS (1995a: table C1.01, and previous versions).

Inflows into IVB have not risen as dramatically as length of duration on it (Berthoud 1993). Holmes *et al.* (1991) found IVB highly correlated with demographic effects (age and poor health), poor labour demand, and poor localities. There appears to be a 'ratchet effect', with the number of IVB claimants rising with rising unemployment but failing to go down when unemployment later falls (Berthoud 1993). The financial structure of IVB does appear to have some significant effects on claimant numbers, but it is not clear whether claimants who 'choose' IVB for these reasons would be out of the social security budget. Pensioners who choose to remain on IVB rather than collect their retirement pensions do so because IVB is worth more, due to tax and benefit advantages. IVB, especially with age-related and earnings-related additions, is more generous than provision for the unemployed. It also gives rise to potentially higher rates of means-tested help for living costs, rent, and council taxes. While subject to medical assessments of incapacity, these are, in general, less continual than the tests of availability for work and job search that would accompany the status of being 'unemployed'. There are IVB work disincentives: replacement rates tend to be quite high. In addition, the age-related additions to IVB, which are more generous for those for whom invalidity began at an earlier age, discourage leaving benefit as duration lengthens and as age increases (a period of work followed by another period of invalidity may result in a drop in benefit income). Studies of GP practices on certification of incapacity have failed to find a 'smoking gun' (Ritchie *et al.* 1993). Practices at unemployment offices in the 1980s encouraged potential unemployed applicants with health problems to define themselves as incapable of work. Thus, while unemployment is crucial to understanding increasing claims for long-term sickness benefits, its effect may be spread throughout the working life and not as concentrated on older workers as earlier research suggests. The causes of increased IVB spending still require more investigation. It is too early to assess the effects of the change to Incapacity Benefit in 1995.

Disability

Spending on disability has grown partly because coverage has grown. These benefits meet the needs that would otherwise be met by means-tested assistance alone. This marked a great change in attitude from that of Beveridge, who saw means-tested assistance as appropriate for 'the cripples, the deformed . . . and moral weaklings' (quoted in Evans and Glennerster 1993: 62). Table 7.11 shows the changing numbers of claimants of Attendance Allowance (AA), Mobility Allowance (MA), non-contributory Invalidity Benefit, and Severe Disablement Allowance (SDA). Claims for disability benefits have grown faster than overall spending on social security (see Table 7.3 for comparison). Taking the period between 1977 and 1991, then, MA has grown at almost 19 per cent per year, AA at 10 per cent per year, and SDA (for which entitlement rules changed in 1983 and hence does not have a consistent time series) at 7 per cent per year. Table 7.11 also shows that these non-contributory non-means-tested benefits are increasingly linked to means-tested assistance. This is because

Table 7.10. INCAPACITY OF OVER 6 MONTHS, EARLY RETIREMENT, AND RETIREMENT

	All long-term incapacity (000s)	Early retirement 1 11–20 years before pension age		Early retirement 2 10 years or less before pension age		Pension Age Retirement Over pension age	
		000s	% of all	000s	% of all	000s	% of all
1973/4	427	93	21.8	254	59.5	20	4.7
1979/80	589	112	19.6	323	54.8	51	8.9
1980/1	626	121	20.5	333	53.2	52	8.8
1985/6	904	178	21.1	457	50.6	92	12.1
1989/90	1295	263	22.4	585	45.2	207	17.6
1990/1	1439	298	23.0	647	45.0	240	18.5
1991/2	1632	342	23.8	703	43.1	268	18.6
1992/3	1827	390	23.9	766	41.9	286	17.5
1993/4	1977	423	23.2	809	40.9	306	16.7
Growth, 1974–1994 (%)	363	355		219		1430	
% of growth attributable to each form of 'retirement'		10.9		35.8		18.5	

Note: Pension age for men is 65 and 60 for women. This means that early retirement measure 1 is women aged 40–49 and men aged 45–54; early retirement measure 2 is women aged 50–59 and men aged 55–64, while 'retired' means over 60 for women and over 65 for men.

Sources: Author's calculations from DSS (1995c: table D1.07) and unpublished data provided by ASD1, DSS

claimants have very low original incomes but also because receipt of these benefits increases the assessment of needs for SB and IS and at the same time is ignored in their calculation. SDA is flat rate over the whole period, while AA and MA do not count as income at all for assistance purposes. It is also due to the proximity of some benefit rates to assistance, especially SDA for example, which in 1977 had over 40 per cent of claimants also claiming assistance. This has risen to over 63 per cent in 1994. Leaving aside the question of take-up, there is evidence that chronic disablement is correlated with very low income (Sainsbury *et al.* 1995) and these factors have increased spending on both these benefits and related assistance.

Since 1992 spending on DLA has grown by 77 per cent (see Table 7A.1). This is in part due to the further extension of coverage. Criteria for disability have been widened for those with lower levels of need (Sainsbury *et al.* 1995). While DLA and SDA are aimed at the working-age disabled, AA has had no upper age limit. Indeed, since 1991, AA has only been available to those over pensionable age. Hence rising numbers of frail elderly people will have had an effect on increased claims and spending. Higher spending also reflects a change in NHS policy and practice. More of the frail elderly are now cared for at home or in private institutions and not in hospital. In part, higher social security spending has taken the strain off the NHS budget.

III. Outputs

I now turn from discussion of spending to consider wider issues of social security performance. I distinguish between 'outputs'—factors which provide evidence of performance of the social security system in aggregate—and 'outcomes', such as effects on the income profile, which are discussed in the next section. Much of the current debate on social security evaluates its aggregate performance. Does it hinder or help individuals and the economy, is it too generous or mean, is it efficient and effective? These issues are addressed below under three main themes.

1. The relationship between state social security and private provision.
2. The changing real and relative value of social security benefits.
3. The secondary effects of means-testing on benefit 'dependency', on incentives, and on the effectiveness of targeting.

All three of these areas have implications for expenditure trends and will further clarify and qualify some of the causal explanations outlined earlier.

Private provision

British social security was based on universal state-provided insurance of a minimum standard with private and voluntary provision as an addition. Private provision in the UK is

Table 7.11. NON-CONTRIBUTORY BENEFITS FOR DISABLEMENT

	Non-contributory Invalidity Benefit/ Severe Disablement Allowance		Attendance Allowance		Mobility Allowance	
	000s	% also receiving assistance	000s	% also receiving assistance	000s	% also receiving assistance
1973	—	—	145	n/a	—	
1977	104	41.3	252	25.4	62	6.5
1979	121	43.8	286	26.6	137	7.3
1980	176	32.4	314	24.8	185	7.0
1984	218	50.5	470	32.8	353	10.5
1989	275	56.7	763	34.7	599	12.9
1990	284	53.9	835	36.9	641	12.8
1991	294	58.5	918	39.3	687	14.4
1992	302	60.3	—	—	—	—
1993	316	61.7	—	—	—	—
1994	326	63.2	—	—	—	—
Growth (%)	213 (1977–94)		533 (1973–91)		1001 (1977–91)	
Average annual rate of growth of benefit (%)	7.0 (1977–94)		10.8 (1973–91) 9.9 (1976–1991)		18.8 (1977–91)	
Average annual rate of claims with assistance (%)	9.7 (1977–94)		12.3 (1976–91)		25.8 (1977–91)	

Note: Attendance Allowance (AA) started in 1972 and Mobility Allowance (MA) in 1976; Non-contributory Invalidity Allowance started in 1976 and was changed to Severe Disablement Allowance (SDA) in 1985. Mobility Allowance and Attendance Allowance for non-pensioners were joined into Disablement Living Allowance (DLA), which is not analysed here.

Source: Author's calculations from DSS (1995a: tables D2.01, E1.03, and A2.24 and DSS (1992: table E2.03).

dominated by occupational and more recently personal pensions. Private market provision for other insurance-based cover has recently been analysed by Burchardt and Hills (1997) but is much less extensive.

Occupational pensions have been the main second pillar of post-war income provision for retirement. Both public and private sector employers have had a strong commitment to contribute to pension schemes. In the private sector such schemes were never spread evenly across all employees and professions and workplaces. The low-paid, manual, and part-time sectors were always disadvantaged and the public SERPS scheme was introduced to deal with such inequity in access and coverage. Table 7.12 shows the changing coverage of the work-force (employees) by occupational pensions. The number of employees contributing to schemes rose during the 1970s and has since fallen back slightly to 10.7 million in 1991. Overall these employees represent around 50 per cent of all employed workers. The composition of these workers has been fairly consistently split between two-thirds in the private and one-third in the public sector. However, the split between women and men has changed significantly. The number of men contributing to pensions has fallen in both sectors and increased numbers of women have largely compensated for this fall. Women contributors in the private sector have risen by 54 per cent over 20 years from 1.3 to 2 million. In 1971 they were around 20 per cent of contributors but by 1991 this had risen to over 30 per cent. In the public sector women were approximately one-quarter of pension coverage in 1971 and by 1991 had risen to 45 per cent, growing from 1.1 to 1.9 million, a growth of 73 per cent.

Those excluded from occupational schemes have had no additional provision, have relied on SERPS, or have joined personal pension schemes. Self-employed professionals have been a particularly strong client group. The 1986 Social Security Act sought to increase personal private provision. Table 7.13 shows that this coverage grew during the 1970s, from 600,000 covered in 1974 to 1 million in 1979. During the 1980s coverage grew more rapidly, and grew at a faster rate before the 1986 Social Security Act came into force. The 1987 to 1989 period saw a one-off surge in business when personal pensions roughly doubled. Either side of this surge, the annual rates of growth show that private pensions were growing at a faster rate before the Act than after. This may be due to greater self-regulation since the mis-selling of that period and may also be due to changes in type of private pension product sold. Table 7.13 also shows that since 1988 there has been a growth in the proportion of private pensions

Table 7.12. OCCUPATIONAL PENSION COVERAGE (MILLIONS OF EMPLOYEES)

	Private sector		Public sector		All	
	Men	Women	Men	Women	Men and women	% of all employed
1971	5.5	1.3	3.2	1.1	11.1	49
1975	4.9	1.1	3.7	1.7	11.4	49
1979	4.6	1.5	3.7	1.8	11.6	50
1983	4.4	1.4	3.4	1.9	11.1	52
1987	4.4	1.4	2.8	2.0	10.6	49
1991	4.5	2.0	2.3	1.9	10.7	48

Source: Government Actuary (1994: Table 2.1).

Table 7.13. PERSONAL PENSION COVERAGE

Financial year beginning March	Personal pension policies in force[a]		Individuals contributing to appropriate personal pensions (%)
	000s	% of which give indexed pension[b]	
1974	600	n/a	n/a
1979	1,600	n/a	n/a
1985	4,461	30	n/a
1987	5,697	32	3,209
1988	7,907	38	3,404
1989	11,640	45	4,179
1990	13,995	46	4,819
1991	15,212	46	5,351
1992	17,429	46	5,679
1993	18,111	49	5,736
1994	18,906	50	5,646
1995	19,913	52	n/a
Average annual growth, 1974–79 (%)	10.7	n/a	n/a
Average annual growth, 1979–87 (%)	17.0	n/a	n/a
Average annual growth, 1988–95 (%)	12.2	16.9[c]	

[a] Pensions in force include lapsed pension policies to which no current contribution is being paid.
[b] Indexation is limited to set assumptions usually 5% or under.
[c] Arithmetic growth rate of numbers of such policies.

Sources: ABI (1996: table 30, and ABI data for previous years); DSS (1997b: table 1.0).

which are index-linked to inflation: they have grown from 38 per cent to 52 per cent of coverage, and are growing faster than overall private pension coverage—16.9 per cent as against 12.2 per cent.

What are the aggregate outputs of personal and occupational provision? Table 7.14 shows that occupational and personal pensions have risen from 54 per cent to over 67 per cent of all pension payments. At the same time, the gross cost to the Exchequer of tax expenditure and contribution rebates in 1994/5 has risen to over £20 billion, equivalent to over 20 per cent of the social security budget for Great Britain but not counted as government expenditure.

The changing value of benefits

Real rates of benefit provide a robust indicator of how the 'generosity' of social security policy has changed. There are two ways in which such generosity can be assessed: the purchasing power of benefit rates, and their relative income standard. Fig. 7.6 shows the real purchasing power of benefits, deflated by the RPI. There has been a small rise in real value of benefits over the whole time period. Basic pension has risen from £54.88 in 1974 to £61.15 in 1996, Unemployment Benefit has risen less overall (from £47.19 to £48.25), and Child Benefit (based on a one-child family) from £7.12 in 1978 to £10.80 in 1996. These changes are not smooth throughout. IVB in 1974 was at rates similar to UB but then changed to mirror pension rates exactly except for the early 1980s, when it lagged slightly behind the basic pension. Child Benefit was uprated significantly before 1979 but remained flat during the early 1980s until 1987, after which it was not uprated until 1991 under the Major Government.

Figure 7.7 shows the same benefits but indicates their changing relative value measured as a proportion of per capita net personal disposable income for the UK. Using this measure it is clear that the overall trend is downwards; benefits now represent a lower proportion of average income than in 1974. This means that the relative incomes of those who rely on benefits have fallen when compared to the rest of the population, in particular with the majority of those with earnings.

Table 7.14. PRIVATE AND OCCUPATIONAL PENSIONERS AND TAX EXPENDITURE OF PENSIONS (£ BILLION AT 1994/5 PRICES)

	Current pensioners in receipt		Tax costs of current contributions	
	Private + occupational pensions (£ billion, cash)	% of total pension provision	Inland Revenue tax expenditure[a]	Estimated value of DSS rebates and incentives
1973/4	3.4	54.2	na	n/a
1979/80	8.5	49.2	n/a	6.5
1985/6	21.4	55.3	n/a	5.3
1986/7	24.7	57.2	13.3	5.7
1987/8	29.1	59.0	13.1	5.2
1988/9	30.2	59.6	12.6	6.1
1989/90	33.9	60.9	13.7	9.3
1990/91	40.2	62.7	13.3	8.8
1991/2	48.0	63.8	12.5	8.1
1992/3	55.9	65.2	12.3	7.6
1993/4	60.8	65.6	12.3	8.6[b]
1994/5	62.5	67.5	12.7	7.4

[a] Gross tax expenditure with no allowance for capital gains on invested funds.
[b] This figure subject to some uncertainty.

Sources: DSS (1995*c*); Inland Revenue (1996: tables 1.6 and 7.10, and previous versions); Government Actuary (1995: tables B1 and E3, and equivalents in previous versions); author's calculations from ONS (1996*b*: tables 4.9 and 7.1, and equivalents in previous versions).

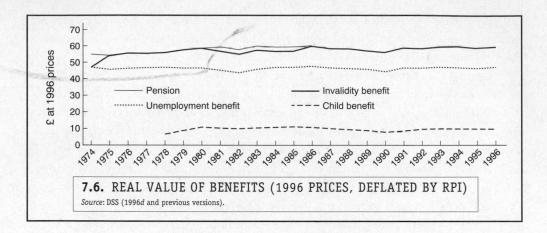

7.6. REAL VALUE OF BENEFITS (1996 PRICES, DEFLATED BY RPI)

Source: DSS (1996*d* and previous versions).

One of the most significant changes in benefit rates has been the change in the value of assistance relative to other benefits. Fig. 7.8 shows that basic rates of National Insurance benefits for retirement and invalidity as a percentage of assistance have fallen from around 102 per cent to 90 per cent. In practice National Insurance benefits may be higher than basic rates, as some people are entitled to additional amounts of pension or to age-related invalidity allowances. The underlying trends are that basic rates are falling to or below assistance levels and that additional benefits are being withdrawn over time—particularly earnings-related elements. Thus the role of assistance grows.

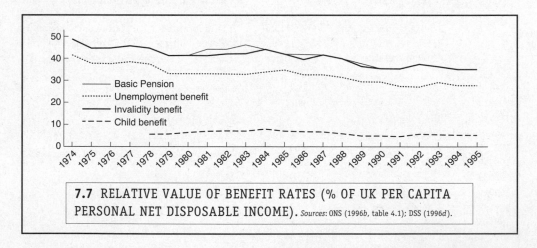

7.7 RELATIVE VALUE OF BENEFIT RATES (% OF UK PER CAPITA PERSONAL NET DISPOSABLE INCOME). *Sources*: ONS (1996*b*, table 4.1); DSS (1996*d*).

Means-tested benefits: Dependency, incentives, and take-up

The rhetorical importance of means-testing lies in its supposed ability to target resources at the poorest and thus to help in restraining spending. How well does this fit with other rhetorical aims of social security: independence, effectiveness, and efficiency?

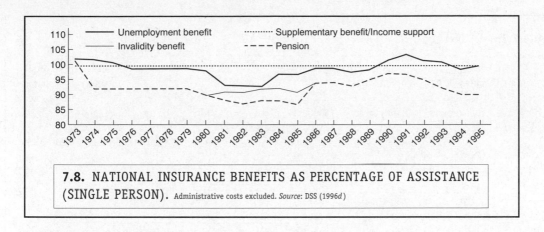

7.8. NATIONAL INSURANCE BENEFITS AS PERCENTAGE OF ASSISTANCE (SINGLE PERSON). Administrative costs excluded. *Source*: DSS (1996*d*)

Dependency Politicians say they worry about benefit 'dependency'. Table 7.15 presents a consistent time series for the growing claimant population for means-tested assistance. It shows that means-tested claimants have grown by 124 per cent since 1973. There are fewer pensioners—they have fallen overall by 14 per cent—and many more unemployed—who have grown by 675 per cent to become the single largest group of claimants. The number of sick and disabled has risen by 150 per cent, and lone parents by 353 per cent. While these growth profiles suggest greater potential dependency, there has also been a growth in the numbers who work; FIS/FC claimants have grown by 447 per cent.

Table 7.16 decomposes claimant growth by the different benefit regimes in order to provide a more consistent analysis of trends over time. Unemployment has been the largest single source of growth in means-tested populations. It accounts for 56 per cent of growth in SB/IS over the whole period of 1973 to 1994, and accounted for 82 per cent of growth between 1973 and 1987. Since 1989 it has accounted for almost 40 per cent of growth. The next largest contribution to growth has been lone parenthood: overall this has constituted almost 27 per cent of aggregate growth of IS/SB. Sickness and disability has risen much faster since 1989. Since 1989 pensioners have also grown, after declining in number under the old scheme. This is partly due to the increased generosity of assistance relative to basic pensions. Pensioners have contributed about 10 per cent of the growth of IS since 1989.

Does this growth necessarily mean increased dependency? Long-term claims from the working-age populations have increased. In 1975 only 12 per cent of unemployed assistance claimants had been claiming for two years or more; in 1992, the last low point, the proportion was 18 per cent and the underlying numbers of unemployed had grown significantly in the mean time. The proportion of long-term lone parents has also grown gradually, from 49 per cent in 1973 to 60 per cent in 1994 (author's own calculations from DSS 1996*a* and previous volumes).

Work incentives One major theme of policy has been to sustain a gap between income on benefit and in work to ensure incentives to work in the face of increasing levels of

Table 7.15. CLAIMANTS OF MEANS-TESTED ASSISTANCE, 1973–1994 (000s)

	Supplementary Benefits (1973–87)[a] Income Support (1988–94)						Family Income Supplement (1973–87) Family Credit (1988–94)	Total means-tested
	Pensioners[b]	Unemployed[c]	Sick/ disabled[d]	Lone parents[e]	Others[f]	All Income Support[g]		
1973	1844	249	280	228	75	2675	98	2773
1979	1720	566	207	306	51	2850	77	2927
1986	1724	2259	301	575	80	4940	202	5142
1989	1437	1331	346	750	298	4161	286	4447
1990	1510	1168	386	788	328	4180	313	4493
1991	1413	1439	433	865	335	4487	328	4815
1992	1470	1770	495	950	404	5088	356	5444
1993	1555	2027	606	1005	449	5643	485	6128
1994	1583	1930	700	1032	430	5675	536	6211
Growth, 1973–94 (%)	−14	+675	+150	+353	473	112	447	124

[a] New scheme growth calculated from start of 1989 as 1988 totals include transitionary arrangements for FIS/FC claimants.
[b] Claimants over pensionable age (men over 65 and women over 60).
[c] Those who must register for work (the rules governing such registration have changed) plus from 1982 all men aged 60 to 64 who are not receiving sickness benefit or in the 'other' category.
[d] From 1988 includes all those who receive SSP or sickness benefit and are not otherwise defined; also includes 60- to 64-year-old men receiving such benefits.
[e] Not including those receiving widows' benefits.
[f] Includes all widows' benefit claimants under 60; since 1982 includes a number of over 60- to 64-year-old men, and, since 1988, lone parents who also receive widows' benefits.
[g] The totals before 1983 are not entirely consistent with those afterwards due to the introduction of housing benefits which lifted an unquantifiable number of claimants from supplementary benefits (mainly affects pensioner totals).

Source: Author's calculations from DSS (1995a: table A2.09), DSS (1995b: table 4.1, 8.1, and 8.2), and previous versions.

unemployment, decreasing relative levels of wages for the unskilled, and increased part-time and temporary working. Benefit policy has changed to both decrease relative value of benefits for the unemployed and to increase use of means-testing. There are then two major problems for ensuring incentives to work:

- To ensure that benefit rates are not close to or greater than in-work income (the replacement ratio). Where this occurs there may be an *unemployment trap*.
- To ensure that those working on the margins of benefit entitlement are able to improve their incomes through work. The side-effect of means-testing is that benefit is reduced as income rises alongside the incidence of tax and social security contributions on increased earnings. The combination of these may produce very high marginal tax rates—where net income only rises by less than 50 pence for each pound earned. Where this effect is pronounced there is a *poverty trap*.

Table 7.16. THE GROWTH OF MEANS-TESTING

	Supplementary Benefits (1973–87) Income Support (1988–94)						Family Income Supplement (1973–87) Family Credit (1988–94)	Total means-tested
	Pensioners	Unemployed	Sick/ disabled	Lone parents	Others	All SB/IS		
Growth, 1973–94								
Annual average rate of growth (%)	−0.7	10.2	4.5	7.5	8.7	3.6	8.4	3.9
Contribution to growth	−8.7% of SB/IS	56.0% of SB/IS	14.0% of SB/IS	26.8% of SB/IS	11.7% of SB/IS	87.3% of total	12.7% of total	
Growth, 1973–87 (old schemes)								
Annual average rate of growth (%)	−0.5	16.4	1.7	7.5	2.5	4.4	6.0	4.5
Contribution to growth	−5.3% of SB	82.4% of SB	3.3% of SB	18.0% of SB	1.4% of SB	94.8% of total	5.2% of total	
Growth, 1989–94 (new schemes)								
Annual average rate of growth (%)	2.0	7.7	15.1	6.6	7.6	6.4	13.4	6.9
Contribution to growth	9.6% of IS	39.6% of IS	23.4% of IS	18.6% of IS	8.7% of IS	85.8% of total	14.2% of total	

Source: Author's calculations from Table 7.15.

Benefits have fallen relative to incomes over the period. Thus, incentives to work, in general, have improved. However, a more accurate discussion of replacement ratios has to relate to available rates of pay for the unemployed—which are lower than average income or average wages. Table 7.17 shows that there has been a substantial reduction in numbers facing replacement ratios above 70 per cent since 1985. This is both a reflection of changing benefit policy—the 1986 Act made significant reductions in means-tested benefits for the unemployed (Evans *et al.* 1994; Evans 1996*a*)—and of changing wage levels. However, such improvements should also be viewed alongside the changing composition of the benefit population. Increasing numbers of lone parents and sick claimants may have, in part, viewed

Table 7.17. REPLACEMENT RATIOS FOR THE WORKING POPULATION (000s)

	1985	1990/1	1994/5	1995/6
100%+	60	15	10	15
90–99%	210	30	35	35
80–89%	730	130	190	165
70–79%	1,870	430	505	510
Total over 70%	2,870	605	740	725

Source: DSS (1997*a*: figure 32, and previous versions).

improvements should also be viewed alongside the changing composition of the benefit population. Increasing numbers of lone parents and sick claimants may have, in part, viewed poor replacement ratios as a reason for not being designated as 'unemployed'. Overall, such outcomes are consistent with the intended effects of policy changes instituted in the 1980s to improve incentives. The unemployment trap *is* smaller in its effect.

A contra indicator of such policy success is shown in Table 7.18. The numbers *in* employment who face high marginal tax rates have risen substantially. The poverty trap has grown. The rise in the provision of means-tested in-work benefits, together with that in claimants who work less than 16 hours while claiming assistance (24 hours between 1988 and 1992, and

Table 7.18. NUMBER IN EMPLOYMENT FACING A PARTICULAR MARGINAL NET INCOME DEDUCTION RATE (000s)

	1985	1991/2	1994/5	1995/6
100%+ on Income Support	211	165	184	171
Other 100%+	70	0	0	20
90%	130	55	120	135
80%	290	205	370	435
70%	290	400	640	700
60%	450	405	660	720
50%	680	405	665	725
Total over 50%	2,121	1,635	2,639	2,906
Total as % of employed workforce in Great Britain[a]	8.7%	6.4%	10.6%	11.6%

[a] Workforce numbers are those for June in 1985 and for September for the remaining years.

Sources: DSS (1996*a*: table A2.25), ONS (1996*d*: table 1.1, and previous versions); DSS (1997*a*: figure 34).

workers who have marginal tax rates of 50 per cent and over. In aggregate this has risen from 8.7 per cent of the employed workforce in 1985 to 11.6 per cent in 1995/6. There has been a decrease in the worst effects of the poverty trap: fewer pay over 100 per cent. But the increased numbers claiming Family Credit have meant that the numbers facing very high marginal tax rates had returned to 1985 levels by 1995/6, and there has been a marked increase in those losing between 60 and 89 per cent of their additional earnings. Part of this increase is also due to the changing nature of work for those on the margins of Income Support entitlement: increasingly part-time and low-paid jobs are available, which means that means-tested in-work benefits have to be claimed to maintain living standards. Research has found little effect of these high marginal tax rates on labour supply (Blundell 1992). Evidence from various surveys (for instance Marsh and McKay 1993; Bryson and Marsh 1996) suggests that few such workers realize the actual nature of the disincentive effects.

Take-up One important measure of benefit performance is the rate of take-up by eligible people. Contributory benefits with clear age-based qualifications have near enough 100 per cent take-up. For pensions and for Child Benefit high take-up results from the fact that forms of claiming are sent at birth and retirement. Take-up of some benefits is actually affected by take-up of others: for instance, a proportion of lone parents do not claim the additional one-parent benefit due to them because they also receive means-tested benefits and they have nothing to gain from receiving it. The take-up of disability and long-term sickness benefits is an under-researched area. Buckle (1988) estimated take-up rates of around 70 per cent to 75 per cent for Attendance Allowance but the medical and care criteria which underlie entitlement mean that a true take-up rate is difficult to measure exactly. Indeed, measuring take-up means recognizing that a claim has to be made and assessed before entitlement can be determined, and hence there may be those who have made a claim and are entitled but have not yet had their benefit determined. There may be those who have been initially refused but are or would be entitled on review or appeal of that decision (see also Sainsbury *et al.* 1995 for a full description and analysis of DLA and AA).

Measurement of take-up rates is usually made in two forms: the *caseload take-up* measure, which is the number of people eligible who do then claim; and the *expenditure take-up* measure, which measures the amount of benefit claimed. Both measures are needed because the amounts not taken up may be small and hence fairly low take-up rates may mask the fact that a high percentage of benefit is nevertheless claimed. Expenditure take-up should also include the amount of benefit underclaimed by existing claimants who do make a claim but for some reason do not receive their full entitlement (Duclos 1991). This point is particularly important for areas of discretionary entitlement (although measuring take-up of discretionary areas of social security—particularly the Social Fund—is very problematic (Huby and Whyley 1996)). It is also important for areas of linked social security entitlements—for instance, the increasing reliance on previous determination of disablement or long-term sickness for means-tested benefits. Thus, for example, a failure to take up an Attendance Allowance may also mean that Income Support is either unclaimed or underclaimed for an elderly disabled person.

Returning to existing measures of take-up, Table 7.19 shows the changing take-up rates for

Table 7.19. TAKE-UP OF MEANS-TESTED BENEFITS PERCENTAGES

Supplementary Benefits and Income Support

	Pensioners		Non-pensioners		All	
	Caseload	Expenditure	Caseload	Expenditure	Caseload	Expenditure
Supplementary Benefits						
1974	76	65	72	77	71	74
1979	65	68	78	84	70	80
1985	n/a	n/a	n/a	n/a	84	91
Income Support (estimates given in ranges)						
1990	n/a	74–83	n/a	89–96	n/a	86–96
1994/5	59–66	73–9	87–92	92–5	76–83	88–92

Family Income Supplement and Family Credit

	Caseload	Expenditure
FIS		
1978/9	51	n/a
1985/6	48	54
FC		
1989	57	67
1994/5	69	82

NUMBERS OF ELIGIBLE NON-CLAIMANTS (000s)

	Supplementary Benefit/Income Support			Family Income Supplement/ Family Credit
	Pensioners	Non-pensioners	All	
1974	572	338	910	(66)
1979	926	319	1245	73
1985[a]			910	218
1994[b]	1059	494	1553	250
Growth, 1979–94 (%)	14	55	25	242

[a] Crude estimates only: 1974 take-up rate for FIS based on 1978/9 levels.
[b] 1994 IS totals based on mid-range caseload take-up estimates; FC populations taken as average annual caseload.

Sources: 1974 figures from SBC (1978); 1979 figures from Hansard (1979: cols. 533–44, Written Answers); 1985 figures from DHSS (1989: tables 48.01–02); subsequent figures from DSS (1996c and previous versions).

means-tested benefits (excluding Housing Benefit). This table has to accommodate several discontinuities. First, it bridges the old and present schemes for means-tested benefits and compares SB with IS and FIS with FC over time. No adjustments have been made to reflect the different underlying rules for these benefits. Second, there have been significant methodological advances in the measurement of take-up and hence estimates made twenty years ago are not 100 per cent comparable with today's. Thirdly, these are official measures of take-up made by the DSS and its forerunners.

What emerges is an overall picture of improving take-up of means-tested benefit over time, although this improvement cannot be exactly measured because of the differences in schemes and measurement. What are the reasons? Better information and more publicity are possible answers. Changing rules of entitlement, especially since 1988, is also a reason (Corden 1995). But another reason could be that increasing numbers of claimants for IS have no other source of income and therefore have to make a claim to have any income at all rather than, say, living on a lower income from other benefits and not claiming the additional top-up from IS. The rise in Family Credit take-up may also reflect the falling real value of earnings of these claimants over time as well as the increased generosity of FC (Evans 1996b) and hence the necessity to claim to maintain a standard of living. Additionally, FC is claimed as a follow-on from IS for many lone parents and hence there is an administrative link with a previous entitlement.

But improved take-up is not an unambivalent success. The growth of the means-tested population means that higher proportions of take-up can still lead to growing numbers of people who do not claim. Some crude estimates of these are shown in Table 7.19. These estimates suggest that the number of families living on incomes below those envisaged by means-tested assistance has grown because of failures to take up entitlement despite increasing *rates* of take-up.

IV. Outcomes

How has social security affected national and personal incomes?

Fig. 7.9 shows the overall relative scale of social security using three measures:

1. Social security benefits as a proportion of gross UK personal income.
2. Expenditure on social security as a proportion of all central government expenditure.
3. Expenditure on social security as a proportion of GDP.

Spending has risen using each of these indicators and has risen over time across fluctuations in the economic cycle, for reasons outlined earlier. Social security represented 10 per cent of all personal income in 1974 and this had grown to 15 per cent by 1994; it was 8.5 per cent of GDP in 1974 and was over 13 per cent by 1994. However, this rate of growth, roughly half as

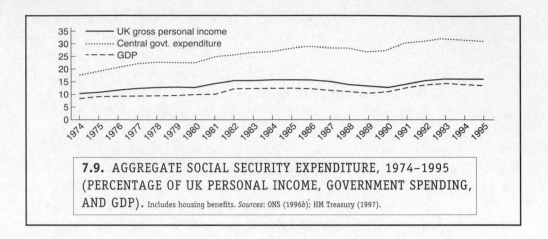

7.9. AGGREGATE SOCIAL SECURITY EXPENDITURE, 1974–1995 (PERCENTAGE OF UK PERSONAL INCOME, GOVERNMENT SPENDING, AND GDP). Includes housing benefits. *Sources*: ONS (1996*b*); HM Treasury (1997).

much again over twenty years, is not as dramatic as the shift of government resources towards social security. In 1974 around 18 per cent of spending was on social security, whereas by 1994 its share had risen to almost 31 per cent. Thus social security spending has grown faster as a proportion of all government spending than its share of national resources would otherwise suggest. This is partly due to social security being demand-led, and to the fact that those demands have grown.

Has this spending mostly gone to the poorest? Overall, between 1980 and 1987 around 70 to 75 per cent of all spending was concentrated on the bottom two quintile groups, and these groups have received between 57 per cent and 64 per cent of spending since 1987. However, if these same figures are viewed differently, and social security is taken as a proportion of each quintile group's income, then there is both a growth over time and a spreading upwards of social security across the bottom three quintiles (see Table 7.20).

Social security and income distribution

There is a growing concern about widening inequalities of income since the mid-1970s (Borrie 1994; Barclay 1995). It is difficult to isolate the role of social security from that of economic, demographic, and social changes and the resulting changes in demand for and outcomes of policy. In broad terms Fig. 7.10 shows that social security has acted to mitigate growing inequality, which has been driven largely by increasing inequality in earnings and increasing inequality in private pension and investment incomes. Social security in these aggregate terms has acted as a brake on income inequality, but its influence on reducing inequality has been increasingly limited over time.

Fig. 7.11 shows the changing composition of the poorest households by family type and economic activity. Both graphs show a declining proportion of pensioners in the quintile. The growing numbers of pensioners have increasingly higher pensions due to private and state schemes maturing (see Tables 7.6, 7.12, and 7.13 above). The proportion of the bottom

Table 7.20a. DISTRIBUTION OF SOCIAL SECURITY SPENDING BY HOUSEHOLD INCOME QUINTILE GROUPS (%)

	Bottom	2	3	4	Top
Old series					
1980	41.6	27.9	12.7	9.5	8.3
1985	38.4	30.3	14.1	9.3	7.9
1987 old	39.0	30.0	14.1	9.6	7.2
New series					
1987 new	33.2	29.1	19.6	11.2	7.0
1990	33.6	29.7	19.2	11.2	6.3
1995	25.8	30.9	21.0	12.9	9.4

b. SOCIAL SECURITY AS A PROPORTION OF HOUSEHOLD GROSS INCOME BY QUINTILE GROUPS (%)

	Bottom	2	3	4	Top
Old series					
1980	92.0	32.8	9.2	5.0	2.7
1985	96.4	48.5	13.4	6.0	2.9
1987 old	95.7	47.7	12.7	5.8	2.1
New series					
1987 new	72.0	41.9	16.5	6.9	2.6
1990	70.0	37.2	13.8	5.6	1.9
1995	72.5	50.8	26.7	8.6	3.3

Note: 1975 to 1987 old series income quintiles calculated on original unequivalent income; 1987 to 1995/6 new series income quintiles calculated on equivalent disposable income.

Source: ONS (1997*c* and previous versions).

quintile group consisting of families with children has grown both from couples and lone parents. There has also been a growth in the proportion of single people in the bottom quintile group. Moving to economic activity, then, the main changes have been an increase in unemployment and an increase in 'other' reasons for economic inactivity—usually sickness and disability and lone parenthood. The bottom quintile is becoming increasingly economically inactive, with fewer full-time workers and only a slight increase in the proportions working part-time.

Other research has shown that the distribution of earnings among households amplifies inequality because of increasing divergence between double-earner households and no-earner households (Gregg and Wadsworth 1996). Means-testing may partly accentuate this trend because working partners may stop work when their partners become unemployed as

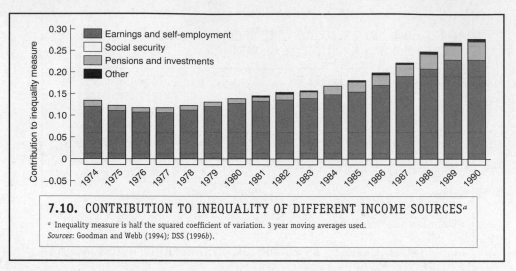

7.10. CONTRIBUTION TO INEQUALITY OF DIFFERENT INCOME SOURCES[a]

[a] Inequality measure is half the squared coefficient of variation. 3 year moving averages used.
Sources: Goodman and Webb (1994); DSS (1996b).

they are faced with strong benefit disincentives. Real income growth for the poorest workers, i.e. those on the margins of Income Support levels, is unlikely to occur in the jobs they currently hold. Substantial improvements in earnings are most likely through promotion or job mobility and/or their partner also being employed (Bryson and Marsh 1996).

Thus it is not only the changing composition of and causes of low income that have influenced social security spending (and that have been influenced by it), but also the changing risk of being poor. This experience of risk has not been equally shared by all. Fig. 7.12 shows the changing risks of falling into the bottom quintile group since 1974. The elderly have experienced decreased risks of being in the bottom fifth: around a quarter of couples and single pensioners were that poor in 1974, but only around an eighth of both groups in 1993 (shown as family types); 28 per cent of individuals over 60 were in the bottom fifth in 1974 but only 13 per cent in 1993. Thus the risks of being poor if you are a pensioner have on aggregate fallen by around 50 per cent. The single non-pensioner's risk has risen from 5 per cent to 9 per cent and couples without children from 3 per cent to almost 5 per cent. Most of this increased risk will be due to increased levels of unemployment. The risk for couples with children has remained largely unchanged, while lone parents have, surprisingly, become slightly less at risk, a fall from 25 per cent to 21 per cent. But lone parents still have the highest risks of all family types of being poor.

The risk profiles by economic activity show far less variation and are far flatter over time than those defined by family type (except for the over-60s mentioned above). The self-employed have a slightly increased risk, but the underlying samples are not reliable enough to provide estimates of how risk has actually increased. The conclusion is that relying on part-time work, being unemployed, or being economically inactive carries a very high risk of being relatively poor, but the risk of being amongst the relatively poorest fifth has fallen slightly for them all. There are more casualties of economic, social, and demographic changes competing for the poorest slots in society.

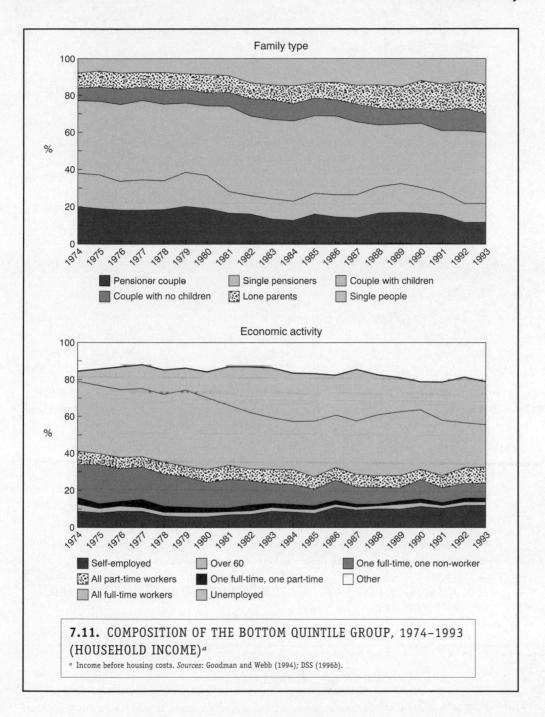

7.11. COMPOSITION OF THE BOTTOM QUINTILE GROUP, 1974–1993 (HOUSEHOLD INCOME)[a]

[a] Income before housing costs. *Sources*: Goodman and Webb (1994); DSS (1996b).

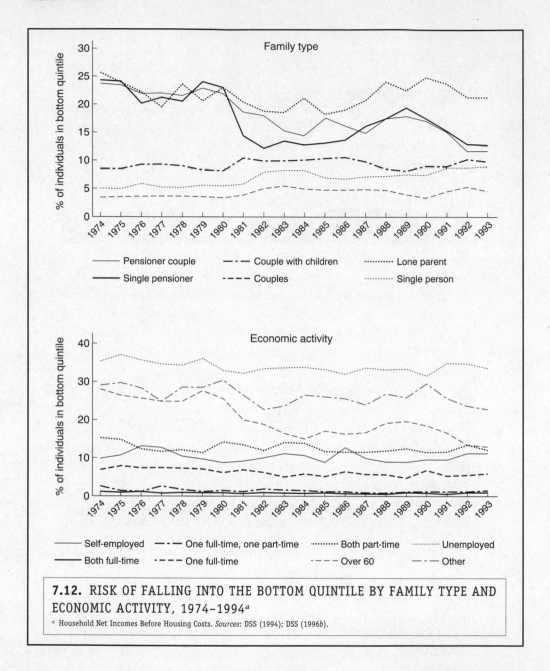

7.12. RISK OF FALLING INTO THE BOTTOM QUINTILE BY FAMILY TYPE AND ECONOMIC ACTIVITY, 1974–1994[a]

[a] Household Net Incomes Before Housing Costs. *Sources*: DSS (1994); DSS (1996b).

Poverty and social security

In the 1970s and early 1980s the frequently used poverty standard was based on the social assistance safety net. The number of families living in poverty was measured mostly as those with an income under 140 per cent of assistance (a standard inherited from the ground-breaking study by Abel-Smith and Townsend (1965)). While this was not an 'official' government measure of poverty it was produced by Government and became an implicit, yet flawed standard. In the mid-1980s, partly as a reflection of the 1986 Social Security Act and the need to accommodate permanently a mass claimant population on assistance, the definition of poverty changed. Indeed, it is possible to argue that 'poverty' as a state concept of commitment disappeared. The Prime Minister and Social Security Minister argued vehemently against any minimum standard of living incorporated within benefit rates. They claimed that poverty was meaningless if the result of improving benefit rates was that more people were in poverty. In place of poverty came a new relativism in which the poor were viewed as merely less well off than the majority, rather than in 'poverty' as such. To measure the incidence of low income (note, not 'poverty') the DSS moved to produce an annual analysis of households below average income. The effect of this change was that attention focused on low income as a proportion of mean or median household income, and there has been a general move towards the EU standard of 50 per cent of mean income (or expenditure) by commentators.

Moving away from a policy standard has not, however, altered the fact that policy on benefits alters the poverty measure. A relative measure of poverty is affected by the distribution of earnings, benefits, and other income and the changing populations who rely on these income sources. The numbers claiming assistance-level benefits and the level of their benefits therefore influence mean or median income. It is also influenced by the incomes of the remainder of the population. Thus average income, and any proportion of it used to measure low income or poverty, has been pulled down by a growing population relying on means-tested benefits and pushed up by those who rely on earnings and private investments. One of the fundamental aims of social security is poverty relief (see Section I above), and social security fulfils this function amongst others. Piachaud (1997) estimates that, without social security, the number of households in poverty (defined as having below 50 per cent of mean income) would rise from 18 per cent to 35 per cent in 1995/6.

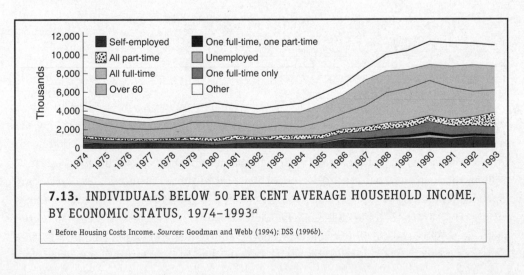

7.13. INDIVIDUALS BELOW 50 PER CENT AVERAGE HOUSEHOLD INCOME, BY ECONOMIC STATUS, 1974–1993[a]

[a] Before Housing Costs Income. *Sources*: Goodman and Webb (1994); DSS (1996b).

Fig. 7.13 shows the growing numbers of people who live in households below 50 per cent of average income, which is taken as a consistent relative poverty measure between 1974 and 1993. The total number of people living in relative poverty has more than doubled over twenty years, rising from 4.7 million to 11.2 million. The major reasons for this have been unemployment and economic inactivity. Table 7.21 shows the arithmetic growth between the two end years (which are not exactly comparable in the economic cycles). Unemployment is the main cause of growing poverty—almost one-third of all growth can be attributed to it. A further fifth of growing poverty is due to 'other' forms of economic inactivity such as sickness, disablement, and lone parenthood, and yet a further fifth is due to part-time working. Amongst the employed, the self-employed have also made poverty grow (but note that there are some strong caveats about the treatment and reporting of self-employed incomes in the underlying data—DSS 1996b). Overall, unemployment and economic inactivity have caused 60 per cent of the growth in poverty. So far, we have only discussed the relative income changes in the population. Fig. 7.14 shows that the real income levels of the poor have risen less fast than the rich between 1979 and 1993/4, and that incomes after housing costs have actually fallen in real terms for the poorest decile.

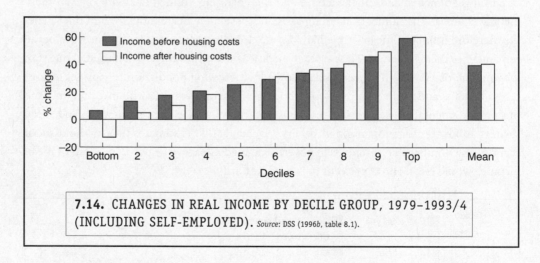

7.14. CHANGES IN REAL INCOME BY DECILE GROUP, 1979–1993/4 (INCLUDING SELF-EMPLOYED). *Source:* DSS (1996b, table 8.1).

As a combined effect of changes in incomes, unemployment levels, and social security policy the final legacy of the years since 1974 has been a huge growth in the proportion of the population relying on means-tested benefits. The number of people in families who rely on means-tested provision for their basic income has risen from around 4.4 million to almost 12 million, that is from 8 per cent to almost 21 per cent of the whole population (excluding Housing Benefit—see Chapter 5). Increasingly children are being born and raised in families relying on IS. The number of children in families claiming SB/IS has risen faster than overall claimant growth, and the number of such children under 5 has risen faster still. In 1974 only 6.4 per cent of all under-16s relied on SB; by 1994 this had risen to just over a quarter of all

Table 7.21. CAUSES OF GROWTH OF POVERTY: ECONOMIC STATUS OF INDIVIDUALS LIVING IN HOUSEHOLDS BELOW 50% OF AVERAGE INCOME, 1974 AND 1993 (000s)

	Self-employed	All full-time work	One full-time, one part-time	One full-time only	Part-time only	Over 60	Unemployed	Other	Total
1974	446	85	48	386	343	1850	523	1019	4701
1993	1176	126	158	836	1599	2424	2535	2365	11219
Growth	730	41	110	450	1256	574	2012	1346	6518
Growth (%)	164	48	229	117	366	31	385	132	139
Attributable proportion of growth (%)	11	<1	2	7	19	9	31	21	100

Sources: Goodman and Webb (1994) and DSS (1996b).

Table 7.22. POPULATION RELIANT ON MEANS-TESTED SOCIAL SECURITY, GREAT BRITAIN, 1974–1994

	Population in families receiving Assistance and FIS/FC (000s)	% of whole population
1974	4,381	8.0
1979	4,658	8.5
1986	9,016	16.3
1990	7,979	14.3
1994	11,726	20.7
Growth,1974–94	168%	

Sources: DSS (1995: table A2.01) and unpublished ONS population estimates.

such children (25.6 per cent). Younger children were more at risk—rising from 6.6 per cent in 1994 to 29.1 per cent in 1994 (author's calculations from DSS 1996*a* and previous versions).

In Brief

- Overall real spending has grown by 109 per cent between 1973/4 and 1995/6. The largest contributors to such growth are contributory benefits (pensions and invalidity benefits in the main) and means-tested benefits.
- The move away from contributory spending towards more means-testing has accelerated over the period and is attributable to both increasing demands (mostly from unemployment and lone parenthood) and a change in the policy response, which has prioritized 'targeting' through means-testing.
- Growth in pension spending has been due to three primary factors: demographic factors, benefit indexation, and the maturation of earnings-related pensions (SERPS). Spending on elderly people has caused over one-third of all increased spending.
- Spending on sick and disabled people has also grown faster than overall spending. Two-thirds of spending on contributory invalidity benefit has been to those over 40 who have 'retired early'. Non-contributory spending on disabled people has grown as the scope of benefits has grown and demand has increased. Increased demand is partly because of more frail elderly people, but demand from the working-age population has also grown.
- Despite the increased generosity and coverage of state pensions, private provision has not been 'crowded out'—quite the reverse. Two-thirds of all pension provision is

now from occupational and personal pensions. Tax spending on contributions to these schemes has grown but is not treated as government spending.
- The result of moving to means-tested provision has been a large increase in the population who rely on it—from 8.0 per cent in 1974 to almost 21 per cent in 1994. Unemployment and lone parenthood account for over three-quarters of this growth. The secondary effects of means-testing are that poor workers—now 12 per cent of the employed workforce—face strong disincentives. There have been gains in efficiency from improved replacement ratios and improved rates of take-up.
- Despite the move to means-testing, benefits are not noticeably targeted more on those with low income, and despite more spending on social security and more targeting on low income, poverty has grown.

Negative aspects of this summary should not be taken as unambivalent indictments of policy making. The results of policy promises have brought real increases in incomes for pensioners, and coverage for the disabled has grown. Demands have grown and social security has had to respond to higher numbers of poor employed people, increased rates of economic inactivity and unemployment, and more pensioners living longer. The growing numbers relying on means-tested benefits reflects withdrawal of social insurance cover—in particular for unemployment. 'Rolling back the state' has led, in part, to growing costs of social security. Social security has increasingly become a reactive ambulance, picking up the casualties of social, economic, and ideological change. It would be perverse to blame motorway accidents on ambulances, even though they appear every time there is one.

Further Reading

BARR, N. (1993). *The Economics of the Welfare State*, London: Weidenfeld and Nicolson, especially chapter 5 and part 2.

DILNOT, A. W., and WALKER, I. (1989), *The Economics of Social Security*, Oxford: Clarendon Press.

HILLS, J. (ed.), *New Inequalities: The Changing Distribution of Income and Wealth in the United Kingdom*, Cambridge: Cambridge University Press.

HILLS, J., DITCH, J., and GLENNERSTER, H. (1994), *Beveridge and Social Security: An International Retrospective*, Oxford: Clarendon Press.

TIMMINS, N. (1995), *The Five Giants: A Biography of the Welfare State*, especially parts 4–6.

ANNEXE

Table 7A.1. BENEFIT EXPENDITURE (£ MILLION AT 1995/6 PRICES,

	1973/4	1974/5	1975/6	1976/7	1977/8	1978/9	1979/80	1980/1	1981/2	1982/3
Contributory benefits (GB)										
Retirement pension[b]	17704	19118	20410	21436	22022	22582	22605	22824	23963	24994
Widows' benefits	1575	1670	1684	1642	1552	1510	1444	1383	1366	1337
Unemployment benefit[c]	1118	1153	1944	2116	2095	1890	1674	2776	3363	2767
Invalidity benefit[d]	1555	1713	1911	2139	2344	2512	2551	2494	2707	2939
Sickness benefit[d e]	2185	2047	1988	2053	2154	2081	1679	1418	1344	1022
Statutory sick pay[e f]	0	0	0	0	0	0	0	0	0	0
Death grant	84	75	64	57	50	48	41	35	34	31
Industrial disablement/ injuries benefits	579	611	640	651	653	661	638	622	632	64
Industrial death benefit	84	92	98	98	97	96	92	91	93	94
Maternity allowance	173	173	171	251	253	314	321	323	312	280
Statutory maternity pay	0	0	0	0	0	0	0	0	0	0
Other contributory benefits	7	7	7	6	6	6	5	4	4	4
Total contributory	25062	26659	28919	30448	31226	31699	31051	31970	33818	34110
Non-contributory, non-means-tested (GB)										
Retirement pension	179	164	145	136	120	111	92	82	77	74
War pension	1053	1099	1105	1071	1033	1017	962	919	947	930
Attendance allowance	232	334	412	432	476	502	515	564	652	743
Invalid care allowance	0	0	0	7	10	12	10	11	12	15
Invalid pension/SD allowance	0	0	51	129	147	206	218	234	257	284
Mobility allowance	0	0	0	31	66	141	203	271	342	435
Disability living/working allowances; ILF, motability	0	0	0	0	0	0	0	0	0	0
Industrial disablement/ injuries benefits	0	0	0	0	0	0	0	0	0	0
Industrial death benefit	0	0	0	0	0	0	0	0	0	0
Child benefit[g]	6464	6034	6422	6561	5811	5311	7146	6384	6664	6752
One-parent benefit	0	0	0	0	21	66	110	132	150	168
Maternity grant	97	81	64	57	50	48	41	35	32	30
Total non-contributory, non-means-tested	8025	7711	8199	8425	7733	7413	9297	8632	9132	9430
Means-tested (GB)										
Supplementary pension/ pensioner income support[h]	539	592	599	715	790	1827	1721	1778	2194	2383
Supplementary allowance/ non-pensioner income support[h i]	1870	2107	2664	3067	3179	2763	2495	2758	3970	5805
Family income supplement/ family credit	78	64	51	69	84	72	69	91	130	173
Social fund	0	0	0	0	0	0	0	0	0	0
Total means-tested	2486	2763	3315	3851	4053	4661	4285	4628	6294	8362
Christmas bonus	513	495	0	0	327	302	259	223	211	199
Total benefits	36086	37629	40433	42724	43339	44075	44893	45454	49456	52101
Administrative costs (GB)[j]	1667	1960	2400	2161	2088	2000	1964	2025	2263	2420
Total Social security spending (GB)	37754	39590	42833	44886	45427	46076	46857	47479	51719	54521
Social security spending (NI)[k]	975	1115	1197	1272	1292	2898	2497	2097	2031	2000

ADJUSTED BY GDP DEFLATOR)[a]

1983/4	1984/5	1985/6	1986/7	1987/8	1988/9	1989/90	1990/1	1991/2	1992/3	1993/4	1094/5	1995/6
25752	25629	26371	27450	27461	26452	26568	26977	28600	28711	29434	29482	29962
1359	1318	1272	1274	1229	1169	1094	1057	1132	1066	1086	1048	1016
2638	2649	2527	2678	2151	1522	941	1034	1796	1892	1725	1332	1102
3299	3596	3735	4129	4349	4618	4925	5266	6142	6676	7382	7902	7906
467	468	439	276	283	264	262	257	307	391	381	351	0
881	853	867	1169	1231	1235	1218	1118	784	734	687	82	36
30	29	29	28	4	0	0	0	0	0	0	0	0
659	648	655	686	670	626	608	0	0	0	0	0	0
95	92	92	94	82	81	76	0	0	0	0	0	0
248	270	261	259	75	37	39	40	35	34	34	28	29
0	0	0	0	283	344	367	373	386	428	439	492	524
43	2	3	1	1	1	2	1	2	1	1	2	
35432	35555	36249	38048	37818	36348	36099	36124	39183	39937	41171	40718	40577
72	65	65	70	54	49	45	43	40	39	38	36	36
923	913	924	910	878	839	823	977	1083	1245	1343	1176	1258
872	967	1091	1203	1314	1379	1488	1642	1910	1670	1875	2013	2194
18	18	21	161	270	238	236	247	319	371	462	539	617
321	396	423	440	432	434	444	510	667	688	734	796	820
536	598	671	794	873	928	987	1049	1189	73	0	0	0
0	0	0	2	1	3	14	29	53	2217	3023	3322	3929
0	0	0	0	0	0	0	623	662	650	648	665	670
0	0	0	0	0	0	0	71	72	68	70	59	58
7028	7178	7105	6971	6737	6207	5824	5456	5810	6104	6319	6272	6332
189	201	213	229	239	246	255	272	279	296	295	296	310
30	30	27	22	0	0	0	0	0	0	0	0	0
9989	10367	10539	10800	10799	10324	10116	10920	12084	13420	14805	15175	16224
2220	2583	2673	2312	2429	2549	2631	2735	3050	4008	4114	4071	3888
7364	7902	8681	9439	8721	7463	6753	7157	8873	10646	11418	11634	11752
217	212	207	249	264	542	546	587	701	999	1262	1478	1739
0	0	0	0	42	205	167	184	235	227	245	224	251
9801	10697	11561	12000	11457	10758	10096	10663	12859	15879	17039	17407	17630
192	186	178	178	170	162	155	144	140	138	142	139	139
55414	56806	58527	61026	60244	57593	56467	57851	64265	69374	73157	73439	74570
2541	2661	2589	2750	2924	2946	3095	3207	3419	3660	3987	3822	3587
57955	59466	61116	63776	63168	60539	59562	61058	67684	73034	77144	77261	78157
2167	1870	1929	2039	2044	1995	1813	2013	2161	2353	2522	2635	2684

Martin Evans

Table 7A.1. *Continued*

	1973/4	1974/5	1975/6	1976/7	1977/8	1978/9	1979/80	1980/1	1981/2	1982/3
Total Social security spending (UK)	38729	40705	44030	46157	46719	48974	49354	49576	53750	56522
Expenditure as a % of all public spending	18.8	17.7	19.1	20.4	21.9	21.8	21.4	21.0	22.6	23.1
Expenditure as a % of GDP	8.2	8.6	9.4	9.6	9.4	9.6	9.4	9.8	10.6	10.9
Housing-related benefit payments[f]	3858	2966	2829	2947	2960	2825	2590	2815	4087	4920

[a] Excluding spending on housing-related benefits (Housing Benefit/rent rebate and Income Support/Mortgage Interest). Spending on Council Tax Benefit/rate rebate is also excluded.
[b] Includes spending on earnings-related component (SERPS and graduated pension).
[c] Became contributory Jobseekers' Allowance in October 1996.
[d] From April 1995 Sickness Benefit and Invalidity Benefit were merged to become Incapacity Benefit.
[e] The introduction from 1983/4 of Statutory Sick Pay meant that the majority of Sickness Benefit claims were met through employers after this date.
[f] Before April 1994 employers received a payment from the DSS of 80% of their Statutory Sick Pay obligations. This reimbursement scheme was abolished in April 1994, so that the cost fell wholly on employers, except for a small element of residual payments when employers experienced exceptionally high sickness bills.
[g] Includes the estimated cost of Child Tax Allowances (see HM Treasury 1980) before 1978.

1983/4	1984/5	1985/6	1986/7	1987/8	1988/9	1989/90	1990/1	1991/2	1992/3	1993/4	1094/5	1995/6
60123	61337	63045	65815	65211	62534	61375	63070	69845	75387	79666	79896	80841
24.3	24.2	25.0	25.9	25.6	25.3	23.8	24.3	26.4	27.0	27.6	27.1	27.0
11.2	11.2	11.1	11.0	10.4	9.6	9.2	9.5	10.7	11.6	11.9	11.5	11.4
4829	5266	5682	5974	5841	5739	6148	6962	8513	9919	11114	11707	12177

^{h} The pre-1983/4 figures have been adjusted to exclude the housing-related element of Supplementary Benefit, using estimates based on data from Social Security Statistics.

^{i} Excludes the cost of all Income Support and Supplementary Benefit assistance to cover mortgage interest payments.

^{j} Taken from DSS (1997: table 3.10, and earlier equivalents). Expenditure by local authorities in administering Housing Benefit, and expenditure by other departments in administering superannuation payments, is excluded.

^{k} Excluding Housing Benefit/rent allowance.

^{l} Memorandum item—see Chapter 5 of this volume for details. The present chapter excludes expenditure on Housing Benefit and rent rebate/allowance, both in Great Britain and Northern Ireland, and spending on Income Support/Mortgage Interest. Note also that some of the cost of Housing Benefit is met through local authority housing accounts rather than by central government, and hence is excluded from the DSS annual report (DSS 1997a).

Sources: DSS (1997a: table 1, and equivalents for earlier years); HM Treasury (1997: table 3.1); NIO (1997: table 12.8, and equivalents for earlier years).

8 Welfare with the Lid On

Howard Glennerster

I. Public Expenditure on Welfare

The lid on

THE economic crises of the mid-1970s changed the course of welfare history not only in the United Kingdom but throughout the industrialized world. Yet perhaps the discontinuity has been greatest in the United Kingdom. A welfare 'leader' for most of the century up to the end of the 1940s, the United Kingdom remained welfare-expansionist if not a leader until the mid-1970s. The share of the nation's income taken by the state and spent on welfare state purposes grew steadily for most of the century until 1976. It rose from about 2 per cent of GDP at the turn of the century to over a quarter by the mid-seventies. From then on and until the end of the century, if the new Labour Government is to be believed, the share of the nation's spending that has been taxed and spent for social welfare purposes will have ceased to rise. In Table 8.1 we show the annual rates of increase in spending at 1995/6 prices (GDP deflator-based) as well as the percentage of all public expenditure taken by the welfare state and its percentage of GDP since 1973/4. We can see that the share of the GDP taken by social spending in 1995/6 was similar to that in 1975/6. The rise in the share that took place in the 1990s was partly recession-induced and is planned to fall back by the end of the century in the plans of the new Labour Government announced in July 1997. Welfare spending was, however, taking a larger share of government spending—up from 50 to 60 per cent. In Fig. 8.1 we decompose welfare state spending into its service elements from 1973/4 in real terms.

With the exception of the pre-1992 election cycle, public spending on welfare has been remarkably constrained during the period covered in this book compared with most of the past century. It could be described as 'welfare with the lid on'. Why?

There are a number of possible reasons. These include the following:

- In the period since 1945 government had taken nearly two-thirds of all the additional incomes generated by individuals and enterprises and used them for social purposes

Table 8.1. PUBLIC EXPENDITURE ON THE WELFARE STATE, OVERALL TRENDS, UNITED KINGDOM[a]

	Year-on-year increase in welfare spending (%)	Spending on welfare as a % of general government expenditure	Spending on welfare as a % of GDP
1973/4		50.3	21.9
1974/5	12.9	50.9	24.9
1975/6	2.6	52.1	25.7
1976/7	3.6	55.3	25.9
1977/8	−4.7	55.8	24.0
1978/9	1.5	53.8	23.7
1979/80	1.2	52.9	23.3
1980/1	1.5	52.6	24.4
1981/2	1.0	52.6	24.8
1982/3	2.2	52.3	24.7
1983/4	4.2	53.8	24.8
1984/5	1.0	53.1	24.5
1985/6	1.3	54.0	23.9
1986/7	4.5	56.0	23.8
1987/8	1.3	56.6	23.0
1988/9	−1.2	57.6	21.8
1989/90	0.8	55.6	21.6
1990/1	3.3	57.2	22.4
1991/2	8.4	60.9	24.7
1992/3	6.6	61.3	26.3
1993/4	3.7	61.6	26.6
1994/5	2.0	61.6	26.1
1995/6	0.7	60.2	25.8

[a] Calculated from real spending at 1995/6 prices.

Sources: Data in previous chapters.

of one kind or another, not all of it for social policy objectives as defined in this book but requiring higher levels of taxation nevertheless (Glennerster 1995). In addition to sustaining a welfare state the UK continued to try to maintain world-power status through this period and to spend more on defence than any of its neighbours or comparable competitors. These demands eventually became unsustainable.

- The crisis of 1976 forced a change because for several years running the real post-tax purchasing power of the average family in the UK fell. Faced with rising private consumer market possibilities, voters found this intolerable. Public attitudes to welfare taxing and spending changed for the worse (Whiteley 1981). They were to change back in the aftermath of the resulting cuts.
- International trade competition, to which the UK was more exposed than most

Howard Glennerster

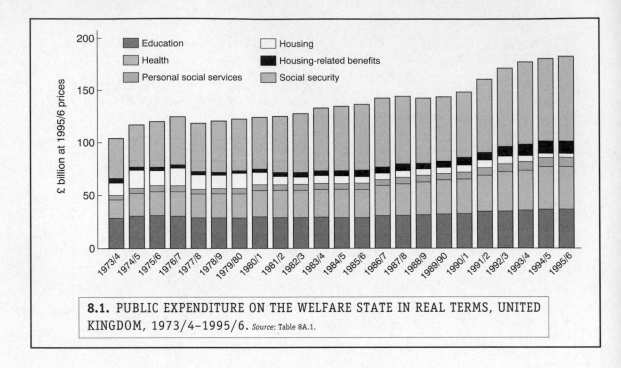

8.1. PUBLIC EXPENDITURE ON THE WELFARE STATE IN REAL TERMS, UNITED KINGDOM, 1973/4–1995/6. *Source:* Table 8A.1.

countries, made it politically difficult merely to transfer the costs of welfare from general taxation onto employers. Higher indirect taxation was imposed but that, too, proved unpopular.

- International movements of capital, both financial and human, to areas with low taxes exerted a downward pressure on taxation the world over. In most advanced countries the 1980s and 1990s were a period of stabilizing overall tax rates (ONS 1996*e*).

Thus, both internal political and external economic pressures forced down the spending lid. This happened in most economies. Social spending levelled off at the kinds of levels it had reached when the economic climate changed. Britain was able to do this more quickly than other countries because of its unitary style of government and Treasury control. The corporatist welfare regimes of the continent of Europe found the task more difficult but, in the late nineties, they were set to do the same under the cloak of the European convergence criteria required by the Maastricht Treaty.

Social pressures remained

Yet the social demands that had led the state steadily to increase its spending on health and income support, education, and the care of the elderly had not gone away and the social casualties of global competition increased those pressures. As incomes rose, people wanted to see the standards of their education and health care grow. Also, relative costs continued to increase. The capacity to treat patients expanded faster than the very moderate pace of economic growth. So, too, did the demand for higher education. The poverty of part of the population grew dramatically for reasons that have to do with technological change and international competition as well as the collapse of Keynesian full-employment goals. Pressures for pay increases in the public sector added to the difficulties. The cost of paying those in the public sector cannot be permanently held down by reducing their rewards compared to the rest of the workforce—not, at least, without undermining the standards of service they provide. It is not merely that the lid has been put on but that the steam pressure in the pot has been rising too.

Other states of welfare

It would not be surprising in the circumstances if Titmuss's (1958) other redistributive systems—fiscal welfare, occupational welfare, private household-financed welfare—had merely grown to take the place of the unmet expectations. As we have seen from previous chapters this has happened to some extent. The fall in the share of the GDP spent by the state on education has been replaced by private spending. While the percentage of those going to private schools has not risen dramatically it has been rising after a full three-quarters of a century in which it had been falling. Though the proportion of the population in occupational pension schemes has remained very stable the number in personal private pension schemes has grown substantially. Spending on private domestic help in the home by old people has risen to replace the withdrawal of state services. Above all, the scale of state-provided housing has declined sharply. Yet we must not exaggerate this trend. The numbers taking out private health insurance grew in the 1980s but then fell back in the 1990s to only 11 per cent of households. Moreover, many of those policies covered only part of the scale of risk, often limited to non-emergency and short-term care. Very few took advantage of the tax breaks for elderly people to take out private health insurance. The inherent limitations of free markets in health care insurance and that of other forms of risk like unemployment and long-term care have left the state as still the overwhelmingly important provider of health, education, and social care (Burchardt and Hills 1997). The National Health Service has been taking more of the nation's income, as have the personal social services despite the period of restraint. The scale of state subsidy to private housing has grown. Overall, as John Hills (1995*b*) has shown elsewhere, if we do take the total spent by firms and households on the services we have been concerned with in this volume and we include tax reliefs as part of the state's involvement we do not find that the share of total 'welfare activity' funded out of taxation has fallen over the past two decades. It has remained the same (Table 8.2).

The reason for this is that, though individuals ('Other private spending' in Table 8.2) have been spending more, firms have been spending relatively less. The competitive pressures that have led the state to ease back on growing tax burdens have also had their impact on firms. Increasingly, therefore, the state has turned to another form of intervention—legal or state-

Table 8.2. SOURCES OF FUNDS FOR WELFARE (% OF TOTAL FROM EACH SOURCE)

Source of funds	1978/9	1993/4
Earmarked taxes: National Insurance	20	18
General taxes	31	35
Local authority taxes	10	8
Total taxes	61	61
Tax reliefs[a]	5	6
Fees and charges for public services	5	3
Enterprise Welfare	12	8
Other private spending	17	22
Total funds for welfare (£ billion at 1995/6 prices)	174.3	273.5

[a] This line is not comparable with Table 7.14, in that it includes tax relief on pension lump-sum payments but excludes tax relief on pension contributions (reflecting the fact that pension payments are taxable).

required welfare. Le Grand (1997) has suggested that since the state cannot tax people to finance the services we have discussed it is increasingly turning to the law to achieve the same objectives. Rent control is an old example and not a very happy precedent. Requiring private individuals to set aside income for retirement or sickness or care in old age are more recent examples. This approach would have been taken further under the Major Government's proposals in 1997 (see Chapter 7). Firms are now required to pay sickness benefit of a defined kind. Absent fathers are required to pay maintenance, not just by the courts but backed by a statutory agency. The Labour Government elected in May 1997 proposes to legislate a minimum wage. This train of policy could be taken much further.

Restructuring the budget

A long-term goal of Conservative social policy had been to target it more effectively on the poor (Glennerster 1995). The tighter constraints of the period pushed this policy to the fore. It is most obvious in the social security budget, where there was a decisive shift towards means-tested benefits. This was not so much an explicit policy, as we saw in Chapter 7, but it was a consequence of the failure to uprate benefits in line with earnings. This was perhaps the most important spending policy change of the period in this area and, with the rise in social housing rents, pushed many more people into the means-tested welfare state. General housing subsidies to all public housing tenants disappeared and were replaced by means-tested housing benefit. These attempts to target and means-test had other, less desirable side-effects we have discussed—the poverty trap, the disincentive to return to work or take up work—but they were a response to the need to get more from the pot.

In other ways Governments tried to give priority to services that had growing demographic pressures—possibly the most obvious need factor. The health service, faced with a growing elderly population and one that was getting more disabled, gained more resources. Education, faced with a declining or static school population for much of the period, did not do well.

For much of our period the share of the GDP going to the welfare state remained static, increasing in the 1990s again under Major (Fig. 8.1). Though the overall share of the GDP taken by social welfare has not changed that much in two decades the composition of that budget has (Figs. 8.1 and 8.3). Social security came to take a larger share. By 1995/6 it was taking more than health and education together whereas these two services in combination had considerably outweighed the social security budget in 1973/4. The personal social services share and total rose, too, but from a low base.

A less justified but politically understandable strategy was to cut capital spending that would affect tomorrow and be less harsh on today's current spending. Capital spending in the social sector took a hard knock in the late 1970s and has not recovered (Fig. 8.2).

Another way to think about the changes is presented in Fig. 8.3. Despite the relative stability in the share of the GDP for much of the period, the actual sums spent on the welfare state have grown as the economy has grown in real terms.

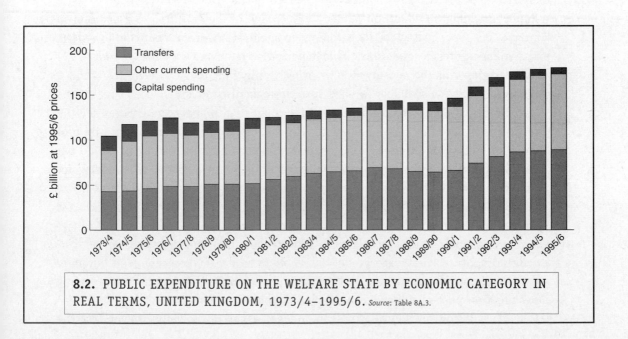

8.2. PUBLIC EXPENDITURE ON THE WELFARE STATE BY ECONOMIC CATEGORY IN REAL TERMS, UNITED KINGDOM, 1973/4–1995/6. *Source*: Table 8A.3.

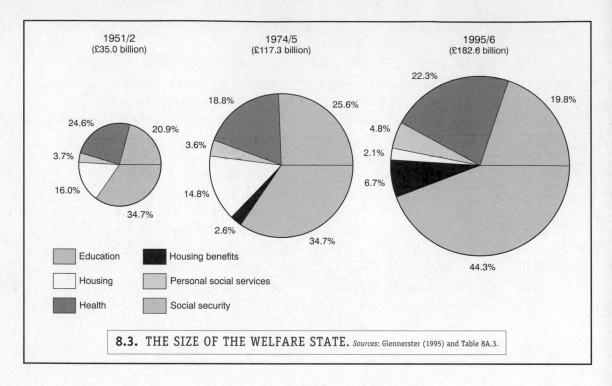

8.3. THE SIZE OF THE WELFARE STATE. *Sources*: Glennerster (1995) and Table 8A.3.

Service-by-service spending patterns

Education entered a stagnant period after the economic crisis.

- Public spending on education fell as a percentage of the GDP from 6.7 per cent in 1975/6 to 4.7 per cent in 1987/8 before rising again, a little, to 5.2 per cent in 1995/6.
- The volume of real resources available to education remained little changed for nearly two decades from the mid-1970s, only rising a little after 1992.
- While the budgets available to each sector remained relatively stable in real terms the number of pupils changed. Thus, as the number of primary-age children fell the resources devoted to each pupil could rise and more nursery places could be provided. Spending on this age group relative to its size actually rose by nearly 60 per cent in the period as a whole. This reflected an increase in per-pupil spending for those in primary school and a larger percentage of pre-school children going to school. Spending per secondary-age child rose by a quarter over the period as a whole in volume terms.
- Higher education's budget was kept relatively stable from the mid-1970s to the mid-1980s despite the rising age group. From 1988/9 real resources expanded in aggregate. But so too, by even more, did the numbers entering higher education. Spending per pupil on post-school education halved in volume terms.
- Private spending on education began to rise, especially towards the end of the

period. It amounted to 0.3 per cent of GDP in 1974. It had risen to 0.9 per cent in 1995.

The National Health Service, in contrast, had demography and political priority on its side. At the very least politicians felt it necessary to be able to assure voters that the service was safe in their hands. Both the volume of resources and the share of the nation's income going to the National Health Service rose in the period of our study and especially so in the periods affected by electioneering. The one exception was the 1997 election.

- At the beginning of our period public spending on the NHS was equivalent to 3.8 per cent of the GDP. At the end it was equivalent to 5.7 per cent.
- In volume terms the real increases amounted to 3.9 per cent per annum in the Labour period of office and 1.8 per cent per annum in the whole period of Conservative rule.
- Needs also grew, especially those of an ageing population. Official figures suggest this amounted to a necessary increase of 0.7 per cent a year. The costs of medical advance may amount to another 0.5 per cent a year. Even so, this combined figure of 1.2 per cent required growth for demographic purposes is still less than the actual volume increase achieved.
- Rising expectations are quite another thing. Some research suggests that demand for health care rises nearly in line with consumers' income and that is rising faster still.
- One measure of frustrated demand is the extent to which individuals who can afford to do so have entered the private market. The Conservative Government extended tax relief to employer-financed health insurance after 1981 and to individuals over 60 after 1989. In 1970 3.6 per cent of the population were covered by personal health insurance schemes. By 1995 this had risen to 10.6 per cent though this had not grown since 1990. The scope of private cover was limited, however, so that benefits actually paid out amounted to the equivalent of only 3 per cent of NHS spending.

The personal social services also did comparatively well during this time, partly through accident and partly through design. In 1976, when Barbara Castle was Secretary of State for Health and Social Services in the Labour Government, she set out to shift health and social service spending towards those groups in the population who had been neglected in the past and who were growing in demographic importance—the elderly, the mentally ill, and the disabled. The personal social services catered for these groups above all others and their budget was partially protected in an otherwise harsh climate. Then, when the Conservatives took power, they relaxed the rules under which the social security budget could be used to support the care of the elderly. Those coming within the Income Support limits could claim to have their fees in private old persons' homes met by the Supplementary Benefit scheme as it then was. This produced a massive increase in the use of such homes funded from public money. When a solution was finally worked out and the practice stopped, the money that had been spent as part of the social security budget was transferred to local authorities. The result was to increase social service departments' budgets far more than would have happened in the normal round of incremental public expenditure bargaining.

- In 1973/4 the state-financed personal social services took 0.7 per cent of the GDP. By 1995/6 the figure was 1.2 per cent. Real spending on these services had risen two and a half times in real terms.
- Fees were accounting for about 14 per cent of the service's income by 1994/5.
- The number of elderly people In residential care had risen from about 130,000 in 1974 to 230,000 in 1995 but the number of local authority provided places had declined sharply from nearly 100,000 to little more than 50,000. From being the dominant providers, local authorities had become the minority providers.
- As a result of the policy shift referred to above (embodied in the 1991 NHS and Community Care Act and implemented in 1993) social security support was withdrawn from new residents in private homes and local authorities could use their new funds to support people in such homes or in the community. In 1992 only 29 per cent of those in private homes were paying for themselves. Two-thirds were financed by social security. By 1995 this had fallen substantially but local authorities had taken over much of that support. The balance of local authority activity shifted to fieldwork, notably with children, and community care.
- The largest proportionate increase in spending was devoted to the mentally ill.

Housing suffered by far the largest cuts of the period, especially in terms of capital expenditure. Indeed in many ways it ceased to have the political salience it once did. Housing policy became an adjunct of social security and urban regeneration.

- Public spending on housing reached 4.2 per cent of GDP in 1974. By 1995 it had fallen to 2.1 per cent, including housing benefits in each total.
- Total public spending on housing of all kinds, capital and current subsidies, fell from the peak of £20 billion (1995/6 prices) in the mid-1970s to just over £15 billion in 1996.
- The composition of this total changed dramatically. General subsidies disappeared. Capital spending on new houses, from being the major component, became a small fraction—less than a fifth. Housing Benefit, the means-tested housing allowance to tenants in all tenures, became the dominant form of spending. Renovation of old stock took precedence over new building.
- The higher rents councils were required to charge and the reduction in the debt-servicing costs as new building dropped enabled councils to spend more on repairs and maintenance. This rose by 4 per cent per annum through the period.
- Tax expenditure on housing (mortgage tax relief) rose to reach a peak of nearly £10 billion in 1990 but was steadily reduced to about £2.5 billion in 1996.
- Housing in all tenures became more expensive.

The social security budget increased most in absolute terms. This was not the result of deliberate and open-handed generosity, indeed the very reverse. It rose because of the rising numbers who had no jobs or were on such low pay that they became entitled to Income Support or suffered from family breakdown. Economic, demographic, and social changes provided the driving force. Social security was the residual legatee. Here again the composition of the budget changed significantly. This did reflect policy.

- In 1973/4 social security spending amounted to 8.2 per cent of the GDP. By 1995/6 this had reached 11.4 per cent, excluding Housing Benefit and its predecessors in both cases.
- Total social security spending more than doubled in real terms from 1973/4 to 1995/6.
- Spending on means-tested benefits grew more than sixfold.
- Spending on the unemployed rose nearly fourfold while that on the elderly less than doubled.
- Spending on the sick and disabled grew more than two and a half times.
- Average payments to pensioners rose by about a fifth in real terms from 1973 to 1996.
- The largest increase was the payment to members of SERPS, the state earnings-related pension introduced by the Labour Government in 1978.
- The numbers in occupational pension schemes remained about the same—more women but less men. About half the employed population were members of such schemes in 1971 and in 1991. However, the numbers retiring with an occupational pension did continue to rise as the post-war cohorts that had entered such schemes reached retiring age.
- Numbers with personal private pensions rose dramatically with the help of tax incentives introduced in the 1980s. In 1974 600,000 policies were in force. By 1995 the figure was 20 million.
- Tax expenditure on tax relief to occupational and private pension schemes and their members amounted to £13 billion 1994/5 or nearly as much as was spent on helping all families with children.
- Various attempts were made to reduce the extent of the poverty trap facing families who were on means-tested benefits, notably following the Fowler Reviews. Though the number of families facing an effective tax rate of over 100 per cent was reduced the number facing a tax rate of over 50 per cent increased from 8.7 per cent of those employed to 11.6 per cent.

Overall generalizations are not easy to make about this pattern of spending. Inertia certainly played its part (Rose and Davies 1994). Governments inherit a vast range of obligations from past legislation and budgets are more difficult to cut and redesign than roll forward. The structure of the welfare budget has changed, however, as we have seen. This has partly been a response to social security safety net obligations to the poorest groups that were difficult to repeal or not to honour. Not to have done so would have undermined the broader economic strategy of the Thatcher Government to force down inflation by increasing unemployment and restructuring the economy. Yet, within the social security budget old obligations were abandoned or eroded—the ending of wage-related sickness and unemployment benefit, the abolition of Unemployment Benefit, and the eroding of retirement pensions' value relative to earnings.

In the previous volume we discussed the political economy thesis that when cuts came they would be least directed at the services the middle-class median voter benefited from or was employed in or both (Le Grand and Winter 1987). The middle class can be seen as more effective in bringing its interests to bear in the battle for funds, both as users and as professional providers. Thus those services with a powerful middle-class user involvement and a powerful professional interest, like the Health Service, will do well. This, too, seems to have some support from the present findings. Public housing, the most pro-poor service, has lost quite heavily. The real value of benefits to the poorest on social security has remained stable through the period since 1975 while earnings have risen. The NHS, from whom most of the population benefit, has done well in relative terms and so has higher education in the last part of the period, measured in access rather than spending per student. Yet, other measures were taken to reduce middle-class benefits, notably mortgage tax relief and student maintenance. Overall, 'in kind' spending during the period was rather more concentrated on the poor than before (Sefton 1997). We discuss this more below. Pure middle-class voter power theories emerge with only some support.

At the same time rational public interest theories of budget allocation also gain some support. Those budgets where there was demographic growth—health and personal social services—did relatively well, while education lost out. There was a needs case to be made for such an outcome. As in the last volume, all the main theories can draw some comfort from this analysis but no one theory dominates.

II. Outcomes

Despite the fact that state welfare has been working within a tightly constrained budget for two decades it has continued to deliver many of its traditional objectives. That is a tribute to the economic efficiency of much of the basic institutional structure as well as to some of the reforms that were undertaken in the period. That is not to say that what has been delivered has matched people's rising expectations—a point to which we will return. However, it is important to recognize what has been achieved.

Education

If the goals of successive governments in the 1950s and 1960s had been increasing access and staying-on rates and reduced class size, those of the 1970s, 1980s, and 1990s shifted towards improving basic standards of achievement and tilting education towards economic objectives, including training and extended opportunities beyond school. Results were mixed.

- Information on basic standards of literacy and numeracy over time are sketchy but international studies of maths attainment suggest that Britain compares relatively poorly with other leading industrialized countries, occupying a middle position in an international league table of standardized mathematical knowledge. British children's levels of attainment and their relative international standard had not changed much in the thirty-year period from 1964.
- On the other hand their achievements in science at the age of 13 outclassed those in almost all European and English-speaking countries. Britain's relative position also improved slightly over the period. This may have to do with the age at which we teach science in our curriculum but it suggests that generalizations from levels of maths scores to the whole schooling system may be over-pessimistic.
- Spending per pupil does not seem to be a significant variable in school performance.
- The spread of achievements between children remains wider than in most comparable countries and is highly correlated with poverty, which has been growing massively.
- Despite this, the percentage of 18-year-olds gaining one or more passes at A level has doubled since the early 1970s and most rapidly since the mid-1980s. The proportion of school-leavers staying on to get some kind of school-leaving qualification has increased dramatically. In 1970, before the school-leaving age was increased to 16, before most schools were comprehensive, and before the introduction of the common school-leaving exam, 44 per cent of all children left school with no graded results in a leaving exam. By 1993 that figure had fallen to 4 per cent.
- Britain produces far fewer young people with vocational training than most other countries at an equivalent level of economic sophistication. One of the reasons lies in the poor private rates of return such qualifications earn.
- Even so, the human capital content of the labour force has increased substantially since 1974. Of those born before 1935 only 15 per cent had qualifications of A level or above. For those born in the ten years after the 1944 Education Act (1945–54) the figure rises to 33 per cent. For those born between 1955 and 1964, mostly educated in our period of study, the figure rises to 40 per cent.
- Entry to higher education remains class-biased but there has been a steady equalization in levels of access by social class at every level of occupational status when account is taken of the changing occupational structure of the population.
- There has been a substantial improvement in the examination achievements of girls and in their access to higher education. Girls now perform better than boys at both A level and GCSE.
- Ethnic minorities have been catching up with and in some cases outperforming other

groups. In secondary school Asian students have outperformed others while Afro-Caribbean students have performed as well as their white peers. In terms of relative progress in secondary school all ethnic minorities outperformed white children.

All this has been achieved within the severely constrained education budget we outlined above.

Health

Measures of the health of the nation—morbidity and mortality and long-term incapacity—respond to far more complex social changes than mere alterations in health service coverage and organization. Nevertheless they are of relevance.

- Life expectancy rose throughout the period.
- Some forms of inequality apparently continued to widen. The age-standardized mortality rates of professional-class males in 1970–2 were half those of unskilled workers. They were a third of these rates in 1991–3.
- There are difficulties with this measure of inequality, particularly over time. It only applies to men of working age and the share of each class group in the total population has changed substantially. An overall measure of population inequality—the Gini coefficient for the distribution of age at death—shows that there has been a fall in inequality over the whole population in age at death.
- On the other hand more people report suffering from chronic illness. This is linked to the ageing of the population and to higher levels of unemployment. Manual workers are more likely to report long-standing or restricting illness and professional workers are increasing their advantage.
- *Health of the Nation* priority concerns have showed only patchy results to date.
- The number of people treated by the NHS has continued to rise. The activity index rose by 1.7 per cent from 1974/5 to 1978/9. It rose by 2.15 per cent a year from 1979/80 to 1990/1 and by 4.14 per cent from 1991/2, when the reforms took effect, to 1995/6.
- For the first period, however, resources grew faster than activity, suggesting a fall in efficiency. From 1979/80 to 1991/2 annual activity grew more than expenditure (1.4 per cent compared to 0.72 per cent in spending). In the period since the reforms activity has grown at nearly twice the rate of expenditure (4.1 per cent per annum compared to 2.1 per cent for expenditure), a marked improvement in efficiency.
- Visits to the doctor are related to social class. Those in the manual group, and especially the unskilled and semi-skilled group, visit the GP much more frequently. This difference in patterns of use has grown since 1974. More unskilled workers and fewer professional workers are going to see their GP now than were in 1974.
- Standardizing for medical need, there is something close to equality of access to pri-

mary care for those in equal need and this has not changed greatly over the eleven years for which we have figures.

- Quality of services and convenience may have improved, with primary care and GP fundholders provoking some of these improvements since 1991.
- Satisfaction with the NHS declined through the 1980s, increased immediately after the reforms of the early 1990s, but has since declined again to its 1980s levels.

Personal social services

The relative achievements of the personal social services are more complex. In the face of a sharply rising demographic demand these social and community health services only partly kept pace. Individuals at home had to rely more on private domestic help. Use of the personal and community health services varied by the type of service, as did reliance on private alternatives.

- The use of home helps employed by the local authority by those aged 65 and over fell slightly from 9 to 8 per cent from 1980 to 1994/5. The use of private home helps has risen from 4 to 7 per cent of the group since 1990 alone. A fifth of those living alone employed private domestic help in 1994/5.
- Use of the district nurse by those unable to get out also fell, especially for those living with others.
- The use of day centres fell. Only 3 per cent of old people used them in 1994/5 compared to 5 per cent in 1980.
- More people received meals on wheels.
- The spouse or partner has continued to provide the main source of help with self-care, bathing, domestic tasks, walking, and going on public transport.
- The range and choice of services offered may have improved. Certainly more services are provided privately by profit and non-profit organizations. There are no systematic measures of quality or satisfaction over time.

Housing

As in the case of health and education the standards of housing enjoyed by the population rose in the period.

- The goal of extending owner-occupation to most of the population succeeded. Its share of the total stock rose from 52 per cent in 1973 to 67 per cent in 1995.
- The proportion of households living without basic amenities or central heating fell substantially. The number of households lacking one or more amenities fell from 17.4 to 1 per cent between 1971 and 1991.

- Fewer people were living in overcrowded conditions in 1994 (13 per cent) compared to 1974 (22 per cent). But overcrowding worsened after 1990.
- Improved housing conditions affected all socio-economic groups, except that, in some respects, the lowest fifth fell behind after 1979.
- Overall satisfaction levels rose between the 1970s and 1994. Council tenants continue to be dissatisfied with repair services. Unhappiness with the neighbourhood has increased.
- For the disadvantaged few, housing access grew worse. There was an increase in numbers in temporary accommodation and in those sleeping rough through the 1980s. Matters improved somewhat in the first half of the 1990s.
- Housing became more expensive in relation to incomes and the costs of Housing Benefit rose steeply. Owner-occupiers' costs fluctuated. Net interest payments were high in the late 1980s but had fallen by 1995. The economic cost of being an owner-occupier had, nevertheless, risen over the period.
- The over-rapid rise in prices and extension of owner-occupation in the late 1980s led to a crisis in the early 1990s, with high mortgage arrears, repossessions, and negative equity.
- Tenures became more sharply polarized by income. By 1994 76 per cent of those in council houses were in the poorest two-fifths of the income distribution compared to 51 per cent in 1979.

The overall distributive effects of in-kind welfare services

As earlier chapters have emphasized, redistribution from rich to poor is only one part of the welfare state's objective but it is its most important moral purpose. Social security *is* heavily redistributive towards the poor, as we saw in Chapter 7. However, it is frequently claimed that some services in kind—health, education, personal social services, and housing—are pro-rich or at least pro-middle class. Le Grand (1982) was the leading exponent of this view, challenged by Powell (1995). Yet, if we take all these services together, what is the picture and what has been the overall effect of the policy changes we have discussed in this book? How has the distribution of the 'social wage' altered?

Three competing propositions have been advanced.

1. Since 1979, under the Conservatives, welfare spending has been successfully targeted on the poor whereas before it was wasted on the affluent.
2. Alternatively, it is claimed that there has been an increasing 'middle-class capture' of the welfare state.
3. Growing prosperity, producing higher tax revenues, has trickled down to the poor and offset the growing inequalities in the labour market (Cooper and Nye 1995).

Official statistics on income distribution, such as those on households with below-average incomes (HBAI), exclude services in kind, and those which include them, like the series which appears in *Economic Trends*, are only available on a consistent basis since the late 1980s. However, Sefton (1997) has produced estimates on a consistent basis from 1979 to 1993 (see Fig. 8.4). This shows, on a basis consistent with the HBAI series, estimates of the value of health and education, housing subsidies, and personal social services going to

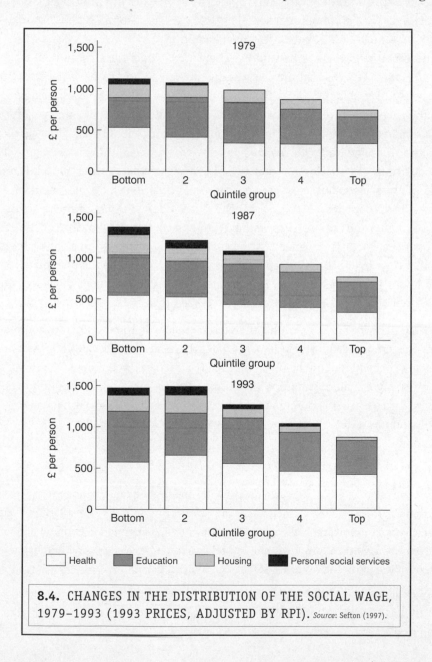

8.4. CHANGES IN THE DISTRIBUTION OF THE SOCIAL WAGE, 1979–1993 (1993 PRICES, ADJUSTED BY RPI). *Source*: Sefton (1997).

successive fifths of the income distribution. The figures are in real terms adjusted for general inflation.

Sefton's results suggest that *none* of the three propositions above is correct.

- Welfare services in kind are pro-poor overall (housing and personal social services especially so). Those in the lower income groups receive more in absolute terms than those in higher income groups and did so in 1979. This pro-poor bias did increase slightly over the period but real spending also increased for all groups. Though there is evidence of greater targeting it is not dramatic.
- On the other hand there is not much evidence of middle-class capture either. Health and education services that are received by all income groups have been maintained or increased in value, but overall receipts remain greater for the lower income groups with the exception of higher education. Given that much of the cost of paying for these services comes from the higher income groups the redistributive effect is significant.
- Despite this, compared with the changes in cash incomes, the social wage only had a modest effect in slowing the growth of income inequality in the period. It reduced the growth in inequality measured by the Gini coefficient by a maximum of a fifth. This estimate depends on using a general price index to deflate service spending. If we use a volume-price basis, as we have done in this book, allowing for the costs of each service, there is no effect on the real incomes of the poorest fifth. Their cash incomes rose by 6 per cent. Depending on what we think has happened to productivity levels in services the rise in their 'income', including services, lies between 6 and 13 per cent at a time when average incomes rose by 40 per cent.

What has happened in our period is therefore both less dramatic and more complex than some of the simple accounts. Those who think there has been a vanishing welfare state increasingly concentrated on the poor will already have been disappointed. Yet, with the lid firmly on spending, the distribution of welfare services in kind could only do a limited amount to turn back the economic and social tides which increased social inequality between the 1970s and the 1990s.

Social security

Cash benefits also acted as a brake on growing inequalities in earnings, private savings income, and pensions. They formed a growing proportion of the poorest families' income. Social security has been largely the residual legatee of widening inequality in the labour market, not least through non-employment, but reliance on it has also contributed by increasing the extent of the disincentives to work.

- Numbers living in households with below 50 per cent of the average income rose from 4.7 million in 1974 to 11.2 million in 1993. Unemployment and economic inactivity accounted for 60 per cent of that growth.

- Real income levels of the poor have risen less fast than those of the rich and have actually fallen in absolute terms for the poorest decile since 1979 on some definitions of income.
- The number of people in families who rely on means-tested income support of one kind or another has risen from 4.4 million to almost 12 million or from 8 to 21 per cent of the population. This has had a pronounced effect on work incentives. Attempts to mitigate these effects through the Fowler reforms of the mid-1980s had little effect.

In short, despite the combined effects of a somewhat more pro-poor redistribution from the in-kind welfare services such as health, education, and housing and the increased targeting of cash social security benefits, the gap between rich and poor grew. The driving force was not social welfare policy but a combination of the widening of rewards in the labour market and labour market inactivity combined with the decline in benefit levels relative to earnings and tax policy, roughly in that order of importance.

Moreover, despite the steady but gradual improvement in rates of treatment in the NHS, much greater participation in post-school education, and improved housing standards, dissatisfaction with the welfare system grew. Performance and quality standards were rising even faster in the rest of the economy. Not only did expenditure on cars more than double in real terms, spending on recreation and cultural services nearly quadrupled, insurance and other financial service spending quadrupled, and foreign holiday spending more than quadrupled, but the quality of those products rose too. TV programmes could be videoed, computers came to the ordinary person, and the Internet was added to its capacity. No wonder 1 per cent per annum increases in the performance of the NHS in the 1980s caused frustration.

III. The future: ways forward

What, then, are the challenges that face the Labour Government elected in 1977 at the end of our period of study? The demands on the human services we have discussed are rising. The ability of the nuclear family to provide care is declining. Both parents are at work and their capacity to invest time in their children is reduced. Children's capacity to care for their dependent elderly parents is lower as their parents' average levels of dependency rise. Families are less secure. The labour market and the rigours of international competition are creating a wider income distribution with more people caught in low-income traps. More redistribution through taxes and benefits has been necessary merely to temper the rise in inequality caused by the labour market. At the same time the quality expected of the mainline services like education and health has risen as the quality of services provided in the private market has risen. Where is the welfare state to go, caught between rising expectations, rising demands, rising costs, and an unchanging share of the nation's resources?

1. Take off the lid

It would be possible to relax the constraints under which the welfare state has operated in the past twenty years. Demography is not such a problem for the UK as it is for many of our competitors. The UK underwent its major demographic transformation between 1940 and 1980. We have also been very sparing in our spending on health and our promises to future pensioners. Current service and benefit standards could be sustained for the rising elderly population at the cost of increasing the share of the GDP devoted to social policy by 5 percentage points over the next half-century or one per cent a decade. This would mean that the UK would reach 1990 European levels of spending by the middle of the next century (Hills 1993). However, that does not meet the problem of rising expectations. To deliver enough to meet them would cost far more. Nor does there seem much enthusiasm for raising substantial additional taxes.

This could change if the public could see a direct relationship between the higher taxes they pay and the service outcomes they say they want. There are ways to do this (Hills 1995b)—a specific addition to the social security contribution to finance improvements in long-term care, a hypotheticated health tax, an income-contingent loan repayment or a graduate tax to pay for higher education (recommended by the Dearing Committee 1997 and long advocated by the author!), mandatory contributions to private or public pension schemes.

Both public opinion and economic theory could support some extension of taxes on 'public bads', that is, the social costs that individuals place on others by their actions. These include pollution and congestion costs. Imposing taxes that brought home to individuals the social costs they imposed on others would produce more efficient outcomes and some revenue too.

2. Get more out of the pot

Another, not mutually exclusive, strategy would be to continue to try to get more out of the existing tax pot by increasing the efficiency and responsiveness of the current services. We have seen that quasi-market reforms to education, health, and housing in the 1980s did, to some extent, succeed in doing this (see Chapter 4 and Le Grand and Bartlett 1993). To unravel these reforms and return to a command-and-control form of central direction and monopoly provision for these services would undermine their future. Equally, because this route has been tried and only been partially successful, the chances of making much progress in this way alone seem remote. Decentralization, distinct from, though often going with, quasi-markets, has produced gains in the administration of housing estates, schools, and community care, particularly in their range of choice and responsiveness to consumers (Power 1987; Glennerster and Turner 1993).

Sometimes, and again housing is a good example, public capital can be made to go further by being mixed with private capital. Local, not-for-profit housing companies that attract private capital with some public support are a model. They put private savings to work. They spread the risk to the private investor; they enable investment to take place for social purposes without expanding the public borrowing requirement. But they can also involve local tenants in the future of their own homes and communities. They break down massive local housing bureaucracies to a human scale and enable managers to identify with the success of the agency. Joint enterprises between local people who want to start a local small business to serve meals or undertake care for an ethnic community with a not-for-profit agency and a state-guaranteed loan would have the same advantages. It would make the capital pot go further. There is scope for more public–private partnerships in capital ventures. At the same time opportunities are limited. If there are risks the state will have to pay private capital to take them. If it gives guarantees to private companies to use their buildings that could be costly. The complex rules to prevent abuse built into the Conservative Government's Private Finance Initiative meant that little happened.

3. Concentrate on the essential ingredients

It may well be that neither of the preceding strategies will be enough. If that is so, there will have to be a fundamental reappraisal of what the state should be doing. This might mean that the state should retreat to its core concerns and concentrate on doing them really well. What are Government's core concerns in the social field?

First and foremost, only the state can be involved in sustaining the lives of the poorest—redistribution of income to the poor. This not only involves support to those with no jobs but support to those in jobs but with such low income that they cannot sustain a minimum standard of life, especially if they have children. Charity alone, in an advanced economy that is not a theocratic state, seems incapable of undertaking this vast task. Second, and closely linked, it is in the wider community interest and in the interests of the institutions of the state itself to prevent groups within it becoming so far separated from the mainstream of that society and so alienated that they no longer truly form a part of it. Neither of social cohesion, a sense of nationhood or the social control necessary for social order can survive such a situation for very long. This means the state has to be concerned with strategies for social inclusion, whether they are directed to excluded ethnic groups or disadvantaged or disabled individuals or to communities that are caught in a downward cycle of exclusion and deprivation.

Thirdly, the state has to be involved to some extent in redistribution over a lifetime (Le Grand 1995). It is here that hard decisions may be necessary. Such redistribution is complementary to the function of private insurance markets and indeed private households and extended families. To some extent, the more the state does, the less families and private individuals do. On the other hand the private market is either not interested in some kinds of risk-taking or will only provide cover at prohibitive cost because the uncertainties are so great or are linked to economic cycles, or there are other market failures (Burchardt and Hills 1997).

This does not apply to all forms of life-cycle redistribution, however. Pensions are the most obvious example. Yet here, too, there are many who will not be able to work for long enough in their lives at stable jobs to produce an adequate pension. The state will then have either to contribute for them or top up their pension on retirement. The uncertainties of the stock market also become of central importance. The state would continue to have a large and uncertain liability and one that might grow if individuals saw that they could avoid contributing to private schemes but the state would bail them out. This route is fraught with difficulty, but so, too, is doing nothing and allowing the social security budget so to constrain the health and education services that people who can afford to do so opt out of these into private health and education.

Other candidates for less state support are university students and those who have the capital to support themselves in old age even at the expense of reducing their bequests. It is not clear that the state ought to have a role in preserving inheritances at the expense of high-quality health and education services. The state may help students borrow to get through university but in a harsh world it is not clear they should not contribute to the cost of an education that will on average put them in higher income brackets. Deciding what is the core state role and what is not is going to be the central task for politicians seeking to secure the future of welfare.

4. Stop stoking up the fire under the pot

Other policies of Government have made social policy's task even greater. Pressures have grown because so many more people are unemployed or have left the labour market early. This is partly the result of macro-economic policy but benefit policy also discourages recipients from returning to work. This is where initiatives to encourage the long-term unemployed back into the labour force, taken forward in the July 1997 Budget, are so important. However, many long-run strategies to reduce welfare demands—education and training, welfare-to-work schemes, etc.—actually increase pressures in the short run.

5. Use more pots

We have already shown that there are many agencies responsible for human welfare, not just the state. Some romantics would like to see the traditional family return to what is seen as its traditional role: caring, educating, and saving for lifetime insecurities. It already does this to a very great degree, in fact, as it always has. Indeed in many ways it may be doing this more now than it ever did. In the nineteenth century few people lived to their eighties or even their seventies. Yet this pot is looking increasingly fragile as more is expected of it—dual earning and paid-work responsibilities, longer childhood, more intensive parental involvement at school, heightened emotional expectations of marriage and the freedom to break the marriage contract. Looking to this institution to solve our welfare problems, as many on the New Right do, looks unduly optimistic.

One of the things that has become increasingly evident in our period is that there are many different ways in which the state can achieve its welfare objectives—far more than was evident to its founders fifty years ago. The state may provide services funded from taxation—old-style welfare-statism. It may give money to individuals or other agencies and let them decide how to spend these resources on defined purposes like pre-school day care and education, or it may lend the money to individuals to spend on higher education, recovering it later. Or it may give money to non-state organizations like GP fundholders or GP commissioning groups to spend state money on behalf of their patients. The state may require people to spend a part of their income in a given way—saving for retirement, for example—but leave them free to decide which pension scheme to join. Le Grand (1997) has called this 'legal' or regulated welfare. Burchardt (forthcoming) has elaborated these varied ways in which welfare objectives can be pursued. Many give the individual much greater decision-power on both how much and how money is spent. In a consumerist world this is likely to enhance the attractiveness of the welfare enterprise. It also carries the danger that the more explicit the redistributive features of the system, the less the middle class will continue to sign on. Balancing the inclusiveness and the redistributive features of the system with its capacity to appeal to the median voter is going to be difficult but we now have a richer variety of means to achieve the social objectives the founders of the old welfare state had in mind.

Further Reading

BURCHARDT, T., and HILLS, J. (1997), *Private Welfare Insurance and Social Security*, York: Joseph Rowntree Foundation.

FALKINGHAM, J., and HILLS, J. (1995), *The Dynamic of Welfare*, Hemel Hempstead: Harvester.

HILLS, J. (1993; 1997), *The Future of Welfare: A Guide to the Debate*, York: Joseph Rowntree Foundation.

—— (1995b), 'Funding the Welfare State', *Oxford Review of Economic Policy* 11:3, 27–43.

LE GRAND, J. (1997), 'Knights, Knaves or Pawns? Human Behaviour and Social Policy', *Journal of Social Policy*, 26:2, 149–69.

—— and BARTLETT, W. (1993), *Quasi-Markets and Social Policy*, London: Macmillan.

SEFTON, T. (1997), *The Changing Distribution of the Social Wage* (STICERD Occasional Paper No. 21), London: London School of Economics.

WORLD BANK (1994), *Averting the Old Age Crisis*, Washington, DC: World Bank.

ANNEXE

Table 8A.1. PUBLIC EXPENDITURE ON THE WELFARE STATE, UNITED KINGDOM

	1973/4	1974/5	1975/6	1976/7	1977/8	1978/9	1979/80	1980/1	1981/2	1982/3
Education	27.5	30.0	30.3	29.9	27.8	27.7	27.5	28.5	28.0	28.1
Health	18.3	22.0	23.5	23.7	23.0	23.5	23.6	25.9	26.2	26.6
Personal social services	3.6	4.2	4.7	4.8	4.2	4.3	4.6	4.8	4.8	4.8
Housing	11.9	17.4	15.1	17.3	14.3	13.5	14.6	12.3	8.3	7.0
Housing-related benefits	3.9	3.0	2.8	2.9	3.0	2.8	2.6	2.8	4.1	4.9
Social security	38.7	40.7	44.0	46.2	46.7	49.0	49.4	49.6	53.8	56.5
All welfare services	103.9	117.3	120.4	124.8	118.9	120.7	122.1	124.0	125.2	127.9

Sources: Equivalent tables in previous chapters.

Table 8A.2. PUBLIC EXPENDITURE ON THE WELFARE STATE AS A PROPORTION OF NATIONAL

	1973/4	1974/5	1975/6	1976/7	1977/8	1978/9	1979/80	1980/1	1981/2	1982/3
Education	5.8	6.4	6.5	6.2	5.6	5.4	5.2	5.6	5.5	5.4
Health	3.9	4.7	5.0	4.9	4.6	4.6	4.5	5.1	5.2	5.1
Personal social services	0.8	0.9	1.0	1.0	0.8	0.8	0.9	1.0	0.9	0.9
Housing	2.5	3.7	3.2	3.6	2.9	2.6	2.8	2.4	1.6	1.4
Housing-related benefits	0.8	0.6	0.6	0.6	0.6	0.6	0.5	0.6	0.8	0.9
Social Security	8.2	8.6	9.4	9.6	9.4	9.6	9.4	9.8	10.6	10.9
All welfare services	21.9	24.9	25.7	25.9	24.0	23.7	23.3	24.4	24.8	24.7

Sources: Equivalent tables in previous chapters and HM Treasury (1997: table 3.1).

(£ BILLION AT 1995/6 PRICES)

1983/4	1984/5	1985/6	1986/7	1987/8	1988/9	1989/90	1990/1	1991/2	1992/3	1993/4	1994/5	1995/6
28.5	28.1	27.9	29.4	30.1	30.4	31.7	31.8	33.1	34.0	34.6	36.0	36.1
27.1	27.4	27.8	29.3	30.7	31.7	32.2	33.2	35.6	38.0	38.9	40.9	40.7
5.0	5.1	5.5	5.8	5.6	6.0	6.3	6.7	7.0	7.3	7.8	8.1	8.89
7.7	7.4	6.5	6.1	6.8	6.1	6.0	6.7	6.8	6.9	5.7	4.8	3.9
4.8	5.3	5.7	6.0	5.8	5.7	6.1	7.0	8.5	9.9	11.1	11.7	12.2
60.1	61.3	63.0	65.8	65.2	62.5	61.4	63.1	69.8	75.4	79.7	79.9	80.8
133.3	134.6	136.4	142.5	144.2	142.5	143.6	148.4	160.9	171.5	177.8	181.3	182.6

INCOME, UNITED KINGDOM (% OF GDP)

1983/4	1984/5	1985/6	1986/7	1987/8	1988/9	1989/90	1990/1	1991/2	1992/3	1993/4	1994/5	1995/6
5.3	5.1	4.9	4.9	4.8	4.6	4.8	4.8	5.1	5.2	5.2	5.2	5.1
5.0	5.0	4.9	4.9	4.9	4.9	4.8	5.0	5.5	5.8	5.8	5.9	5.7
0.9	0.9	1.0	1.0	0.9	0.9	0.9	1.0	1.1	1.1	1.2	1.2	1.2
1.4	1.3	1.1	1.0	1.1	0.9	0.9	1.0	1.1	1.1	0.9	0.7	0.6
0.9	1.0	1.0	1.0	0.9	0.9	0.9	1.1	1.3	1.5	1.7	1.7	1.7
11.2	11.2	11.1	11.0	10.4	9.6	9.2	9.5	10.7	11.6	11.9	11.5	11.4
24.8	24.5	23.9	23.8	23.0	21.8	21.6	22.4	24.7	26.3	26.6	26.1	25.8

Table 8A.3. PUBLIC EXPENDITURE ON THE WELFARE STATE BY ECONOMIC CATEGORY,

	1973/4	1974/5	1975/6	1976/7	1977/8	1978/9	1979/80	1980/1	1981/2	1982/3
Transfers[a]	42.1	43.0	45.9	48.2	48.8	51.1	51.4	51.8	57.0	60.4
Other current spending	46.3	55.7	58.7	59.8	57.1	58.1	58.9	62.2	60.8	60.6
Capital spending	15.4	18.7	16.0	16.7	13.1	11.5	11.8	10.0	7.4	6.9
All spending on welfare services	103.9	117.3	120.4	124.8	118.9	120.7	122.1	124.0	125.2	127.9
Capital as a % of total welfare spending	14.8	15.9	13.3	13.4	11.0	9.5	9.6	8.1	5.9	5.4
Spending on welfare as a % of GGE[b]	50.3	50.9	52.1	55.3	55.8	53.8	52.9	52.6	52.6	52.3

[a] Expenditure on housing-related benefits, social security (bar administration costs), and educational grants.

[b] The General Government Expenditure (GGE) definition of public spending includes privatization proceeds and differs from the government's preferred measure of public spending, GGE(X). See HM Treasury (1997: 5) for details.

Sources: Equivalent tables in previous chapters and HM Treasury (1997: table 3.1).

Table 8A.4. COMPOSITION OF PUBLIC EXPENDITURE ON THE WELFARE STATE, UNITED

	1973/4	1974/5	1975/6	1976/7	1977/8	1978/9	1979/80	1980/1	1981/2	1982/3
Education	26.5	25.6	25.2	24.0	23.4	22.9	22.5	23.0	22.4	22.0
Health	17.7	18.8	19.5	19.0	19.3	19.4	19.3	20.9	20.9	20.8
Personal social services	3.4	3.6	3.9	3.8	3.5	3.5	3.7	3.9	3.8	3.8
Housing	11.4	14.8	12.5	13.9	12.0	11.2	11.9	9.9	6.6	5.5
Housing-related benefits	3.7	2.5	2.3	2.4	2.5	2.3	2.1	2.3	3.3	3.8
Social Security	37.3	34.7	36.6	37.0	39.3	40.6	40.4	40.0	42.9	44.2

Sources: Equivalent tables in previous chapters.

UNITED KINGDOM (£ BILLION AT 1995/6 PRICES)

1983/4	1984/5	1985/6	1986/7	1987/8	1988/9	1989/90	1990/1	1991/2	1992/3	1993/4	1994/5	1995/6
63.9	65.4	67.5	70.3	69.3	66.6	65.6	68.1	76.5	83.5	88.9	90.0	91.6
61.2	61.3	61.9	65.3	66.8	68.4	69.3	71.5	75.2	78.5	81.0	84.3	84.5
8.2	7.9	7.1	6.8	8.1	7.5	8.6	8.9	9.3	9.4	7.9	7.1	6.4
133.3	134.6	136.4	142.5	144.2	142.5	143.6	148.4	160.9	171.5	177.8	181.3	182.6
6.2	5.9	5.2	4.8	5.6	5.3	6.0	6.0	5.8	5.5	4.5	3.9	3.5
53.8	53.1	54.0	56.0	56.6	57.6	55.6	57.2	60.9	61.3	61.6	61.6	60.2

KINGDOM (% OF TOTAL WELFARE EXPENDITURE)

1983/4	1984/5	1985/6	1986/7	1987/8	1988/9	1989/90	1990/1	1991/2	1992/3	1993/4	1994/5	1995/6
21.4	20.9	20.5	20.6	20.9	21.3	22.1	21.4	20.6	19.8	19.5	19.9	19.8
20.3	20.4	20.4	20.6	21.3	22.3	22.4	22.4	22.1	22.2	21.9	22.6	22.3
3.7	3.8	4.1	4.1	3.9	4.2	4.4	4.5	4.3	4.2	4.4	4.5	4.8
5.8	5.5	4.7	4.3	4.7	4.3	4.2	4.5	4.2	4.0	3.2	2.6	2.1
3.6	3.9	4.2	4.2	4.0	4.0	4.3	4.7	5.3	5.8	6.3	6.5	6.7
45.1	45.6	46.2	46.2	45.2	43.9	42.7	42.5	43.4	44.0	44.8	44.1	44.3

Bibliography

ABEL-SMITH, B. (1958), 'Whose Welfare State?', in N. MacKenzie (ed.) *Conviction*, London: MacGibbon and Kee.

—— and Townsend, P. (1965), *The Poor and the Poorest* (Occasional Paper on Social Administration No. 17), London: Bell.

ABI [Association of British Insurers] (1996), *Insurance Statistics Yearbook 1985–1995*, London: ABI.

ARBER, S. and GILBERT, G. N. (1989), 'Men: The Forgotten Carers', *Sociology* 23: 1, 111–18.

—— and GINN, J. (1995), 'Gender Differences in Informal Caring', *Health and Social Care in the Community* 3, 19–31.

ARROW, K. (1973), 'Higher Education as Filter', *Journal of Public Economics* 2, 103–216.

ASSESSMENT OF PERFORMANCE UNIT (1988), *Science at Age 15: A Review of APU Findings 1980–84* London: HMSO.

ATKINSON, A. B., and MICKLEWRIGHT, J. (1989), 'Turning the Screw: Benefits for the Unemployed 1979–1988', in A. Dilnot and I. Walker (eds.), *The Economics of Social Security,* Oxford: Oxford University Press.

—— HILLS, J. and LE GRAND, J. (1987), 'The Welfare State' in R. Dornbusch and R. Layard (eds.), *The Performance of the British Economy,* Oxford: Oxford University Press.

AUDIT COMMISSION (1986a), *Performance Review in Local Government: A Handbook for Auditors and Local Authorities (Social Services),* London: HMSO.

—— (1986b), *Making a Reality of Community Care,* London: HMSO.

—— (1989), *Housing the Homeless: The Local Authority Role,* London: HMSO.

—— (1993), *Taking Care,* London: HMSO.

—— (1994), *Finding a Place: A Review of Mental Health Services for Adults,* London: HMSO.

—— (1996a), 'Balancing the Care Equation: Progress with Community Care', *Community Care Bulletin* no. 3 (Mar.), London: HMSO.

—— (1996b), *What the Doctor Ordered: A Study of GP Fundholders in England and Wales*, Vol. 1 *Report*. London: HMSO.

BACON, R., and ELTIS, W. (1976), *Britain's Economic Problem: Too Few Producers*, London: Macmillan.

BAGGOTT, R. (1994), *Health and Health Care in Britain,* Houndmills: Macmillan.

BALDWIN, S., PARKER, G. and WALKER, R. (eds.) (1989), *Social Security and Community Care,* Avebury: Gower.

BARCLAY, P. (1995), *The Joseph Rowntree Foundation Inquiry into Income and Wealth*, Vol. 1 *Report*. York: Joseph Rowntree Foundation.

BARR, N. (1975), 'Labour's Pension Plan—A Lost Opportunity?', *British Tax Review* 2, 102–13 and 3, 155–74.

—— (1993: 1998), *The Economics of the Welfare State,* Oxford: Oxford University Press.

—— FALKINGHAM, J., and GLENNERSTER, H. (1994), *Funding Higher Education*, Poole: BP Educational and LSE.

Bibliography

BEBBINGTON, A., and KELLY, A. (1995), 'Expenditure Planning in the Personal Social Services: Unit Costs in the 1980s', *Journal of Social Policy* 3:24, 385–411.

BECKER, G. S. (1964), *Human Capital,* Princeton: Princeton University Press.

BEER, S. (1982), *Britain Against Itself,* London: Faber.

BELL, C. (1995), 'In a Different League?', *British Journal of Curriculum and Assessment* 5:3, 32–3.

BELSKY, J, and EGGEBEEN, D. (1991), 'Effects of Maternal Employment and Child Care Arrangements on Pre-schoolers' Cognitive and Behavioural Outcomes', *Developmental Psychology* 27:6, 932–45.

BELTRAM, G. (1984), *Testing the Safety Net: An Enquiry into the Reformed Supplementary Benefit Scheme* (Occasional Paper on Social Administration No. 74), London: Bedford Square Press.

BENNETT, R., GLENNERSTER, H, and NEVISON, D. (1992*a*), 'Investing in Skills: To Stay On or Not to Stay On', *Oxford Review of Economic Policy* 8:2, 130–45.

—— —— —— (1992*b*), *Learning Should Pay,* Poole: BP Educational.

—— —— —— (1995), 'Investing in Skill: Expected Returns to Vocational Studies', *Education Economics* 3:2, 99–117.

BENZEVAL, M., and JUDGE, K. (1995), 'Access to Health Care in England: Continuing Inequalities in the Distribution of GPs', *Journal of Public Health Medicine* 18, 33–40.

—— —— and WHITEHEAD, M. (1996), *Tackling Inequalities in Health: An Agenda for Action,* London: King's Fund Institute.

BERTHOUD, R. (1989), 'Social Security and the Economics of Housing', in A. Dilnot and I. Walker (eds.), *The Economics of Social Security,* Oxford: Oxford University Press.

—— (1993), *Incapacity Benefit: How Will the New 'Medical Assessment' Work?,* London: Policy Studies Institute.

BESLEY, T., HALL, J., and PRESTON, I. (1996), *The Demand for Private Health Insurance: Do Waiting Lists Matter?* (Working Paper Series No. W96/7), London: Institute for Fiscal Studies.

BEVERIDGE REPORT (1942), *Social Insurance and Allied Services* (Cmd. 6404), London: HMSO.

BLACK REPORT (1980), *Inequalities in Health: Report of a Research Working Group,* London: Department of Health and Social Security. Reprinted in Townsend *et al.* (1992).

BLAUG, M. (1984), 'Education Vouchers: It All Depends What You Mean', in J. Le Grand and R. Robinson (eds.), *Privatisation and the Welfare State,* London: Allen and Unwin

BLAXTER, M. (1990), *Health and Lifestyles,* London: Routledge.

BLUNDELL R. (1992), 'Labour Supply and Taxation: A Survey', *Fiscal Studies* 13:3, 15–40.

—— DEARDEN, P., and MEGHIR, C. (1995), *The Determinants and Effects of Training in Britain* (mimeo), London: Institute for Fiscal Studies.

BORRIE, G. (1994), *Social Justice, Strategies for Renewal: The Report of the Commission on Social Justice,* London: Vintage.

BRADSHAW, J. ,and DEACON, A. (1986), 'Social Security', in P. Wilding (ed.), *In Defence of the Welfare State,* Manchester: Manchester University Press.

BRAMLEY, G. (1993), 'Quasi-markets in Social Housing', in J. Le Grand and W. Bartlett (eds.), *Quasi-markets and Social Policy,* Basingstoke: Macmillan.

BRENNAN, M., and CARR-HILL, R. (1996), *No Need to Weight Community Health Programmes for Resource Allocation?* (Centre for Health Economics Discussion Paper 146), York: University of York.

BRITTON, M. (ed.) (1990), *Mortality and Geography,* London: HMSO.

BROWN, M. (1972), 'Inequality and the Personal Social Services', in P. Townsend and N. Bosanquet (eds.), *Labour and Inequality*, London: Fabian Society.

BRYSON, A., and MARSH, A. (1996), *Leaving Family Credit*, London: HMSO.

BRYSON, C. (1995), *Trends in Attitudes to Health Care 1983 to 1985*, London: Social and Community Planning Research.

BULMER, M. (1987), *The Social Basis of Community Care*, London: Allen and Unwin.

BURCHARDT, T. (forthcoming), *Boundaries between Public and Private Welfare*, London: London School of Economics.

—— and HILLS, J. (1997), *Private Welfare Insurance and Social Security: Pushing the Boundaries*, York: Joseph Rowntree Foundation.

BURKE, K., and CAIRNCROSS, A. (1992), *Goodbye Great Britain: The 1976 IMF Crisis*, New Haven: Yale University Press.

BURROWS, R. (1997), *Contemporary Patterns of Residential Mobility in Relation to Social Housing in England* (Centre for Housing Policy Research Report), York: University of York.

BURTLESS, G. (ed.) (1996), *Does Money Matter?: The Effect of School Resources on Student Achievement and Adult Success*, Washington, DC: Brookings Institution.

BUXTON, M. S., and KLEIN, R.(1978), 'Allocating Health Resources' (Royal Commission on the National Health Service, Research Paper No. 3), London: HMSO.

CAF [Charities Aid Foundation] (1996), *Dimensions of the Voluntary Sector: How the Voluntary Sector is Changing*, London: CAF.

CANTER, D., DRAKE, M., LITTLER, T., MOORE, J., STOCKLEY, D., and BALL, J. (1989), *The Faces of Homelessness in London*, Guildford: University of Surrey Department of Psychology.

CASTLE, B. (1975), speech at the Local Authority Social Services Conference, 28 Nov.

CAVE, M., DODSWORTH, R., and THOMPSON, D. (1992), 'Regulatory Reform in Higher Education in the UK: Incentives for Efficiency and Product Quality', *Oxford Review of Economic Policy* 8:2, 79–102.

CBO [Congressional Budget Office] (1987), *Educational Achievement: Explorations and Implications of Recent Trends*, Washington, DC: CBO.

CHALLIS, D., and TRASKE, K. (1997), 'Community Care', in P. Mayer, E. Dickinson, and M. Sandler (eds.), *Quality Care for Elderly People*, London: Chapman and Hall Medical.

CHETWYND, M., and RITCHIE, J., with REITH, L., and HOWARD, M. (1996), *The Costs of Care: The Impact of Charging Policy on the Lives of Disabled People*, York: Joseph Rowntree Foundation.

CHEW, R. (1995), *Compendium of Health Statistics* (9th edn.), London: Office of Health Economics.

CHR [Centre for Housing Research] (1989), *The Nature and Effectiveness of Housing Management in England*, London: HMSO.

CIPFA [Chartered Institute of Public Finance and Accountancy] (1985), *Personal Social Services Statistics 1984/5 (Actuals)*, London: CIPFA.

—— (1995), *Education Statistics 1993–94 Actuals Incorporating the Handbook of Unit Costs*, London: CIPFA.

—— (1996), *Personal Social Services Statistics 1994/5 (Actuals)*, London: CIPFA.

CLOTFELTER, C.T. (1996), *Buying the Best: Cost Escalation in Higher Education*, Princeton: Princeton University Press.

COHEN, D. K. (1996), 'Standards-Based School Reform: Policy Practice and Performance', in H. Ladd (ed.), *Holding Schools Accountable*, Washington, DC: Brookings Institution.

Bibliography

COLLINS, E., and KLEIN, R. (1980), 'Equity and the NHS: Self-reported Morbidity, Access and Primary Care', *British Medical Journal* 281, 1111–15.

COOPER, A., and NYE, R. (1995), 'The Rowntree Enquiry and "Trickle Down" ', *Hard Data* No. 1, London: Social Market Foundation.

COOPER, J. (1983), *The Creation of the Personal Social Services 1962–1974,* London: Heinemann.

CORDEN A. (1995), *Changing Perspectives on Benefit Take-up*, London: HMSO.

COUNCIL OF MORTGAGE LENDERS (1997), *Housing Finance 33* (Feb.).

COX, C. B., and DYSON, A. E. (eds.) (1969), *Fight for Education; A Black Paper,* London: Critical Quarterly Society.

CRESSWELL, M., and GRUBB, J. (1987), *The Second International Mathematics Study in England and Wales,* Windsor: NFER-Nelson.

CROOK, A. D. H., HUGHES, J., and KEMP, P. A (1995), *The Supply of Privately Rented Homes: Today and Tomorrow*, York: Joseph Rowntree Foundation.

CROSLAND, C. A. R. (1956), *The Future of Socialism*, London: Cape.

CSO [Central Statistical Office] (1974), 'The Incidence of Taxes and Social Service Benefits in 1973', *Economic Trends* (Dec.), London: HMSO.

—— (1976), *Social Trends 1976,* London: HMSO.

—— (1979), *Social Trends 1979,* London: HMSO.

—— (1980), *Social Trends 1980,* London: HMSO.

—— (1988), *Social Trends 1988,* London: HMSO.

—— (1989), *Social Trends 1989,* London: HMSO.

—— (1995), *Social Trends 1995,* London: HMSO.

—— (1996), *Social Trends 1996,* London: HMSO.

CULLIS, J., and JONES, P. (1986), 'Rationing by Waiting Lists: An Implication', *American Economic Review* 76, 250–6.

CVCP [Committee of Vice-Chancellors and Principals] (1996 and previous edns.), *Higher Education Pay and Prices Index,* London: CVCP.

DAHRENDORF, R. (1995), *Report on Wealth Creation and Social Cohesion in a Free Society,* London: The Commission on Wealth Creation and Social Cohesion.

DAY, P., KLEIN, R., and REDMAYNE, S. (1996), *Why Regulate? Regulating Residential Care for Elderly People,* London: Polity Press.

DEARING COMMITTEE (1997), *Higher Education in the Learning Society*, London: The Committee of Inquiry into Higher Education.

DEPARTMENT FOR CATHOLIC EDUCATION (1997), *Struggle for Excellence: Catholic Secondary Schools in Urban Poverty Areas*, London: Catholic Bishops' Conference.

DES [Department of Education and Science] (1963), *Higher Education* (Robbins Report), Cmnd. 2154, London: HMSO.

—— (1966), *Progress in Reading 1948–64* (Education Pamphlet No. 50), London: HMSO.

—— (1967), *Children and their Primary Schools* (Plowden Report) London: HMSO.

—— (1972), *Education a Framework for Expansion,* London: HMSO.

—— (1974), *Educational Disadvantage and the Educational Needs of Immigrants* (Cmnd. 5720), London: HMSO.

—— (1975a), *A Language for Life* (Bullock Report), London: HMSO.

—— (1975b), *Income of Non-university Teachers: Report of Inquiry* (Houghton Report: Cmnd. 5878), London: HMSO

—— (1977a), *Education in Schools* (Cmnd. 6869), London: HMSO.

—— (1977b), *A Study of School Building,* London: HMSO.

—— (1978), *Primary Education in England: A Survey by HM Inspectors of Schools,* London: HMSO.

—— (1979), *Aspects of Secondary Education in England: A Survey by HM Inspectors of Schools,* London: HMSO.

—— (1981), *West Indian Children in our Schools* (Cmnd. 8273), London: HMSO.

—— (1982), *Mathematics Counts,* London: HMSO.

—— (1985a), *Better Schools* (Cmnd. 9467), London: HMSO.

—— (1985b), *The Development of Higher Education in the 1990s* (Cmnd. 9624), London: HMSO.

—— (1985c), *Education for All* (Swann Report; Cmnd. 9453), London: HMSO.

—— (1985d), *The Curriculum from 5–16* (HMI Curriculum Matters Series No. 2), London: HMSO.

—— (1987), *The National Curriculum 5–16: A Consultation Document,* London: DES.

—— (1988), *Top-up Loans for Students* (Cm. 520), London: HMSO.

—— (1991), *Higher Education: A New Framework* (Cm. 1541), London: HMSO.

DESAI, S., CHASE-LANSDALE, P. L., and MICHAEL, R. T. (1989), 'Mother or Market? Effects of Maternal Employment on the Intellectual Ability of 4-Year-Old Children', *Demography* 26:4, 545–61

—— MICHAEL, R. T, CHASE-LANSDALE, P. L. (1990), 'The Home Environment: A Mechanism through which Maternal Employment Affects Child Development', paper presented to the Population Association of America Meeting, Toronto, May.

DfE [Department for Education] (1995a), *Departmental Annual Report: The Government's Expenditure Plans 1995–6 to 1997–8* (Cm. 2810), London: HMSO.

—— (1995b), *Educational Statistics Bulletin,* London: DfE.

DfEE [Department for Education and Employment] (1997a), *The Contribution of Graduates to the Economy: Evidence to the Dearing Enquiry,* London: DfEE.

—— (1997b), *Departmental Annual Report,* London: DfEE.

DHSS [Department of Health and Social Security] (1971), *Better Services for the Mentally Handicapped* (Cmnd. 4683), London: HMSO.

—— (1975), *Better Services for the Mentally Ill,* London, HMSO.

—— (1976a), *Sharing Resources for Health in England: Report of the Resource Allocation Working Party,* London: HMSO.

—— (1976b), *Priorities for the Health and Personal Social Services in England: A Consultative Document,* London: HMSO.

—— (1977a), *Priorities in Health and Personal Social Services: The Way Forward,* London: HMSO.

—— (1977b), *Forward Planning of Local Authority Social Services* (Circular 2ASSL (77/13)), London: DHSS.

—— (1981a) *Care in Action: A Handbook of Policies and Priorities for the Health and Personal Social Services in England,* London: HMSO.

—— (1981b), *Growing Older* (Cmnd. 8173), London: HMSO.

—— (1985a), *Reform of Social Security* (Cmnd. 9517), London: HMSO.

—— (1985b), *Reform of Social Security: Programme for Action* (Cmnd. 9691), London: HMSO.

—— (1985c), *Housing Benefit Review: Report of the Review Team* (Cmnd. 9520), London: HMSO.

—— (1988), *Community Care: Agenda for Action* (The Griffiths Report), London: DHSS.

—— (1989), *Social Security Statistics 1989,* London: HMSO.

DIGBY, A. (1989), *British Welfare Policy: Workhouse to Workfare,* London: Faber.

DILNOT, A. and WEBB, S. (1989), 'The 1988 Social Security Reforms', *Fiscal Studies* 9:3, 26–53.

Bibliography

DISABILITY ALLIANCE (1988), 'Briefing on the First Report from the OPCS Surveys of Disability: "The Prevalence of Disability among Adults" ', London: Disability Alliance.

DIXON, J., DINWOODIE, M., HODSON, D., POLTORAK, T., GARRETT, C., RICE, P., DONCASTER, I., and WILLIAMS, M. (1994), 'Distribution of NHS Funds between Fundholding and Non-fundholding Practices', *British Medical Journal* 306, 30–4.

—— HARRISON, A., and NEW, B. (1997), 'Funding the NHS: Is the NHS Underfunded?', *British Medical Journal* 314, 216–19.

DoE [Department of the Environment] (1971), *Fair Deal for Housing* (Cmnd. 4728), London: HMSO.

—— (1977*a*), *Housing Policy: A Consultative Document* (Cmnd. 6851), London: HMSO.

—— (1977*b*), *Housing Policy Technical Volume*, London: HMSO.

—— (1978), *National Dwelling and Housing Survey*, London: HMSO.

—— (1982), *English House Condition Survey 1981. Part 1: Report of the Physical Condition Survey*, London: HMSO.

—— (1983), *English House Condition Survey 1981. Part 2: Report of the Interview and Local Authority Survey*, London: HMSO.

—— (1985), *Housing and Construction Statistics 1974–1984*, London: HMSO.

—— (1987), *Housing: The Government's Proposals* (Cm. 214), London: HMSO.

—— (1988), *English House Condition Survey, 1986*, London: HMSO.

—— (1993), *English House Condition Survey 1991*, London: HMSO.

—— (1996), *Annual Report 1996* (Cm. 3207), London: HMSO.

—— (1997*a*), *Housing and Construction Statistics 1985–1995*, London: The Stationery Office.

—— (1997*b*), *Annual Report 1997* (Cm. 3607), London: The Stationery Office.

DoH [Department of Health] (1989*a*), *Working for Patients* (Cm. 555), London: HMSO.

—— (1989*b*), *Caring for People*, London: HMSO.

—— (1991), *The Patient's Charter*, London: HMSO.

—— (1992), *The Health of the Nation: A Strategy for Health in England* (Cm. 1986), London: HMSO.

—— (1994*a*), *Registers of People with Physical Disabilities (General Classes) at 31 March 1993, England*, London: Government Statistical Service.

—— (1994*b*), *Department of Health Statistical Bulletin* (Mar. 1994), London: Department of Health.

—— (1995*a*), *The Patient's Charter and You* (Pamphlet No. H51/005 776 40k 2RP (23)), London: Department of Health.

—— (1995*b*), *Variations in Health*, London: Department of Health.

—— (1995*c*), *Summarized Accounts 1994/5*, London: HMSO.

—— (1996*a*), *Choice and Opportunity. Primary Care: The Future* (Cm. 3390), London: HMSO.

—— (1996*b*), *Health and Personal Social Services Statistics for England 1996*, London: HMSO.

—— (1996*c*), 'Community Care Statistics 1995' (*Department of Health Statistical Bulletin* 1996/), London: Department of Health.

—— (1996*d*), *Primary Care: Delivering the Future* (Cm. 3512), London: HMSO.

—— (1996*e*), (*Department of Health Statistical Bulletin* 1996/19), London: Department of Health.

—— (1996*f*), *Private Hospitals, Homes and Clinics Registered under Section 23 of the Registered Homes Act 1984, Financial Year 1995–96*, London: Department of Health.

—— (1996*g*), *Summarized Accounts 1995/6*, London: The Stationery Office.

—— (1996h), 'Elective Admissions and Patients Waiting: England at 30 September 1995' (*Department of Health Statistical Bulletin* 1995/2), London: Department of Health.

—— (1996i), *Children's Day Care Facilities at 31 March 1995, England*, London: Government Statistical Service.

—— (1996j), 'Waiting Times for First Outpatient Appointments in England: Quarter Ended 30 September 1996' (*Department of Health Statistical Bulletin* 1997/2), London: Department of Health.

—— (1997a), 'Elective Admissions and Patients Waiting: England at 30 September 1996' (*Department of Health Statistical Bulletin* 1997/1), London: Department of Health.

—— (1997b), 'Provisional Waiting List Figures, 31 December 1996' (Department of Health Press Release 97/043, dated 19 Feb. 1996, London: Department of Health.

—— (1997c), 'Provisional Waiting List Figures, 31 March 1997' (Department of Health Press Release 97/106, dated 22 May 1997), London: Department of Health.

—— (1997d), *The Government's Expenditure Plans 1997–98 to 1999–2000: Departmental Report* (Cm. 3612), London: HMSO.

—— (1997e), *Better Value for Money in Social Services: A Review of Performance Trends in Social Services in England*, London: Department of Health.

DONNISON, D. (1982), *The Politics of Poverty*, Oxford: Martin Robertson.

DOWLING, B. (1997), 'Fundholding and Waiting Times: Beyond the Anecdotal Evidence', *British Medical Journal* 315, 290–2.

DREVER, F., WHITEHEAD, M., and RODEN, M. (1996), 'Current Patterns and Trends in Male Mortality by Social Class (Based on Occupation)', *Population Trends* 86, 15–22.

DSS [Department of Social Security] (1993), *The Growth of Social Security*, London: HMSO.

—— (1995a), *Social Security Statistics 1995*, London: HMSO.

—— (1995b), *Income Support Statistics: Quarterly Enquiry May 1994*, Newcastle: DSS.

—— (1995c), *National Insurance Fund Account 1993–94* (House of Commons Paper HC404, Session 94/95), London: HMSO.

—— (1996a), *Social Security Statistics 1996*, London: HMSO.

—— (1996b), *Households Below Average Income*, London: HMSO.

—— (1996c), *Income-Related Benefits: Estimates of Take-up in 1993/4*, London: DSS.

—— (1996d), *The Abstract of Statistics for Social Security Benefits and Contributions and the Indices of Retail Prices and Average Earnings*, Newcastle: DSS.

—— (1997a), *Social Security Departmental Report: The Government's Expenditure Plans 1997–98 to 1999–2000* (Cm. 361), London: The Stationery Office.

—— (1997b), *Pension Scheme Contributors 1986/87 to 1994/95*, Newcastle: DSS.

DUCLOS, J-Y. (1991), 'The Take-up of State Benefits: An Application to Supplementary Benefits in Britain using the FES' (STICERD Welfare State Discussion Paper WSP/71), London: London School of Economics.

DUNCAN, G. J. (1994), 'Families and Neighbours as Sources of Disadvantage in the Schooling Decisions of White and Black Adolescents,' *American Journal of Education* 103, 20–53.

DUNNELL, K. (1997), 'Are We Healthier?', in M. Murphy and J. Charlton (eds.), *The Health of Adult Britain 1841–1994*, London: HMSO.

DYNARSKI, M., SCHWAB, R., and ZAMPELLI, E. (1989), 'Local Characteristics and Production Function: The Case of Education', *Journal of Urban Economics* 26, 250–63.

Bibliography

ECKSTEIN, H. (1959), *The English Health Service*, Oxford: Oxford University Press.

ENTHOVEN, A. (1985), *Reflections on the Management of the National Health Service* (Occasional Paper No. 5), London: National Provincial Hospitals Trust.

ERENS, B., and GHATE, D. (1993), *Invalidity Benefit: A Longitudinal Study of New Recipients*, London: HMSO.

ESTRIN, S., and PEROTIN, V. (1989), *Creeping Privatisation: Old Age Homes in Britain and France* (mimeo), London: London School of Economics.

EVANDROU, M. (1992), 'Challenging the Invisibility of Carers: Mapping Informal Care Nationally', in F. Laczko and C. Victor (eds.), *Social Policy and Older People*, Aldershot: Avebury.

—— (1995), 'Paid and Unpaid Work: The Socio-economic Position of Informal Carers in Britain', in J. Phillips (ed.), *Working Carers and Older People*, Aldershot: Avebury.

—— (1996a), 'Health Care Utilisation in Britain: Socio-economic Variations', paper presented to the British Society of Population Studies Annual Conference, St Andrews, Sept.

—— (1996b), 'Unpaid Work, Carers and Health', in D. Blane, E. Brunner and R. G. Wilkinson (eds.), *Health and Social Organisation: Toward a Health Policy for the 21st century*, London: Routledge.

—— (1997), 'Building a Future Retirement: Towards a Policy Agenda', in M. Evandrou (ed.), *Baby Boomers: Ageing in the 21st Century*, London: Age Concern England.

—— and FALKINGHAM, J. (1995), 'Gender, Lone-parenthood and Lifetime Incomes', in J. Falkingham and J. Hills (eds.), *The Dynamics of Welfare*, London: Prentice Hall/Harvester Wheatsheaf.

—— —— (1997), 'Growing Old in Twenty-First Century Britain: The Experience of Four Cohorts 1974–1993' (STICERD Welfare State Discussion Paper WSP/128), London: London School of Economics.

—— and WINTER, D. (1992), 'Informal Carers and the Labour Market in Britain' (STICERD Welfare State Discussion Paper WSP/89), London: London School of Economics.

—— FALKINGHAM, J., and GLENNERSTER, H. (1990), 'The Personal Social Services: Everyone's Poor Relation but Nobody's Baby', in J. Hills (1990).

—— —— LE GRAND, J., and WINTER, D. (1991), 'Equity in Health and Social Care', *Journal of Social Policy* 21, 489–523.

EVANS, M. (1996a), 'Fairer or Fowler? The Effects of the 1986 Social Security Act on Family Incomes', in J. Hills (ed.), *New Inequalities: The Changing Distribution of Income and Wealth in the United Kingdom*, Cambridge: Cambridge University Press.

—— (1996b), 'Giving Credit Where It's Due? The Success of Family Credit Reassessed', (STICERD Welfare State Discussion Paper WSP/121), London: London School of Economics.

—— (1996c), 'Housing Benefit Problems and Dilemmas : What Can We Learn from France and Germany?' (Welfare State Discussion Paper WSP/119), London: London School of Economics.

—— and GLENNERSTER, H. (1993), 'Squaring the Circle: The Inconsistencies and Constraints of Beveridge's Plan' (STICERD Welfare State Discussion Paper WSP/86), London: London School of Economics.

—— PIACHAUD, D., and SUTHERLAND, H. (1994), 'Designed for the Poor—Poorer by Design? The Effects of the 1986 Social Security Act on Family Incomes' (STICERD Welfare State Discussion Paper WSP/105), London: London School of Economics.

FALKINGHAM, J. (1997), 'Who are the Baby Boomers? A Demographic Profile', in M. Evandrou (ed.), *Baby Boomers: Ageing in the 21st Century*, London: Age Concern England.

—— and HILLS, J. (1995), *The Dynamics of Welfare*, Hemel Hempstead: Harvester.

Bibliography

FEINSTEIN, C. H. (1972), *National Income, Expenditure and Output of the United Kingdom 1858–1965*, Cambridge: Cambridge University Press.

FELCE, D., TAYLOR, D., and WRIGHT, K. (1992), *People with Learning Disabilities* (NHS Management Executive: DHA Project in Epidemiologically Based Needs Assessment), Leeds: NHS Management Executive.

FERLIE, E., and JUDGE, K. (1981), 'Detrenchment and Rationality in Personal Social Services', *Policy and Politics* 9:3, 313–14.

FINCH, J., and GROVES, D. (1980), 'Community Care and the Family: A Case for Equal Opportunities', *Journal of Social Policy* 9:4, 487–511.

—— (eds.) (1983), A *Labour of Love: Women, Work and Caring*, London: Routledge and Kegan Paul.

FLOUD, J., HALSEY, A. H., and MARTIN, F. M. (1956), *Social Class and Educational Mobility,* London: Heinemann.

FOOT, M. (1975), *Aneurin Bevan 1945–1960*, London: Paladin.

FORD, J., and KEMPSON, E. (1997), *Bridging the Gap? Safety-nets for Mortgage Borrowers* (Centre for Housing Policy Research Report), York: University of York.

FORSTER, D. (1976), 'Social Class Differences in Sickness and General Practitioner Consultations', *Health Trends* 8, 29–32.

FOSTER, C., JACKMAN, R., and PERLMAN, M. (1980), *Local Government Finance in a Unitary State*, London: Allen and Unwin.

FRANKEL, S., and WEST, R. (1993), *Rationing and Rationality in the National Health Service: The Persistence of Waiting Lists*, Basingstoke: Macmillan.

GAL, J. (1997), 'Categorical Benefits in Welfare States: Findings from Britain and Israel' (STICERD Welfare State Discussion Paper WSP/132), London: London School of Economics.

GARDINER, K., and HILLS, J. (1992), 'What Price Housing? Valuing "Voluntary Transfers" of Council Housing', *Fiscal Studies* 13:1, 54–70.

GARNHAM, A., and KNIGHTS, E. (1994), *Putting the Treasury First: The Truth about the Child Support Act*, London: Child Poverty Action Group.

GEORGE, V., and WILDING, P. (1984), *The Impact of Social Policy*, London: Routledge.

GIBB, K., and MUNRO, M. (1991), *Housing Finance in the UK*, Basingstoke: Macmillan.

GILES, C., JOHNSON, P., MCCRAE, J., and TAYLOR, J. (1996), *Living with the State: The Incomes and Work Incentives of Tenants in the Social Rented Sector*, London: Institute for Fiscal Studies.

GLASS, D. (1954), *Social Mobility in Britain*, London: Routledge and Kegan Paul.

GLENNERSTER, H. (1980), 'Prime Cuts: Public Expenditure and Social Service Planning in a Hostile Environment', *Policy and Politics* 8:4, 367–82.

—— (1985), *Paying for Welfare*, Oxford: Blackwell.

—— (1991), 'Quasi-markets for Education?', *Economic Journal* 101:408, 1268–76.

—— (1995), *British Social Policy since 1945*, Oxford: Blackwell.

—— (1996), 'Vouchers and Quasi-vouchers in Education', in M. May, E. Brunsdon, and G. Craig (eds.), *Social Policy Review No. 8*, London: Social Policy Association.

—— (1997), *Paying for Welfare: Towards 2000*, Hemel Hempstead: Prentice Hall/Harvester Wheatsheaf.

—— and LE GRAND, J. (1995), 'The Development of Quasi-markets in Welfare Provision in the United Kingdom', *International Journal of Health Services* 25, 203–18.

Bibliography

GLENNERSTER, H. and LOWE, W. (1990), 'Education and the Welfare State: Does It Add Up?', in J. Hills (1990).

—— and TURNER, T. (1993), *Estate-based Housing Management: An Evaluation*, London: HMSO.

—— and WILSON, G. (1970), *Paying for Private Schools*, London: Allen Lane.

—— POWER, A., and TRAVERS, T. (1991), 'A New Era for Social Policy: A New Enlightenment or a New Leviathan?', *Journal of Social Policy* 20:3, 389–414.

—— MATASAGANIS, M., OWEN, P., and HANCOCK, S. (1994), *Implementing GP Fundholding: Wild Card or Winning Hand?*, Milton Keynes: Open University Press.

GLYNN, S., and OXBORROW, J. (1976), *Interwar Britain: A Social and Economic History*, London: Allen and Unwin.

GOODIN, R., and LE GRAND, J. (1987), *Not Only the Poor: The Middle Classes and the Welfare State*, London: Allen and Unwin.

GOODMAN, A., and WEBB, S. (1994), 'For Richer and Poorer: The Changing Distribution of Income in the United Kingdom 1961–91' (IFS Commentary No. 42), London: Institute for Fiscal Studies.

GOULD, F., and ROWETH, B. (1980), 'Public Spending and Social Policy: The United Kingdom 1950–1977', *Journal of Social Policy* 9:3, 337–57.

GOVERNMENT ACTUARY (1994), *Occupational Pension Schemes 1991*, London: HMSO.

—— (1995), *National Insurance Fund Long-Term Estimates: Report by the Government Actuary on the Third Quinquennial Review of the Social Security Act 1975* (House of Commons Paper HC160, Session 1994/95), London: HMSO.

GRAY, J., and JESSON, D. (1996), *Times Educational Supplement*, 29 Nov., 5.

—— —— and JONES, B. (1984), 'Predicting Differences in Examination Results between LEAS: Does School Organisation Matter?', *Oxford Review of Education*, 10:1, 45–61.

GRAY, J., McPHERSON, A. F., and RAFFE, D. (1983), *Reconstructions and Secondary Education: Theory, Myth and Practice since the War*, London: Routledge and Kegan Paul.

GREEN, A., and STEEDMAN, H. (1993), *Educational Provision, Educational Attainment and the Needs of Industry*, London: National Institute of Economic and Social Research.

—— —— (1997), 'Into the Twenty-First Century: An Assessment of British Skill Profiles and Prospects' (Centre for Economic Performance), London: London School of Economics.

GREEN, H., THOMAS, M., ILES, N., and DOWN, D. (1996), *Housing in England 1994/5*, London: HMSO.

GREGG, P., and WADSWORTH J. (1996), 'More Work in Fewer Households', in J. Hills (ed.), *New Inequalities: The Changing Distribution of Income and Wealth in the United Kingdom*, Cambridge: Cambridge University Press.

GRIFFITH, J. A. G. (1965), *Central Departments and Local Authorities*, London: Allen and Unwin.

HAAG, M. (1990), *Discovery Guide to Egypt*, London: Michael Haag Ltd.

HALL, P. (1976), *Reforming the Welfare*, London: Heinemann.

HALSEY, A. H. (1991), 'Failing Education', in R. Jowell, L. Brook, and B. Taylor (eds.), *British Social Attitudes: The 8th Report*, Aldershot: Dartmouth.

—— HEATH, A. F., and RIDGE, J.(1980), *Origins and Destinations*, Oxford: Oxford University Press.

HAM, C. (1992), *Health Policy in Britain*, London: Macmillan.

HANSARD (1979), *Official Report*, London: HMSO.

HANUSHEK, E. A. (1986), 'The Economics of Schooling: Production and Efficiency in Public Schools', *Journal of Economic Literature* 24, 1141–77.

—— (1996), 'School Resources and Student Performance', in Burtless (ed.) (1996).

HARRIS, B., KEYS, W., and FERNANDEZ, C. (1997), *Third International Mathematics and Science Study, Second National Report*, Slough: National Foundation for Educational Research.

HARRISON, A., DIXON, J., NEW, B., and JUDGE, K. (1997a), 'Funding the NHS: Can the NHS Cope in Future?', *British Medical Journal* 314, 139–42.

—— —— —— —— (1997b), 'Funding the NHS: Is the NHS Sustainable?', *British Medical Journal* 314, 296–8.

HEATH, A. (1984), 'In Defence of Comprehensive Schools', *Oxford Review of Education* 10:1, 115–23.

HECLO, H., and WILDAVSKY, A. (1974), *The Private Government of Public Money*, London: Macmillan.

HELLEVIK, O., and RINGEN, S. (1995), 'Class Inequality and Egalitarian Reform', Oxford: Oxford University Department of Applied Social Studies (mimeo).

HEMS, L., and PASSEY, A. (1996), *The UK Voluntary Sector Statistical Almanac*, London: NCVO Publications.

HENDERSON, V., MIESZKOWSKI, P., and SAUVAGEAU, Y. (1978), 'Peer Group Effects and Educational Production Functions', *Journal of Public Economics* 10, 97–106.

HILLS, J. (ed.) (1990), *The State of Welfare: The Welfare State in Britain since 1990*, Oxford: Clarendon Press.

—— (1991), *Unravelling Housing Finance: Subsidies, Benefits and Taxation*, Oxford: Clarendon Press.

—— (1993; and 1997), *The Future of Welfare: A Guide to the Debate*, York: Joseph Rowntree Foundation.

—— (1995a), *Income and Wealth. Volume 2: A Summary of the Evidence*, York: Joseph Rowntree Foundation.

—— (1995b), 'Funding the Welfare State', *Oxford Review of Economic Policy* 11:3, 27–43.

—— (ed.) (1996), *New Inequalities: The Changing Distribution of Income and Wealth in the United Kingdom*, Cambridge: Cambridge University Press.

—— and MULLINGS, M. (1990), 'Housing: A Decent Home for All at a Price within their Means?', in Hills (1990).

—— and SUTHERLAND, H. (1991), 'The Proposed Council Tax', *Fiscal Studies* 12:4, 1–21.

—— DITCH, J., and GLENNERSTER, H. (1994), *Beveridge and Social Security: An International Retrospective*, Oxford: Clarendon Press.

HM TREASURY (1944), *Employment Policy* (Cmd. 6527), London: HMSO.

—— (1971), *Public Expenditure to 1975–76* (Cmnd. 4829), London: HMSO.

—— (1978), *The Government's Expenditure Plans 1978–79 to 1981–82* (Cmnd. 7049), London: HMSO.

—— (1979a), *The Government's Expenditure Plans 1979–80 to 1982–83* (Cmnd. 7437), London: HMSO.

—— (1979b), *The Government's Expenditure Plans 1980–81* (Cmnd. 7746), London: HMSO.

—— (1980), *The Government's Expenditure Plans 1980–81 to 1983–84* (Cmnd. 7841), London: HMSO.

—— (1981), *The Government's Expenditure Plans 1981–82 to 1983–84* (Cmnd. 8175), London: HMSO.

HM TREASURY (1982), *The Government's Expenditure Plans 1982–83 to 1984–85*, Vol. 2 (Cmnd. 8494 II), London: HMSO.

—— (1986), *The Government's Expenditure Plans 1986–87 to 1988–89* (Cmnd. 9702), London: HMSO.

—— (1989), *The Government's Expenditure Plans 1989–90 to 1991–92* (Cm. 601–21), London: HMSO.

—— (1996a), *Public Expenditure Statistical Supplement (The Grey Book)*, London: HMSO.

—— (1996b), *Tax Ready Reckoner and Tax Reliefs*, London: HM Treasury.

—— (1997), *Public Expenditure: Statistical Analyses 1997–8* (Cm. 3601), London: HMSO.

Bibliography

HOBCRAFT, J., and KIERNAN, K.(1995), 'Becoming a Parent in Europe' (STICERD Welfare State Discussion Paper WSP/116), London: London School of Economics.

HOME OFFICE (1959), *Committee on Children and Young Persons* (Cmnd. 1191), London: HMSO.

—— (1968), *Local Authority and Allied Personal Social Services* (Seebohm Report; Cmnd. 3703), London: HMSO.

HOPE, T., and HOUGH, M. (1988), 'Area, Crime and Incivilities: A Profile from the British Crime Survey', in T. Hope and M. Shaw (eds.), *Communities and Crime Reduction*, London: HMSO.

HOUSE OF COMMONS HEALTH COMMITTEE (1996), *Public Expenditure on Health and Personal Social Services: Memorandum Received from the Department of Health* (HC698) London: The Stationery Office.

HOUSE OF COMMONS (SOCIAL SERVICES COMMITTEE) (1982), *Public Expenditure on the Social Services Session 1981/2* (HC306i–v), London: HMSO.

HUBY, M., and WHYLEY, C. (1996), 'Take-up and the Social Fund', *Journal of Social Policy* 25:1, 1–18.

IAEP [International Assessment of Educational Progress] (1992), *A World of Difference*, Boston: Educational Testing Service.

ILEA [Inner London Education Authority] (1981), *Literacy Survey*, London: ILEA.

ILLSLEY, R., and LE GRAND, J. (1987), 'The Measurement of Inequality in Health', in A. Williams (ed.), *Health and Economics*, London: Macmillan.

—— —— (1993), 'Regional Inequalities in Mortality', *Journal of Epidemiology and Community Health* 47, 444–9.

INLAND REVENUE (1996), *Inland Revenue Statistics 1996*, London: HMSO.

JONES, H. O. W. (1992), 'The Conservative Party and the Welfare State 1942–55' London University Ph.D. thesis.

JOSEPH ROWNTREE FOUNDATION (1995), *Inquiry into Income and Wealth. Volume 1: Report; Vol. 2: A Summary of the Evidence*, York: Joseph Rowntree Foundation.

—— (1996), *Meeting the Costs of Continuing Care: Report and Recommendations of the Joseph Rowntree Inquiry*, York: Joseph Rowntree Foundation.

JOWELL, R., and AIREY, C. (1984), *British Social Attitudes: The 1984 Report*, Aldershot: Gower.

—— WITHERSPOON, S., and BROOK, L. (1986), *British Social Attitudes: The 1986 Report*, Aldershot: Gower.

KANAVOS, P., and MOSSIALOS, E. (1997) 'The Methodology of International Comparisons of Health Care Expenditures' (LSE Health Discussion Paper No. 3), London: London School of Economics.

KARN, V. (1993), 'Remodelling a HAT: The Implementation of the Housing Action Trust Legislation 1987–92', in Malpass and Means (1993).

KENNY, D., and EDWARDS, P. (1996), *Community Care Trends: The Impact of Funding on Local Authorities*, London: The Local Government Management Board.

KEYS, W., HARRIS, S., and FERNANDES, C. (1996), *Third International Mathematics and Science Study, First National Report, Part 1*, Slough: National Foundation for Educational Research.

KIERNAN, K. (1995), *Transition to Parenthood: Young Mothers, Young Fathers and Later Life Experiences* (STICERD Welfare State Discussion Paper WSP/113), London: London School of Economics.

—— and ESTAUGH, V. (1993), 'Cohabitation, Extra-marital Childbearing and Social Policy' (Occasional Paper No. 17), London: Family Policy Studies Centre.

KING'S FUND (1997), 'Management Costs' (press briefing), London: King's Fund.

KIRKUP, B., and DONALDSON, L. (1994), 'Is Health Care a Commodity? How Will Purchasing Improve the National Health Service?', *Journal of Public Health Medicine* 16, 256–62.

KLEIN, R. (1983), 'The NHS and the Theatre of Inadequacy', *Universities Quarterly* 37, 201–15.

—— (1995), *The New Politics of the National Health Service*, London: Longman.

—— DAY, P., and REDMAYNE, S. (1996), *Managing Scarcity: Priority Setting and Rationing in the National Health Service*, Buckingham: Open University Press.

KLEINMAN, M. P. (1988), 'Where Did It Hurt Most? Uneven Decline in the Availability of Council Housing in England', *Policy and Politics* 16:4, 221–33.

KNAPP, M. (1987), 'Wrong Numbers', *Social Services Insight*, 17 July, 20–3.

KOGAN, M. (1978), *The Politics of Educational Change*, London: Fontana.

LABOUR PARTY (1976), *Annual Report*, London: Labour Party.

—— (1997), *New Labour: Because Britain Deserves Better* (election manifesto), London: Labour Party.

LAING, W. (1994), *Laing's Review of Private Health Care*, London: Laing and Buisson Ltd.

LAING and BUISSON LTD. (1995), *Care of Elderly People: Market Survey 1995*, London: Laing and Buisson Ltd.

—— (1996a), *Laing's Review of Private Health Care 1996 and Directory of Independent Hospitals, Nursing and Residential Homes and Related Services*, London: Laing and Buisson Ltd.

—— (1996b), *Care of Elderly People: Market Survey 1996*, London: Laing and Buisson Ltd.

LAMBERT, R. (1964), 'Nutrition in Britain 1950–60' (Occasional Paper on Social Administration No. 6), London: Bell.

LAWSON, N. (1984), 'The British Experiment' (The Mais Lecture), *Public Money* 4:2, 45–8.

—— (1992), *The View from No. 11: Memoirs of a Tory Radical*, London: Bantam Press.

LE GRAND, J. (1978), 'The Distribution of Public Expenditure: The Case of Health Care', *Economica* 45, 125–42.

—— (1982), *The Strategy of Equality: Redistribution and the Social Services*, London: Allen and Unwin.

—— (1991a), *Equity and Choice: An Essay in Economics and Applied Philosophy*, London: HarperCollins.

—— (1991b), 'The Distribution of Health Care Revisited', *Journal of Health Economics* 10, 239–45.

—— (1991c), 'Quasi Markets and Social Policy', *Economic Journal* 101, 1256–67.

—— (1995), 'The Market, the State and the Redistribution of Lifetime Income', in J. Falkingham and J. Hills (eds.), *The Dynamic of Welfare: The Welfare State and the Life Cycle*, Hemel Hempstead: Harvester Wheatsheaf.

—— (1997), 'Knights, Knaves or Pawns? Human Behaviour and Social Policy', *Journal of Social Policy* 26:2, 149–69.

—— and BARTLETT, W. (1993), *Quasi-Markets and Social Policy*, Houndmills: Macmillan.

—— and WINTER, D. (1987), 'The Middle Classes and the Welfare State under Conservative and Labour Governments', *Journal of Public Policy* 6, 399–430.

—— —— and WOOLLEY, F. (1990), 'The National Health Service: Safe in Whose Hands?', in Hills (1990).

LEAT, D., and GAY, P. (1987), *Paying for Care: A Study of Policy and Practice in Paid Care Schemes* (Policy Studies Research Report No. 661), London: Policy Studies Institute.

LEATHER, P. (1983), 'Housing (Dis?)Investment Programmes', *Policy and Politics* 11:2, 215–29.

—— and MORRISON, T. (1997), *The State of UK Housing: A Factfile on Dwelling Conditions*, Bristol: The Policy Press.

LEVIN, P. (1997), *Making Social Policy: The Mechanisms of Government and Politics, and How to Investigate Them*, Milton Keynes: Open University Press.

Bibliography

LONDON MATHEMATICAL SOCIETY (1995), *Tackling the Mathematics Problem*, London: Royal Statistical Society.

LONSDALE, S., LESSOF, C., and FERRIS, G. (1993), *Invalidity Benefit: A Survey of Recipients*, London: HMSO.

LOW PAY UNIT (1995), 'Quiet Growth in Poverty', *The New Review of the Low Pay Unit* (Nov./Dec.), 8–11.

LOWE, R. (1989), 'Resignation at the Treasury: The Social Services Committee and the Reform of the Welfare State 1955–7', *Journal of Social Policy* 18:4, 505–26

—— (1993), *The Welfare State in Britain since 1945*, London: Macmillan.

—— (1994), 'A Prophet Dishonoured in His Own Country? The Rejection of Beveridge in Britain 1945–70', in J. Hills, J. Ditch, and H. Glennerster (eds.), *Beveridge and Social Security*, Cambridge: Cambridge University Press.

McCARTHY, M. (1986), *Campaigning for the Poor: CPAG and the Politics of Welfare*, London: Croom Helm.

McGUIGAN, S. (1997), *Compendium of Health Statistics* (10th edn.), London: Office of Health Economics.

MACK, J., and LANSLEY, S. (1985), *Poor Britain*, London: Allen and Unwin.

McKEOWN, T. (1976), *The Role of Medicine*, London: Nuffield Provincial Hospitals Trust.

MACLEOD, I., and POWELL, E. (1952), *The Social Services: Needs and Means*, London: Conservative Political Centre.

MALPASS, P. (1989), 'The Road from Clay Cross', *Roof*, Jan.–Feb.

—— and MEANS, R. (eds.) (1993), *Implementing Housing Policy*, Buckingham: Open University Press.

MARSH, A. and McKAY, S. (1993), *Families, Work and Benefits*, London: Policy Studies Institute.

MAYNARD, A. (1991), 'Developing the Healthcare Market', *Economic Journal* 101, 1277–86.

MEADE, J. E. (1978), *The Structure and Reform of Direct Taxation*, London: Allen and Unwin.

MHLG [Ministry of Housing and Local Government] (1953), *Houses: The Next Step* (Cmd. 8996), London: HMSO.

—— (1957), *Local Government Finance* (Cmnd. 209), London: HMSO.

—— (1968), *Old Houses into New Homes* (Cmnd. 3602), London: HMSO.

MIDWINTER, E. (1986), *Caring for Cash: The Issue of Private Domiciliary Care*, London: Centre for Policy on Ageing.

MILL, J. S. (1991 edn.), *On Liberty* (1st pub. 1859), in J. Gray (ed.), *On Liberty and Other Essays*, Oxford: Oxford University Press.

MILLS, C., JONSSON, J. O., and MULLER, W. (1996), 'A Half Century of Educational Openness? Social Class, Gender and Educational Achievement in Sweden, Germany and Britain', in R. Erickson and J. O. Jonsson (eds.), *Can Education be Equalised: the Swedish Case in Comparative Perspective*, Boulder, Colo.: Westview Press.

MINISTRY OF SOCIAL SECURITY (1954), *Report of the Committee on the Economic and Financial Problems of the Provision for Old Age* (Phillips Committee; Cmd. 9333), London: HMSO.

MoH [Ministry of Health] (1944), *A National Health Service* (Cmd. 6502), London: HMSO.

—— (1956), *Report of the Committee of Enquiry into the Cost of the National Health Service* (Guillebaud Committee: Cmd. 9663), London: HMSO.

MOSSIALOS, E. (1997), 'Citizens' views on healthcare systems in the fifteen member states of the European Union', *Health Economics* 6, 109–16.

MULLINS, D., NINER, P., and RISEBOROUGH, M. (1993), 'Large-scale Voluntary Transfers', in Malpass and Means (1993).

MURNANE, R. J., WILLETT, J. B., and LEVY, F. (1995), 'The Growing Importance of Cognitive Skills in Wage Determination', *Review of Economics and Statistics* 77:2, 251–64.

NATIONAL AUDIT OFFICE (1987), *Community Care Developments*, London: HMSO.

—— (1995), *Health of the Nation: A Progress Report*, London: HMSO.

NATIONAL COMMISSION ON EDUCATION (1993), *Learning to Succeed*, London: Heinemann.

NATIONAL HEALTH SERVICE MANAGEMENT INQUIRY (1983), *Report*, London: DHSS.

NETTEN, A. (1991), 'Coming of Age: The Cost of Social Care Support' (Personal Social Services Research Unit Discussion Paper 742), Canterbury: University of Kent Personal Social Services Research Unit.

NEW, B., and LE GRAND, J. (1996), *Rationing in the NHS: Principles and Pragmatism*, London: King's Fund.

NEWTON, J. (1991), *All in One Place: The British Housing Story 1971–1990*, London: Catholic Housing Aid Society.

NHSE [National Health Service Executive] (1996), *Annual Report 1995/6*, London: Department of Health.

NINER, P. (1989), *Homelessness in Nine Local Authorities: Case Studies of Policy and Practice*, London: HMSO.

NISBET, J., WATT, J., and WELSH, M. (1972), *Reading Standards in Aberdeen*, Aberdeen: Aberdeen University Press.

NOCON, A. (1994), *Collaboration in Community Care in the 1990s*, Sunderland: Business Education.

NORTHERN IRELAND OFFICE (1997), *Northern Ireland Expenditure Plans and Priorities: The Government's Expenditure Plans 1997–98 to 1999–2000* (Cm. 3616), London: The Stationery Office.

NUTTALL, S., BLACKWOOD, R., BUSSELL, B., CORNELL, M., COWLEY, A., GATENBY, P., and WEBBER, J. (1993), *Financing Long-Term Care in Great Britain*, London: Institute of Actuaries.

O'DONNELL, O., and PROPPER, C. (1991a), 'Equity and the Distribution of UK National Health Service Resources', *Journal of Health Economics* 10, 1–19.

—— —— (1991b), 'Equity and the Distribution of UK National Health Service Resources: A Reply', *Journal of Health Economics* 10, 247–50.

OFFICE OF HEALTH ECONOMICS (1987), *Compendium of Health Statistics* (6th edn.), London: Office of Health Economics.

ONS [Office for National Statistics] (1996a), *Economic Trends Annual Supplement 1996/7* (No. 22), London: HMSO.

—— (1996b), *United Kingdom National Accounts (The Blue Book) 1996*, London: HMSO.

—— (1996c), *New Earnings Survey 1996*, London: HMSO.

—— (1996d), *Labour Market Trends*, London: HMSO.

—— (1996e), 'An International Comparison of Taxes and Social Security Contributions (1984–1994)' (*Economic Trends* No. 516 and previous editions), London: HMSO.

—— (1996f), *Annual Abstract of Statistics 1996*, London: HMSO.

—— (1997a), *Annual Abstract of Statistics 1997* [previous editions produced by the CSO], London: HMSO.

—— (1997b), *Social Trends 1997*, London: HMSO.

—— (1997c), 'The Effects of Taxes and Benefits on Household Incomes, 1995' (*Economic Trends* No. 520), London: HMSO.

Bibliography

ONS [Office for National Statistics] (1997*d*), *United Kingdom National Accounts (The Blue Book) 1997*, London: HMSO.

—— (1997*e*) *Economic Trends*, March 1997 No. 520, London: HMSO.

OPCS [Office of Population Censuses and Surveys] (1977), *General Household Survey 1974*, London: HMSO.

—— (1980), *General Household Survey 1978*, London: HMSO.

—— (1981), *General Household Survey 1979*, London: HMSO.

—— (1982), *General Household Survey 1980*, London: HMSO.

—— (1987), *General Household Survey 1985*, London: HMSO.

—— (1989), *General Household Survey 1987*, London: HMSO.

—— (1992), *General Household Survey 1990*, London: HMSO.

—— (1994*a*), *Birth Statistics* (Series FM1), London: HMSO.

—— (1994*b*), *Mortality Statistics: General* (OPCS Series DH1), London: HMSO.

—— (1994*c*), *People Aged 65 and Over* (Series GHS No. 22 Supplement A), London: HMSO.

—— (1996), *Living in Britain: Results from the 1994 General Household Survey*, London: HMSO.

OSBORN, A. F., and MILBANK, J. E. (1987), *The Effects of Early Education*, Oxford: Oxford University Press.

—— BUTLER, N. F., and MOMES, A. C. (1984), *The Social Life of Britain's Five Year Olds*, London: Routledge.

PARKER, R. (1981), 'Tending and Social Policy', in E. M. Goldberg and S. Hatch (eds.), *A New Look at the Personal Social Services*, London: Policy Studies Institute.

PARTON, N. (1985), *The Politics of Child Abuse*, London: Macmillan.

PATON, C. (1992), *Competition and Planning in the National Health Service: The Dangers of Unplanned Markets*, London: Chapman and Hall.

PEACOCK, A., and WISEMAN, J. (1961), *The Growth of Public Expenditure in the United Kingdom*, London: Allen and Unwin.

PIACHAUD, D. (1986), 'Disability, Retirement and Unemployment of Older Men', *Journal of Social Policy* 15:2, 145–62.

—— (1997), 'Social Security and the Prevention of Poverty: Reconstructing the Research Agenda', paper presented to the Foundation for International Studies on Social Security Conference, June 1997, Sigtuna, Sweden.

PIERSON, P. (1994), *Dismantling the Welfare State? Reagan, Thatcher, and the Politics of Retrenchment*, Cambridge: Cambridge University Press

PISSARIDES, C. (1982), 'From School to University: The Demand for Post-compulsory Education in Britain', *Economic Journal* 92:367, 654–67.

POWELL, M. (1995), 'The Strategy of Equality Revisited', *Journal of Social Policy* 24:2, 163–85.

—— (1997), *Evaluating the National Health Service*, Buckingham: Open University Press.

POWER, A. (1987), *Property without People*, London: Allen and Unwin.

—— and TUNSTALL, B. (1995), *Swimming against the Tide : Polarisation or Progress on 20 Unpopular Estates, 1980–1995*, York: Joseph Rowntree Foundation.

PRAIS, S. J. (1995), *Productivity, Education and Training: An International Perspective*, Cambridge: Cambridge University Press.

PREST, A. R. (1983), 'The Social Security Reform Minefield', *British Tax Review* 1, 44–53.

PROPPER, C. (1990), 'Contingent Valuation of Time Spent on NHS Waiting Lists', *Economic Journal* 100, 193–200.

Bibliography

PUBLIC SCHOOLS COMMISSION (1970), *Second Report*, London: HMSO.

RANDALL, G., and BROWN, S. (1993), *The Rough Sleepers Initiative: An Evaluation*, London: HMSO.

RICHARDS, E. (1996), *Paying for Long-Term Care*, London: Institute of Public Policy Research.

RICHARDS, M. (1996), *Community Care for Older People: Rights, Remedies and Finances*, Bristol: Jordan Publishing.

RITCHIE, J., WARD, K., and DULDIG, W. (1993), *GPs and IVB—A Qualitative Study of the Role of GPs in the Award of Invalidity Benefit*, London: HMSO.

ROBERTSON, D., and SYMONS, J. (1995), *'Do Peer Groups Matter?': Peer Group versus Schooling Effects on Academic Attainment* (Centre for Economic Performance Discussioin Paper No. 311), London: London School of Economics.

ROBINSON, R., and LE GRAND, J. (1994), *Evaluating the NHS Reforms*, London: King's Fund Institute.

ROBITAILLE, D. F., and GARDEN, R. A. (1989), *The IEA Study of Mathematics Contexts and Outcomes of School Mathematics*, Oxford: Pergamon.

ROMER, P. M. (1993), 'Idea Gaps and Object Gaps in Economic Development', *Journal of Monetary Economics* 32, 338–69.

ROSE, R., and DAVIES, P. L. (1994), *Inheritance and Public Policy: Change without choice in Britain*, New Haven: Yale University Press.

ROYAL COMMISSION ON THE NATIONAL HEALTH SERVICE (1979), *Report* (Cmnd. 7615), London: HMSO.

RUTTER, M., MAUGHAN, B., MORTIMORE, P., OUSTON, J., and SMITH, A. (1979), *Fifteen Thousand Hours: Schools and their Effects on Children*, London: Open Books.

SAINSBURY, R., HIRST, M., and LAWTON, D. (1995), *Evaluation of Disability Living Allowance and Attendance Allowance* (Department of Social Security Research Report No. 41), London: HMSO.

SAMMONS, P. (1995), 'Gender, Ethnic and Socio-economic Differences in Attainment Progress: A Longitudinal Analysis of Student Achievement over Nine Years', *British Educational Research Journal* 21:4, 465–85.

SAUNDERS, P. (1990), *A Nation of Home Owners*, London: Unwin Hyman.

SBC [Supplementary Benefits Commission] (1978), *Take-up of Supplementary Benefits*, London: HMSO.

SCHEFFLER, R. (1989), 'Adverse Selection: The Achilles Heel of the NHS Reforms', *The Lancet* 29 Apr.: 950–2.

SCHMITT, J. (1993), *The Changing Structure of Male Earnings in Britain 1974–88* (Centre for Economic Performance Discussion Paper No. 122), London: London School of Economics.

SCOTTISH HOME AND HEALTH DEPARTMENT (1964), *Children and Young Persons* (Kilbrandon Report; Cmnd. 2306), Edinburgh: HMSO.

SCOTTISH OFFICE (1980), *Scottish Annual Abstract of Statistics* (No. 9), Edinburgh: HMSO.

—— (1997), *Serving Scotland's Needs: The Government's Expenditure Plans 1997–98 to 1999–2000* (Cm. 3614), London: The Stationery Office.

SEFTON, J., and WEALE, M. (1995), *Reconcilation of National Income and Expenditure: Balanced Estimates of National Income for the United Kingdom, 1920–90*, Cambridge: Cambridge University Press.

SEFTON, T. (1997), *The Changing Distribution of the Social Wage* (STICERD Occasional Paper No. 21), London: London School of Economics.

SELDON, A. (1986), *The Riddle of the Voucher*, London: Institute of Economic Affairs.

SHELTER (1994), *Annual Report 1993/94*, London: Shelter.

Bibliography

SMAJE, C. (1995), *Health, 'Race' and Ethnicity: Making Sense of the Evidence*, London: King's Fund.

—— and LE GRAND, J. (1997), 'Ethnicity, Equity and the Use of the Health Services', *Social Science and Medicine*, 45:3, 485–96.

SMITH, D. J., and TOMLINSON, S. (1989), *The School Effects of Multi-Racial Comprehensives*, London: Policy Studies Institute.

SNOWER, D. (1993), 'The Future of the Welfare State', *Economic Journal* 103, 700–17.

SPROAT, I. (1996), *House of Commons Official Report* (Hansard), 23 July.

STARK, J. (1987), 'Health and Social Contacts', in Health Promotion Research Trust, *The Health and Lifestyle Survey*, London: Health Promotion Research Trust.

START, K. B., and WELLS, B. K. (1972), *Trend of Reading Standards 1970–71*, Slough: National Foundation for Educational Research.

STEEDMAN, H., and GREEN, A. (1996), 'Widening Participation in Further Education and Training: A Survey of the Issues (A Report to the Further Education Funding Council)' (Centre for Economic Performance Special Report), London: London School of Economics.

—— —— BERTRAND, O., RICHTER, A., RUBIN, M., and WEBER, K. (1997), 'Assessment, Qualifications and Standards: The UK Compared to France, Germany, Singapore and the USA: Technical Report' (Centre for Economic Performance Discussion Paper), London: London School of Economics.

STIGLITZ, J. E. (1975), 'The Theory of "Screening" Education and the Distribution of Income', *American Economic Review* 65, 283–300.

SWAIN, V. (1993), 'Social Relationships and Health', in B. Cox, F. Hippert, and M. Whichelow (eds.), *The Health and Lifestyle Survey: Seven Years On*, Aldershot: Dartmouth.

TAUBMAN, P. J., and WALES, T. J. (1973), 'Higher Education, Mental Ability and Screening', *Journal of Political Economy* 81, 28–55

TAWNEY, R. H. (1931), *Equality*, London: Allen and Unwin.

TAYLOR-GOOBY, P. (1995), 'Comfortable, Marginal and Excluded', in R. Jowell, J. Curtis, A. Park, L. Brock, and D. Ahrendt (eds.), *British Social Attitudes: The 12th Report*, Aldershot: Dartmouth.

THAIN, C., and WRIGHT, M. (1995), *The Treasury and Whitehall: The Planning and Control of Public Expenditure, 1976–1993*, Oxford: Clarendon Press.

THATCHER, M., (1993), *The Downing Street Years*, London: HarperCollins.

TIMMINS, N. (1995), *The Five Giants: A Biography of the Welfare State*, London: HarperCollins.

TITMUSS, R. (1958), *Essays on the 'Welfare State'*, London: Allen and Unwin.

—— (1968), *Commitment to Welfare*, London: Allen and Unwin.

TOWNSEND, P. (1957), *The Family Life of Old People*, London: Routledge and Kegan Paul.

—— (1979), *Poverty in the United Kingdom: A Survey of Household Resources and Standards of Living*, Harmondsworth: Penguin.

—— and BONSANQUET, N. (1972), *Labour and Inequality*, London: Fabian Society.

—— WALKER, R., and LAWSON, R. (1984), *Responses to Poverty: Lessons from Europe*, London: Heinemann.

—— WHITEHEAD, M., and DAVIDSON, N. (1992), *Inequalities in Health: The Black Report and the Health Divide*, London: Penguin Books.

TRINDER, C. (1987), 'Public Service Pay', in M. Levitt (ed.), *New Priorities in Public Spending*, London: Gower.

—— (1997), 'Pay Review: Overview of the Main Issues', paper presented to the AUT/NATFHE Conference on Pay Review, Apr.

VIET-WILSON, J.(1994), 'Condemned to Deprivation? Beveridge's Responsibility for the Invisibility of Poverty', in Hills *et al.* (1994).

VIZARD, P. (1997), *Reconciling Health Expenditure Figures* (STICERD Welfare State Research Note WSP/RN/31), London: London School of Economics.

WALKER, A. (ed.) (1982), *Community Care : The Family, the State and Social Policy*, Oxford: Blackwell.

WALKER, C. (1983), 'Changing Social Policy: The Case of the Supplementary Benefits Review' (Occasional Paper on Social Administration No. 70), London: Bedford Square Press.

WEBB, A., and WISTOW, G. (1982), 'The Personal Social Services', in A. Walker, (ed.), *Public Expenditure and Social Policy*, London: Heinemann.

—— —— (1986), *Planning, Need and Scarcity*, London: Allen and Unwin.

—— —— (1987), *Social Work, Social Care and Social Planning*, London: Longmans.

WEINER, M. J. (1981), *English Culture and the Decline of the Industrial Spirit 1850–1980*, Cambridge: Cambridge University Press.

WELSH OFFICE (1979), *Health and Personal Social Services Statistics*, Cardiff: Welsh Office.

—— (1982), *1981 Welsh House Condition Survey*, Cardiff: Welsh Office.

—— (1988), *1986 Welsh House Condition Survey* (rev. edn.), Cardiff: Welsh Office.

—— (1997), *Departmental Report 1997: The Government's Expenditure Plans 1997–98 to 1999–2000* (Cm. 3615), London: The Stationery Office.

WEST, A., and PENNELL, H. (1997), 'Educational Reform and School Choice in England and Wales', *Education Economics*, forthcoming.

—— WEST, R., and PENNELL, H. (1995), 'Financing of School-based Education: Changing the Additional School Needs Allowance', *Education Economics* 3:3, 265–75

WHITEHEAD, C. (1997), 'Changing Needs, Changing Incentives: Trends in the UK Housing System', in P. Williams (ed.), *Directons in Housing Policy*, London: Paul Chapman Publishing.

WHITEHEAD, M. (1992), 'The Health Divide', in Townsend *et al.* (1992).

—— EVANDROU, M., HAGLUND, B., and DIDERICHSEN, F. (forthcoming), 'The Health Divide Widens in Britain and Sweden, but What's Happening to Access to Care?', *British Medical Journal*.

WHITELEY, P. (1981), 'Public Opinion and the Demand for Social Welfare in Britain', *Journal of Social Policy* 10:4, 435–75.

WHITFIELD, K., and WILSON, R. A. (1991), 'Staying On in Full-Time Education: The Educational Participation Rates of 16-Year-Olds', *Economica* 58, 391–404.

WHITTY, G., EDWARDS, T., and GERWITZ, S. (1993), *Specialisation and Choice in Urban Education: The City Technology College Experiment*, London: Routledge.

WHO (World Health Organisation) (1985), *Targets for Health for All*, Copenhagen: WHO.

WILCOX, S. (ed.) (1996), *Housing Review 1996/97*, York: Joseph Rowntree Foundation.

—— BRAMLEY, G., FERGUSON, A., PERRY, J., and WOODS, C. (1993), *Local Housing Companion: New Opportunities for Council Housing*, York: Joseph Rowntree Foundation.

WILDING, P. (1986), *In Defence of the Welfare State*, Manchester: Manchester University Press.

WILLIAMS, P. (ed.) (1997), *Directions in Housing Policy*, London: Paul Chapman.

WILLMOTT, P. (1986), 'Social Networks, Informal Care and Public Policy' (Research Report No. 655), London: Policy Studies Institute.

WISTOW, G. (1997), 'Community Care Services', in NHS Confederation, *NHS Handbook 1997/8* (12th edn.), Tunbridge Wells: JMH Publishing.

Bibliography

WISTOW, G., KNAPP, M., HARDY, B., FORDER, J., KENDALL, J., and MANNING, R. (eds.) (1996), *Social Care Markets: Progress and Prospects*, Buckingham: Open University Press.

WOLFENDEN COMMITTEE (1978), *The Future of Voluntary Organisations*, London: Croom Helm.

YOUNG, R., and WISTOW, G. (1996), *Domiciliary Care: Growth and Stability? Report of the 1996 Survey of the UK Home Care Association Members*, London: UK Home Care Association.

Index

Index

Index

Index

imputed rents 144
public funding 144–5
see also housing; mortgage interest relief
Oxford Review of Education, comprehensive education 64

'Parker Morris' standards 126
Parker, R. 199, 243
part-time workers, social security 266
Parton, N. 194
Patient's Charter 81–3, 85
  hospital waiting lists 99–101
  see also NHS
Paton, C. 81
Pearson, M. 38
pensions 271, 273–4, 285, 287, 302
  graduated 274
  longevity 274
  occupational 282–4
  private 282–4
  value 285
  see also elderly; social security
Pensions Act (1973) 22
personal social services (PSS)
  aims 192–3
  charges 206–8, 210, 211; regional variations 208
  children in care 216, 231
  children prioritized 194
  day care 216–18, 220–1
  equity 192
  ethnicity 246
  expenditure 194, 200–29, 230, 253, 255, 256, 315–16;
    by client group 208–10; by families 239–40;
    current vs capital 204; growth 211
  funding structure 197
  future 245–6
  and GDP 203, 316
  goals 189–200
  health care vs social care 205, 254
  independent sector and private funding 198–200,
    238, 255
  informal care sector 242–5, 255
  joint finance 205–6
  local authorities 204–5, 206, 209, 211, 215–27
  'mixed economy of care' 198–200, 235–6
  monitoring 197–8
  outcomes 246–53, 321
  outputs 229–46
  priorities 218–22
  private provision 253
  private sector 233–5
  public expenditure restraint 198
  residential care 223, 226, 231–5; privately funded
    199
  social class 246
  social integration 192

usage and income distribution 249
voluntary sector 198–199; charities 240–2
see also community care; disabled persons;
  domiciliary care; elderly; residential care
Phillips Committee (1954) 20
physical disabilities, provision for people with 225–7
Piachaud, D. 277, 299
Pierson, P. 12
Pissarides, C. 47
Plowden Report 42
Poll Tax 130
Polytechnic Funding Council 34
polythechnics 34
Poor Law authorities 190
poverty:
  exam performance 63
  and social security 294–6, 298–302
  see also low-paid employment; social security
poverty trap 288–91
Powell, E. 21
Powell, M. 322
Power, A. 326
Prais, Prof. S. J. 29, 49, 51, 52, 53
Prest, A. R. 261
Primary Care (White Paper 1996) 84
Priorities 194
Private Finance Initiative (White Paper) 84, 89
private health care 96–8
private medical insurance 94, 97–8
  NHS waiting lists 99
private pensions 282–4
Propper, C. 99
public expenditure, change of policy 14

Quality Adjusted Life-Year 109–10

race *see* ethnicity
Randall, G. 130
Rate Support Grant 126–7
Rent Act (1957) 21
rented accommodation *see* tenants
residential care 232–8, 254, 316
  and community care 231–5
  elderly 221
  personal social services 208
  see also community care; personal social services
    (PSS)
Resource Allocation Working Party 77–8
Revenue Support Grant 205
Richards, E. 243
Richards, M. 218
Right to Buy 126–7, 131, 139, 153, 185
  see also housing
Ritchie, J. 279
Robbins Report 28
Robertson, D. 65

Index